MONKEYS, MEN, AND MISSILES

By the same author

FROM APES TO WARLORDS: AN AUTOBIOGRAPHY 1904–46

THE SOCIAL LIFE OF MONKEYS AND APES
FUNCTIONAL AFFINITIES OF MAN, MONKEYS AND APES
A NEW SYSTEM OF ANATOMY
THE OVARY (ED.)
GREAT ZOOS OF THE WORLD (ED.)

SCIENTISTS AND WAR
BEYOND THE IVORY TOWER
NUCLEAR ILLUSION AND REALITY
STAR WARS IN A NUCLEAR WORLD

MONKEYS, MEN, AND MISSILES

An autobiography
1946–88

SOLLY ZUCKERMAN

W • W • NORTON & COMPANY
New York   London

Copyright © 1988 by Solly Zuckerman
First American edition, 1989.

Printed in the United States of America.

Library of Congress Cataloging-in-Publication Data

Zuckerman, Solly Zuckerman, Baron, 1904–
Monkeys, men, and missiles: an autobiography, 1946-88 / Solly
Zuckerman. — 1st ed.
p. cm.
Originally published in Great Britain in 1988.
1. Zuckerman, Solly Zuckerman,—Baron,—1904– 2. Zoologists—
Great Britain—Biography. I. Title
QL31.Z93A3 1989
591′.092′4—dc19
[B]   88–37239

ISBN 0-393-02689-2

W. W. Norton & Company, Inc., 500 Fifth Avenue, New York, N.Y. 10110
W. W. Norton & Company Ltd., 37 Great Russell Street, London WC1B 3NU

1 2 3 4 5 6 7 8 9 0

To my grandchildren, Hester and Sebastian

CONTENTS

CONTENTS

ILLUSTRATIONS

(Unless otherwise stated all photographs come from the personal collection of the author)

ix

ILLUSTRATIONS

ACKNOWLEDGEMENTS

I sat down to write this book some years ago, basing myself at the start entirely on memory. Then came the laborious task of checking and rewriting, combing pocket diaries, letters and odd notes that I had kept, as well as books and papers that I had published. I have had to consult the biographies of many who come into my story, as well as reports of parliamentary and other proceedings and, to the extent that has been permitted, official records. In addition, I have asked friends and colleagues to read chapters or pages which deal with events in which they played a part.

I am immensely grateful to all who have helped in my efforts to assure the factual accuracy of what I have written, and in particular to Peter Krohn FRS, Dr Peter Dallas Ross, Dr Anita Mandl and Tom Spence (Part I); Sir Terence Morrison-Scott, Dr Eirwen Owen, and Dr Marcia Edwards (Part II); Paul Willert and Peter Krohn (Part III); Sir Arnold Hall FRS, Marshal of the RAF Sir Michael Beetham, Sir Clifford Cornford, Dr Glyn Owen, and Lord Watkinson (Part IV); John Rubel, Glyn Owen, B.T. Price (Part V); Dr H.I.S. Thirlaway, B.T. Price, William ('Bill') Walton (Part VI); Dr Fergus Allen (Part VII); Sir Hermann Bondi FRS and Glyn Owen (Part VIII).

The cartoons that are reproduced in the text were given to me by the late Sir Osbert Lancaster, that sophisticated writer and designer of operatic and ballet decor. To the public at large he was best known as the witty and satirical 'pocket' cartoonist of the *Daily Express*.

To Roy Jenkins (Lord Jenkins of Hillhead) and to Philip Ziegler, my editor, I owe very special thanks. Both have read every word, with the former alert to references to ministerial matters in which he was involved, and the latter wisely advising me to omit matters tangential to my main story. I would also like to thank Sir Robert Armstrong who, in the discharge of his formal duty as Secretary to the Cabinet, saw to it that I did not transgress any of the conventions relating to official secrecy, and who drew my attention to a few points which needed amendment. Joan, my wife, helped in many ways, but particularly in the choice of illustrations.

I am also deeply indebted to the University of East Anglia, my academic base since my retirement from Birmingham, and to the Wolfson Foundation and Wellcome Trust for grants to the University to help support my assistant, Gillian Booth, and my 'archivist', Deirdre Sharp. To both of them I am deeply indebted for their endless patience as I drafted and redrafted, and for helping in my checking. I can truly say that I would not have embarked on this book without their help.

INTRODUCTION

The course that my life has taken since the end of the Second World War has turned out to be even less predictable than it was in the years that went before. In the first part of my autobiography, *From Apes to Warlords*, I wrote that I had been moved along by one accident after another, with no clear goal in sight and with no intention of ever following a narrow professional career. What I mostly wanted as I approached my twentieth year was to leave South Africa, and to settle in England. I was born in the Cape in 1904 and had gone to a school where competitive sports, in which I had neither interest nor aptitude, counted far more than did scholarship. My substitute athletic activity, mountaineering, accidentally provided the environment out of which emerged my first scientific interest – the biology of the baboon. In those days one came across the animal wherever one climbed in the wild country of the Cape.

I entered the University of Cape Town as a medical student at the age of seventeen, and after three years gained the BA degree. In the following two I worked for an MA, which I was awarded when I was twenty-one. During those two years, and without denying myself any of the social life there was to enjoy, I read widely, and embarked on an enquiry into the growth of the baboon skull. I imagine that by then I saw myself carrying on with scientific research, not in South Africa, but in England, where great things waited to be savoured. So there I went in January 1926, ostensibly to embark on the clinical part of a doctor's training, but with no intention of becoming a practising doctor, and with an undeclared resolve never to return to the land of my birth.

In London, two years later, I gained my medical qualification. I had already been appointed the Zoological Society of London's Research Anatomist, an appointment that lasted five years. There followed a spell of a year and a half at Yale, where I declined a permanent appointment. I had also declined an invitation to fill the Chair of Anatomy at the Peiping Union Medical College, an institution that was supported in China by the Rockefeller Foundation. At the age of thirty, I returned to England, to a research fellowship and lectureship in Oxford in the Department of Anatomy. There I established a colony of monkeys that I needed for my researches. With the approach of war, I was asked in 1939 to carry out an experiment to see whether monkeys that were restrained in a trench were concussed when a bomb was exploded in the ground nearby. This innocent beginning led to other studies of the wounding effects of weapons, and then, when England came under attack by the Luftwaffe, to the establishment and direction of a national casualty survey. From there a short, but again accidental, step moved me into the world of the warlords – first to the staff of Lord Mountbatten, Chief of Combined Operations, and then, in 1943, to the Mediterranean theatre where I became planning adviser on strategic air operations to Air Chief Marshal Sir Arthur Tedder, Deputy to General Eisenhower, the Supreme Commander. It was in the same capacity that I served both of them, as well as Air Chief Marshal Sir Trafford Leigh-Mallory, the Commander in Chief of the Allied Expeditionary Air Forces, in the Normandy invasion and in the operations that followed.

That, in brief, is the outline of the story that I told in *From Apes to Warlords*, and which ended, after the defeat of Hitler's Germany, with my return to Oxford as an anatomist.

The present volume is an account of the three parallel and overlapping careers that have together filled the years since then. At one and the same time I have been a 'full-time' professor and head of a large university department, the chief executive of the Zoological Society of London, and therefore of the London Zoo, and a government servant. Somehow or other, but without preconceived design, these three interests became woven into a coherent and stimulating pattern of life.

PART I

Birmingham

From Oxford to Birmingham

From autumn 1946 until 1969, that is to say for close on twenty-five years, Birmingham was our home and its university my academic base.

I had not wanted to leave Oxford, where I had been since 1934, but Wilfrid Le Gros Clark, the head of the department in which I then worked, had made it clear that life would become difficult for me were I not to take up the Chair of Anatomy that the Birmingham authorities had kept open for me from before the war – the Birmingham University Calendar had in fact started to list me as their Professor of Anatomy in 1943, well before I had decided whether I wanted the post. It was not within Le Gros Clark's power to deprive me of my Oxford appointment but, as early as March 1944, he had written to say that, were I to decide to remain in Oxford after the war, the plans he was making meant that I would be deprived of much of the space that my research students and I had occupied during the thirties.

Part of the trouble with Le Gros Clark was that the more I had become involved in the study of wounding mechanisms, and then in the analysis of air raids, the more I had to be away from Oxford. My absences became ever more frequent when I was appointed in the spring of 1942 Scientific Adviser to Lord Mountbatten, the Chief of Combined Operations, with the unexpected consequence that I spent most of 1943 in the Mediterranean theatre of war.

Le Gros Clark sent his letter when I was back in England, for at the beginning of 1944 I had also been appointed Scientific Adviser on Air Planning for the invasion of Europe. My academic future was then far from my thoughts. Indeed I had little time even for the affairs of my wound-ballistics team – the Oxford Extra-Mural Unit – which was still busy with its experimental and analytical studies, and which Le Gros Clark had started suggesting should be closed down. Nonetheless, on the next occasion that I was in Oxford, I acknowledged his letter verbally, without committing myself.

Life with Le Gros had its ups and downs. He was the acknowledged senior professor of anatomy in the country and, apart from myself, was the only anatomist who was then a Fellow of the Royal Society. As the doyen of the subject in Britain, he had considerable powers of patronage in the appointment of anatomists to other universities.

We had known each other for years – he had wanted me to join forces with him shortly after I had qualified in medicine and long before he was appointed to Oxford – but my apparently endless energy and multifarious activities and interests as often as not aggravated the bouts of depression to which he was subject. So did my varied and seemingly glamorous social life which, so he once warned me, would prove my undoing. But he also took pleasure in my scientific achievements. And in his autobiography he acknowledged that I had been a considerable help to him in reorganizing and replanning the Oxford Department of Anatomy in the mid-thirties.

In my ignorance, Birmingham University seemed an unattractive prospect. Even if my department-to-be was housed in splendid new premises that were far grander than those at Oxford, I neither had the inclination nor the ambition to resurrect what was nonetheless a somewhat run-down part of the University. It was also clear that, when the fighting stopped, winding up my Extra-Mural Unit would take time. I would have to arrange for the disbandment of a relatively large staff. We not only occupied the rooms in the Department of Anatomy where the work had started in 1939, but had overflowed into another university department, and had also taken over a house as the central HQ for my Casualty Survey. More than that, two large prefabricated-hut laboratories had been built for our experiments on blast and high-velocity fragments. A mass of equipment had to be disposed of, and a home found for our numerous records. Before the fighting had stopped, I had also been appointed scientific director to the British Bombing Survey Unit, which the Government had set up to analyse the strategic results of the bombing offensive against Germany. And as if that were not enough, I had become a member of a central advisory committee on scientific affairs which the post-war Labour Government had set up almost as soon as it came to power in 1945.

For a time I flirted with an idea that was put to me by Roy Harrod, one of Oxford's most distinguished economists and a senior member of Christ Church, the college by which I had been adopted. Roy was influential in its affairs, and saw a way by which I could remain in Oxford, but divorced from the University's Anatomy Department. The idea had its attractions, but I did not pursue it. I was then asked whether I would like to be considered for the vacant Chair of Anatomy in University College, London, to which Le Gros Clark would have moved in 1939 had the war not broken out. But as luck would have it, the amiable interview which I had with a few members of the Electoral Board came to nothing. J.Z. Young, another Oxford friend and a zoologist, was later appointed to the chair.

I say 'as luck would have it' because my subsequent years in Birmingham could not have proved more rewarding. I cannot imagine any other university treating me as generously as I was treated there, or allowing me as much freedom as I was to enjoy.

My wife Joan, who had seen relatively little of me in the last two years of the war, was sympathetic and understanding during the uncertain months before I decided that we would move to Birmingham. But her patience wore thin when I started to search for a new home. Since I saw myself returning from week to week to dine in Christ Church, a house somewhere between Oxford and Birmingham seemed to me to be the obvious choice. There were any number of empty ones on the market after the war, but most were far too big either for our needs or for our means as, indeed, they must have been for the families that had lived in them before the war. In all, and I counted them as I went along, I looked over more than a hundred houses before we settled in Edgbaston, the late Regency and Victorian suburb of Birmingham. Occasionally Joan accompanied me on my housing forays, with our infant son, Paul, in a baby-basket on the back seat of the car. My idea of what we wanted became less and less realistic as the number of houses which I inspected grew. One Edgbaston house on which I had set my heart was as big as a fair-sized country house, and had a 'garden' that covered nine acres. Joan, not without reason, said that I had lost all sense of proportion.

Number 6 Carpenter Road, the lease of which I finally bought, had been built for the kind of gracious living that depended on a plentiful supply of domestic servants. It was little more than a mile from the centre of the city, but in those days no buildings could be seen either

5

from our main sitting room or from the garden which, running as it did into those of its neighbours, made it seem as though we were living on the edge of a spacious park. The lay-out of the house needed changing and modernizing, and the work took much longer than we anticipated because of the stringent post-war building regulations.

The central part of the Birmingham Medical School and its main teaching hospital – known today as the Queen Elizabeth Hospital – formed a complex that had been completed just before the outbreak of war, on a site contiguous with the main University campus. The driving force in the establishment of the new school was Dr Stanley Barnes, a delightfully independent character. He was a bachelor, and a brother of the then Bishop of Birmingham who was renowned in ecclesiastical circles for his advanced and outspoken views.[1]

In Oxford I had managed to avoid serving on any committee other than one that had been set up *ad hoc* to consider the establishment of what is now the Oxford School of Psychology, Philosophy and Physiology. I therefore had little experience of university administration. But I enjoyed the meetings of the Birmingham Medical Faculty Board, first under the chairmanship of Stanley Barnes, then under that of his successor as Dean, Sir Leonard Parsons, a distinguished paediatrician,* who in turn was followed by A.P. Thomson – Sir Arthur Thomson as he became – and the last of the part-time consultant professors to occupy the post.

While a few of my new colleagues on the Faculty Board, which was both inbred and conservative in outlook, regarded me with suspicion, the others could not have been more welcoming. I already enjoyed a national scientific reputation, and had had what was referred to as a 'good' war. The general hope was that I would build up a strong scientific department. What is more, no-one minded that I proposed to carry on with my non-academic activities in Whitehall, probably because most of my new colleagues were clinical consultants who themselves did not abide by any strict academic timetable. They were not at all surprised when, from the start of my appointment, I spent a day or two a week, more often two or three, in London.

The board had only recently begun to meet in the new school, and its

---

*He was later (1948) elected to the Royal Society, a rare honour in those days for a clinician.

members were generally treated with condescension by the Faculty Board of Science and Engineering, the body that had dominated the University campus from the turn of the century. Stanley Barnes later told me that he was sorry that the Medical Faculty had moved at all. This was after he had retired from the deanship, and at a time when the National Health Service was being formed. 'Had I known they were going to nationalize medicine,' he said over a glass of sherry, 'I would not have spent all those years getting the two hospitals together and raising all that money to build a new medical school and hospital – just to have it taken over by those socialists.'

His successors, Parsons and Thomson, were far more resigned to the change. Indeed, A.P. Thomson tried to play a part in the negotiations that brought the medical consultants into the National Health Service, a move which some of his less-enthusiastic colleagues unkindly viewed as a manoeuvre designed to increase his chances of replacing Lord Moran, Winston Churchill's doctor, as President of the Royal College of Physicians. One day 'A.P.' came to my room and said that he had been told that Aneurin ('Nye') Bevan, the Minister of Health, was a friend of mine. There was, he went on, some misunderstanding about the terms that were to be offered to consultant physicians and surgeons, and there would be less opposition if the Minister would agree to this, that and the other. Perhaps, he went on, I could mention his worries the next time I saw Bevan. I asked whether he would like me to try to get an immediate answer. He said yes. I picked up the telephone and managed to get through to Nye, to whom I explained that I had with me a leading Birmingham consultant and colleague who wanted to clear up some ambiguities. Nye seemed to know about A.P. and about the issues which he had raised, and gave reassuring answers. The questions meant nothing to me, but when A.P. brought the matter up a few days later at a meeting of the Royal College of Physicians in London, Moran, who was in the chair, upstaged him by saying that he had already settled the problem, and that he also knew how Thomson had got his information. There were no flies on Moran. A.P. never did become President of the College.

But if A.P. was not as distinguished a clinician or as widely respected as were his two predecessors, he was certainly a nimbler and more receptive chairman of a faculty meeting. For the convenience of the clinicians, the board met late on a Friday afternoon at monthly

7

intervals. On one occasion I arrived from London to find my colleagues about to decide that the two vast glass screens which now separate the spacious foyer of the Medical School from the library – the latter was built after the main building – should be etched in small panels depicting medicinal herbs. A.P. asked what I thought of the sketches that were being passed around. I replied that floral decorations seemed more appropriate for the curtains of a drawing room or kitchen. 'What do you suggest instead?' he asked, to which I replied, 'Why don't we have life-sized reproductions of the anatomical figures in Vesalius's *Fabrica?*' – the famous anatomical work that was published in 1543. 'Why not?' said A.P., and all agreed. There they are today, a most conspicuous imprint of whatever influence I exercised as a professor in Birmingham.

Science and Engineering constituted the outstanding faculty in Birmingham, and its board counted among its members a number of internationally famed men, including Sir Norman Haworth, a chemist and a Nobel Laureate; Mark Oliphant, the Australian nuclear physicist who had been one of Rutherford's most distinguished disciples in Cambridge; and Rudolf Peierls, the theoretical physicist who, together with a fellow refugee, Otto Frisch, had been encouraged by Oliphant to spell out for the first time how an atomic bomb of practicable size could be made. Another of the many outstanding wartime achievements of Oliphant's department was Randall and Boot's invention of the cavity magnetron, a device that had revolutionized radar, and without which Britain and America might well have lost the air war.

Haworth was 'number one' among the University's professors, and he made it his business, as did Oliphant, to give me whatever support I needed in bringing about changes in the department that I had taken over. They also appointed me a member of their board.

After I had settled in, I also attended a few meetings of the Senate, which in those days met, not in the grand chamber it graces today, but in a dreary room in the basement of Aston Webb's main university building, still the finest architectural feature of what has become a tightly-packed campus.

The Senate was presided over by the Vice Chancellor, Raymond Priestley. Priestley, who had served as the Secretary General of Faculties in Cambridge University, and for three years as Vice Chancellor of the University of Melbourne, was celebrated not only as a university administrator, but also as a polar explorer – he had been a member of both Scott's and Shackleton's expeditions to the South Pole, about which he reminisced with enormous interest and pleasure. He also told me that he had not been the Priestley whom the Council of the University thought they had invited to be interviewed for the post of vice chancellor. But it was too late for them to retract when, during the course of the meeting, this became apparent. Who the other Priestley was I never did learn.

Oliphant shared my view that the Senate was far too big and conflicting in its interests to be an effective forum for determining University policy in a period when higher education was expanding rapidly. By then I had become Deputy Chairman of the Government's Advisory Council on Scientific Policy, and Chairman of its most important sub-committee, that on Scientific Manpower. With Oliphant of the same mind, we therefore drafted a paper proposing that a small executive committee of the Senate be set up to 'process' the issues which the whole Senate could then decide. Older hands opposed us, but in the end we prevailed, both of us being appointed founder members of what at first was a body of about ten, presided over by the Vice Chancellor. I served for two years, and from then on, until I left Birmingham, I rarely attended any meetings of the Senate or of its sub-committees. But I tried never to miss the monthly boards of the Medical Faculty.

The Department of Anatomy

The Birmingham chair had fallen vacant in 1938 on the resignation of Professor R.D. Lockhart, who had returned to Aberdeen to fill a Regius chair of the university of which he was a distinguished graduate. Lockhart was a delightful character, and a conventional anatomist of the old school. I got to know him well on his frequent and welcome visits to Birmingham, where he showed an enormous interest in the changes that I was introducing. He lived to the age of 93, enjoying fame as a cultivator of roses and rhododendrons.

In the interval between his resignation and my formal acceptance of the chair, Charles Smout, a medical man and anatomist, had acted as head of the department. Charles was a strict disciplinarian, and was celebrated for his lectures on the female pelvis. Apart from him, the staff that I inherited consisted of Walter Brandt, a man of the highest decorum and a refugee professor of anatomy from Gottingen – one of a few non-Jewish academics who had fled from Hitler's Germany; Sam Green, a young Birmingham medical graduate, who had just been demobilized; and an American embryologist called Reagan. Reagan was a superb microdissector and illustrator. He was also one of the most eccentric people with whom I have ever had to deal. He avoided contact with people; he was always untidy, with his clothes stained either with gravy or with some laboratory chemical; and rumour had it that he had fled from America because of a homosexual scandal. I had no idea where he lived until I discovered that his room in the department was also his home. His bed was mounted on tables, for when he slept he liked to have as little space as possible between himself and the ceiling. He cooked and ate in his room, and an unpleasant smell seeped from under his door, which he always kept locked. He washed in the students' lavatory, and one evening was found stark naked having a bath in a big white sink with which the dissecting room was furnished. I decided that a stop had to be put to this eccentric domesticity. Bill Pardoe, the department's head technician, said he would find a way of moving poor Reagan into a room so small that there would be nowhere for him to hide even a folding bed. That took time, for Reagan knew what I was doing, but in the end Pardoe succeeded.

I never did learn how to deal with Reagan. His genius as a micro-dissector was widely recognized among a small and very specialized group of scholars, one of whose leaders was Professor Kenneth Franklin, FRS, an Oxford physiologist. Franklin was a celebrated medical historian, and an authority on William Harvey, the discoverer of the circulatory system of the blood. Reagan had promised to provide him with a chapter and a series of special illustrations for a book that he was producing. From time to time Franklin would turn up to see Reagan, but Reagan would have vanished. Then one day, after the book had appeared, but minus Reagan's contribution, a fat parcel addressed to Franklin was brought to my office by a worried Pardoe. Having spoken to Franklin over the telephone, I asked Pardoe to remove the first layer of wrapping. On the second was an instruction, saying that Franklin was not to remove the next layer unless he undertook to publish, without change, all that was in the parcel. Pardoe and I looked at each other, and I said, 'Go on.' The third layer had an even more abrupt instruction. To this day, I have no idea whether or where Reagan's superb illustrations were ever reproduced, nor do I know where they are now. When Reagan died in 1965, dealing with his effects was not easy.

Pardoe was a professional jack-of-all-trades, if there can be such a thing. He had three technicians under him. One was Ernie Sims, who looked after the bodies which the first and second year medical students dissected. Sims had served in the Machine Gun Corps during the First World War, and had been wounded and twice mentioned in despatches. He was a considerable character and a perfectionist in the preparation of bodies for dissection. The second was Willie Tranter, who was essentially Sim's understudy. The third was Tom Spence, who had been recently demobilized from the RAF. Tom was avid to learn, and also had an enquiring mind. One day he surprised me with a paper he had written describing the South-American practice of head-shrinking. It took little encouragement to make him go further, and in due course – and with a certain relaxation of university rules – he obtained the degree of BSc, and a place on the academic staff. Tom retired in 1980, after serving the University for thirty-six years, and having held every rank from technician to senior lecturer. During these years he published a book and numerous scientific papers. It was a remarkable achievement for a man who had left school at the age of fourteen without even the equivalent of one of today's O levels.

As a condition of my acceptance of the Chair, the authorities had agreed to provide me with quarters in which to pursue my experimental work, and also to establish four new lectureships, plus associated staff. Three of my wartime colleagues had already decided to throw in their lot with me: Peter Krohn, who had been a pupil of mine in Oxford; Alexander ('Sandy') Thomson, the soldier who had attached himself to me in January 1943, when the 8th Army entered Tripoli; and Peter Eckstein, the refugee scientist who had kept some of my prewar experimental researches alive. The fourth post, which I had originally intended for another of my wartime staff, who then changed his mind, was filled later. One of the new technical and secretarial posts which had also been agreed was filled by a member of my Oxford wound-ballistics team. Sergeant Barney Campion, ex-RAF, was appointed to a second. Barney had been assigned to me in mid-1943 in North Africa as a 'clerk', and had remained in the Mediterranean theatre until the end of the war as a member of the Bombing Survey Unit that I had set up in Sicily. I then arranged for him to join me in Birmingham.

The new Anatomy School comprised a magnificent dissecting hall and lecture theatre, and a number of unequipped rooms. There were two or three old microscopes, but not a single balance on which to weigh chemicals or tissues. Under the direction of Smout, Sims and Pardoe kept the dissecting room in so spotless a state that at the start of each session it was turned – minus bodies – into a tearoom in which the parents of those students who had been fortunate enough to secure a place in the school were entertained. Half of an enormous museum that was allocated to the department housed a heterogeneous collection of skeletal material and anthropological specimens, including numerous stone-age implements, with little in the way of labels to explain their provenance. The transformation of the department into what it became a few years later was not just a case of making a desert bloom. It was more like a seismic upheaval.

As was then the practice in all British medical schools, students worked for five full terms in the dissecting room, and were also expected to attend regular lectures on the structure of the body. Anatomy was also treated as a subject that had little connection with the study of the functions and chemistry of living tissue. Of my wartime colleagues who came with me, I was the only one who had ever been taught the anatomy of the old textbooks. Fortunately my colleagues on the Faculty Board raised no objections to the appointments I was making, and by agreement with Peter Gilding, the Professor of Physiology, I also proposed to pursue experimental studies which in some schools would have been regarded as part of his discipline.

Talk about the reform of the medical curriculum had long been in the air, with the trend of most discussion focusing on the need to introduce into the curriculum both a sense of the social needs which the medical practitioner should try to satisfy, and the spirit of an intellectual rather than a didactic education. Would-be reformers kept talking about the desirability of departing from descriptive instruction to an education that had as its basis a general scientific understanding of the mechanisms underlying the processes of health and disease. It was also widely realized that, with the growth of knowledge, particularly in the clinical subjects, the medical curriculum was becoming over-crowded, and students over-burdened.

In my time, however, every professor was master of his own house, and it would have been a rare one who would have surrendered part of the time allotted to him in the curriculum in order to allow more for a colleague. In this respect, the heads of anatomical departments had long been regarded as the worst sinners, and the subject had come to be looked at askance. But at the same time anatomists were custodians of a part of the medical curriculum which, however belittled, no one seemed anxious to jettison. The result was that the subject had come to be regarded as the Cinderella of the medical sciences.

As I saw it, there was no point in uncluttering the subject of unimportant detail merely to create a vacuum which would be filled, according to the taste of the individual teacher, by borrowings from another subject. To begin with, I therefore proposed the abolition of conventional lectures on the structure of the body. I then proposed that the student should not be made to spend the conventional five terms working in the dissecting room; three would be enough.

Early in 1947 I spelt all this out in a paper that was published in *The*

Lancet, and in which I wrote that 'in the belief that half-measures were not likely to solve the fundamental difficulties, we have in Birmingham taken the radical step of completely reintegrating the subject [anatomy] with physiology. The term reintegration is used advisedly, for it is only relatively recently that the two disciplines went their separate ways.'[1] In the three years that followed, I published a few brief reports whose purpose was to show that reducing the time the student spent on structural anatomy did not undermine any part of the foundation which was needed for his further medical studies. Because it would have been inappropriate if only my name had appeared as the author of a paper that dealt with the combined study of form and function, I got Gilding to add his name to a paper which I prepared in 1953 for the First World Conference on Medical Education that called for the full integration of anatomy and physiology.[2] Gilding's heart was not in the project; all he wanted was a quiet life. Integration meant work, and he was not prepared to make any changes in a departmental curriculum whose pattern he had set nearly twenty years before. We remained on good terms, but I had to lower my reforming sights as I continued to reorganize my department.

With the help of my staff I produced an atlas and guide to dissection under the title *A New System of Anatomy*.[3] It took all of ten years to write, mimeographed version after version being tried out on each new annual intake of students. In those days the human body was seldom dissected in Denmark, and Birmingham was one of the British schools to which Danish students came during the long vacation to do their practical anatomy. They, too, proved a most valuable set of 'guinea pigs' for the text I was trying to achieve. I experimented with several methods of illustration before deciding to rely mainly on touched-up photographs of actual dissections, and here the good nature, patience and tolerance of Pardoe and Spence in complying with my exigent demands is something I shall never forget. But there had to be an end to chopping and changing, and in 1959 I submitted my typescript and illustrations to the Oxford University Press. The book went through many impressions and, with the help of two of my old colleagues, a second edition was prepared and published in 1981. Since the book has already been in use in several medical schools for some thirty years, I feel justified in claiming that I suceeded in my objective of reducing the drudgery of dissection.

I also embarked on the enormous task of transforming our half of the school's big museum into a teaching museum. As it turned out, however, we did not have the resources to finish the job in the way I had planned. Moreover, and much to our surprise, most students thought that there must be a catch in what we were doing. Simple visual displays and models were not trusted in those days. What had not been read either in Gray's or Cunningham's big textbooks of anatomy was suspect. The late Mark Longman, then the head of the publishing house that bears his family name, invited me to a dinner to mark the centenary of the appearance of *Gray's Anatomy*. He told me that the book was so well-known, and still in such demand, that its sale alone would guarantee modest prosperity for a publisher even if he were never to issue another book.

But sorting out the essential bread and butter work of the Anatomy Department was only a background for ever more exciting ventures.

The Faculty Boards of Medicine and Science jointly agreed that I could launch a novel course for the BSc degree in which, instead of being subjected to formal training, students would spend a year carrying out research. The few who were selected to do this were guided in their choice of problem towards one of the main lines of enquiry that were being pursued in the department. It was the fact that these all derived ultimately from my early interest in the story of human evolution which distinguished my own from almost all other departments of anatomy and physiology in the country. My preoccupation with hormonal mechanisms, and in particular those that control the reproductive processes, was born out of the analysis I had made of the social behaviour of monkeys and apes. Our neurological researches stemmed partly from studies of the hormonal acceleration of growth, and partly from an analysis of certain forms of behaviour. We housed a large collection of monkeys, some of which were the survivors of the colony of animals on which I had started to work in Oxford in 1934. As our programme of research fanned out, it was obvious that more space was necessary. I had no difficulty in getting the necessary funds from the Research Councils and from such private foundations as the Wellcome and the Ford. While we were waiting for proper quarters to be provided for my animal colony, a temporary home for the few monkeys I had brought with me was found in a large room that had been used to store the coffins which, in those days, were made by

15

Pardoe. In order to free the room, we started buying coffins as and when they were needed. (The Anatomy Act requires that after they have been dissected, bodies have to be given a formal burial.) The Wellcome Trust later provided funds for even bigger animal quarters than those built by the University. By the mid-sixties my department was attracting more research funds from outside sources than the rest of the Medical Faculty put together.

It has always been my belief that any reasonable student can be taught to appreciate the pleasures of personal discovery – even if not all to the same extent. Each BSc student had his own tutor to direct his work and reading, at the start either myself, Peter Krohn or Anita Mandl, a research worker who came to us in 1948 from the London Hospital. There were no lectures, but we organized seminars, many of them on topics remote from the medical curriculum, and given by colleagues from other universities. The original intention had been that the new 'course' would be a joint one between anatomy and physiology. But once again Gilding found it less wearisome to manage his students in a conventional way. He even forbade them to spend time listening to A.J. Ayer talking about scientific method, or Frank Yates on the new horizons of enquiry which the computer was going to reveal, or J.D. Bernal on X-ray crystallography.

Not long after I had launched my new variety of BSc course, I was asked by the editor of the Birmingham students' medical magazine to write an article explaining what was going on in the Anatomy Department. I began by saying that

> Scientific research is never as clear-cut in practice as in theory. A true account of the history of an enquiry usually reads less like a detective story, with its orderly procession from clues to discoveries and to the final leap of imagination which elucidates the whole problem, than like the accounts of early voyages of exploration. . . . A man might spend half his life beating up and down the coast of America in search of a Northwest Passage . . . but never reaching his Indies. The research worker bent on advancing some particular branch of biology might end in much the same way. His successes would depend partly on his skill in continually adjusting the direction of his enquiries, as well as their purpose, in relation to all and sundry of his observations – and partly on his

16

judgment in deciding which plants, and which animals, were worth collecting on the way.[4]

I went on to say that 'someone with a conventional view' of anatomy might well wonder why an anatomy student should be training a rat to run an intricate maze; another carrying out some chemical operation in front of a scaffolding of glass and rubber tubing; a third trying to net a monkey; a fourth, in semi-darkness, glued to a microscope; and a fifth busy with a calculating machine, establishing the statistical significance of differences in the measurements of skulls. These, I pointed out, were some of the many shapes which research may assume in an anatomical department today.

There was criticism that my BSc course was too elitist – the number of students who could be dealt with rarely exceeded five or six a year. But adverse comment soon died down. Students had to work hard, far harder than did the average undergraduate I had known in prewar Oxford, and before long the department, which evolved into a small community of scholars, was working a seven-day week, with lights burning well into the night not only on weekdays but also at weekends. At the end of their year's work the BSc students had to pull together the results of their researches into a properly bound thesis before they presented themselves for a lengthy a lengthy examination by professors from other universities. But none of this harsh treatment dampened the enthusiasm of those who had elected to take the course. Some enjoyed the thrill of seeing their theses accepted for publication in scientific journals. As often as not, their work posed new questions that called for investigation by one of the next crop of BSc students. A few became so keen on the work they were doing that, instead of returning to their medical studies, they applied for grants with which to continue with their own researches, so sacrificing the prospect of a secure career in medicine for the chance of an academic appointment. Those who completed their clinical studies soon found themselves being competed for as 'housemen' by the clinical professors.

My responsibility as Head of Department did not come to an end when, in January of 1960, I became Chief Scientific Adviser to the Ministry of Defence. A condition that I made when I accepted the appointment was that, if the University authorities agreed, I would remain in full executive charge of my department without a salary.

Despite the fact that my new appointment meant that from then on I was usually in London during the week, and often abroad, the department continued to grow and to prosper. Sandy Thomson and, after him, a later recruit to the staff, Peter Dallas Ross, a Cambridge graduate, took over the administration and the supervision of the routine teaching, while Peter Krohn, Anita Mandl and I continued to wield the whip over our young research workers. In 1958 our team was strengthened by the recruitment of Sir Francis Knowles who, when a master at Marlborough College, had made a name for himself through his research work on the hormones of shrimps. I had met him in the thirties when he was an Oxford undergraduate, and my colleagues on the Faculty Board were persuaded that, although Francis knew nothing about human anatomy, his knowledge of the ultra-microscopic structure of tissues would make him a useful addition to our staff, which by then also included some five of the students who had taken the BSc course.

In due course our research interests became so well defined that the department was divided into five quasi-autonomous sub-departments, of which one was under Peter Krohn, and another under Eric Ashton. Eric had been one of the first of my BSc students. Peter Krohn was elected to the Fellowship of the Royal Society in 1963 and Francis Knowles in 1966. They might well have been followed into the Society by Anita Mandl, had I not abided by custom and told her that I proposed putting her name forward as a candidate. A few days later she came to tell me not to do so, since she intended to resign her lectureship. I sometimes ask myself whether the happy life she has enjoyed since then, and her success as a sculptor, have really made up for the loss that British science suffered when she decided to leave the laboratory.

By the late sixties we had become one of the most flourishing departments in the whole University, and by the time I retired from the chair in 1968, some twenty of the BSc students, research fellows or junior members of staff who had passed through my hands, had become heads of departments in other universities, or full professors on individual merit. That, I would say, was the most rewarding outcome of the years I spent in Birmingham.

3

Eggs, Humours and Skulls

In 1964, on an occasion when the Royal College of Surgeons convened its Annual General Meeting in the Birmingham Medical School, I was called upon to deliver an address to mark my election as an Honorary Fellow of the College, of which I was already a Member. I called it 'The Natural History of an Enquiry', my theme being the origin of the female egg or germ cells, one of the three main lines of enquiry that were being pursued in the department.[1]

During the course of the research that I was carrying out in Oxford before the war, I had made a chance observation which led me to suppose that sex hormones could be used to regenerate the menopausal ovary, and so make it possible for women to conceive and bear children after their normal reproductive life had come to an end. At that time the conventional view was that new egg cells are produced throughout reproductive life, and that the process stops abruptly at the menopause. This was almost the first piece of prewar research to which I returned when I settled down in Birmingham. Confusion soon set in. Some of my new observations simply did not fit. I therefore decided to go back to square one, and to examine the evidence that was the foundation of the conventional teaching, and which had been the basis of my – as it was to turn out – incorrect hunch. It was not convincing. There have often been pieces of scientific dogma, particularly in the biological sciences, that have become conventional wisdom without having been subjected to critical scrutiny.

I therefore decided to re-examine my new findings in the light of a contrary hypothesis which had been the accepted teaching up to the end of the nineteenth century, namely, that women are born with a finite number of germ cells, which are used up during reproductive life. It was only then that they began to make sense. I designed further experiments, and a series of new microscopical enquiries. The results made it clear that the nineteenth-century view of the subject, which had been proposed by Waldeyer, a German microscopist, was the correct one.

Although ramifications of the work were going to be pursued for many years, mostly by Anita Mandl and the BSc pupils she tutored, I soon judged that I had enough evidence to 'go public', and to try to overturn what was manifestly a false hypothesis that had far-reaching practical implications. My opportunity came in 1950 in the form of an invitation to attend a conference of American endocrinologists that was due to take place at Franconia in New Hampshire. Apart from the pleasure I would get from seeing many of my American scientific colleagues, accepting the invitation also meant that I would have the chance of spending a few days with E.E. Cummings, the poet, and his wife Marion who, since it was late summer, would still be at their New Hampshire farm at Silver Lake, not many miles from the tourist hotel where the meeting was due to take place. We had been friends since the early thirties, when I was at Yale.

The audience included most of the then leading research workers in the field of reproductive physiology, and I was given an hour to deliver my address. Dr Carl Hartman, a prominent American scholar, was in the chair. For years his work on monkeys had run on lines parallel to my own, and there had once been talk of his coming to work with me in England, an idea he thought funny since he was much the senior in years. Before the meeting began, he told me that he had with him some lantern slides which demonstrated that the formation of egg-cells (oogenesis) could be stimulated in mature rhesus monkeys by means of hormones, slides which I could throw on the screen in order to reinforce the point he thought I was going to make.

The slides were not shown. Instead Carl began the customary laudatory remarks a chairman makes when a speaker sits down by saying that he had listened with attention to my tale and stood there both 'convinced and convicted' – he, like myself, had uncritically fallen under the sway of the prevailing hypothesis. He ended his remarks with the statement that the story I had outlined had convinced him that 'Waldeyer must have been right after all.' He could not have been more generous.

It was also an academic triumph. Much of practical value depended on knowing whether there were natural limits to the formation of egg-cells in the human ovary. But triumph or not, it did not mean that those members of my audience who had not worked on the subject had followed my critique, nor that the incorrect textbook story would be altered overnight. Much more work had to be done before the false doctrine was buried.

The meeting has remained a vivid memory. I had driven to it with a party of physiologists from Yale, having broken my journey in New Haven to spend a few hours with John and Lucia Fulton. John was the professor who had arranged my sojourn at Yale in 1933 and 1934. Most unusually for me, I had started a headache before I got to the Fultons'. By the time I was deposited at the Franconia hotel, it had developed into one of those fierce migraines that is associated with the loss of part of one's vision. The only thing to do was retire to bed. My paper was to be the opening one of the conference, and when I woke next morning I had only partly recovered. But I spoke for the full hour that had been allotted to me, conscious all the time of the hammering in my head. After I had finished, my still-defective vision made it difficult to focus on whoever it was in the audience who had put a question or made a comment.

At the end of the meeting, I was driven to a rendezvous where I was picked up by Marion Cummings and taken to Joy Farm. Unlike Marion, Cummings was not even mildly interested in what I had to say about the meeting. Most of the time he just sat on the verandah at the back of the house, which opened on to fields that had once been cleared and cultivated, but which were now becoming covered by trees that grew like weeds. It was always fun conversing with him, even when the noise of mechanical saws felling trees in woods behind his property made him wince. Cummings pretended not to like the modern world. Marion took his moods, if that is how they should be described, in her stride. They did not interfere with either her housekeeping and shopping, or her hobby, photography. Not long after I had returned to England, I read something that Cummings had published and which denigrated science. I wrote protesting. Back came the reply: '. . . it hadn't occurred to ignorant me that you might be a scientist; I'd have sworn . . . that my favorite rogue was a human being.'[2]

The second of the main fields of research to which I returned as soon as circumstances allowed was that of the mechanisms whereby the hormonal and nervous systems act together in controlling the functions of the body. The science of hormones – endocrinology – was in its infancy, and an endless series of questions seemed to be calling for answers – as indeed they continue to do. I had had the good fortune in my early work on the reproductive cycle of monkeys to make some critical observations that helped determine the time when ovulation occurs in the monthly menstrual cycle, and more important, to propose an adequate general hypothesis to explain the hormonal control of the phases of the cycle. That problem was of considerable interest at the time, and my own researches, which were published in a lengthy series of papers, most of them in the *Proceedings of the Royal Society*, were being pursued in parallel with, but quite independently of others that were being carried out by endocrinologists in the United States. The foremost of the American workers was George Corner who, after elucidating the way an ovarian hormone called progesterone prepares the lining of the uterus for the implantation of the fertilized ovum, had shifted his interest to the study of the menstrual cycle, and had hit upon the same explanation of its control as I had. As he records in his autobiography, on announcing his discovery in 1937, he 'was happy to mention that Solly Zuckerman had stated in the same year as I a conception of the antagonism of progesterone to estrogen [a second ovarian hormone] in the primate cycle, practically identical with mine. Solly and I, then as now cordial friends, had no reason to contend for priority in this matter.' He went on to say that so far as he knew, 'the basic hypothesis of an antagonistic effect of progesterone upon estrogen has never been disputed; in fact, a good deal of evidence has accumulated to support it, and the whole concept is now generally accepted'.[3] Corner added that our hypothesis was basic to an understanding of the way the birth-control pill worked.

In parallel with this research, I was pursuing the notion that the endocrine functions of the ovaries might be under some kind of nervous control, an idea which I abandoned after some two years of fruitless experimental work. I then turned my attention to the more direct problem of how it is that light mediates the annual reproductive rhythm in so many species of animal – the most familiar example being the battery-hen which, when kept under regular conditions of artificial light, lays eggs throughout the year.

The animal that I chose to study was the ferret, which in England normally has a restricted breeding season that lasts from mid-March to September. But ferrets that are kept in artificial light during the winter can be made to come into heat precociously, while those kept continually in the dark exhibit no regular rhythm. The eyes are clearly the primary receptors in the sequence of events, in the same way as the ovaries, through the hormones they produce, constitute the terminal reactor in the system. Between the two is the all-important pituitary gland, a small endocrine organ that is attached by a stalk to the base of the brain, and which exercises a kind of controlling function over the rest of the body's endocrine system. Students used to be taught that the pituitary is 'the conductor of the endocrine orchestra', and for all I know, they may still be in some schools.

The trouble, however, is that the part of the pituitary that does the controlling has no obvious nerve supply. How, therefore, are its very precise functions stimulated by nervous impulses? A Cambridge anatomist, Geoffrey Harris, proposed that nervous impulses that start in the eye travel to the minute region of the brain – called the hypothalamus – where the pituitary stalk starts. Here the impulses cause the release of specific chemical substances – chemotransmitters – which, according to Harris, passed down the vessels of the stalk to stimulate the pituitary to produce its own specific hormones which, in turn, stimulate the other endocrine organs of the body – for example the ovary and the thyroid gland. While this hypothesis was little better than speculation, it caught on for lack of any better explanation.

I was sceptical. The validity of the hypothesis was critically dependent upon three basic propositions, each of which had to stand up to experimental test. I designed a series of experiments to test two of them, and by 1953 had assembled enough evidence to throw serious doubt on what by then had become known as the pituitary–portal hypothesis. That year I had been invited to deliver the Addison Memorial Lecture at Guy's Hospital in London. Addison was the physician who had published a monograph in 1855 in which he ascribed the disease that is still known by his name to a disorder of the adrenal glands, structures whose endocrine function was not known at the time. I decided to use the opportunity to deliver my critique, which I entitled 'The Secretions of the Brain'. I enjoyed the occasion, mainly because, when preparing the lecture, I had delved into the original literature about the 'bodily humours', and in so doing had realized that the pituitary–portal hypothesis, with its presumption of multifarious chemicals being produced by a finite number of nerve cells in a small part of the brain, each exercising a specific bodily function, was a re-run of the medieval belief that four humours control the state of the body.

Two years later I delivered a much more direct critique of the hypothesis at a seminar that was devoted solely to the subject. I was already too late. My criticisms led to no better explanation, whereas the naive mechanistic hypothesis at which they were directed made everything appear so simple that, true or false, it was something to which to cling. But I continued my experiments, helped by a small team of students, at the same time as scores of workers in other laboratories tried – with highly conflicting results – to extract from the minute hypothalamus, chemotransmitters or 'releasing factors' which, when injected into an experimental animal, were supposed to cause the pituitary gland to release one or other of the specific hormones that control the hormonal output of the secretory cells of the ovaries or of the adrenal glands.

In 1970 I published my last review of the subject, asserting in my concluding paragraph that the hypothesis about the pituitary portal vessels is 'beyond direct experimental proof', and that it had no more scientific value than the ancient belief 'that through the [pituitary] gland passed the phlegm, one of the four humours of the body, to percolate through the olfactory nerves to the front part of the base of the skull and so into the nose. We have now abandoned the view that health depends on the balance between the phlegm and the three other humours of the body, blood, yellow bile and black bile. I am prepared to bet that in due course the pituitary-portal theory will follow the humours to the same graveyard of abandoned hypotheses where they now rest.'[4]

I did not have to wait long. The chemical nature of some of the hypothalamic chemotransmitters was unravelled some years later, an achievement for which Professors Guillemin, Schally and Yalow shared a Nobel Prize in 1977. Since then other workers have managed to extract precisely the same chemicals, with identical properties, from tissues that have no connection whatever with either the hypothalamus or any other part of the brain.

*　　*　　*

The third main field of enquiry to which I returned after the war concerned the question of man's evolutionary origins, a subject that had fascinated me from my earlier years in South Africa. A number of new fossils were being unearthed in South, and then East Africa, all of which were being hailed as unique 'missing links' in our ancestry. Public interest was considerable, and stories about our new fossil relations could not be kept out of the papers. While my renewed interest in the subject could not have been regarded as better than desultory, it soon brought me into a running debate with Le Gros Clark. He, too, had long been interested in the subject and, like me, had at first been highly sceptical about the new claims that were being made by South African anthropologists. Suddenly, however, he changed his views. From then until his death he became obsessed with the subject, and it was largely because of his support that the view that the South African fossils – the Australopithecines – represent a stage in man's evolution has become part of conventional teaching, even if a precarious part. The subject being what it is, the *obiter dicta* of authority count far more than does dispassionate study. Who is likely to forget the story of the Piltdown Skull?

With the help of Eric Ashton, I started to check statements that had been made about differences in the dimensions of the teeth of the African fossils and those of living apes and man. The results confirmed my doubts. Le Gros Clark was much annoyed. I had failed to appreciate that what was a sideline interest to me had become his main preoccupation. He was not, however, prepared to sit down to see where and why our findings diverged. Any view contrary to what he was then expounding he regarded as a personal affront – with the result that he opposed almost everything on the subject that emanated from my department.

In order to help challenge our findings, he turned to Jacob Bronowski – why Bronowski, we never did discover – to provide an alternative statistical approach to the problem. Whatever else he may have been, Bronowski was not an authority on statistics. By profession he was a geometer, and an authority on William Blake, the eighteenth-century poet and painter; that was before he became a TV personality and a popular philosopher. As I once wrote, during the war we had found him 'a great waster of time', who 'impressed people by always suggesting some alternative mathematical approach to problems of

25

analysis which had already been dealt with by simpler and perfectly adequate methods'[5] – usually propounded by Frank Yates, my wartime colleague and the doyen of British statisticians. It must have pleased Bronowski to be called in by Le Gros Clark to help refute what I was saying about the latest fossil finds.

Unfortunately, a statistical error had crept into one of our calculations. In comparing the measurements of the teeth of living apes with the published dimensions of those of the South African fossils, we had used a formula devised for us by the author – not Yates – of a much-used textbook on statistics. The formula proved to be defective, and it introduced a systematic error into the comparisons. But since the error applied to both sides of our equations, it made little difference to the conclusions that we were drawing.

Ironically it was not Bronowski who discovered the error. That was done by Frank Yates, whom I had asked to comment on a short article that Bronowski had published in *Nature*. As soon as my attention had been drawn to the mistake, I published a correction, at the same time pointing out that the error was of little significance to the conclusions we had drawn. But Le Gros Clark seized on 'the error of root 2', as I had styled it, and paid no more attention to its lack of significance than did Bronowski to the strictures later made by Yates of his own statistical pronouncements. I can still see Bronowski, in one of his celebrated TV programmes, with a plaster cast of the first Australopithecine fossil skull in his hand, telling the world of his continuing sense of wonder as he contemplated that spectral human ancestor.

In 1951 I delivered the Wood Jones Memorial Lecture in the University of Manchester to the title, 'Art and Science in Anatomical Diagnosis'.[6] My main point was that those anatomists who believe that the eye can recognize critical diagnostic features in a fragment of bone have been proved wrong so often that the immediate diagnosis which the unaided eye provides should always be regarded as suspect. Any tendency to assurance in these matters should, I said, be exorcised, since the evolutionary inferences we base on structural comparisons are in the end only speculations.

This last remark was certainly not intended as a dig at Le Gros Clark, although the occasion may not have been well-judged since the lecture commemorated a man whom he had much admired, but who had never returned the compliment. The debate between the

Birmingham and Oxford schools then started to be regarded as a feud that was damaging the image of the discipline of anatomy. Le Gros died in 1971, and I sometimes find myself wondering what he would have made of the constant overturning by an ever-growing number of fossil hunters of his firm pronouncements about the Australopithecines. The biometric studies that I started in Birmingham are still pursued, in the United Kingdom and in Australia, by two of my old pupils, Charles Oxnard and Jim Moore (Ashton died in 1985). Unfortunately, the many sound papers and books which they – now styled the 'Birmingham school of palaeontologists' – have published have not yet succeeded in bringing discipline to a field of study that should have a place among the sciences. But I am sure that that day will come.

I have written only about three of the main lines of enquiry in which I was engaged in Birmingham. Peter Krohn, Francis Knowles and other members of staff developed their special fields. The results of our work are recorded in scores of scientific papers and monographs. We were an enormously active and enthusiastic department. For fifteen years we edited the *Journal of Endocrinology*, taking it in turns to do the donkey-work which editorship entails. We were assiduous in our support of several scientific societies, and also organized and attended national and international seminars on subjects that related to our work.

By the time I retired from the chair in 1968, the staff of the department, including research fellows and technical assistants, had grown from eight to about 125. I and others regarded Peter Krohn as the natural successor to the chair, but he decided that he did not want the administrative responsibility, and boldly but regretfully retired from academic life. The Birmingham authorities then decided that Francis Knowles, even if an FRS, was not enough of an anatomist to succeed – although he was later elected to the Chair of Anatomy in King's College, London, where, alas, his career was cut short by a sudden and fatal heart-attack. In the end, John Eayrs, another of my first batch of BSc students, was persuaded to resign the chair he already held in the University of London, and to return to Birmingham to take my place.

My departure in 1968 was marked by a sentimental dinner given by the department. Everyone was there. We were like a large extended family. I was presented with a handsomely bound volume of the printed

27

reports that I had had to submit to the University authorities every year, and which gave the titles of nearly nine hundred scientific papers that we had published during the period of my stewardship (and of which I was the author or part author of nearly a quarter). I was also given a handsome snuff-box that had been made by a Birmingham silversmith who would have been known to my early-nineteenth-century predecessor, Sands Cox. A farewell dinner was also organized by the board of the faculty, while the University, having appointed me a Professor Emeritus, awarded me the honorary degree of Doctor of Laws. The Earl of Avon (Anthony Eden as he was better known), was Chancellor, and presided over the occasion in the Great Hall. I have just reread the short oration that I had to deliver, and fear that it was more than a little pompous.

4

Social Life in Birmingham

Number 6 Carpenter Road was about a mile from the Medical School and about the same distance from the centre of the city. With workmen constantly in and out of the house, our first year was far from pleasant. The winter of 1946–7 was one of the coldest on record. The railways had been brought to a standstill. Coal was rationed – and it was impossible to keep warm. Paul, who was just a year old when we left Oxford, was followed a year after we had moved by our daughter, Stella.

In Oxford, all our neighbours had some connection with the University. In Birmingham, academics were scattered over a wider area, which was a pity as many were very interesting people – and not only in their specialist fields. I saw all too little of Mark Oliphant; he lived nearly ten miles from us. A Professor Garner lived fairly close by. He was one of the University's top engineers, but had also written a definitive text on English delftware. His other hobby was the Cromwellian period of English history. It was usually assumed, so he told me, that genius had died during the years of the Commonwealth, whereas it was as creative a period as any other. He enjoyed showing me his collection of books and memorabilia, one of the most outstanding in the world, of the five years of Cromwell's Protectorship. We got to know Thomas Bodkin, who was the Professor of Fine Arts during our first few years in the University. Bodkin, who before coming to Birmingham had been Director of the National Gallery in Dublin, was an immensely entertaining man, and great fun at dinner parties.

The Barber Institute over which Bodkin presided – and which he had designed – is a gem of a building, and contains a priceless collection of classical and impressionist paintings, the bulk of which Bodkin had himself bought in the late thirties and during the war years. A condition of the Barber benefaction was that the Institute should also house a collection of portraits of Dame Martha Barber. This obligation Bodkin fulfilled by arranging that the architect left a space between two walls just wide enough for hanging the canvases. During his time the Institute was usually shut to undergraduates, but he enjoyed showing friends round, and would even open the Institute at night to take a party of our dinner guests round, as a special treat unlocking a door to show us the narrow corridor where he had hung the portraits of Lady Barber. Bodkin's successor was Ellis Waterhouse, who took a house near us, and with whom we soon became friends. Ellis was more knowledgeable than his predecessor. On the first occasion that he and his wife dined with us, he cast his eye over the pictures in our sitting room, and with barely a smile said: 'How strange to gaze at half a dozen landscapes to not a single one of which one could attach a name.' I had my own assignations for all but one of them.

Among other interesting members of the University staff were three whom I helped to recruit. The first was Lancelot Hogben. In 1941 Lancelot had written to me saying that he had heard that Birmingham's then Professor of Zoology, Harold Munro Fox, proposed moving to London, and that he, Hogben, who at the time was Regius Professor of Natural History in Aberdeen, would like to succeed him. But, so he wrote, the dignity of his chair made it impossible for him to apply for the Birmingham post in the customary way – he would have to be invited as I had been. I let Priestley know what Hogben had in mind, and he was duly elected – not without misgivings on the part of some members of the Science Faculty who knew that however stimulating a teacher, and however brilliant an experimental zoologist, Hogben had been a focus of controversy in every academic post that he had previously held. Their concern turned out to be fully justified.

About a year after his appointment, Hogben was seconded to the War Office in London, where he had taken charge of 'medical statistics'. He was still there when in 1946 I received another letter saying that he was not prepared to continue as a member of the Science Faculty, where he was persecuted by Haworth. Hogben always needed a persecutor, and he had elected Haworth to that office from the moment he arrived in the University. Could I take some soundings, he asked, and see whether a chair in Medical Statistics could be created in the Medical Faculty? I broached the matter with Parsons, the Dean, and with A.P. Thomson. In spite of their doubts because of Hogben's eccentricities, both became keen on the idea. The National Health Service was about to be launched, and there would be an opportunity to assemble statistics about the prevalence and genetics of diseases in the Birmingham area. I prepared a paper setting out the proposal, which was then discussed with the regional authorities, who in turn gave their support. Hogben duly resigned from his chair in the Science Faculty and was appointed to one in Medicine.

Despite what happened later, I never regretted the representations that I had made on his behalf. Lancelot had a brilliant mind. I had been much influenced by a book that he had published in 1932 under the title, *The Nature of Living Matter* – a vigorous rebuttal of the philosophies of Holism and Vitalism. In his first few years as Professor of Medical Statistics I found his company invigorating, but then, not satisfied with regarding Haworth as his sole persecutor, he started to invent additional enemies among his colleagues in the Medical Faculty. He frequently dropped round to see me, and over a drink – sometimes too many drinks – he would pour out his complaints.

One night, not long after Haworth's retirement, the telephone rang, and there was Lancelot, paraphrasing over and over again in a slurred voice Churchill's defiant call after the Dunkirk disaster, 'I shall fight you on the beaches, on the landing grounds', and so on. Realizing that he was drunk, I asked, 'Where are you? Shall I come and pick you up?' He just kept repeating his cry, and then hung up. I telephoned Enid Charles, his wife, herself a distinguished statistician, to ask whether she knew where he was. She didn't, and didn't seem to care. They parted not long afterwards. From that moment I became Lancelot's hate-figure. Joan was delighted. It meant an end to those late-night sessions of woe and drinking.

After he retired from Birmingham, Lancelot served for two years as Vice Chancellor of the University of British Guiana, before settling in Wales to devote himself to what had always been one of his passions, the study of language. Suddenly, out of the blue, I started to receive letters from him, as though there had never been a rift in our friendship. He went on writing to the end, and I was sad when I read of his death. 'Gip' Wells wrote an excellent biographical memoir for the Royal Society, but I wish someone would one day take Lancelot as the subject of a full-length biography. Through his writings, including such popular works as *Mathematics for the Million* and *Science for the*

Citizen, Lancelot added much to the intellectual vigour of his time, both before and after the war.

When Lancelot left the Chair of Zoology, I wrote to Peter Medawar in Oxford to see whether he was interested in the succession. He was, and I suggested to my colleagues in the Science Faculty that they would be wasting their time if they looked further. Only thirty-two at the time, Peter was clearly one of the more outstanding biologists in the country. In those days, the Faculty Boards of the University were responsible for nominating to the Senate names for higher appointments – they may still be for all I know. Haworth was delighted that Hogben was being transferred from his faculty, and suggested that I should invite Peter to Birmingham on the next occasion that the Science Faculty Board was to meet. He came, and the members of the board were every bit as impressed as I expected them to be. There and then he was told that he could regard himself as appointed. Reporting to the Senate would be a mere formality.

Not long afterwards, Peter and his wife Jean (one of whose tutors I had been when she was an Oxford undergraduate) spent a weekend with us in order to meet a few of the more prominent figures in the University. At the dinner party we had arranged, he was talking animatedly to Lady Priestley, the Vice Chancellor's wife, who was on his right, and did not notice that he was about to be served. He made a sudden gesture and the inevitable happened – the dish which our maid was holding spilt into his lap. He ignored the incident, and I had to insist on his leaving the table to change into a spare pair of my evening trousers. When he returned he immediately took up the conversation where he had left off. One could always be sure that nothing would put Peter off, as became apparent in 1969, by when he was a Nobel Laureate and President of the British Association for the Advancement of Science.

That year Exeter was the venue for the Association's annual meeting, and in accordance with custom, Peter, as President, had to read the Lesson at a service in Exeter Cathedral. As he stood in the high pulpit, he realized that something was going wrong, but even though in intense pain, he continued to the end of his reading. A verger had to help him down the steps to his pew. What had happened was a sudden massive cerebral bleeding. As he tells in his autobiography, Jean realized that something awful was happening, and had him moved to the local hospital, from where he was transferred to the Middlesex Hospital in London to be operated upon. He survived, but handicapped by a paralysis that affected the whole of his left side. But Peter did not give up. Helped by Jean, he continued to work and write, to the benefit of an ever-appreciative audience, until his death in 1987.

John Squire was the third of my recruits to the University. During the war he had been a member of the Army Operational Research Group and, like me, he had been a student at University College Hospital Medical School in London. When the Birmingham Chair of Pathology fell vacant in 1948, I suggested that instead of appointing, as most of my colleagues wanted, a classical pathologist – that is to say, someone whose main business was to perform post-mortems and relate what they discovered to the clinical history of the patient – we should elect someone who employed experiment to discover the underlying causes of disease. John was then directing a Medical Research Council unit in the Birmingham Accident Hospital. I went to see him. He liked the idea, and in due course was selected for the vacant chair. No better appointment could have been made. Before long the Birmingham school became recognized as one of the most forward-looking medical schools in the land.

A fourth effort at recruitment failed. A lectureship in physiology had fallen vacant, and I thought that Andrew Huxley, then a young lecturer in Cambridge, was the very man to invigorate the Physiology Department. He came to stay, and I introduced him to Gilding, who unfortunately thought otherwise. I doubt if Sir Andrew Huxley OM, Nobel Laureate and past President of the Royal Society, and now Master of Trinity College, Cambridge, has any cause for regret.

The three appointments in which I did succeed added to the number of like-minded friends in the University. It also meant that we entertained an ever-widening social circle. Members of my staff and BSc students were in and out of the house, often to meals. The Medawars soon found a house not far from ours. So did Alastair Frazer, the Professor of Medical Biochemistry and Pharmacology. Suddenly people started dropping in after the monthly Friday faculty meetings. We gave parties for my BSc students and members of staff, with a large one every Christmas. We met and made lasting friends among the older families of Birmingham, some of whom had gone out of their way to seek us out and welcome us after we had settled in.

Friends turned up from London and Oxford to see how we were getting on. One way and another, we soon seemed to be having house-guests almost every weekend. Some, like Julian Huxley and John Young, were frequently with us. American friends came to stay.

The annual degree-giving ceremony was a major event in the life of the University. Saturday was the big day, and it was the custom for the University to give a dinner on the preceding night – white tie, tails and decorations. On several occasions honorary graduands stayed with us, and it soon became our habit to entertain one or two of them on the Saturday night, inviting for the occasion the Vice Chancellor and his wife, together with other friends from the University.

One year, after I had become Chief Scientific Adviser to the Ministry of Defence, I successfully proposed for an honorary degree the late Admiral Rickover, a brilliant naval engineer and the 'father' of the American nuclear navy (and the 'stepfather' of our own). A colleague in the Ministry of Defence had told me that in recognition of his services to the Royal Navy during the Second World War, 'Rick' had been awarded the CBE. Since it was in the highest degree unlikely that he would have brought the insignia with him – given that he even remembered that he had been so honoured – I borrowed one for the occasion. When he came downstairs dressed for the University dinner, I showed it to him and suggested that he should allow me to fit the ribbon and cross round his neck. He looked surprised, but agreed when he saw that I was bemedalled and after I had told him that it would be the polite thing to do since it was a rare thing for a foreigner to have been awarded the honour. We arrived a little late, and I intro-duced the Admiral to the Chancellor and Vice Chancellor in the ante-room where those who were to sit at the top table were drinking sherry. As we moved into the big room, where all the other diners were standing, many bedecked with medals and orders, Rickover stopped and exclaimed in a loud voice, 'Jesus, a nation of heroes.' No-one seemed to mind.

Another event which for a time seemed to bring us guests year after year was the annual British Jewellers' Association dinner, the only 'national' dinner that by tradition took place in Birmingham, and at which Ministers and prominent public figures were always the main guests. On the occasions when one of them stayed with us, I was usually invited to the dinner. The first time this happened I met Ivan Shortt, a

Birmingham silver-plater, who, as President for the year, was in the chair. It was a very lucky encounter. In my travels between London and Birmingham I was in the habit of stopping at an antique shop in Warwick where from time to time I found pieces of furniture that were needed to fill the empty spaces of our new house. I became friends with Mr Grainger Brown, the owner, a man with a deep knowledge of the crafts of the cabinet-maker and of the silversmith. One day he encouraged me to buy a set of four telescopic candlesticks (alas, since stolen), made of Old Sheffield Plate – poor man's silver as it used to be called at the end of the eighteenth century. That was the beginning of what became all but an obsession.

The process of making 'Sheffield silver' had been discovered in 1743 by a man called Boulsover, who accidentally found that when a thin sheet of silver is tightly applied to a clean block of copper, which is then forced through rollers at a high temperature, the two metals fuse. The process was made obsolete by the far cheaper and less demanding one of silver electroplating, which Elkingtons, a Birmingham firm, perfected in the 1830s. Many years later, collectors started to turn their attention to the original Sheffield Plate, and books started to appear on the subject.

At the dinner at which I met Ivan Shortt, I was told that he was the country's greatest expert on old plate, and that his firm, Ellis & Co., owned about a third of the dies that Matthew Boulton had used in his Soho plating factory in the latter half of the eighteenth century. I decided that when next I bought a piece of old plate I would seek his opinion. In due course a wine-cooler was sent to me on approval, and I telephoned to ask whether I could bring it to his factory in Birmingham's Soho district to see whether it was a genuine piece of old plate or only modern electroplate. He replied that it would be more convenient for him to call at Carpenter Road on his way home one evening. Unfortunately I was away when he turned up. Joan received him, and was amused to report that Mr Shortt had said that if more than £5 was being asked for the cooler, I should send it back – a piece of advice she welcomed since she did not approve of my squirrel-like collecting habits (for a long time she liked telling how I had once gone hunting for a small round table and had returned with three).

I rang Mr Shortt to thank him, and was promptly invited to lunch at his factory, which, along with the rest of the old buildings of Soho, was demolished at the end of the sixties. That visit was a remarkable experience. In addition to a modern and flourishing electroplating business, Ellis's was then the best repair shop for old plate in the country. In one room of the factory were craftsmen whose job it was to repair bent or broken pieces and, when necessary, replace damaged silver gadroons or handles – for Ellis's had the patterns for most of the decorative pieces that embellished eighteenth-century silver. One of the firm's prize possessions was Matthew Boulton's own pattern cupboard. I wonder where it is now? Several pine doors were hinged together to open like the leaves of a book, on which were pinned different gadroons, handles, and other embellishments from which Boulton's clients would choose what they wanted, as they would from a pattern-book of cloth. In a bigger room were dozens of pieces that had come in the week before, and which Mr Shortt was in the process of sorting. Shelves in a third were loaded with pieces of old plate – odd candlesticks, teapots, sugar-bowls – waiting to be 'married', as Ivan Shortt put it, to the rest of the set to which they belonged, and which he was certain would sooner or later turn up in the course of his purchasing expeditions. A vast dungeon of a basement housed Matthew Boulton's steel dies.

In those days there were also many bric-a-brac shops in Birmingham, and a few days after my visit to the factory, I spotted in a window a pair of rubbed candlesticks which I thought might be Old Sheffield Plate. I went in and saw that they carried Matthew Boulton's mark. Having bought them for a song, I sent them with my compliments and thanks to Ivan Shortt. His acknowledgement came in the form of an invitation to dine. Not surprisingly there was good silver on his table, including a set of four candlesticks. After dinner he, his wife and I moved to his sitting room – Joan had been unable to come – and continued talking about the history of Birmingham and its 'thousand trades', and about Mr Shortt's work as a magistrate and prison-visitor. When I left, he saw me to the door, where he presented me with a parcel which he said I was not to open until I got home. It contained the set of four candlesticks that had graced his table – or an identical set – made in Matthew Boulton's factory.

There was no turning back. I became a fan of Ivan Shortt, and a collector. No one from the University had been near him before, and he seemed delighted to teach me how to tell Old Sheffield Plate from

36

electro- and other plated articles, and one maker from another. As often as I could, I would call on him at about eleven o'clock on a Sunday morning, and drive with him to his Soho works where he would show me the new pieces that had been channelled his way. When he thought I had learnt enough about the subject, he got into the habit of asking what I thought of a particular piece, and whether I could spot if there was anything wrong with it – for many items had been repaired, often badly. He would then correct me, and so prepare me for my next lesson. He also allowed me to buy at the price he had paid – in those days, not much – any pieces which struck my fancy, repairing them if necessary. We would then return to his house, to carry on talking over a glass of whisky until it was time for me to return home. Friends to whom I described my fascinating new world of Sheffield Plate and the ancient plating works of Ellis & Co., asked if they too could visit the place. Ivan Shortt was always delighted. John Betjeman, who was spending a weekend with us, came with me, and I can still recall his exclamations of pleasure as the time fled in that dark and dusty relic of the Industrial Revolution. A poet of the present, John always hankered after the disappearing past. The exquisite Rosamond Lehmann was another guest, and it gave me a lot of pleasure to see her against so strange a background. There were other things to show our friends, for Birmingham was full of marvellous remains, if one knew where to look.

Ivan Shortt died a few years before we left Birmingham, and I was very touched when his widow gave me, as a memento of our friendship, the small silver box in which he had always carried his 'heart pills'.

Well before I left Oxford I had managed to acquire the ovary of a mature whale in order to check the belief that the egg-cells of these vast mammals are no bigger than those of a mouse. After our move, I deposited the specimen in the Birmingham City's municipal abattoir cold-store – it was far too big to be kept in the departmental refrigerator. One day Peter Krohn reminded me that we had the specimen, and suggested that we cut out a piece in order to see what it looked like. We made a few microscopic sections, and were amazed to discover that between the cells surrounding the egg-cells were any number of small crystals. We knew that the ovarian sex-hormones were crystalline substances that belong to a class of chemicals called sterols – of which the one best known today is cholesterol because of its presumed connection with heart disease. Desmond Bernal was an international authority on steroid chemistry and, as a leading X-ray crystallographer, had played a critical part in elucidating the molecular structure of the first ovarian hormones. A high proportion of the British molecular biologists who later won Nobel prizes were his disciples. I telephoned to tell him what we had discovered and to say that the crystals were almost big enough to be picked out with a needle. We were wondering whether they were the natural, the real, female sex-hormone, or one of its precursors.

The next day I took some to London, and, soon after, Bernal telephoned to say that the crystals were unique. Could he have more? For two or three weeks we organized a despatch service to deliver specimens to his laboratory at Birkbeck College, where he was Professor of Physics. Excitement mounted; we were on the verge of being told what the natural hormone of the ovary was. And then came another telephone call. The technician whose business it was to measure the distances between the spots on the X-ray pictures of the crystals had been making a systematic error. Remeasurement had shown that our crystals were the common steroid substance, cholesterol. We returned to our previous work and for all I know the whale ovary may still be in the Birmingham cold-store. I cannot remember that it was ever again disturbed by us.

Not long after this incident, Bernal came up to give a seminar, and the occasion turned out to be the end of our friendship. He was staying with us, and we had been talking after dinner about all manner of things. At one moment the conversation turned to the part that Byzantium had played in the development of Western culture. He was fascinating. But suddenly he turned it all round. Western culture was disintegrating. We lived in a world made unstable by its class and economic structure. We were 'having to build buttress after buttress' – I can hear him now – to keep the rickety structure of society upright. The process could not continue. We could not go on trying to make our science accord with the world as it was. The only framework within which the knowledge and culture that man had gained over the ages could be secure was that of an organized society, and that meant a Marxist society. We could no longer afford the privilege of going on as we were. We had to accept the inevitability of a rationally designed framework for the development of human knowledge and human institutions.

Neither Joan nor I had interrupted so far, but suddenly I jumped up and turned on him, declaring that I didn't give a damn about his politics; he could believe what he liked, but no-one was going to make me conform to some pre-designed framework which defined what was right and what wrong. If I happened to be wrong, that was one of my liberties. Desmond became more and more silent as I continued, his big head sinking into his chest. I do not remember him going up to bed nor did I see him before he left next morning.

I saw him again only twice before his death, nearly twenty years after my outburst. The first occasion was at an anniversary dinner of the Royal Society at which, in the customary manner of those days, I was wearing dress clothes with decorations. He came up to Joan and me to say that he would be ashamed to wear the insignia of national honours – a bizarre remark since it must have been one of the few occasions on which he had worn a dinner jacket. The second was at the Royal Institution in 1967. He had come to hear me delivering an address to the theme 'the scientist in public affairs'.[1] By then he had suffered two strokes, and was in a wheelchair. I sought him out after the lecture, but his speech was so affected that I could not understand what he was trying to say. When I was appointed to the Order of Merit in 1968, he wrote to congratulate me, in script which his paralysis had made all but indecipherable. It was an extraordinary letter. 'I may join,' he wrote, 'but with a slight difference, the notes of your various Establishment friends on your OM. I am sure that scientifically and technically it was fully deserved, I saw you demonstrating it in France and the Med, but I at least must deplore the uselessness of so much good science being devoted to war science even when used against the Nazis. . . . So in memories of past work together.D.'[2] I found the reference to the Nazis amazing. I kept wondering if, in the light of events, he would have preferred them to have won.

The abrupt end to my friendship with Bernal was mirrored, as I was to discover much later, by a similar break in his relations with a number of artist friends to whom he had been introduced by Margaret Gardiner and me. In Margaret's charming book about Barbara Hepworth, she quotes a letter, in which Barbara wrote, 'I was shocked to the bone by Des's remark about political illiteracy – it sounds so incredibly snobbish.'[3] Presumably Bernal had been trying to recruit her to the Communist Party, giving her the same lecture as he had given me about his political, almost religious, convictions. 'Who is capable of giving most to society?' Barbara went on. 'Who told him it was bad to explore? It is, alas, just one more proof of the disastrous result of toeing any party line. . . . Des has provoked the most violent and bitter antagonism from many quarters during the last few months. . . . It is this religious fanaticism of his – this blind doctrinism – which shocks me so.' I was not alone.

As a natural dissenter, Des would have easily fitted into that group of brilliant scientists who, in the late eighteenth century, formed the Lunar Society, the men who in their efforts to promote the first Industrial Revolution were automatically pitting themselves against the existing social and economic order. I had never heard of the Society before we moved to Birmingham.

In 1939 the University had invited me to deliver the William Withering lecture, a lecture that commemorates the discoverer of the heart stimulant, digitalis. Soon after we had moved, I learnt that Edgbaston Hall, a grand house about a quarter of a mile from Carpenter Road, had once belonged to Withering, and that he had been a leading figure of a small dining club that had also included Joseph Priestley, the famous Dissenter and the father of modern chemistry, Matthew Boulton, Erasmus Darwin (Charles's grandfather), Josiah Wedgwood, the founder of the pottery that still bears his name, and James Watt, the man who perfected the steam-engine. Withering was also the co-founder of the Birmingham General Hospital which had become part of the Medical School to which I now belonged. I read what I could about all these men, and then encouraged my new colleagues in the faculty to hold a dinner in Edgbaston Hall – which had become the headquarters of a golf club – on the occasion of the annual Withering lecture, usually held at the time of year when the foxglove, from which digitalis was extracted, was flowering in many of the Edgbaston gardens.

Robin Whitworth, a prewar friend who came back into our lives when he was moved from London to a senior post with the BBC in Birmingham, was fascinated by the story. He was a highly cultivated man, and suggested that we should resurrect the Lunar Society, but as the Lunar Society of the Air, a project that he was sure his BBC colleagues would encourage. A series of dinners would be arranged at a BBC establishment close to Edgbaston. Microphones would be concealed in a bowl of flowers, and the best dinner that rationing allowed would be served, together with all the wine and port we could possibly drink. All I had to do was get together some like-minded friends and 'converse freely and brilliantly' without using any script. I fell in with the idea.

The 'guests' at our first dinner, on 18 February 1950, were A.P. Thomson, Mark Oliphant, and John Squire from the University, J.M. Mackintosh, a specialist in social medicine, and Richard Titmuss, a well-known social historian, whom I had invited up from London. It was a memorable occasion, but for the wrong reasons. I cannot remember what it was we were supposed to be discussing, but what with drinking too much, and interrupting each other all the time, poor Robin was unable to make anything of the recording. Undeterred, he decided to repeat the performance, but in a more disciplined way. That time it worked, and a programme resulted which was put on the air. On this occasion the participants were Leonard Parsons, Peter Medawar, Charles Madge – of Mass Observation fame and now a Birmingham professor – A.P. Thomson and myself from the University, and Titmuss. Further dinners, to which I invited different guests,* provided five more programmes. Even if we were perhaps somewhat highbrow, Robin and his Birmingham controller expressed themselves well-satisfied with the series. I was meant to edit the transcripts for publication as a book, but I soon lost interest. Nor, despite Robin's urging, did a projected second series of programmes of the Lunar Society of the Air ever materialize.

A few of the politicians who sat for constituencies in or close to Birmingham also used to drop in at Carpenter Road. There was Patrick Gordon-Walker, a prewar colleague from Oxford, and the Member for Smethwick. He was a cabinet minister in Attlee's second government. Roy Jenkins was a frequent guest. He had become the Member for the Stechford constituency in 1950, and both of us were friends of Hugh Gaitskell. We met Woodrow Wyatt, who sat for Aston

*A.J. 'Freddie' Ayer, the philosopher; Julian Huxley; John Wolfenden, later Vice Chancellor of Reading University and Lord Wolfenden; Sargant Florence, Birmingham's Professor of Commerce; Tom Howarth, then the headmaster of King Edward VI School in Birmingham; Patrick Blackett; Arthur Lewis, the economist; and Noel Annan (later Lord Annan), then a Fellow of King's College, Cambridge.

and who, when he came to Birmingham, preferred to spend the night with his local party agent in a 'back-to-back' in his constituency, where one tap served a row of houses, rather than to enjoy the comfort of Edgbaston. Hugh Fraser, who sat for a constituency to the north of Birmingham, was a constant visitor, as was Jenny Lee, Nye Bevan's wife, who represented a constituency that bordered on Hugh's.

On one occasion, Hugh Fraser and I had arranged to travel together to Birmingham. As we were about to pass on to the platform at Paddington, a man came up and asked if I could lend him a pound. Of course, I said, handing one over. Hugh looked back as we walked down the platform, and asked who the 'shifty character' was. It was Laurence Cadbury, the head of the well-known firm, and one of the Birmingham dignitaries by whom we had been befriended. 'And, what's more,' I said to Hugh, 'he's also on the Court of the Bank of England.' Years later, when I told Laurence's son, Adrian, the story, I learnt that Laurence was so absent-minded that when he travelled to London his wife Joyce used to check that he had his keys and just enough money to pay his way. On that occasion he had lost the lot.

Hugh Gaitskell stayed a few times, as also did the Bevans. Nye once telephoned to ask whether he could spend the night after he had finished with a political meeting in a large hall near the centre of the city. We arranged that I should pick him up at one of the side-doors. He emerged looking disconsolate, and in reply to my question whether the meeting had gone well, he replied, 'Awful, there was no-one there against me.' Nye and Jenny were always excellent company. Nye's curiosity about my work and interests was endless. 'What is the relevance of your work on reproduction in monkeys to the problem of human population?' 'Tell me, what is that logical positivism about which your friend Freddie Ayer writes? What's he getting at?' By then Freddie had started to change the slant of his first book, *Language, Truth and Logic*, to what is set out in its successor, *The Foundations of Empirical Knowledge*. I did my best to explain what I thought he was getting at. Nye listened and then, with that slight and engaging stammer of his, provided me with a better version of what I had been trying to say, and one that I imagine would have been welcomed by Freddie.

One of the attractions of Number 6 was my cellar. In 1956, I was invited by an old prewar friend, Gaston Mayer, to lecture at the University of Bordeaux, to which he had moved from the University of

Strasbourg, where he had been throughout the war. Gaston's main experimental interests, like mine, were in hormone physiology, and I was more than a little daunted at the prospect of lecturing in French. The theme which I chose was the interaction of the nervous and hormonal systems of the body.[4]

During the course of my visit I was entertained by the university authorities, and introduced to the magnificent cuisine of the region. But the best was to come. Gaston's closest friend at the University was Raymond Pautrizel, the Professor of Parasitology and Immunology. Raymond was married to the niece of an elderly bachelor, Raymond Dupin, one of the great wine-growers of the Medoc, and the proprietor of a vineyard called Grand Puy Lacoste. M. Dupin invited me to luncheon in his dilapidated chateau in the country – he himself lived in Bordeaux – his guests being the Mayers and the Pautrizels, and two other members of his family. The food was exquisite and the wines superb, in a meal that lasted every bit of three hours. My appreciation was so obvious that I was straightaway invited back.

Since then Joan and I have managed to visit Bordeaux almost yearly. We have been treated as members of the Dupin family, and encouraged to bring our own friends, provided, of course, that they like good wine.

In addition to growing his own wine, M. Dupin was a considerable shipper, and he invited me to select from his extensive cellars in the old part of Bordeaux any wine I liked, on the understanding that he would arrange to have it delivered to Carpenter Road. All I had to do was pay his bill and that of his Liverpool agent, who would take care of all the rest. But, said M. Dupin, why didn't I see whether any of my wine-loving friends in England would trust my judgment and join in? Nothing could have been easier, so once a year the hall of 6 Carpenter Road became converted into a temporary warehouse from which cases of wine were distributed to my 'partners' in the enterprise. Joan then made the obvious suggestion that it would be just as simple for the agent to despatch the cases direct to their respective owners. From then on I was able not only to enjoy my visits to the University of Bordeaux, but also an annual wine-tasting, both in Dupin's cellars in the city and at his chateau in the Medoc. We also had wine-tasting weekends at home, usually with the same nucleus of friends, among them Jack and Frankie Donaldson and Ralph and Coney Jarvis, at whose lovely house, Doddington in Lincolnshire, we frequently stayed for Christmas – children and all. I think that a lot of nonsense is written about wine connoisseurs, but there was something gratifying in being regarded as a bit of an expert, and in always having good wine on our table.

I also became much interested in the academic affairs of my two Bordeaux friends, and particularly in a curious enterprise of which Pautrizel was both a financial and scientific patron. It concerned a 'black box' that had been invented by a self-taught electrical technician named Antoine Priore, and which was supposed to emit electromagnetic waves that stimulated the defence mechanisms of the body. Unfortunately, the extravagant claims that Priore had made about the ability of his black box to arrest the growth of cancer attracted great publicity, and 'L'Affaire Priore' soon became the subject of national debate. Powerful reputations were involved. Priore had served in the Italian Navy during the war, and after the capitulation of his country in 1943, had been imprisoned by the Germans. He managed to escape and had made his way to western France, where he served with the Maquis in the Dordogne. Chaban-Delmas, the Mayor of Bordeaux, a considerable war hero, and twice Prime Minister of France, became one of his supporters. The Académie des Sciences was called in, in effect to say 'true or false', and Professor Robert Courrier, the Secrétaire Perpétuel and a scientific colleague of mine from the midthirties, asked Pautrizel to design a precise series of experiments to see whether Priore's machine had any influence whatever on the healing mechanisms of the body. Raymond designed impeccable experiments, using as his 'model' the trypanosome organism that causes sleeping sickness. The more involved he became, the more clear-cut were his results. The machine's emanations did have an effect. Then came a cry that Priore was somehow or other perpetrating a fraud on a renowned but innocent scientist. Pautrizel and Chaban-Delmas encouraged me to follow the story, and I gave an account of what was happening to the *Sunday Times*.[5] Before the '*Affaire*' could be settled, Priore died of a stroke, and it turned out that only he was able to operate the apparatus in such a way that it worked. Pautrizel's reputation as a scientist in his own field did not suffer, but his determination to get to the bottom of the affair lost him a number of powerful academic friends. Maybe one day someone will discover the secret of Priore's 'black box'.

*   *   *

There were never any empty moments during the twenty-five years that Birmingham was our main base. The time that was left over from my departmental activities was filled by work that I brought from London. I managed to get a lot done on train journeys. The schools that Paul and Stella attended were close enough to make visiting easy. Joan became involved in various voluntary civic jobs. She became the WVS* regional Children's Welfare organizer, and arranged a holiday scheme for poor children. By the time we left Birmingham, she was sending about a thousand away to camps or to private homes in the country for their summer holidays. The Director of the City Museum and Art Gallery, Trenchard Cox, and the Director of Art, Mary Woodall, became close friends, and Joan was appointed to the governing body of the Birmingham College of Art and Design. For a short time before we left the city she was also a magistrate. Birmingham, in fact, became so much part of our lives, that Joan set about writing a short book on its history.[6]

In the first few years after the war Joan and I managed an occasional summer holiday in France. I was also able to get up to Scotland for a week's stalking with Michael Noble on the hills of Ardkinglas, the estate that he and his brother John shared. Michael, who was married to one of Joan's cousins, had been on my staff for part of the war, in the first two years of which I had been introduced to the sport. I found it absorbing.

Then, in 1949, I bought as a summer home two small adjoining derelict cottages in Burnham Thorpe, about two miles from the North Norfolk coast. Many old Edgbaston houses were then being pulled down, and a demolition contractor whom I had got to know encouraged me to buy bits and pieces that 'might come in useful' in the reconstruction of the cottages, which he suggested could then be called Edgbaston Grove – not, as they became, the Forge House to commemorate the fact that for generations one of the cottages had been the home of the village blacksmith. When I exchanged the Forge House for our present home, the Shooting Box, more fragments of old Birmingham were needed in its reconstruction, including an eighteenth-century oak staircase that had once graced what was reputed to be the first wine shop ever to be opened in Birmingham.

*Women's Voluntary Service.

Another relic, which is now part of our Norfolk home, was presented to me as a parting gift by Birmingham's civic authorities. In Victorian times some Birmingham streets were furnished with ornate ironwork public lavatories, familiarly known as Homes of the Iron Convenience. One of the most conspicuous was in the Bristol Road, only a few hundred yards from the Town Hall. Having learnt that it was about to be demolished, I got the idea that its magnificent cast-iron panels and its pagoda-like iron roof could be reassembled to make an elegant summerhouse. I made some enquiries, but decided that the idea was far too expensive a 'folly'. I then forgot all about the matter. Some months later the City authorities wrote to say that they proposed sending me the iron 'convenience' as a memento. I can see it now as I write, some two hundred yards away, a delightful summerhouse at the side of a stream.

Once Paul and Stella had gone away to school and then to university, most of our holidays were spent with them in Norfolk. I was often asked what I did there. Shoot? – no. Sail? – no (not strictly true). Golf? (Burnham Thorpe is not far from a famous coastal course) – no. What do you do? Shrimp and collect pebbles, I would answer. I loved walking along the miles of deserted sandy beach, or spending hours shrimping with a big net, wading in the sea to the sound of sea birds. The north Norfolk coast is an ornithologist's paradise.

Paul and Stella had started to regard Norfolk as their home well before I retired from the Chair of Anatomy. In 1967 we accordingly sold our Birmingham house, and for a few years became tenants of Francis Knowles. Number 6 Carpenter Road still stands, scheduled for preservation, I understand, as a good example of the architecture of its period. During the course of visits to Birmingham, I have once or twice asked to be driven past it. Strangely I never get the feeling that it was once my home.

PART II

The Zoo

5

The Secretary of the Zoological Society

Of the half a dozen or so scientific societies of which I was a member, that of endocrinology, which I had helped found, became the most relevant to the work I was doing in Birmingham. I had also been one of the two founders of what today is the Society for the Study of Animal Behaviour, but my interest in its affairs had dwindled.[1] The Anatomical Society, to which I had been elected in 1926, had also become a secondary interest: many years after I had become one of the Society's senior members, I was 'sounded out' about my willingness to become its president, but I declined the honour. The Royal Society, to which I was elected in 1943, demanded more of my time. I was accorded the rare distinction of serving on its council for three terms, the maximum normally being two unless a Fellow becomes one of the Society's three officers. I enjoyed chairing a committee which the Society had set up soon after the war to consider ways of speeding the publication of scientific journals, which were then in a very bad way.[2] But the institution which in the end took up most of the time that I could spare from my academic activities was the Zoo – or to give it its full title – the Zoological Society of London.

My association with the Society began in 1926 when I delivered my first scientific paper at one of its meetings. In 1928, I was appointed the Society's 'Prosector'. It was during the period that I occupied that post that the pattern of most of my future scientific interests became defined. Early in 1932, in my final year as Prosector, I published my first book, *The Social Life of Monkeys and Apes*.[3] My second, *The Functional Affinities of Man, Monkeys and Apes*,[4] was completed just before my appointment came to an end. After that, and until the end of the war, my main connection with the Zoological Society had been

49

through my friendship with Julian Huxley, who in 1935 had become its Secretary, a post from which he resigned in 1942.

The vacancy that Julian's more or less enforced departure had created had been filled by Dr Sheffield Neave, a wealthy entomologist, and the man who had helped draw attention to the fact that the practice of paying the Secretary a handsome salary, plus perks, contravened the Society's charter and bylaws. Julian Huxley was the Society's last paid Secretary.

In 1953 I received a letter from Lord Chaplin, then the Society's Secretary, asking whether I would allow the Council to nominate me as one of its members. I was flattered. I remembered the Council as having consisted of distinguished elders of biological science, together with a few wealthy amateur naturalists, and I saw no reason to suppose that its prestige had dwindled. Anthony Chaplin, who was an amateur composer as well as an amateur zoologist, told me that it was not obligatory to attend the Council's monthly meeting. Since I was usually in London on the day of the week that it met, it seemed that were I to accept, I would be adding little to my already crowded London programme.

The Zoo had suffered severely during the war. Many of its staff had joined the armed forces; animals had had to be 'put down' lest they escaped – the reptile house was practically depopulated; the flower gardens and lawns had been turned over to potato and other vegetable crops; and bombs had caused a fair amount of damage. The Zoo was still in a very dilapidated state when I joined the Council, and restoration was obviously going to prove a formidable task. The Society had few financial reserves, and unlike other national zoos, was not in receipt of subventions from public funds, although the land it occupies in Regent's Park is Crown property for which only a 'peppercorn rent' was paid. Added to that, building work was strictly controlled during the immediate post-war years. Bombed-out people obviously came before bombed-out animals. The Zoo, however, then benefited from the fact that there were few competing attractions in London. It still drew crowds, and the birth of a polar-bear cub known as Brumas attracted three million visitors in 1950 – a record number, and almost twice what today would be regarded as a reasonable annual attendance figure.

The Society had also always enjoyed much free publicity, and several national newspapers then employed regular Zoo correspondents. In the days when I was Prosector, it used to be said that 'Zoo news' – a birth or the arrival of a rare creature – came second only to murder in public interest. But for a few years, what had been appearing always seemed to be bad news – rows between the Fellows and the Council about what should be done to resurrect the Regent's Park Gardens, rumours of staff dissatisfaction and, in particular, an open quarrel which simply would not die between George Cansdale, a Zoo official whose appointment had been terminated by the Council, and Dr Harrison Matthews, then the Society's Scientific Director. I had no idea what the trouble had been.

Noisy meetings of the Society kept making the headlines, with one lot of Fellows calling for the resignation of the Council, another for the reinstatement of Cansdale, and a third crying for Harrison Matthews's blood. In 1950 Field Marshal Lord Alanbrooke, who for most of the war had been the UK's senior Chief of Staff, and who was also a keen amateur ornithologist, had been persuaded to become the Society's President. He resigned in 1954, having no doubt been disappointed in his expectation that his life with the Council and staff of the Zoo would be quieter than the one he had enjoyed in his daily – and nightly – wartime encounters with Winston Churchill. He was succeeded by Sir Landsborough Thomson, the Second Secretary of the Medical Research Council. Landsborough was a somewhat staid character who had spent his life in public service. He was an acknowledged authority on bird migration.

When I joined the Council, I had no more than a nodding acquaintance with any of its members – other than J.Z. Young. Most were complete strangers, and some were clearly not of the calibre of the men who had formed the governing body of the Society when I was its Prosector. After yet another stormy meeting of Fellows which, as a member of Council, I felt in duty bound to attend, Anthony Chaplin decided that he, too, had had enough. He then approached me, saying that he wanted me to take his place, as did Landsborough Thomson, the President, and Terence Morrison-Scott, the Treasurer. So, too, did Harrison Matthews. I dithered for some weeks, but agreed after I had been assured that now that the 'Cansdale affair' had been put to rest, the Society and the Zoo were back on the rails. Anthony was sure that I would find the job of Secretary a sinecure, and that little more would be expected of me than of an 'ordinary' member of the Council. So it was that I became the Secretary, unaware that in accordance with

51

the Society's Royal Charter, the Secretary, even if unpaid, was the chief executive not only of the Council, but also of the Society.

My state of innocence was soon shattered. Without informing the Council, but with the best of possible intentions, Harrison Matthews had arranged that a few Père David deer from the herd that was maintained in the Society's Whipsnade Park should be sent to China, where the last representatives of the species had perished during the Boxer Rebellion of 1900. The source of the Whipsnade stock was nearby Woburn Park, in which the 11th Duke of Bedford, when President of the Zoological Society, had collected together in the early years of the century every Père David deer that he could from zoos which earlier on had managed to obtain a specimen or two.

In the 1950s, however, the British Government had no diplomatic ties with China, and some members of Council were indignant that the Scientific Director had acted without the Council's authority. At the meeting where the matter blew up, it became clear that I should have been aware of what had been done. Having whispered to Harrison Matthews that it might be politic for him to leave the room, I apologized profusely to the Council for my ignorance, acknowledged that the responsibility had been mine, and said that, since the animals were already in China, all that could now be done was to explain the circumstances formally to the Foreign Secretary. A few days later Terence Morrison-Scott, with whom I had rapidly got on the friendliest terms, appeared with me at the Foreign Office before Lord Reading, then the Minister of State (and my father-in-law!). The affair was settled with a smile.

My education continued fast. In my first year on the Council, I had failed to attend a reception given for Fellows by the President, and not knowing what kind of affair it was, I made no comment when a second one was arranged by Harrison Matthews with, presumably, Landsborough Thomson's approval. This time I attended and stayed for about an hour. I was much taken aback by the lavish hospitality that was being accorded to several hundred Fellows and their guests, into many of whose eager hands, when I was leaving, I saw keepers literally throwing bottles of champagne. I wondered where the money came from to pay for such largesse.

Not long after this strange sight, a friend who was close both to Princess Margaret and me telephoned to say that she had heard that I was now the Society's Secretary, and wouldn't it be fun to organize a ball in the Gardens for the Princess? Fine, I said, provided I was not expected to do anything myself. Ring up so-and-so, I advised, and he'd make the arrangements. When I was next in the Zoo's offices, Mr Westwood, an elderly, stooped chain-smoker who was the Society's accountant, came to warn me that throwing the Gardens open for a ball, even one for Princess Margaret, would endanger the Society's status as a charity. 'What about the President's reception and all that champagne?' I asked. The answer was that 'however regrettable that occasion, the guests were Fellows and the friends of Fellows.' 'But,' I went on, 'didn't Julian Huxley throw parties when he was Secretary?' The answer was, yes. But Westwood felt that there was something I needed to know. The story was fascinating.

In 1930 a Mr George de Arroyave Lopes, of whom the Society had never heard before, left part of his estate, worth about £80,000, in trust to the Society, provided it complied with certain modest conditions. Mr Lopes's brother decided to challenge the will on the grounds that the Society had not adhered to the strict terms of its Royal Charter – 'the advancement of zoology and animal physiology and the introduction of rare and curious subjects of the animal kingdom', and so had forfeited its charitable status. For example, it had at times allowed a band to play in the Gardens. It also charged for elephant rides. What did this have to do with the advancement of zoology? The Society also ran a catering service. Was this advancing zoology? The case came up in the High Court before Mr Justice Farwell, who decided in favour of the Society. People came to the Zoo, so he declared, to be educated and entertained. How much closer could children come to the subjects they were studying – the elephant, for example – than to ride on their backs? Visitors to the Zoo also needed to eat, and the Society could not be expected to provide food and drink free of charge. In effect Judge Farwell's ruling meant that the justification for the Zoo's catering establishment was that it was needed when the Gardens were open to the general public – and at such times only. Private balls or parties were 'not on'. I told Westwood to inform my would-be organizer friend that the ball was off, but that in due course I would arrange a private dinner party for the Princess.

I was disconcerted by what I was learning, and started to talk to keepers who had been there during the five years I had been Prosector.

It became obvious that there was a lot of disaffection amongst the staff about conditions of service. There was no clear ladder for promotion. The Society's pension fund was not assured, and there was something arbitrary about the way the Council dealt with pensioners. There were no staff-rooms. The quarters for the maintenance and buildings staff were primitive in the extreme. Staff organization was divided. A national trade union to which a few belonged was campaigning hard to add to its numbers from the majority, who were members of a 'company' or 'house' union. The Gardens were shabbier than they needed to be. To find out what was wrong, all I had to do was look around. I did, and that is how the Zoo became another part of my life.

6

A Foretaste of Trouble

I shared what I was learning with Landsborough Thomson and particularly with Terence Morrison-Scott. Helped by Frank Yates, I analysed the Zoo's annual attendance figures, and discovered that if Fellows who enjoyed the privilege of free entry to the Gardens had paid the same gate fees as did the general public, receipts from their attendances would have far exceeded the total they contributed in annual subscriptions. Our Fellows were therefore not contributing to an educational charity, but benefiting from it. The analysis also showed that the practice of excluding paying visitors from the Gardens on Sunday mornings – when entry was restricted to Fellows and their friends – was depriving the Society of about a third of its potential revenue. We did not have to dig deeply to see that what money the catering department made in the summer, when attendances were at their best, barely covered the wages and salaries of the catering staff during the winter.

Westwood had already explained why it was legally impossible for the Society to try to increase its revenues by opening the restaurant at night, when the gardens were closed to the public. A friend with whom I discussed the matter suggested that the way to overcome this hurdle without infringing our charter and bylaws was to set up a subsidiary company to which the Society would lease the Zoo's restaurant at such times as it was not needed by the public – that is to say, when the Gardens were shut. If the shares in such a company were donated to the Society, the latter would benefit as if it were a trading company. Given that this was within the law, Landsborough Thomson and Morrison-Scott agreed that it was the sensible thing to do.

I started to dream about the many other things that could be done. Plans that had been drawn up after the war for the rebuilding of the Gardens had had to be set aside for lack of funds. They had not taken into account the desirability of landscaping the Zoo into the whole of Regent's Park, of which it occupies the northern 36 acres, and from the rest of which it is separated by a high turfed ridge which I was told had been formed from the rubble of bombed houses from neighbouring Camden Town. I discussed the idea with two other friends, first with the late Earl of Rosse, who was then Chairman of the Georgian Group, a body of people who were concerned to preserve what was architecturally important in Georgian England, and then with Sir Hugh Casson, a distinguished architect, and later President of the Royal Academy. Hugh had been the Director of Architecture for the 1951 Festival of Britain. Sitting on the balcony of the Zoo's restaurant, I asked them to imagine what the Gardens would look like if, instead of a ridge made of rubble, its southern boundary were a man-made stream fed by water from the canal which runs through the most northern part of the Gardens. In my mind's eye was a vista of Regent's Park with the dome of St Paul's standing out in the distance, as I believe it did when the Zoo was laid out in the early part of the nineteenth century.

I discussed my many ideas with Landsborough Thomson and Terence Morrison-Scott, and while Landsborough was cautious, Terence soon shared all my enthusiasm. But on some matters we had to move gently. What I had come to realize was that little could be achieved unless the Society's name stood higher in public esteem than it had been doing recently. There were a few members of the Council who were certainly no help from this point of view. They were interested only in trivialities, such, for example, as the possibility that some of our gatekeepers occasionally 'fiddled' – a matter which, in deference to their views, I had to investigate, even though I knew that the loss of a few pounds hardly mattered against the background of our real financial problems.

By statute every year five members of the Council retired and five new names were put forward for election, with the Council's nominees almost inevitably being accepted unopposed at the Fellows' AGM. The process of deciding the Council's nominations began at its November meeting. The chair called for suggestions, and names were then voted on by a show of hands. In my first two years as Secretary, I doubt if I put forward any name. I found the procedure almost irresponsible. At the beginning of my third year, Landsborough and Terence agreed that we had to find a way of electing to the Council more influential Fellows than those who had been elected in the preceding two years. I suggested that the three of us, as the officers, should decide on five or six names, then invite the Council to put forward further names, and that, as Secretary, I should then write round to all the members of the Council, listing the names that had been proposed, and indicating how each of them could contribute to the affairs of the Society. As a result of this procedure we managed to elect for that year: Lord Glenconner, whom I particularly wanted because he was chairman of a national insurance company; Dr Cecil Hoare, who was an FRS – I was concerned that we should raise the scientific stature of the Council; Sir Allen Lane, the publisher of Penguin Books; Michael Perrin (now Sir Michael), the head of the Wellcome Foundation; and Frank Yates. They all happened to be friends.

I went to see Sir Edward Muir, the Permanent Secretary of the Ministry of Public Building and Works, to which the Zoological Society paid its annual 'peppercorn rent'. I wanted Muir to know what was happening, and to understand the difficulties. Above all, I wanted to see what help he could provide in bringing about the changes which seemed essential if the Society were to continue to act as the custodian of so ancient a national institution as the Regent's Park Zoo. Muir listened sympathetically, and indicated that he would give what help he could – but without specifying what it would be. Years later he showed me a minute that he had sent his Minister after my visit. It was a fair statement of the problems which the Society was then facing, and included a sentence to the effect that I had taken on a very difficult job, but that he, Muir, had said nothing to discourage me. But my visit did have one significant result. The 1961 Crown Estates Act was then being prepared for presentation to Parliament, and a new clause was introduced that changed our annual peppercorn lease for one of a renewable term of years, the charge for which was to be at the discretion of the Government – none was ever levied. Given that his Treasury colleagues agreed, another clause entitled our main landlord, the Minister of Works, to allow the Zoo to incorporate ten more acres of Regent's Park. Without this, the change in our southern boundary which I then had in mind, could never have been achieved. It still remains to be done.

If my new-found interests were to bear fruit, the time had come for me to get some administrative help. I already realized that no one man could carry the executive responsibilities that rested on Harrison Matthews' shoulders. On paper he was both the director of a major scientific society and the chief administrator of a famous London amenity. It was an impossible burden for a man who had practically no supporting staff. It was his job to organize regular scientific meetings and edit publications, at the same time as he was supposed to maintain an oversight of the Society's day-to-day financial affairs and all that happened in the Gardens. He was helped by a single secretary–typist, a slim, elderly spinster named Miss Gay, who had been in the Society's employ since 1912. She was the repository of all confidential Council matters, and also served as secretary to the officers of the Society. Her only interest in life other than the Zoo was St Paul's Cathedral.

To my great good fortune I managed to recruit Miss Eirwen Owen. She had been Deputy Regional Commissioner for Wales during the war, and had wide administrative experience. She joined me in January of 1957, in my third year as Secretary. Next I went to see Sir Thomas Padmore, the Second Secretary of the Treasury. I told him that, while I had already managed to find my own administrative assistant in Miss Owen, it was essential that the Zoo had on its staff a high-powered administrator to look after its day-to-day management. As a possible candidate Padmore suggested one of his colleagues, a Treasury under-secretary, whom I had already met. After a few days during which he studied our annual accounts, he told me that he could see serious trouble ahead for the Society, and that the job was not for him. Padmore had also told some of our mutual Whitehall colleagues of my visit, for within a few days Sir Edward ('Eddie') Playfair, then the Permanent Under-Secretary at the War Office, telephoned to suggest that I should look to the armed forces as well as the civil service. The following day Sir Hugh Stockwell, the general who had been the force-commander of the ill-fated Suez operation, and who was now Military Secretary, that is to say the member of the Army Council responsible for promotions, came to find out what the job entailed. But the news had spread even further. Not a day later I was visited by a wartime friend who was now Vice Chief of the Air Staff, and who was about to retire from the RAF. He thought that the job would suit him. I was taken aback by the level of interest that the post had stimulated, and said that I would have to consult. The following morning General Stockwell again turned up at my Whitehall office and said that he'd been thinking that perhaps he was the very man we were looking for. I was more than startled. Two 'four-star' officers after the job!

Before I had decided what to do next, I received a message asking me to call on Field Marshal Sir Gerald Templer, then the Chief of the Imperial General Staff. Templer started by asking in his characteristically blunt but friendly way what on earth I thought I was doing trying to 'hijack' his Military Secretary.

'Stop messing around, Solly, and I'll find you the right man.' I was soon visited by Major General Charles Dalton, then the Director of Manpower Planning in the War Office. I was impressed. So were Landsborough and Terence. Dalton was appointed Controller, taking up his appointment in December of 1957. He and Eirwen Owen complemented each other perfectly.

By then I had started to make enquiries about opening the restaurant for evening functions. Because the Society's own lawyers were discouraging, I decided that higher legal opinion should be sought. Terence, Mr Westwood, Harrison Matthews and I, together with a senior member of the firm of solicitors who looked after the Society's affairs, called on 'learned counsel'. His view was that a company of the kind which I had in mind would endanger the Society's status as an educational charity. I asked for a second opinion. Once again the same contingent of four from the Zoo turned up in another barrister's chambers. When the Society's solicitor started to explain the problem, I interrupted and said that I would do the talking. By then Terence was used to my ways. I began by saying that we were going to set up a company to which we would lease the Society's catering department when the menagerie was closed. 'What we want to know from you is the best way to do this without causing trouble for the Society.' The barrister was amused by this approach, gave his advice and in due course a company, Zoo Restaurants Ltd, was set up. The two shareholders, to wit, Terence and myself, then made a deed transferring our £1 shares to the Society which, as an educational charity, would be able to recover the tax from the concession-fee that it received from the company. Terence and I then had to attend in person at a licensing authority office in Hampstead to arrange the transfer from the Society to the new company of a licence to sell alcohol, and to show that we were fit persons to hold such a licence. From then on, the catering department, instead of frequently making a net annual loss, returned a profit to the Society's general funds. Some twenty years later I arranged very generous terms for the transfer of the running of the Zoo's catering establishments to a national catering company.

About the same time as this was being done I also arranged with Sidney Bernstein* to set up a television unit in the Gardens. Sidney had just been granted the franchise to form Granada Television, which he agreed would bear the costs of the Zoo venture. Dr Desmond Morris, later to become well known as the author of a popular book entitled *The Naked Ape*, was appointed director of the unit. The hope that the programmes which the unit produced would add significantly to the Society's funds was fulfilled in the first few years, but revenues gradually tailed off, and in 1964 the unit was closed down.

Both these moves were welcomed by the Council. But in so far as the Society's financial fortunes were concerned, they were small beer compared to what the Society would gain if the Gardens could be opened to the public on Sunday mornings. Exclusive entry was, however, a privilege very dear to most of the Society's Fellows, and a sacred cow to some members of Council. I could see no future for the Zoo if it was not sacrificed.

*Now Lord Bernstein.

7

The Zoo Rebels

The Sunday privilege had a long history. The Society had been founded in 1826, and in its early days its menagerie was open only to Fellows and their friends. After a few years, and because money was needed to pay for the running of the Gardens, members of the public were admitted, on payment, on weekdays and Saturdays, to which Sunday afternoons were added after the Second World War. As I saw it, the Fellows' privilege of exclusive entry on Sunday mornings might have been justified before the First World War, when their subscriptions accounted for about 25 per cent of the Society's total revenues. It was an entirely different matter now that the figure had dropped to 6 per cent. The calculations which Yates and I had made showed that it was during Sunday afternoons – two hours at most in the depth of winter – that the public made proportionately their greatest contribution to the Society's revenues, a conclusion which merely reflected the obvious fact that Sunday was everyone's day off. Indeed what the public paid on Sunday afternoons far exceeded the total of Fellows' subscriptions. As I put it in the Society's annual report for 1957, 'The stage had been reached in the history of the Society in which the Fellowship was threatening to be a financial impediment to the discharge of the purpose of the Royal Charter, and was therefore threatening the very existence of the Society itself.' Once they had seen the figures, Landsborough and Terence were at one with me about what was needed. So, too, was the majority of the Council, to which I had spelt out the problems as persuasively as I could. From 3 November 1957, the Gardens were accordingly thrown open to the public on Sunday mornings as well as afternoons.

There were immediate protests. At a crowded general meeting two months later, a 'rebel' group of Fellows, styling themselves the FZS

Committee,* and chaired by a Mr R. J. Knowles, the Mayor of the
London Borough of Hendon, challenged the Council both about
Sunday openings, and about certain changes in the bylaws which the
Council wished to introduce. The press was present, and the meeting
turned out to be one of the stormiest in which I have ever participated. I
had expected trouble. Indeed, before the meeting the senior member

*For Sollgr,
Me too! With much love
from Osbert*

*'I know nothing about it, but
personally I'm on the side of
x the mammals!'*

Osbert Lancaster –
undated

of the Gardens staff had sent me a letter urging me to 'flay the hyenas &
jackals. . . . Give it to them good and proper, and gladden the hearts of
those who are forced to "look on" but are nevertheless solidly behind
you.' I had accordingly consulted my wartime colleague, Leslie Scarman, who was now a barrister (and who today is Lord Scarman, until
retirement a Lord of Appeal) to get him to check whether I could go

*Fellows of the Zoological Society Committee.

62

even further than I had in my draft of the text from which I proposed to read, in order 'to expose the so-called rebels' and to let 'the public know that what they had given to the press had been a tissue of lies'.

There were moments at the meeting when I all but lost my temper. Sitting close to the front was one Fellow whom I knew to be a High Court Judge. He was indignant about the disappearance of the Sunday privilege. In answer to one of his remarks, I heard myself saying, 'If ever you have to advise us in a different capacity [meaning the courts], I trust your mind will be more open than it now is.' This particular exchange got into the papers. It was all being recorded.

The amendments to the bylaws which the Council was proposing were, first, to increase the annual subscriptions of Fellows – they had not been changed for well over a hundred years, despite the vast fall in the value of the pound; second, to restructure the Fellowship, sub-dividing it into 'Ordinary' and 'Scientific' Fellows; and third, to introduce a new class of subscribers, to be called Associates. By statute, proposals of this kind had to be put to the whole Fellowship in a postal ballot, proxies being allowed. At the end of the meeting it was clear that, if the Zoo rebels went on protesting, it was going to be a close-run thing.

I went to bed thoroughly dispirited, and worrying lest the rebuke I had delivered to the High Court Judge would lead to the defeat of the Council. Very early next morning I had to fly to Paris for a meeting of the Science Committee of NATO. I paid practically no attention to the early items on the agenda, and at the first break dashed out to buy the English newspapers – expecting to discover that once again the Society had suffered a bad press. To my great relief all the papers supported the Council. *The Times* did so in one of its main editorials. A piece by Chapman Pincher, then one of the best known reporters in the land, pleased me particularly. Its headline read 'Zoo Rebels Routed'. People in the quality and popular press – whom I had been quietly cultivating in the Zoo's interest – were clearly no less keen to help than were my Whitehall friends. Editors had often given me space to write about the Zoo's problems. I returned to the NATO table, and for the first time that morning the affairs of the Zoo fled from my mind. When I returned to London I found a number of letters of congratulation. But the rebels were certainly not yet routed.

A postal ballot of all the Fellows, who then numbered about five thousand, had had to be carried out before the general meeting which was to decide on the proposed amendments to the bylaws. A majority voted in favour, and accordingly it was decided to put the new bylaws into effect. But within a few months all our new arrangements were disrupted when Mr Knowles, the leader of the 'rebels', let it be known that he proposed to challenge the validity of the vote in the High Court, his argument being that the new bylaws had been approved by only a majority of those Fellows who had bothered to vote, and not by a majority of all the Fellows, which he claimed was what was meant by the wording of the relevant clause in the Society's statutes.

No-one in the Council wanted to be taken to the courts. A few, who sympathized secretly with the Zoo rebels, were clearly opposed. The Society's lawyers suggested that we should be represented in the High Court by Sir Andrew Clark, a prominent barrister who specialized in cases where matters of contract were in question. My own choice had been Mr Charles Russell.* When I went to brief Sir Andrew in his chambers, he could not have been less encouraging, and I feared for the worst when he bluntly declared that the Council did not stand a chance. The case came up in the High Court before Mr Justice Roxburgh. I attended the hearing – the only member of the Council to do so – to hear Clark pleading our case, with his every sentence indicating that he believed that he was fighting a lost cause.

Suddenly the Judge called for an adjournment – I felt he was either bored or extremely tired. In the corridor I made no bones about letting our solicitors know how displeased I was by our counsel's performance, and asked whether the hearing was likely to continue in the way it had begun. Something that was said made me wonder whether we could not ask to have the hearing adjourned. I wanted to change our counsel. I was told that it would be unusual to do so, but that it had been done. 'In which case,' said I, 'let it be done again.' I was sure that I could count on Landsborough and Terence to back me up. The public explanation for the adjournment was that there would not be enough time before the end of the legal term for the case to be dealt with adequately.

An adjournment having been granted, Clark was thanked for his services and Charles Russell asked to represent the Society. Some six months later the case came up again before another High Court Judge,

*The late Lord Russell.

64

a Mr Justice Vaisey, who was then in his early eighties. Again I attended, only to be flabbergasted, as was Charles Russell, when the judge declared in favour of the rebels. It was a simple matter of the law. On his interpretation, the wording of the bylaw meant approval by a majority of the Fellows, and not just by a majority of the Fellows who took the trouble to vote.

This decision left the Council, and indeed the Society, in an absurd position, since for all practical purposes it meant that no change could ever be made in the bylaws, unless every person who subscribed to the Society voted in a ballot. A *Times* editorial was outspoken in its condemnation of the judgment. Russell agreed that there was no alternative to an Appeal, a move which the Council approved, but not without the few who sympathized with the rebels making their dis-agreement clear.

The hearing in the Appeal Court took place some three months later. During that time I gave every minute that I could to the affairs of the Society. Everything seemed to be happening at once. I kept my Whitehall friends informed about the way things were going. The Government had an interest. The Zoo was a national institution which did not cost the Exchequer a penny. If the Appeal Court upheld the High Court judgement, it was inevitable that the management of what was the national Zoo by a private society would become impossible, and that the Government would have to step in. Even though we had decided to go to Appeal, I was therefore advised that it would be prudent to prepare a Private Bill about the future of the Zoo for presentation to Parliament. At the least the Society would have to be given a new charter. Since the Government Bill to deal with the Crown Estates was still being prepared, my Whitehall friends advised that we could tack the business of the Zoo onto it. When I told Landsborough and Terence about this, they agreed that I should move as I thought fit.

I took other advice. Shortly after the war Israel Sieff and his brother-in-law Simon Marks, the joint heads of Marks and Spencer, had invited me, as a so-called pioneer of operational research, to join their well-known firm as some kind of consultant. I declined the invitation – I could not see myself in the business world – but the result was that Israel and I became friends. He was a fascinating character, much involved in good works, and also celebrated for his table and cellar. He invited members of his family to dine so that I could tell them about the happenings at the Zoo, and about my worries about the legal costs which the Society would have to bear in fighting the case.

'There's no problem about that,' said Israel. 'I'm going to give so much. You' – going round the table – 'will give so much, you so much,' and so on. I left much heartened. Within a day a second benefactor appeared. I received a letter from Raymond Russell, a member of the Society whom I had not met before. He thought that the High Court decision was a disaster, and offered to help in whatever way he could. Attached to his letter was a cheque for £100. That was the beginning of a friendship which lasted until Raymond's death in an accident a few years later.

Then came another letter. Sir James Duncan wrote from Scotland to say that he had just read about the troubles that were plaguing the Zoo. Since he was a Fellow, he wondered why I hadn't asked him to help. It turned out, however, that his name was not on the register of Fellows. When I wrote to tell him this, he replied saying that some mistake must have been made, since he was a Life Fellow, that is to say a subscriber who had compounded all his dues in a single payment. What had happened was that the name of James Duncan had been dropped from the list of Fellows when he became a baronet. Ah, I said to myself, how many Life Fellows are there in the Society, and with how many have we lost touch? If it were obligatory that every Fellow had to vote, it would be impossible to establish what constituted a majority when the size of the whole electorate was unknown. I let Charles Russell know about Sir James Duncan, and what I thought were the implications.

Mr Knowles next announced that he was going to put up his own list of candidates for election to the 1959 Council. Being well experienced in local politics, he had already canvassed effectively. In those days a bound list of all Fellows, giving their addresses, used to be published annually. Mr Knowles had written around, and a number of prominent people appeared to have agreed to their names being used as supporters of his candidates. He had also collected enough money to prepare a manifesto attacking the Council. And worse, he had enough contacts in Fleet Street to plant pieces critical of the Council.

Raymond Russell and I set about organizing the opposition. Since it was inappropriate to do this from the Society's offices, my department in Birmingham and his flat in London became our campaign head-

A pelican meets the Queen, 1967, London Zoo. From left to right,
Overseer Newson (front), Charles Dalton, Terence Morrison
Scott, S.Z., Colin Rawlins.

Before and after. Above, the canal banks at the Zoo in 1960; below, the banks today, with the Snowdon Aviary on the left, the Cotton Terraces on the right and, spanning the canal, the Casson Bridge.

Above, the old lion house. Below, the New Lion Terraces.

With Dickie Mountbatten at the opening of the New Lion
Terraces, 1976.

Three Presidents. William Henderson (right), current President
of the Zoological Society, Prince Philip, previous President, and S.Z.

quarters, from which letters and telephone calls went out far and wide. We organized one committee of 'friends' consisting of professional scientists, and chaired by Sir Gavin de Beer FRS, then the Director of the Natural History Museum, and another of amateur zoologists, which was led by the late Earl of Cranbrook, a well-known naturalist.

Mr Knowles had, however, blundered when he released the names of some of the Fellows who had promised him their support. Among them was a distant member of the Royal Family. There was also a prominent surgeon whom I knew well, and who had allowed his name to go forward as one of Mr Knowles's nominees for the Council. I wrote to all on Mr Knowles's list whom I knew, and explained the situation. Not one of those to whom I wrote said that they had ever met Mr Knowles or knew what he was up to. In view of my letter they were withdrawing their support.

Raymond and I derived a lot of pleasure designing an elaborate election manifesto, which we proposed to send to the 5000 Fellows whom we knew would be receiving the one that Mr Knowles was preparing. We were helped by Guy Mountfort, one of Britain's best-known ornithologists, and at the same time the managing director of a prominent public relations firm. The cost did not worry us, because I had asked several friends to contribute to the small fund that Israel Sieff and Raymond had started, and which Raymond looked after – indeed, he himself had guaranteed to cover the entire cost if we ran short of money. Our manifesto was an elegant production, a typographical gem in red and black. Accompanying it was a slip signed by seven Fellows – including Raymond and Guy Mountfort – extolling the merits of the five people whom the Council were nominating for election. The seven signatories became the nucleus of a body that we later called 'The Friends of the Society'.

Everything then had to go into reverse. The Appeal Court heard the case towards the end of March 1959, and unanimously upturned the decision of the High Court. The judgement was, of course, a great relief to all who had been working to hold the rebels at bay. Landsborough had found the public row a great strain. Terence, who had spurred me on and supported me unhesitatingly in all my reforming but combative zeal, was enthusiastic. To commemorate the event I asked Ivan Shortt to search for a silver salver with the date mark of

1759. On the reverse side I had engraved (to Ivan's horror, since it is wrong to deface antique silver) the words:

> To the Hon. Charles Russell from the Zoological Society of London, in recognition of his demonstration, two hundred years after this tray was made, that the whole, being greater than the sum of its ascertainable parts, is indivisible into exact halves.

Alas, only photographs of the salver survive. Years later Russell told me that it had been among a number of things that had been stolen by a burglar.

I had not known when the Appeal was going to be heard, and it so happened that I had invited Hugh Molson, then the Minister of Works in Harold Macmillan's government, to lunch on what turned out to be the very day that the newspapers reported the decision. Molson was full of congratulations, but I imagine much relieved by the fact that the London Zoo would not now be encumbering the Crown Estates Bill which it was his responsibility to steer through Parliament. A note from our Head Keeper which read, 'Congratulations, now forward!', pleased me particularly, as did one from Miss Owen who wrote that, if I had not been so determined to fight it out, 'it would never have happened, and the faint hearts' would have rested content.

8

Reforms

Within a matter of days after the Appeal Court decision, I received a letter from Mr Knowles saying that he was resigning from the Society, and that the Council election would therefore be unopposed. His resignation was followed by several others, including two Fellows who had been members of the Council! Mr Knowles had been ordered by the Appeal Court to pay half of the Society's legal costs, but despite the financial undertakings that he had given when he started the litigation, the money was not forthcoming. Fortunately, the residue of the funds which Raymond and I had already raised, plus some further monies collected by the 'Friends', of which body the Duke of Devonshire had now agreed to be Chairman, covered the rest, leaving a balance of about a hundred pounds which was transferred to the Society's general funds.

After our years of strife, Landsborough, now approaching seventy, had had enough of the presidency, and early in 1960 he decided not to seek re-election, although he was prepared to serve as an ordinary member of the Council. It was then agreed that I should approach HRH Prince Philip, who had already spoken to me about his interest in the conservation of wildlife, to see whether he would honour the Society by becoming its President. I warned him that our troubles were not yet over, but that we were confident that he would be able to control our meetings were they ever again to become stormy. He accepted, and in 1961 presided over his first Annual General Meeting, on an occasion when, as Secretary, I had to explain the constitutional changes that we hoped to achieve with a new charter. The temper of the meeting could not have been more different from those of the previous few years, and the new President told the audience that he had been looking forward to a much more argumentative gathering. Prince Philip made a point of presiding over the AGMs for the seventeen years that he was President, and he often took the chair at the Council meetings by which they were preceded. Once he accorded the Society the honour of inviting the Council to meet at the Palace. He was assiduous in reading all Council papers, and I made it a rule to discuss with him any major matter that concerned the Society.

A legitimate complaint of some of the rebels was that few Fellows were given an opportunity to play a part in the affairs of the Society. Up to the time of my Secretaryship, the Council had only three advisory committees of any consequence: one to which the Society's pathologist and prosector reported; one which dealt with publications, meetings, and the library; and a third, today styled the Gardens and Parks Committee, on which, as on the Finance Committee, only members of the Council then served. The Council agreed that three more committees should be immediately established, one on education, one on animal husbandry and welfare, and one on collections policy. Others were added in due course, so that when I left the Council some twenty years later, more than a hundred Fellows, in addition to those on the Council itself, were concerned in the management of the Society's affairs.

With our legal problems out of the way, and the public able to enter the Gardens at any time on a Sunday, we were able to turn our attention once again to our longer-term financial problems. When Yates and I had analysed the seasonal fluctuations in our revenues, I was surprised to discover that the Society did not benefit as much as I thought it should from the large sums that accumulated in our current bank account at times of peak attendances. Changes in our financial management were then put in hand, especially after Michael Behrens, a City banker whom I had met through Michael Perrin, joined the Council. Michael Behrens was responsible for setting up a buildings replacement fund, it being my hope, which vanished into thin air once inflation took hold of the economy in the seventies, that one day the fund would be big enough to pay not only for repairs, but also for new developments.

We turned our attention to staff organization and trade union representation, where we were helped by Sir Harold Emmerson, the Permanent Secretary of the Ministry of Labour (now the Department of Employment) – I had met him frequently when he was Permanent Secretary of the Ministry of Works before Edward Muir took his place.

He put me in touch with Mr Thomas Williamson,* the General Secretary of the bigger of the two national unions with which we had to deal. He fully appreciated that labour unrest could not be tolerated in an organization that was concerned with the care of animals. The Council readily agreed to take his advice and to follow Local Authority awards on wages. I then proposed an additional scheme whereby our professional posts were equated with corresponding grades in universities.

Pension arrangements obviously had to be dealt with at the same time. The reason why I had early on become worried about this problem was that a superficial analysis of the ages of our employees had indicated that the potential burden of pensions which the Society had to face was way beyond what could be met out of what in effect was our revenue account. That is where Christopher Glenconner helped. In 1957 he arranged for the general manager of the big insurance company of which he was Chairman to carry out an actuarial survey of our potential pension liability. This indicated the size of fund that would have to be established for an assured scheme. The staff were consulted, and Council then approved the rest.

The representatives of every public authority to whom I had turned for advice had been ready to help, and the longer-term problems of the Zoo were becoming clear. Hugh Casson, whom the Council had by now appointed consultant architect, was working with Mr Stengel-hofen, the Society's own architect, in the preparation of yet another master plan for the development of the Regent's Park Zoo. Many European zoos had been destroyed during the war and were being entirely rebuilt, but we knew little about what they were doing. When in Washington in 1958 on business, I took time off to visit the national zoo – which receives all its funds from the Federal Government. I discovered that its director, who had only recently been appointed, knew nothing about what was happening in European, and little about what was happening even in other American, zoos – he did not seem to know as much as I did about the San Diego Zoo, which I had visited when I was lecturing at the California Institute of Technology.

I returned to London by way of New York, where I looked up Fairfield Osborn, an old acquaintance who was President of the

*Later Lord Williamson.

71

Trustees of the New York Zoological Society, and who, as a pioneer of the conservation movement subsequently became Chairman of the US Conservation Foundation, to which he recruited me as a kind of associate member. I asked him about the Chicago Zoo. He knew nothing about it. 'Isn't it about time,' I suggested, 'that someone launched a zoo quarterly or yearbook to tell us what we are all trying to do? What about our two societies starting one and sharing the costs?' Shortly after my return to London Fairfield wrote to say that his board had no money, but was ready to give the venture their 'moral support'. I replied politely, and at the same time urged the Council to agree that we should go ahead on our own, and publish an *International Zoo Yearbook*. The first volume, for which I wrote a foreword, appeared in 1960, and the most recent, the twenty-sixth, in 1987. The *Yearbook* receives contributions from far and wide, and is now known by zoo directors the world over as the 'Zoo Bible'.

In 1957 the Council also agreed to launch a full-time educational programme for London schoolchildren. The education authorities of the London County Council (LCC) were consulted, and I addressed a meeting of London teachers, who gave the venture their enthusiastic support. A grant of £3500 which I secured from the Nuffield Foundation helped pay for the conversion of an abandoned Victorian animal house into a lecture theatre. Today the Zoo's Education Department has a full-time staff of six, and caters every year for some 70,000 pupils in a fine new building which was partly paid for by a grant that I secured from the Wolfson Foundation, and to which the Inner London Education Authority added a section as its own natural history teacher-training centre.

Early in 1959 I also got the Council's approval for another educational venture. From the days of its foundation, the Society had organized general scientific meetings, for the discussion of diverse zoological subjects. I suggested that we should now launch a programme of scientific symposia to bring together workers who were engaged in research in particular areas of zoological science where rapid progress was being made. The first symposium took place later that year. By the time I retired from the Council, fifty volumes of symposia had been published.

In order to give further emphasis to the Society's standing as a scientific institution, I had written to all the professors of zoology and anatomy in the country, and to many biological research workers as well, urging them to become Scientific Fellows. The Council now allowed me to establish a series of annual awards.

Soon after the Society had been granted its Royal Charter in 1829, a very handsome medal had been struck to a design of Thomas Landseer, the brother of the more famous Edwin, and for some years bronze and silver and, extremely rarely, gold versions had been awarded to individuals for services either to the Society or to zoological science. But it was years since any had been awarded. We decided not to change the regulations that affected the Society's original medal, except in so far as it was agreed that a bronze version would be awarded annually to a worthy member of the Gardens staff. What I suggested were additional awards, one to be called the Prince Philip Prize, to be competed for by schoolchildren; another, the Thomas Henry Huxley Award, for the author of the best PhD zoological thesis of the year; and a third, to be called after Stamford Raffles, the founder of the Society, to be awarded – although not necessarily annually – to a really outstanding non-professional zoologist whose work had contributed materially to the advancement of the subject. The question was, where was the money to come from?

I again approached Sidney Bernstein, who agreed that the awards should not be medals or books, but a piece of sculpture or a painting, so as to remind zoologists that there were fields of creative endeavour other than science. Knowing that Henry Moore was one of my oldest friends, Sidney suggested that I should approach him, and if he was willing to give me three small pieces, he, Sidney, would pay for the casting. And so it turned out.

I spoke to Henry and then spent some hours with him at his studio in the country discussing what abstract themes might be appropriate for what we had in mind. It was fun watching him arrange small pebbles in a form that one could imagine signified some zoological idea. In due course he presented the Society with an edition of seven of each of three pieces, a small one for the Prince Philip Prize, a slightly bigger one for the T.H. Huxley award, and a still bigger one for the Raffles. The cost to Sidney, if I remember rightly, was no more than about £2000.

But that was in 1961. All went according to plan until the fifth year, when Eirwen Owen told me that now that Henry Moore's work was so

73

sought after, the insurance premium to cover the short period that the three Moore pieces were not in a bank vault cost almost as much as had the casting. As we obviously could not go on awarding such valuable prizes, I got Henry Moore's agreement to our suspending the award of his sculptures, and to disposing of the remainder to form a fund with which to sponsor young artists who could be commissioned to provide further series of prizes. I asked Henry to advise me where to turn, and in due course he suggested a young and at the time not very well known sculptor, 'Lis' Frink.* I saw her. She agreed to help. To fill the gap until she had a suitable piece, and to provide for the other awards, I bought a few small bronzes from David Wynne. Lis in due course surfaced with a series of her now well-known wild boars (for which I obtained funds from an anonymous source). When all but one of the boars had been awarded, her work, too, had become so sought after and costly that they again had become too valuable to give as prizes (only one of a second series, a baboon, was ever awarded). Again I had to seek permission to sell the final boar and the remaining baboons for my prizes fund. To fill the gap this time, Michael Behrens stepped in and donated a series of seven small sculptures of a heron by Tapio Wirkkala, a Finnish artist.

When the time came for me to retire from the Zoo, I realized that if the Council were to have a stock of awards to carry it over the next twenty years or so, I would have to move fast. The result is that the Society now has a series of striking bronzes of a hippo by Anita Mandl.† It has become the Stamford Raffles award for amateur zoologists. Some time before this, we had decided that the Prince Philip Prize would have to be a bronze medal, and we were fortunate in being allowed to use the winning entry – a head of Stamford Raffles – in a competition for students of art and design that had been organized by the Royal Society of Arts. For the Thomas Henry Huxley award, I turned to Jonathan Kingdon, one of the finest animal artists of this

*Today Dame Elisabeth Frink, RA.
†I knew in Birmingham that sculpture was her hobby. One day she nervously asked whether I would go with her to the Art School to look at a head she had done of me. I exploded. 'How could you have done one? I have never sat for you?' She then explained that she had sat so often on my left while I tore her manuscripts to shreds that she knew my left profile well, but that she was uncertain about the other side. She had done the head from memory, and please would I help her. Years later I bought a bronze of the head she did.

century, and a keen zoologist. I had already written a foreword to a folio volume of his drawings which the Wellcome Trust had subsidized, and had bought one of his drawings of the West African red mangabey. I then discovered that he was also a sculptor and medallist. He undertook to produce two series of ten medals, both of which depict T.H. Huxley's head in relief on one side, and with the obverse of one series showing a red mangabey and the other the head of a zebra.

Henry Moore gave me an 'artist's copy' of the piece that he had done for the Stamford Raffles prize, and I had bought a boar from another series of the animal that Lis Frink had sculpted, as well as a copy of her baboon. They are an everyday reminder of the fact that I had met some of my first artist friends, among them Henry Moore, Barbara Hepworth, and John Skeaping, when I was the Society's Prosector.

9

The Search for Funds

Unfortunately none of the new ventures that an increasingly enthusiastic Council endorsed was generating the kind of money that would be needed to launch a building programme. In my first year on the Council, and before I became Secretary, a new animal hospital and quarantine station for Regent's Park had been sanctioned out of the Society's own funds. But that satisfied only one urgent need. Providing proper quarters for our works and supplies staff was another. I had been so appalled when I discovered what they were like that I insisted that all the members of the Council saw with their own eyes how awful the situation was. In 1958 it was therefore agreed that a new works and supplies building should be built, again out of the Society's own reserves, a move which was very popular with our gardens and menagerie staff – 'people before animals' was a slogan they liked.

But every new development cried out for more to be done. We had a new hospital, but no facilities for anyone to pursue adequate enquiries into causes of death. Every day we were throwing into the incinerator the carcases of animals which, if properly studied, could conceivably provide the knowledge which would reduce the number of deaths, and which might even help in the treatment of human disease. I wrote a paper proposing that a laboratory for the study of comparative medicine should be established and, with the blessing of the Council, went out to seek funds. My first port of call was the recently established Wolfson Foundation, whose Chairman was then the first Lord Nathan, a lawyer and ex-MP. I had lunch with him, explained what it was all about, and left him my paper, which in effect was an application for a major grant.

I had, of course, told many friends about my dream of an Institute of Comparative Medicine, and about my conviction that it could increase our understanding of human disease. I was not surprised, therefore,

when Leslie Farrer-Brown, the first Director of the Nuffield Foundation, asked me to call on him. He had heard that I had approached the
Wolfson Foundation with an imaginative idea, and he wanted to know
more about it. In due course the Trustees of the Nuffield Foundation
provided the funds for the building that now bears its name.

At the time I happened to be engaged in talks with the Ford
Foundation of America, which had made the problem of population-
growth one of its major concerns. They knew of my researches into the
physiology of reproduction, and wanted to know whether I could
intensify my work on reproductive physiology, in the hope that this
would help bring closer the day when enough would be known to
devise an easy and practicable method of birth control. This, I knew,
was a highly simplistic view, but I nonetheless put forward two
proposals which the Foundation agreed. The first was that I would
intensify the work I was doing in Birmingham, and the second that I
would recruit three research workers to the staff of the London Zoo to
investigate the reproductive cycle of species other than those normally
studied in university laboratories.

Since I was sceptical about the value of crash programmes in fields of
basic research, I persuaded the Foundation to agree a fifteen-year term
for both grants, the money to be paid in two capital sums. The
Foundation further agreed that if the Zoological Society spent the
amount that their actuaries had calculated should be used each year,
regardless of where the money came from, the capital sum which they
were offering could be invested. So it was that the Ford grant became the
main component of what is now the Society's assured scientific fund
which, when I resigned the Presidency in 1984, had a value of more than
half a million pounds. The same arrangement could not be made with
the grant to Birmingham, where the capital sum that had been provided
was used to buy an annuity of £16,000 a year. When I retired from the
University, I arranged for this to be paid to the Society's laboratories.
Together the annual sums so paid amounted to about £100,000.

As soon as financial support from the Ford Foundation was assured,
I approached Sir Henry Dale, then the Chairman of the Wellcome
Trust (which had already supported my work in Birmingham), and told
him that the Zoo now needed laboratory facilities to carry out the work
we had undertaken to do. In due course the Trust provided the funds
that were needed to build in Regent's Park the Wellcome Institute of

77

Comparative Physiology which, with the Nuffield Institute of Comparative Medicine, forms what is now the Institute of Zoology. Once space and the necessary long-term support had been assured, I set about recruiting the necessary staff, our first appointment being Idwal Rowlands, an old colleague who was then on the staff of the National Institute for Medical Research. He became the Society's Senior Research Fellow in charge of the new programme of work.

But all this was science. Our animal houses were in a shocking state, and the only rebuilding that we had so far embarked upon was the hospital and the works and supply complex. Hugh Casson and Stengelhofen had produced their outline plan for a new Gardens – and also a detailed plan of what is now the Casson bridge over the Grand Union Canal. The hospital and works building, and the establishment of an assured pensions fund, had exhausted the Society's reserves. If Regent's Park and Whipsnade were to be adequately reconstructed and developed, we would not only have to borrow from the banks, but would also have to look for large sums from private benefactors and, if possible, secure money from the Government – which, after all, had been saved by the Appeal Court decision from having either to take over full financial responsibility for the Regent's Park Gardens, or responsibility for shutting it down. If there had to be a national zoo, I saw no reason why it had to be the responsibility of a private society that was not supported by public funds.

Experience suggested that there was little point in launching a public appeal. In 1945, shortly after the end of the war, a campaign to raise money for a building fund from Fellows and the public had proved a failure. A second and later campaign, which was run by a professional firm in order to raise funds for the Institute of Comparative Medicine, was also far from a success. Had it not been for a donation of £30,000 that I induced the late Henry J. Heinz II to contribute, the total sum raised would have barely paid the fees of the firm.

The first big benefaction that we received came about almost by accident. One day I read in the papers that Jack Cotton, a Birmingham property magnate, had donated £100,000 to the Royal College of Surgeons. This was in 1960. The little I had heard of Cotton did not suggest that he was the kind of person with whom I was likely to get on. When I enquired about him from one of my Birmingham 'Establishment' friends, he wrinkled his nose and advised me to have nothing to do with the man. Ivan Shortt also thought that Jack Cotton was 'bad news'. But they had a link. Birmingham's small Jewish community had a far longer history than the larger ones of other provincial cities, and the Cotton family had supported the synagogue for at least three generations. Jack Cotton had, however, fallen out with the Jewish community, and he and Ivan Shortt were no longer friends. Even so I asked Ivan whether he knew Cotton well enough to tell him that I'd like to meet him. He did, and within a day I got word that Cotton was expecting to hear from me.

Towards the end of a busy day in 1960, the first year in which I doubled as a Birmingham professor and as Chief Scientific Adviser to the Minister of Defence, I telephoned Mr Cotton. 'My name,' I said, 'is Zuckerman, and I wonder whether you could spare the time to give me some advice?' 'I know all about you,' said Cotton. 'What advice do you want, and when do you want it?' 'As soon as possible,' I said, and was surprised when he said, 'Well, it's now ten to six. I'll be waiting for you here at six.' My office was not far from the Dorchester Hotel where Jack Cotton had his headquarters, so I suggested 6.30. I was there on the dot. In one hand he held a glass of whisky, in the other a cigar. Eyeing me shrewdly, he began by asking what I would like to drink, and whether I'd like a cigar. I accepted the drink. He then asked what advice I wanted. 'You are in the property business,' I said, 'and as Secretary of the Zoological Society I have discovered that we have a freehold house which I think should be sold.' 'I don't deal in that kind of property,' said Cotton. 'If that is what you want, ring Mr so-and-so – he will help you. Now what have you really come to see me about?'

All this took less time than it takes to tell the story. I took a deep breath and said, just as bluntly, 'Well, Mr Cotton, if you want to know, I wished to see the man who I am told is a very smart and powerful businessman, but who has just given £100,000 to the College of Surgeons, about which I assume he knows little or nothing' – I spoke, I told him, as a member of the College. Did he think that his £100,000 would either help him live longer or, now that we had a National Health Service, significantly improve the health of the country? For a few moments he was silent with anger. He then asked where I thought his money should go. I had already been so rude that there was nothing for it but to continue. I therefore replied that I understood that he was making millions out of land that was not being economically used. If he had money to throw about, it should therefore go back to the land – to the country's public parks. The fact that I had an interest in Regent's Park was neither here nor there. If he wanted to give money to the Zoo, well and good, but if not, there were any number of other public parks that could benefit from his generosity. He listened silently, and when I had finished my drink, I was surprised to hear him say, 'Come and see me again.' I did. I had never met anyone like him, and I imagine I was just as much a novelty to him.

Cotton had become a national figure as the wizard of the post-war property boom. Managers of investment funds and insurance companies, bankers and property developers, all wanted to be associated with him. He invited me to dine at the Dorchester, but it was embarrassing to be with someone who behaved like a pop star, constantly waving to other diners, and to whose table came person after person to whom I would be introduced. He seemed to know everybody, and everybody seemed to want to know him. After the second such dinner, I said that it was impossible to have a conversation in the Dorchester dining room, and suggested that he should dine with me at my club. I liked his caviare – he entertained lavishly – but I certainly did not like the sample of people who buzzed round his table like bees round a honey-pot. He took the hint gracefully, and after one or two meals with me, he suggested that we should always dine in his hotel suite. And so we did. He seemed to like my company, without ever wanting to know what I did, and I enjoyed getting to know so magnetic a man with interests that were so strange to me.

Not many weeks after we had got to know each other, he promised to donate to the Society £200,000 – at today's values around £2 million – which was the figure I then thought would be sufficient to pay for the reconstruction of Decimus Burton's ancient giraffe house which, because of its historical interest, was a 'listed' building. He telephoned one day and asked me to drop round to discuss the gift. I was with him the next morning, and was introduced to a Mr Lindgren, his confidential man of business. 'I've asked Freddie to arrange for the payment of the £200,000 I said I would give you.' Jack then turned to a window to look down at the traffic in Park Lane, while Mr Lindgren got out his pen and consulted a sheet of paper that he was holding. The money, he said, could be paid in two or four instalments, whichever I wanted. Before he could say another word, I blurted out that Mr Cotton should not be allowed to give £200,000 when he could give a quarter of a million. 'But this says £200,000,' Mr Lindgren replied, as he looked at his notes. There was a moment's silence before Jack turned round and said 'He's quite right. Yes, a quarter of a million sounds so much better.'

It was the middle of the morning, but we had a drink before I left to telephone the good news to Prince Philip and to Terence. It was by far the largest gift the Society had ever been given in the 150 years of its history. Indeed, the de Arroyave Lopes bequest of 1930 was the only other benefaction of any significance the Society had ever received.

With the grants from the Wellcome and Ford foundations, this meant that in 1960 the Zoo had become richer by £550,000. I wrote without exaggeration in the Council's report for that year, that Mr Cotton's gift was 'the key which set in motion the plan for the reconstruction of the Regent's Park Gardens'.

A year later, by when yet another £135,000 had been raised, a grand dinner was organized as an expression of the Society's gratitude to its benefactors, as well as to mark the occasion of Prince Philip's presidency. Unfortunately a torn Achilles' tendon prevented him from presiding, although he insisted up to the last moment that whatever the doctor said, he could 'do the honours', sitting with his injured leg on a chair! Landsborough presided instead. I sat with Prince Philip while he wrote a speech – he has the facility, which I envy, of knowing exactly what he wants to say – which was delivered by his uncle, Lord Mountbatten, who was in the habit of claiming, incorrectly, that he was the senior Fellow of the Society. The company, all in white tie and tails and wearing orders and decorations, included Mr Macmillan, the Prime Minister, and Hugh Gaitskell, the Leader of the Opposition, both of whom spoke. The assembly included other Ministers, and representatives of the country's major learned and scientific societies.

Jack Cotton was much pleased by the occasion, and I then encouraged him to donate £10,000 through the Society to the World Wildlife Fund, of whose British National Appeal Prince Philip had also become President. But that was not the end of his generosity. In 1962 he gave the Society a further £50,000 towards its rebuilding fund. Jack also arranged a drinks party for a dozen or so leaders of financial institutions to whom I outlined the Zoo's problems. While they were impressed by Jack's concern, I seem to remember that only one, the managing director of a large insurance company, was sufficiently moved to contribute a sum of £5000.

On Jack's last visit to the Zoo in 1963, it was clear that he was far from well. As I took him round the terraces named in his honour, he said, 'You've spent much more on this and the Snowdon Aviary than I gave you. Don't worry. I'll make it up.' But he died the following year. The last time I heard his voice was over the telephone. He was speaking from Nassau, where he was recuperating from a heart attack. A well-known American cardiologist had been called in for consultation, and Jack wanted me to discuss his condition with the specialist over the telephone. I insisted that I knew nothing about his heart, that I had never practised medicine, and that since I was not his doctor, what he was asking was highly irregular. 'I know,' said Jack disarmingly, 'and so does Professor deBakey. It would reassure me if you spoke to him and then called me back.' I never did know why my speaking to a distinguished American cardiologist whom I had never met, about a man of whose medical condition I knew nothing, would be reassuring. But I did as Jack asked. He died not long after, and his body was brought back to England for burial. I felt very sad at his funeral.

In his last years Jack had run into a lot of criticism from his business colleagues, and some two years before his death had been moved from the chairmanship of his own company to the purely titular position of president. But whatever may have been his faults in the way he ran his business, no-one could have accused him of meanness. He was more impulsively generous than anyone I have ever met. In addition to his gifts to the Zoo, I encouraged him to make a significant donation to an appeal which the Royal Society had launched.

Only once did I go too far with him. When attending a meeting in Paris, I had lunched with Sir Frank Roberts, then our ambassador to NATO, and had admired a small picture that hung in his dining room. The artist turned out to be Ernest Risse, a little-known French painter of whom Lady Roberts had become a patron. I was later introduced to him, and was particularly impressed by one of his larger pieces. When I next saw Jack, I told him that I wanted him to donate a picture to a public institution, which I didn't name. Fine, he said. If I liked the picture, I should buy it on his behalf. Jack was himself a discriminating collector, and he had a number of marvellous flower pictures by Fantin-Latour. I then arranged for the Risse canvas to be brought to

London, together with some others of his works, in a military aircraft in which Lord Mountbatten was travelling. When the picture arrived in London I told Jack that I wanted him to see it before it was given to the University of Birmingham. His reaction was immediate. He had no wish to see the picture for in no circumstances would he give anything to Birmingham. I could either send it back or pay for it myself. The first alternative being impossible, I was stuck with the second. In due course I loaned the canvas first to the Birmingham Art Gallery, where it hung for more than a year, and then to the University. It now hangs in the Shooting Box, our home in Burnham Thorpe.

10

Government Support

Whitehall friends were following my fund-raising activities closely. They knew that the gifts that had been received so far could not possibly cover the costs of the Zoo's rebuilding programme. They also knew that we were already borrowing from the banks. Sir Richard ('Otto') Clarke, then Second Secretary to the Treasury, agreed that the time had come for the Government to help. Reginald Maudling, at the time the Chancellor, was sympathetic. Otto and I had more than once gone over the Zoo's books, and in 1963, with the blessings of the Council, I accordingly approached the Government for a grant of £1 million – £10 million at today's values – that being the figure that Otto thought was then needed. His colleagues clearly thought otherwise, for in 1964 we were given only £500,000, part grant and part long-term loan.

Otto also engineered a grant of £100,000 from the LCC. My office as Chief Scientific Adviser to the Ministry of Defence was then in the same building as Otto's, and one day when we were discussing the need for a Treasury grant, he picked up his telephone and asked to be put through to Sir Isaac Hayward, then Leader of the LCC. The Government, he told Sir Isaac, was considering making a grant to the Zoological Society, and while a national institution, the Zoo was even more a London amenity. The LCC should therefore make a grant of at least £100,000. He ended the conversation by saying that I would call on Sir Isaac to give him the details. While I do not know what then passed between the Leader and his Council, the Society was soon the recipient of £100,000. It all seemed so easy.

By now we were also receiving the occasional unsolicited donation, but none for more than about one or two hundred pounds. I therefore continued to seek the help of wealthy people whom I knew. Raising money meant doing a fair amount of entertaining, and often an appeal to something less praiseworthy than a potential donor's charitable instincts. The dinner parties which I organized, as well as the ones I had to attend, were generally very enjoyable. They made the Society many powerful friends and patrons, but I sometimes found them more than a burden. As Terence put it, I was destroying my liver on behalf of the Society. Two personal friends who wished to remain anonymous donated £10,000 and £20,000, but I soon became blasé about any donation of less than £100,000 – which I regarded as the unit cost for doing anything in the Zoo. On one occasion I declined an immediate offer of £10,000 when the would-be donor said that if I could wait, he would be able to make it £100,000 – a gift which in the end did not materialize. On another I pushed a cheque for £1000 across the desk of another would-be donor saying that I would accept it when he added another nought or two. He failed to oblige. But I went on trying.

The year 1964 was a good one. First the Wolfson Foundation, of which I later became a trustee, donated £100,000 towards the modernization and extension of the Society's administrative building (the balance later went towards the cost of the Society's educational building). Then Charles Clore, who for a brief moment had joined his property business to that of Jack Cotton, donated £50,000. Clore was far less instinctively generous than Cotton, and far more difficult to woo. Obviously, too, I could not pursue him while Cotton was alive. Clore, unlike Cotton, sought smart company, and pursued beautiful women. His house in London was embellished with fine pictures, but I never felt that he enjoyed them in the personal way that Jack Cotton did either his flower pictures, or a small Rembrandt head that he owned. Clore had a large country estate where he organized shooting parties, without himself getting any pleasure from the sport. Later I persuaded him to add a further £150,000 to the £50,000 he had given so that we could build a pavilion for small mammals. It was officially opened in 1967 by HM the Queen, and continues to be one of the most attractive displays in the Zoo, and one of the best in the world for exhibiting nocturnal creatures.

Prince Philip and Terence cheered me on, and rejoiced when some new benefaction enriched the Society. One stands out in my memory as something special. It was a gift of a quarter of a million pounds from Sir Michael Sobell. Sir Michael had for long been one of the great postwar benefactors to charitable causes, and I must have been one of scores of supplicants for his charity. No-one could have been more gracious in the way he responded.

I spoke to him early in 1969, and he replied by saying that he would make a gift to me personally as a recognition of the fact that even though I was not actively associated with the Jewish community, my public services had brought it credit. I wrote back saying that I was grateful for what he had said. A few days later I received a confirmatory letter that ended: 'I repeat that it has given me a great deal of pleasure to be able to do this for you personally.' This gift paid for the building now called the Sobell Pavilion for Monkeys and Apes. It was formally opened in 1972 by Prince Philip, in the presence of Sir Michael and Lady Sobell.

Except in the case of the big foundations, where one was always dealing with hard professional men, the relationships which I established with private benefactors varied enormously. As individuals they were so different: Sir Michael, the gentle, almost secret, but enormous benefactor to a heap of noble causes; Jack Cotton, lavishly hospitable, boisterous and impetuous, who fully trusted my judgment once I had engaged his personal interest; Charles Clore, shrewd, wondering what he could derive socially from contributing to an out-of-the-ordinary charity such as the Zoological Society, but who in his will left vast sums to other worthy causes in Britain and Israel. On the occasions when I lunched alone with Charles, his butler served only a half bottle of wine for the two of us, where Jack would have opened two bottles. Another man whom I approached, who was able to dispose of large sums from a trust, behaved less like a Midas than a miser, always chipping a few per cent off the donations that he had undertaken to give. But in one very important respect the big donors to the Zoo were alike. Most contributed to other charities. And they often found themselves criticized for having given money to improve the lot of caged animals rather than donating more than they already had to the poor, the aged, and the sick.

Charles Dalton retired in 1967, and Eirwen Owen now had the longest and most intimate knowledge of the way the Society and Zoo had developed over the preceding ten years. Nonetheless it seemed inappropriate to ask her to manage the Gardens the way Dalton had done. Colin Rawlins, a retired Colonial Office official, had just joined us as Director of Zoos, and was too inexperienced in the Society's affairs to be fitted straight away into Dalton's shoes. Dr L.G. Goodwin FRS had become Scientific Director in succession to Harrison Matthews. After much deliberation the Council decided that the administration should take the form of a triumvirate of equals – a director of zoos, one of science, and one of administration – with me concerting their affairs at regular weekly meetings. This was no burden. It was as easy to dash up to Regent's Park for a sandwich lunch with the three Directors as it was to eat sandwiches in my Whitehall office or to lunch in a club. There was once a profile of me in a national newspaper in which it was said that when I got bored with chairing some official committee in Whitehall, I would turn to someone and say, you get on with this, I'm going to the Zoo. As it turned out, after a few months regular meetings were not needed. I saw the three Directors as and when necessary. And there was always the telephone.

But despite the progress we were making as a scientific institution, and all the money that had been raised, the Council knew that we were living dangerously, and that we were always on the verge of financial collapse. During the sixties we could claim that the Government could rely upon us to cover the Zoo's operating costs, at the same time as we insisted that there was no possibility that we could generate the money for new buildings. These had to be financed by donations and grants.

When we had first examined the figures, Otto Clarke had come to the view that the demand to go to the Zoo was 'inelastic' – people would always want to visit it because there was nothing else like it. Before the end of the 1960s, however, that particular claim was beginning to wear thin. Labour and all other costs were rising at a rate which could not be matched by adjusting our gate charges. The interest payments on our bank loans were also an increasing burden. I therefore warned the Society in its Annual Report for 1968 that, in a highly inflationary period, it would be very difficult to find the means 'to continue and complete the rebuilding of the Regent's Park Gardens and of assuring the stability of the Society's affairs'.

When I penned those words, the Council had already agreed that the time had come to make yet another approach to the Treasury. I was then Chief Scientific Adviser to the Government, and my quarters were in the Cabinet Office. Rarely a week passed without my seeing Harold Wilson, the then Prime Minister. I raised the matter with him, and he agreed that I could talk to Roy Jenkins, the Chancellor. It was only five years since we had received a grant from the previous administration, when Maudling was Chancellor. The senior civil servants in the Treasury still understood the nature of the Society's problems, and knew how difficult it was for the Society to continue as the custodian of a national institution without help from public funds.

Encouraged by Roy Jenkins, negotiations were started with the Ministry of Public Building and Works, our titular landlord. The outcome was a loan of £375,000, guaranteed by the Government, from the Bank of England. That was in 1970. At the same time we undertook to cooperate with a firm of management consultants whom the Government had engaged to enquire into our affairs.

The report which they submitted commended all that had been done during the preceding decade, but warned the Government that there was little scope for further economies in the conduct of the Society's business. As the consultants saw it, progress was dependent on the Government itself providing capital funds to add to what we ourselves were raising. In June of 1970 this recommendation was agreed. The Government waived a debt of £250,000 that was a hangover from the Maudling grant, and also provided £650,000 to pay off our other short-term debts. In addition, an indexed grant of £700,000 was made towards the costs of our rebuilding programme to cover the period 1970–74. In the announcement in which these grants were reported to Parliament, one sentence in particular was important. 'In providing the Society with this substantial measure of support, the Government have had in mind that the Zoo has become in fact, if not in form, a national institution, that it is a major London amenity, and also an important tourist attraction.' Roy Jenkins himself had worded this sentence – with me looking over his shoulder.

In the following year I encouraged Walter Annenberg, then the American Ambassador, whose residence in Regent's Park is close to the Zoo, to make a donation of $25,000 to the Society, the first of two grants which I managed to raise from private American sources. The second, of $50,000, was provided by Mrs Brooke Astor, whose munificent gifts to the Bronx Zoo in New York have made it pre-eminent in the zoo world. Finally I managed to persuade Charles Clore to make yet a third grant, one for £200,000 to help complete the New Lion Terraces. We also continued to enjoy the confidence of the Research Councils and the large foundations. Before I retired from the

Council in 1984, the Wolfson Foundation had donated yet another £210,000 to support the work of the Society's Institute of Zoology.

The New Lion Terraces were formally opened by Her Majesty the Queen on the occasion of yet another grand dinner – and one which the President, Prince Philip, was this time able to attend. The ceremony took place in the evening, before an assembly of past and present members of the Council and its committees, and of various public dignitaries, including Ministers and senior officials, and, of course, Charles Clore. The Council had agreed that I could ask the late Sir William Walton OM to compose a fanfare for the occasion. I had always envied the Royal Academy the Arthur Bliss fanfare that is played at its annual dinners, and William was at least as famous a composer of fanfares. He obliged, and it was performed by the trumpeters of the Royal Military School of Music on the arrival of the Queen and Prince Philip. William entitled it the 'Roar of Lions', and dedicated it to me, calling me the 'lion of lions'. I have the original and OUP, his publishers, a copy. I wonder when it will next be played. The occasion and the dinner went off splendidly, and I believe the Queen was almost as pleased as was Charles Clore.

By then I had been Secretary for more than twenty years. To my great regret, Terence retired in 1975, and in the following year I informed the AGM of Fellows that I would not commit myself to completing a further statutory term of seven years as Secretary. A year later Prince Philip, who had held office for seventeen years, also decided to stand down. He had given more time to the Society's affairs than anyone had ever dared expect, and had actively helped in every stage in our progress. I was elected in his place in 1977, but again made it plain that I doubted whether I could serve the full statutory period of five years. But there was more trouble ahead. We were in difficulties over the posts of secretary and treasurer. Aubrey Buxton, who had followed Terence as Treasurer, was too occupied with his own business affairs, and had also accepted a new appointment as Chairman of Independent Television News. Ronald Hedley, who had become Secretary, found that he simply did not have the time for the job and for his post as Director of the Natural History Museum.* For a

---

*Dr Erasmus Barlow, a member of the Council and a medical man, stood in for two years as Secretary until Professor John Phillips, a zoologist, agreed to fill the post. Pressure of other work forced him to resign after two years.

time I found myself behaving less as a President should – as one who presides at meetings – than as a combination of all three officers – President, Treasurer and Secretary. As nothing could be done at the time to rectify the situation, I had to agree to be renominated as President in 1982, but this time on the explicit understanding that, come what may, I was going to resign after two years.

Our financial position grew steadily worse. But my message to the Council always remained the same. If what were regarded as the national zoological gardens were not to be shut down, the Government in the final analysis would have to take financial responsibility, with the Society selling its expert services to whatever new management was put in. We could not be expected to do what no other national zoo would consider possible – operate without a government grant.

Nineteen seventy-eight was the last year when we were financially viable on paper. By the end of 1979 we were debtors, and the signs were that nothing could prevent a continuing decline. Inflation, which had been running at about 9 per cent when Margaret Thatcher became Prime Minister, fluctuated in 1980 between about 15 and 20 per cent. Michael Heseltine had become Secretary of State for the Environment, and thus our landlord. I had already met him, and sought an early appointment to make him aware of the Society's plight. He was interested in the Zoo – he had a small aviary on his estate in the country – and his advice was, 'strike now, the Society will never have a more sympathetic minister with whom to deal than myself. I should like to see a new bird-house and aviaries built.' So far as it went, that was encouraging, but alas it did not go very far, since the next message from the Government was that all public expenditure was going to be curtailed in the fight against inflation. I found an opportunity to warn the new Prime Minister about the situation, and in January of 1981 sent the Secretary of the Cabinet a formal minute which I concluded by saying:

The Society could, of course, give the whole thing up, and just say to the Government and to the GLC, 'Take over our 36 acres of Regent's Park and run it yourself.' But, the chances are that we would then stop being, as at present, a pre-eminent and international institution, a major centre of education and research, and a leading tourist attraction. The public would, I believe, strongly resent such a change. Neither can I see the Zoo being run on a commercial basis as a 'honky-tonk' in a Royal Park.

Obviously the Zoo's problems were small beer to the Government against the background of the major economic problems with which it was wrestling. But throughout 1980 I kept stressing the Zoo's plight in government circles, endlessly repeating my cry, 'You, Government, take us over. Run the Gardens. We'll sell you our expert services to help you manage them, year in, year out.' Ever since I had become Secretary, in report after report, in article after article, I had pointed to the fact that the Society was the only custodian of a national zoo which was virtually unsupported by public funds. I painted the story in the grimmest terms in a foreword which I wrote for the Society's Annual Report for 1980. This was breaking with tradition – there had never been a foreword before. I did the same a year later, during which our financial position had continued to worsen, and in the course of which government officials had once again reviewed our books.

Michael Heseltine then managed to get the Treasury to agree that his department should keep the Society in funds while yet another lot of management consultants considered 'the prospects of the Society becoming self-supporting'. We had entered the era when the new profession of management experts ruled. It was no use my pointing out that the Society had never been self-supporting, if the term implied that it could earn enough to pay not only for the upkeep of the collections but also for new buildings. The battle cry of the day had become 'encourage the profit-centres and eliminate loss-centres'. Lavish praise for what I had done was expressed in the report which the consultants submitted. But the rest revealed an abysmal lack of understanding, not only of the Society's immediate financial problems, but of its functions and responsibilities. To them the Society and the menagerie were one. Nonetheless, the report did recommend that the Government should continue its interim financial support, at the same time as an 'operational plan' was prepared for the three years up to 1986 to reveal whether and how the Society could become self-supporting.

I had to insist that the preparation of such an operational plan was not a job for City consultants, and that only the Society itself knew enough about its scientific institutions and about zoos to prepare such a plan. Weeks passed before officials agreed this simple fact. I then laid out the framework of a voluminous report, the separate sections of which were written by members of the Society's staff, and then coordinated by Eirwen Owen, who generously came out of retirement to do the job. The work took four months and was completed just before I had to take off for a visit to the United States. I approved it formally at the airport, where I signed a letter of transmittal to the Secretary of State. That was in February 1983.

Michael Heseltine had arranged that Lord Gibson, Chairman of the National Trust, should evaluate the plan. He, however, had accepted the chore on the clear understanding that he would report only on the Society's management, and that he could not contribute to the study of the plan itself. About a week later he submitted his report – but not to Michael Heseltine who, after the Falklands War, had been appointed Secretary of State for Defence. His successor until the General Election of June 1983 was Tom King, with whom I had two or three fruitless meetings. Following the Election, Patrick Jenkin became Secretary of State for the Environment. Like his predecessor, he knew little or nothing about our affairs, and, as is only to be expected in such cases, he was mainly guided by his senior officials, who had committed themselves to the earlier consultants' report. It was not until late December 1983, and only after much argument, that this phase of negotiations with the Government ended.

In 1981 and 1982, the Society was provided with nearly £3 million over and above the permitted level of our bank loan. Without this help we could not have kept going. In December of 1983 the department agreed to continue to provide funds, at an estimated rate of £2 million a year, for the period up to March of 1986. This final phase of my negotiations ended with an argument about the terms of the Government's statement to Parliament. I was unprepared to agree that the Secretary of State should include words which implied that the Council was accepting government help on the false understanding that the Society could 'break even' after three years. A textual compromise was reached, in accordance with which the Secretary of State was able to tell Parliament that the Council would use its 'best endeavours' to develop plans aimed at reducing the Society's operating deficit, in the hope that it would be able to do without further government revenue support after 1986. Once the Secretary of State had made his announcement, Roy Jenkins put down a parliamentary question asking whether the Government would now pay off our bank overdraft and provide the Society with money for new buildings. The answer was no to the first question – which was nonetheless a reminder to Parliament that the Government had done just that in 1970 – and a qualified yes to the second. The Government *might* contribute to the Zoo's building programme on a pound for pound basis.

By now I had had more than enough. When it sought public funds, it was the Society that was helping the Government, not the other way round. As a scientific institution and educational charity operating under Royal Charter, the Society could survive without the burden of managing a public amenity. Moreover, were the Zoo ever to be forced into bankruptcy and closed down, it would be the Government, not the Society, that would have to face the public protest.

I resigned from the presidency at the 1984 AGM, and was much pleased by a dinner that was given in my honour by the Council. The company included scores of old friends whom I had persuaded over the years to serve on the Zoo Council and its committees. Prince Philip and Terence spoke – the latter elaborating an apocryphal story of how in a nightclub, with 'bunny girls' on our knees, I had urged Jack Cotton to support the Zoo. If I had ever had to plead the Zoo's case in a nightclub, it would more likely have been with Charles Clore than with Jack. Prince Philip presented me with a magnificently bound 'scrap-book', in which were mounted dozens of newspaper and other articles relating to my efforts on the Zoo's behalf, and photographs of the staff with whom I had worked. A two-day seminar on the part that zoos should play in the conservation of animal wildlife was also organized to mark my departure.

I have sometimes been asked whether I have any regrets about having given as much time as I did to the Society's affairs. My answer has usually been no. On the other hand, I do know that I would certainly have resigned from the Council had I thought that the time I was devoting to the Society's affairs was taking my mind off my academic and governmental duties. But that didn't happen. I usually work fast in concentrated bursts. When I come to a moment of pause, I need to turn to some other problem with which I am concerned. That way of doing things has always left me with masses of time.

I suppose, too, that it was the battle against the 'Zoo rebels' in 1959 that led me to devote so much effort to the Zoo. Over the years I had enjoyed the confidence of the Council. I had been favoured by the goodwill of all the Society's staff. And according to the Operational Plan which was presented to the Government, something like £25 million at 1983 values had been collected during the period I was Secretary – to which could now be added the £7 million more for which, in my final years, I had pestered three Secretaries of State. All had gone to the building of animal houses, and in establishing the Society's research laboratories. Yes, there was a lot to be pleased about. At the end of my last meeting with the Council's Management Committee, Sir Richard ('Sam') Way, then the Treasurer – and one of three ex-Permanent Secretaries whom over the years I had encouraged to join the Council – quoted, in appreciation for what I had done, the words attributed to Christopher Wren's son, '*Si monumentum requiris, circumspice*' – 'If you would see his monument, look around'. I remained silent.

'Zoos', I once wrote, 'exist because the people who want them vastly outnumber those who would like to see them suppressed.' Scientific societies and research institutions exist not because a majority demands that they should, but because of the few who believe that they must. The future of the Zoological Society and its research establishments will definitely depend upon the few.

PART III

An Amateur in Whitehall

CIVIL AFFAIRS

11

The Organization of Civil Science

Shortly before the war ended, Duncan Sandys, then the Minister of Works, had invited Sir Reginald Stradling to become his Chief Scientist. As the director of the Research Department of the wartime Ministry of Home Security, Stradling had sponsored my Oxford Extra-Mural Unit and, at his suggestion, Sandys had invited me to join a Scientific Advisory Committee that he proposed to set up. Then, in July of 1945, during the course of the Potsdam Conference, the Conservative Party lost the general election, and Clement Attlee became Prime Minister. George Tomlinson, who succeeded Sandys as Minister of Works, decided to keep the Sandys Committee in being.

Visions of a new and ideally reconstructed world were then in the air. Bombed areas were going to be quickly cleared. There would be magnificent new housing with a statutory minimum of 900 square feet per family, including a room where, undisturbed, the children could do their homework. Scientists, who during the war had shown their worth outside the laboratory, would help make a reality of a peacetime Utopia. That was before the hard facts began to intrude, before more than a select few appreciated that the country was bankrupt.

I cannot pretend that I was enthused by such meetings of the Ministry of Works Committee as I attended. I remember them mainly because it was there that I first met Harold Wilson, then Parliamentary Private Secretary to Tomlinson. The only other reason I have for remembering the Committee is a group photograph, rather like one of a school football team, with Mr Tomlinson seated in the centre of the front row, and all his senior officials and the members of his Advisory Committee around him.

Six years later Winston Churchill was returned to power. Lord Woolton, Churchill's wartime Minister of Food, was appointed to the office of Lord President of the Council, and in effect he therefore became the Minister for Science in the new Government. Within a short time the Advisory Council of the Ministry of Works was wound up. I remember Woolton telling me that we didn't want scientists poking their noses into people's domestic affairs. 'Who', he wanted to know, 'was to say where Johnny was to do his homework?' I cannot imagine that he had read any of the papers that the Ministry's Council had produced, and I suppose that someone must have cited the business of the minimum requirements for a house as a sample of socialist meddling.

The Barlow Committee, of which I also became a member, was a very different affair. It was set up in December 1945 by Herbert Morrison, Deputy Prime Minister and Lord President in Attlee's Government. I had a hunch that I was asked to join Barlow's small committee, first because none of its other members was a biologist, and second, because I was available. I was still spending part of my time in Whitehall as Scientific Director of the British Bombing Survey Unit.

It is also possible that the suggestion that I should become a member of Barlow's Committee came from Herbert Morrison himself. I had first met him during the war when he was the Minister of Home Security and, as such, the Minister to whom Stradling reported. On the basis of my wartime experiences, I had come to believe that governments never paid sufficient attention to the place of science in public affairs. Some three months before Barlow's committee was set up, I had therefore sent Morrison a short paper in which I had proposed that he should establish a central scientific secretariat – not a committee – in order to ensure that public scientific affairs became better integrated and planned than they had been before the war.[1] My memorandum had been critical about the Scientific Advisory Committee to the Cabinet which, despite its high-sounding title, had enjoyed little authority.

Sir Alan Barlow, the Chairman of the committee which was to commemorate his name, was then the Second Secretary of the Treasury. During the war years, I had got on easily with the military leaders with whom I worked. But I found it unnerving to be sitting at Barlow's table with leaders of the scientific establishment. One was Sir Alfred Egerton, the Physical Secretary of the Royal Society. Another was Sir Edward Appleton, the Secretary of the Department of Scientific and Industrial Research (the DSIR). The three other members were Patrick Blackett,* very much a senior figure in the world of science and also the 'father' of wartime operational research – in so far as anyone deserves that designation; Geoffrey Crowther, then the Editor of *The Economist*; and Sir George Nelson, the Chairman of one of the country's major electrical engineering companies. There were two Assessors, one of whom was C.P. Snow, the chemist–novelist. He represented the Civil Service Commission. During the war years, he had had the responsibility for directing scientists to essential jobs.

Before the war I do not recall ever having heard anyone say that there were too few professional scientists in the country. But a shortage of scientifically trained men and women had certainly revealed itself during its course, and towards its close Alan Barlow had chaired an official inter-departmental committee, the Committee on Scientific Staff, to see what could be done to improve the quality of the scientific Civil Service. The terms of reference now given him by Herbert Morrison were to consider the policies that should govern both the use and the development of the country's scientific resources during the next ten years 'so as to facilitate forward planning in those fields which are dependent upon the use of scientific man-power'.

My awe at being a member of so high-powered a committee soon vanished, and it was not long before I was regarded as a 'Young Turk' and, like Patrick Blackett, a radical. For one thing, I saw no reason why the universities should receive their research funds both by way of the Government's University Grants Committee (UGC) and from the Research Councils. I argued forcibly that the universities should be provided with research money only from the Grants Committee, and that they themselves should decide how it should be spent. The Research Councils should be left to run their own laboratories. This was not a view that was likely to appeal either to the Royal Society, or to the Secretaries of the Research Councils. Some years later I realized that my elders and betters had been far wiser than I on that particular issue.

After deliberating on the evidence submitted by the representatives of the university and scientific worlds, the committee recommended, in a report that was published by the Government, that the country's

*Later Lord Blackett OM, President of the Royal Society.

output of professional scientists, then estimated at about 2500 a year, should be increased as rapidly as possible to 5000 – exclusive of professional engineers and graduates in 'related technologies', of whom no more than about 1000 were being turned out annually.[2] Appropriate noises were made about the need to help the technical colleges, and about the desirability of creating two or three institutes of technology of the quality of the Massachusetts and California Institutes of Technology (MIT and Caltech) in the United States. Our main recommendation – that the government grant to the universities should rise sharply in order to provide them with the means to expand – was immediately accepted.

The best estimate that could then be made was that at the end of the thirties the total number of full-time university students in the UK had been only 50,000, that is to say, about 0.1 per cent of a population of 48 million. We were confident that only a fraction of every age group that had the ability to benefit from a higher education was in fact enjoying one. Today the proportion is about 0.5 per cent.

While there was no problem either about money or about the availability of students, there certainly was one with the universities. Only the provincial or, as they were then called, 'red-brick' universities, were in general willing to expand. Administrative difficulties in London obstructed expansion, but the university authorities were nonetheless ready to try to overcome them. The official representatives of Oxford and Cambridge were not prepared to contemplate more than a temporary increase in order to cope with the expected influx of men and women who were being demobilized from the armed forces. Between them the two ancient universities had housed in 1939 about 11,000 undergraduates; that was the maximum they were now prepared to consider. In the event, the 11,000 has since doubled, for over the years Oxford and Cambridge have shown as little reluctance to grow and to accept whatever money is available, either from the public purse or from private sources, as have other centres of higher education. But we were all over-cautious. Our committee had estimated that it would take five to ten years to double the output of professional scientists. In the event, it took four.[3]

With scientific manpower out of the way, Barlow's committee turned its attention to the question of coordinating the country's scientific effort. In the memorandum that I had sent to Morrison I had urged that civil and defence science should be dealt with by one and the same body. This was not to be. We took evidence from several quarters, but the Chiefs of Staff organization, which during the war had been eager to accept any help that academic and industrial scientists could provide, had decided that they had to have their own central committee to help set research priorities in the defence field. The need for secrecy was a major reason for this decision, especially now that the atom bomb, about which the military then knew little or nothing, had become a reality. Accordingly, and before Barlow was in a position to put forward any recommendation, the Ministry of Defence set up its own Defence Research Policy Committee (the DRPC).

Opinions in Barlow's committee then became sharply divided about the need for a corresponding body to deal with civil science. Egerton did not like the idea of any council that might threaten the freedom of the individual scientist. In his turn, Appleton, whose views reflected those of his two colleagues, the Secretaries of the Medical and Agricultural Research Councils, was concerned lest the quasi-autonomous positions of the latter might be affected if any central body were established. In the end we agreed a benign recommendation that an Advisory Council on Scientific Policy should be set up to advise the Lord President of the Council – to whom the Research Councils reported – 'in the exercise of his responsibility for the formulation and execution of Government scientific policy'.[4] The new Council was appointed in January 1947.

The Advisory Council on Scientific Policy

A week or two before the public announcement of the establishment of the Council, I was taken aback to receive a letter from Morrison inviting me to become a member. I did not know who else had been invited, and I was also aware that my views about what was needed at the centre were not very popular.

The Barlow Report had stated that 'least of all nations can Great Britain afford to neglect whatever benefits the scientists can confer upon her', and it had gone on to say that, if we were to maintain our position in the world and restore and improve our standard of living, there was no alternative but 'to strive for that scientific achievement without which our trade will wither, our Colonial Empire will remain undeveloped and our lives and freedom will be at the mercy of a potential aggressor'.[1] These were brave words, and I believed every one of them.

Despite the fact that defence policy lay outside its terms of reference, great things were therefore expected of the new Council. But I had my doubts. I still suspected that governments did not really appreciate the extent to which both the development of the economy and national security are dependent on the exploitation of scientific knowledge, and I feared that the new Council would prove just as ineffective as had the Cabinet's wartime advisory committee.

Herbert Morrison was not only Deputy Prime Minister, but also chairman of a cabinet committee that was responsible for the coordination of the nation's economic affairs. To head his office, he had recruited E.M. ('Max') Nicholson. I had known Max, an ornithologist, before the war. He had been the Director of PEP (Political and Economic Planning), and during the war had been in charge of 'tonnage allocation' in the Ministry of War Transport, and then Director of the Middle East Supply Centre.

I went to see him to explain my misgivings. He brushed them aside, saying that I had long been protesting about the Government's failure to use science effectively, and that I now had a chance of helping to show what should be done. He also told me that Sir Henry Tizard was almost certain to be the Chairman of the new Council as well as of the Defence Research Policy Committee. He then showed me a list of those who were being invited to serve. I became even more nervous when I saw that Patrick Blackett's name was not among them. Max was not prepared to tell me why Patrick had been left out, but years later, after I had become a full-time civil servant, and had discovered that the names of 'independents' who are proposed as members of central governmental committees are often 'canvassed' around Whitehall, I guessed that the reason had probably been Patrick's forthright opposition to the course Attlee's Government had decided to pursue about the atom bomb.

Sir Henry Tizard was a scientist and administrator of great distinction. He was respected in Royal Society circles as well as in the wider scientific community. He was also well liked by the Chiefs of Staff organization, which trusted him far more than they had Winston Churchill's Scientific Adviser, Lord Cherwell (Professor Lindemann – 'Prof'). One of the reasons why Tizard had left Whitehall for Oxford in 1942 was that Cherwell's influence with Winston Churchill constantly frustrated the work which he, Tizard, was doing as a member of the Air Council and as Scientific Adviser to the Ministry of Aircraft Production. I had known him for some time, although not well, and he was aware of the work I had done during the war. He also sympathized with my views about the place of science in public affairs. My worries somewhat allayed, I wrote accepting the invitation.

When Tizard returned to London, the first thing he had to do was to get back into the swing of things with the Chiefs, and indeed, during the six years that he was Chairman of both the ACSP and the DRPC, he devoted the better part of his time to the latter. For its first year or so, Tizard accordingly got Alan Barlow to act as Deputy Chairman of the ACSP. He then asked me to serve in that capacity. By now I was spending two or three days a week in London, and was able to give far more than casual attention to the matters which came up to the

Council, and to the drafting of its annual reports. I remained Deputy Chairman for fifteen of the seventeen years of the Council's existence.

The understanding was that when Tizard reached retiring age he would be succeeded as Chairman of both the ACSP and the DRPC by Sir John Cockcroft, who was then Director of the Harwell nuclear establishment. John and I knew each other well, and it suited me to continue as Deputy Chairman when he took over. But all these arrangements were disrupted when Churchill returned to power in 1951, and when Cherwell once again became a member of the Government. 'Prof' had no time for the ACSP. In his opinion it was an unnecessary body, and he was convinced that it would be a mistake if Cockcroft, who had already started to arrange the lease of a house in London, left Harwell. Cherwell was agreeable to him becoming Chairman of the DRPC, since in that position he would be helped by a full-time deputy, an Admiralty scientist by the name of Sir Frederick Brundrett. But not the ACSP. Alexander Todd, Professor of Chemistry at Cambridge, was appointed instead.* He and I worked happily together until the Council was dissolved in 1964.

The Council usually met at monthly intervals, and until it was wound up in 1964, we published an annual report in which, in addition to a brief record of our deliberations, useful figures were provided about government expenditure on science and technology and about the numbers of new science graduates who were emerging from the universities. We discussed, but rarely in depth, such topics as the need to encourage particular fields of scientific enquiry, higher education, the lack of a national library of science and technology, and our overseas scientific relations. But few of our recommendations ever led to any specific action.

We touched neither on 'defence science' nor in any significant way on nuclear matters. Shortly after we were set up, Tizard appointed a sub-committee to consider the civil applications of atomic energy, with Sir James Chadwick as Chairman. Cockcroft, who succeeded Chadwick as its Chairman, was the only other member of the ACSP who ever served on this committee, about whose affairs the rest of us were ignorant. I was in the chair of the ACSP on the single occasion when the sub-committee, which remained in being for no more than two

*Later Lord Todd OM, President of the Royal Society.

years, reported to its parent body. The matter of the UK becoming an independent nuclear power was never discussed.

The issue of the independence of the Research Councils became a bone of contention as soon as we started deliberating the respective responsibilities of government departments and the Councils. Before the Second World War only a few departments had executive, as distinct from purely administrative, responsibilities. Exceptions were the Service departments, the Ministry of Pensions, the Post Office, and the Office of Works.* Until the creation of the National Health Service in 1948, the Ministry of Health was responsible for housing policy and for monitoring public health, this being one of the functions which it had taken over when it replaced the Local Government Board. The pre-war Department of Mines was responsible only for safety in mines.† Correspondingly, the Research Councils were quasi-independent bodies which were available for consultation by any branch of government that needed their help. The Department of Scientific and Industrial Research (DSIR) had been set up in 1916, the Medical Research Council (the MRC) in 1920 (having started life as the Medical Research Committee just before the First World War), and the Agricultural Research Council (the ARC) in 1931.

There were two sharply divergent views about the way the Councils should work in relation to government departments. Some (and I was one of them), felt that government departments should either have a major say, or should be in direct control of such research organizations, including those belonging to the Councils, as carried out work which impinged on the statutory responsibilities for which they – the departments – were answerable to Parliament. The representatives of the Research Councils and of the Royal Society thought otherwise. The Councils enjoyed enormous prestige, and Sir Edward Mellanby, the Secretary of the MRC, and Sir Edward Appleton of the DSIR, both of whom were members of the ACSP, also happened to be major scientific figures in their own right. Mellanby had a powerful personality, and he lived by the principle that his job was to support the work of first-class men who had ideas of their own, rather than to find people to work in fields that might be selected in the national interest. In the end the

---

*Later renamed the Ministry of Works, and now part of the Department of the Environment.
†Now part of the Department of Energy.

ACSP compromised by recommending what was essentially a continuation of the *status quo*, namely that the executive Ministries should be responsible for their own scientific affairs, and that the Research Councils should continue to be 'free from administrative control by the executive departments'. However, we did add the further recommendation that those government departments with executive responsibilities as had not as yet done so, should follow the example of departments such as Defence and Agriculture, and appoint chief scientific advisers.

Rereading some of the reports of those early days, I still find myself amazed by the way proposed changes in the existing order, however sensible, were always resisted. For example, the Lord President asked the ACSP to consider 'as a special case' the status of the Government's Building Research Station, which in those days was a DSIR establishment. After the usual exchange of views about the sanctity of the Research Councils, the ACSP recommended that the station should remain with the DSIR, and that the Ministry of Works, which at the time was responsible for a vast rebuilding programme, should appoint a chief scientist and its own scientific advisory council. But, so the ACSP decreed, the Ministry should not have any direct say in the formulation of the programme of work carried out by the DSIR's Building Research Station. To me it seemed ridiculous that a government department that was spending thousands of millions of pounds of public money on housing – and which presumably was aware of the technical needs of the industry – should not be responsible for the country's main building research establishment. In this case, as in others, the Research Councils stood together. If the DSIR were to allow one of its institutes to be transferred to a government department, who could tell which would be the next victim?

In 1966, some two years after I had become Chief Scientific Adviser to the Government, I managed to get the question reopened. The Earl of Longford, who was then the Leader of the House of Lords, was asked by Harold Wilson, the Prime Minister, to decide whether the Ministry of Works should shoulder the responsibility for building research. To help in his enquiry, he was provided with two assessors, Sir Laurence Helsby, then the head of the Civil Service, and myself. After several meetings, Longford recommended that the Building Research Station should be placed under the Ministry. The administrative transfer was made without any protest from the people who worked in the station, nor did it result in any decline in the quality of their work. My view was that the director of the station should also be appointed scientific adviser to the Minister of Works – instead of the Ministry having a different 'scientist' in that position. What, I used to ask myself, can be wrong in principle with the concept of a two-hatted departmental chief scientific adviser, concerned first with the practical problems that relate to a department's statutory responsibilities, and second with the administration of the research bodies that generate the new knowledge which affects those responsibilities?

The usual attitude of the Research Councils also proved an obstacle when it came to closing down institutes that may have outlived their usefulness. There were, for example, several enquiries into the work of the then Fuel Research Station at Greenwich, before part of its programme of work was transferred to the new Warren Spring Laboratory in Stevenage, and the rest dropped.

The only Government Research Station that I can recall being shut down during the fifties was the Institute of Seaweed Research outside Edinburgh. This establishment, which had been set up in 1944 as the Scottish Seaweed Research Association, had done useful work during the war years when explosives factories were in need of a chemical substance – alginate – of which seaweed was a source material. Once the demand for alginates had dwindled – except for the making of ice cream – there was little or no point in the Government subsidizing the station. I was Chairman of the small Committee on Biology and Allied Sciences that was asked to advise what should be done. We were pretty blunt in our recommendation. There was no justification for using public money to support work of little value either to science or to the economy. This time, despite the powerful protest of the Secretary of State for Scotland that the institute was one of the few government research stations north of the border, our recommendation was acted upon. The Research Councils did not protest. The station was not one of theirs. It was later taken over by an American corporation.

In the years that have passed since the ACSP put forward its anodyne recommendations about the place of science in government, the whole world has been transformed through the exploitation of new scientific and technological knowledge. So too have the Research Councils. The old Department of Scientific and Industrial Research started to change towards the end of the fifties, and no longer exists in its original form. The Agricultural Research Council, which became the Agricultural and Food Research Council, has lost a great deal of its power. So far as government is concerned, however, the place of science remains essentially the same as it has always been. My own views on these matters had been formed during the war when I learnt how strategic policy has to keep in step with new scientific and technological developments. What matters in the end is not who manages a piece of research, but whether a scientific point of view is brought to bear on those matters of major national policy that are affected by scientific and technical considerations.

I suppose that at the start we all thought that the ACSP would be doing something like that. Little that we discussed was, however, significant politically. Attlee, by whom the Council was set up, does not refer to it in his autobiography, nor is it mentioned in Kenneth Harris's biography, which is a far more extensive work. As Prime Minister, the matters that came before the Council were of little or no political interest to him. Both the ACSP and DRPC survived through the 1950s and into the 1960s, that is to say, through the premiership of Harold Macmillan and into that of Harold Wilson. It is again a measure of the political insignificance of the issues which both bodies debated that neither Council is referred to in the memoirs of these two Prime Ministers. The DRPC became a forum where mundane matters regarding defence R&D were secretly settled, or supposedly settled, while the ACSP dealt mainly with issues which, however important to the scientific community, were not critical to government.

Some twenty years ago I gave my view of the achievements of the ACSP. As I saw it, the Council was never inhibited 'when it discussed problems in which no other body had a particular vested interest – for example, questions such as the growth and deployment of scientific manpower, the scale of financial support for basic research, or matters concerning certain aspects of our overseas scientific relations. But throughout its existence it not surprisingly found itself impotent, and often baulked, when it came to advising either about the use of scientific and technological resources in executive departments of state, for example, the Defence departments, or about the programmes of the Research Councils.'[2]

Only in 1960, when I became a full-time civil servant, did I begin to realize just how little influence on policy can be exercised by any committee of 'independents' that is not privy to what are the main concerns of government, or to what goes on behind the closed doors of government departments.

13

Scientific Manpower

Scientific manpower was one of the main issues which Morrison wanted the ACSP to keep under review. Some members of the new Council were concerned lest 'expanding' the universities would result in a lowering of university entry standards. Two who were particularly worried were Sir James Chadwick of Cambridge, the physicist who discovered the neutron, and Sir Cyril Hinshelwood, the physical chemist of Oxford, the only man who, I believe, has been at the same time President of the Royal Society and President of the Classical Association. Distinguished not only in their respective fields of science but also in appearance, both were inclined to argue that the entry examination papers for Oxford or Cambridge should be regarded as a national yardstick. After one meeting at which the matter was discussed, John Cockcroft sent me a set of entrance papers to a Cambridge college. In his covering letter he wrote: 'Could you get in? I couldn't.' I answered that I too would have failed.

The topic of the supply of scientists came up at almost every one of the early meetings of the ACSP. Sir Edward Salisbury, then the Biological Secretary of the Royal Society, was quite certain that there would be serious problems of scientific unemployment if the number of scientists coming out of the universities was significantly increased. He had in mind a picture of the sad days of the twenties. I raised the matter privately with Tizard, saying that I thought it ridiculous for the Council to try to monitor the expansion of the universities and the output of scientists by way of an exchange of off-the-cuff opinions. As I saw it, what we needed was a specialist subcommittee made up of representatives of the Government's Central Statistical Office, the University Grants Committee, the schools, industrialists, and the Treasury. Tizard agreed. But once again I had to pay a price for intervening. Tizard declared that he would set up a committee on scientific manpower – but that I had to chair it. And so it came about that for some sixteen years the problem of scientific manpower became one of my continuing interests. In 1964, when I handed over the chairmanship to Sir Willis Jackson, a professor of engineering at Imperial College, the name of the committee was changed to the Committee on Manpower Resources for Science and Technology.

During the years that I was Chairman, the committee was small and intimate. It comprised the Director of the Government's Central Statistical Office, the Permanent Secretary of the Ministry of Education, the Chairman of the UGC, and a senior Treasury representative (which is how I first got to know Eddie Playfair and, later, Otto Clarke, who took his place on the committee). C.P. Snow represented the Civil Service Commission. Our job was to see that the process of university expansion was as orderly as it could be. Up-to-date information about the rate at which the universities were increasing their intake of students and about the output of professional scientists and engineers was readily available. But we had to use every manner of speculative enquiry to obtain indications of future levels of demand.

Sir Gilbert Flemming, the Permanent Secretary of the Ministry of Education, and one of the committee's original members, constantly advised that it was no use pretending that it was possible to predict what the demand would be for physicists or chemists or engineers ten years ahead.* Otto Clarke, while convinced of the need to expand the universities, was also concerned lest the public money that was pumped into the universities was not used sensibly. C.P. Snow, on the other hand, always felt that we were not doing enough, and that the scale of our effort compared poorly with that of other countries, even, I remember, with that of Italy. In private, Otto was scathing about Snow's views. 'If he tells us that we should be moving in that direction,' he would say, 'turn smartly round and go the opposite way – we are more likely to be right.' Snow was more a novelist than a scientist, while Otto was a practical economist with one of the most incisive minds I have ever known. Sir Arthur Trueman, a geologist who was Chairman of the UGC, was the quietest member of the committee. With every

---

*Dame Mary Smieton succeeded Gilbert Flemming as Permanent Secretary of the Ministry of Education on the committee, and I have a memory of her knitting during our meetings. I suppose it was a substitute for the smoking which in those days was so usual around Whitehall tables. It made us seem very homely.

university in the country pressing him day after day for more money, it was a period of great strain for him. He was sitting opposite me at one of our meetings, and I suddenly spotted that one side of his face was beginning to droop. I remembered enough of what I had learnt as a medical student to realize that he was beginning to suffer a minor stroke. I pushed a note across, saying, 'You don't look at all well. Would you like me to suspend the meeting?' He shook his head, but we all became worried as his condition worsened. Finally, I stopped the meeting and Trueman was helped out, still protesting, but in a voice that was no longer his normal one.*

The committee published a number of general as well as specialized reports, of which the last was formally presented in 1963 to the Lord President of the Council, then Lord Hailsham. In my foreword I spoke generally of the changes that had taken place in the seventeen years since I had become involved in the problem of assessing the national need for scientific manpower, and I ended by saying that it was now less a case of the Government needing to encourage young people to continue their scientific education 'in order to provide science graduates for vocational jobs, which is what the problem was until not long ago, than it is of an ever-increasing general demand for a higher education in which science plays a significant part'.[1]

The truth was that I had early on started to lose faith in the statistical and sampling techniques which the committee used in making forecasts of the numbers of chemists, physicists or biologists who would be wanted in the years ahead. My scepticism was revealed all too clearly when I appeared before a committee on higher education that had been set up by the Government in 1961 under the chairmanship of the late Lord Robbins. A critical article about 'manpower forecasting' that was published a few years later, said that I had placed myself 'in the curious position' of supporting proposals to expand the colleges of advanced technology, at the same time as my committee was publishing long-term forecasts that predicted a *surplus* of scientists and engineers by

*That was not the only time in my life as a committee chairman that I encountered a medical disaster. Many years later, when I arrived one morning at the Cabinet Office, I saw Dr Nyman Levin, the Director of the nuclear weapons establishment at Aldermaston, lying outstretched in the foyer. He had been on his way to a meeting of a small secret official committee that I chaired, but had not even managed to get to the lift before suffering a heart attack. The meeting was delayed until I had got him to a nearby hospital where, alas, he died a few days later.

1970.[2] 'Sir Solly', the commentary went on, 'not only abandoned all claims to faith in his own forecasts but also gave the strong impression that, despite the variety of techniques which had been tried since 1946, his committee was really no nearer to developing a reliable forecasting technique for scientists and engineers.'

But if I was sceptical about our own techniques of forecasting, I was every bit as dubious about the 'social-demand approach' adopted by the Robbins Committee. Their view was that the doors of the universities should be opened to all who wished to enter, given that they had satisfied certain arbitrary entrance requirements. I had learnt enough from Otto Clarke and Eddie Playfair to realize that this would lead to so considerable and rapid an expansion of the universities that the Exchequer could never keep pace. Satisfying any 'social demand' costs money, and resources have always to be rationed. Long before the financial crisis that has recently engulfed Britain's universities, Sir Edward Boyle had admitted that the acceptance of the Robbins recommendations by the Government of which he was then the Minister of Education, and particularly the decision to found a number of new universities, had been a mistake. Today, alas, one hears talk of shutting down or down-grading some of the new post-Robbins universities.

In many an address and article that I gave or wrote when Chairman of the Scientific Manpower Committee, I emphasized that while a shortage of scientific manpower was a critical factor, it was certainly not a sufficient reason for the postwar decline in Britain's economic and industrial power. During my encounter with the Robbins Committee, I had in fact said that one of the least reliable ways of finding out about industry's needs for professional manpower is to ask industry itself. What was never revealed, what industrialists themselves probably did not know, was the scale of the investments that they hoped to make – and about their chances of success. As industrialists saw the problem, it was the business of government to produce scientists. Only the stars could tell if, as a consequence, economic resurrection would follow. And they have not told us yet.

Natural Resources (Technical) Committee

A third item that Herbert Morrison had asked Tizard to include in the opening agenda of the new Advisory Council concerned the contribution that science could make to the improvement of 'national productivity'. This very wide question Tizard referred to a small subcommittee that he set up under the chairmanship of Sir Claude Gibb FRS, an industrial scientist. Because of Morrison's notional role as Minister responsible for economic planning, Sir Edwin Plowden,* then head of the Treasury's Economic Planning staff, and, following him, William Strath,† were made members. Within a few months, it was decided that the new subcommittee should become an independent Committee on Industrial Productivity (CIP), with Tizard as Chairman, and answerable, as Parliament was informed in December of 1947, jointly to Herbert Morrison, the Lord President, and to Sir Stafford Cripps who, in replacing Hugh Dalton as Chancellor of the Exchequer, had assumed the Chancellor's traditional role as the minister responsible for coordinating the country's economic affairs.

Tizard had appointed me a member of Gibb's Subcommittee, which then delegated its work to four panels: one on Technology and Operational Research; a second on 'Human Factors affecting Productivity'; a third on Technical Information Services; and a fourth, the Imports Substitution Panel of which, despite my ignorance of economic matters, I was made Chairman. Representatives of all the government departments concerned, including the Cabinet Office and Treasury, were appointed to my panel, together with senior executives of two major manufacturing companies.

*Now Lord Plowden.
†Later Sir William Strath.

At the end of its first year, the Committee on Industrial Productivity published a White Paper. A second followed a year later,[1] but a few weeks after it appeared, Tizard, presumably after consulting with Cripps and Morrison, recommended that the main committee and three of its panels should be dissolved. The explanation was that their work either duplicated or could be better done by other bodies. But the powers-that-be also decided that the Imports Substitution Panel should continue as an independent body and be renamed the Natural Resources (Technical) Committee. I was surprised and pleased. Not only was this a sign that what we had been doing had been worthwhile, but, of all my Whitehall activities, the panel was the one that was then teaching me most, opening as it did a thousand new worlds of which I had been all but totally ignorant before. The committee was not dissolved until 1967.

Rationing of food, clothing, and of almost everything else, was still in force. We were highly dependent on imported manufactured goods and, despite the help provided by America through the Marshall Plan, we lived for years with a perpetual balance of payments problem. To pay for 'essential imports', our manufacturing industry, which during the war years had had to concentrate on the production of armaments, had returned to the production of any goods that could be sold abroad. The pattern of agriculture had to change. During the war farmers had had to produce essential foodstuffs such as milk and wheat. New crops were now wanted, and livestock had to be reintroduced if our supply of domestically grown meat was to be increased. On top of all this, we had to make good the dereliction that had occurred during the thirties when hundreds of farmers had gone to the wall as they tried to grow foodstuffs which, in those days of world depression, could be bought more cheaply in overseas markets.

The economic situation became even more serious in 1950, when the Korean War began. The Americans then started to stockpile almost every commodity they could buy, so pushing up world prices. Agricultural surpluses soon became shortages. The value of such manufactured goods as we could export simply could not match the cost of what we wanted or needed to import. The social dislocations caused by the nationalization of the railways and coal mines, and by the resettlement of men and women demobilized from the forces, did not make matters any easier.

Whatever could be saved from the national import bill was therefore worth saving, provided only that the cost of producing a domestic substitute was not too high. As Chairman of the Natural Resources Committee, I was summoned by Herbert Morrison to a meeting of newspaper proprietors, who were led by the powerful Mr Bartholomew of the *Daily Mirror*, which in those days was fervently pro-Labour. They wanted more newsprint to be imported from Scandinavia. Morrison asked why straw, which traditionally was burnt (in those days no-one objected to the practice on environmental grounds), could not be used to make paper pulp. Someone had provided the Lord President's office with a copy of the *Daily Telegraph* that had been printed in the 1920s on paper made largely from straw. It was passed round the table, and Mr Bartholomew reluctantly agreed to see what could be done. At the same time, I was asked to enquire into straw as a wasted natural resource. The search for a substitute for paper pulp was therefore an early item on the agenda of my committee. But we soon discovered that the cost of bringing straw to collection centres would make its use as a raw material for paper pulp uneconomic, even if the necessary transport could have been organized in a period of strict petrol rationing.

But straw was almost the least important of the matters which my committee considered. When still a panel of the disbanded main committee, we had made a rapid survey of the list of our imports, and had decided that animal foodstuffs – coarse grains and protein 'cattle-cake' – should be dealt with straight away. An adequate supply of these commodities, particularly of protein, was essential for rebuilding the national herd, and imports of cattle-cake had become very expensive. Grass was the obvious substitute. Within a few weeks I became all but obsessed by the need to encourage the better management and use of grass as a source of protein. The task was far from easy. Not only had pastures been neglected in the bad years of the thirties, but thousands of acres of grass had had to make way during the war for cereals and potatoes. It was now a case of trying to get more protein out of a smaller acreage of pasture. Farmers had to be advised and helped. Scarce nitrogenous fertilizer was wanted.

Plowden was convinced that what was needed was a powerful 'grassland campaign', and he spurred me on. There were other grassland enthusiasts. In the days before he had become involved in the analysis of bombing raids, Frank Yates, then head of the Department of Statistics at the Rothamsted Experimental Research Station, had helped reveal that farmers knew very little about the value of fertilizer in the cultivation of arable crops.* Once again I called on him for help. Sir William ('Bill') Slater, who had been a member of my now-defunct dining club, the Tots and Quots,[2] and who was the Chief Scientist in the Ministry of Agriculture, was also enthusiastic. I was given advice by the staff of the Grassland Research Station near Reading, and made a trip to the Hannah Dairy Research Institute outside Glasgow, where Dr William Holmes, a young research worker, was showing how the nutrient value of grass could be greatly increased by heavy dressings of nitrogenous fertilizer. As I travelled between Birmingham and London my eyes would scan the fields on either side of the railway lines, and I would speculate about the potential value of all the neglected pasture land that I could see.

By May 1948, I knew enough to write a lengthy paper on the subject for my panel, which sent it on to the main Committee on Industrial Productivity, by which it was endorsed. Tizard then submitted it both to the Lord President and to the Chancellor. The Chancellor's copy was later shown to me, and I was much pleased to see that his marginal comments indicated full agreement with all our recommendations. Max Nicholson had also sent a minute to Herbert Morrison saying, in effect, 'Just see what the scientists can do. The Imports Substitution Panel has shown within a matter of months how millions of pounds can be knocked off the imports bill.' With the Chancellor's approval, the Government then agreed that the Ministry of Agriculture should be provided with the resources necessary to launch a major grassland campaign.

Shortly before this happened, Herbert Morrison asked me to call on him. He wanted to know whether I had been discussing the matter with Nye Bevan, the Minister of Health, who apparently had been surprisingly enthusiastic about the subject of grass. Other than Hugh Gaitskell, Nye was the only senior member of Attlee's Government with whom I was on personal terms, and in those days he was not expected to back costly agricultural schemes. Morrison was not at all pleased when I told him that I had. 'In future you leave the politics to

---

*The station was part of the Lawes Agricultural Trust.

me,' was all he could say. Morrison was Nye's major enemy in the Cabinet, and Nye had no respect for him. He laughed when I told him the story.

Plowden has often said to me that the grassland campaign was the most useful thing that he and I ever did in Whitehall. I cannot imagine that he meant this seriously, nor do I know whether the part which I played was really crucial. But however it came about, the resurrection of the country's grasslands was a good thing. I still feel sad when I see an ill-kept pasture.

The success of the grassland campaign depended critically on adequate supplies of nitrogenous fertilizer which, like almost everything else, was then a heavy item in our imports bill. And that also meant sulphur, of which there was also a serious shortage. F.H. Braybrook, one of the two industrialists on my committee, brought D.S. Richard, an executive of Courtaulds, the leading British manufacturer of fibres and cloth, to see me. Both were concerned that I should realize that the artificial fibre industry was in a parlous state for lack of sulphuric acid, and they wanted me to understand that if I was studying fertilizers, I should also be aware of the related problems in the production of cloth.

In the quest for sulphuric acid, Richard had been joined by General Wildman-Lushington, and together they had formed the Sulphur Exploration Syndicate. I had first met Wildman-Lushington, a Marine general, when he was Chief of Staff to Lord Mountbatten in Combined Operations. 'Ran' Antrim (the Earl of Antrim), a friend from those days, then offered to help, and to stand in for me when I was not in London. Ran and I were given a room in the Treasury, where we sat laughing at the ridiculous situation in which we found ourselves, two volunteers – neither of us a chemist – who, it was assumed, would know how to produce fertilizer out of thin air, and how to spirit flagons of sulphuric acid into the country. Max Nicholson suggested that all that was now missing was a series of signposts pointing to our room and marked 'To the black market'.

Chemical advice was there for the asking. Patrick Linstead, a member of my committee, and at the time the Director of the now defunct National Chemical Laboratory, took me on a tour of plants that produced sulphuric acid and nitrogenous fertilizer. We went to two of the most primitive and filthy (both now obsolete), the first a coking plant attached to a gasworks, and the second a plant where the acid was made by burning pyrites, that beautiful iron sulphide ore, sometimes known as fool's gold, which was imported, mainly from Spain and Cyprus. We then moved on to a modern catalytic plant somewhere in the North, before ending up at ICI's vast Billingham works, where ammonium sulphate was manufactured from anhydrite, a form of gypsum that was mined on the spot.

That was not the only tour I made in search of sulphur. Early in 1951 I told Braybook, who was about to become head of Shell Chemicals in France, that Joan and I were going to Italy and Sicily for a short holiday. He suggested that it might help if I made some enquiries about the future of the Sicilian sulphur mines. The late Sir John Russell, with his highly attractive wife Aliki, were then at our Embassy in Rome. I knew them well, and sent a message that Joan and I would be passing through Rome on our way to Sicily. Back came a telegram saying, 'expect you to dine, ordinary clothes'. When we got to Rome, we found two extravagantly engraved cards waiting for us at our hotel, one from the Russells inviting us to dinner, and the other, from the Ambassador, to a ball at the Embassy – white tie! When in London in connection with my Whitehall committees, I often dined out and went to parties. But I had not expected that to happen when enquiring into natural resources abroad, and we were without formal clothes. I telephoned to say that we could not accept. John's reply was that since he would be wearing tails, I could borrow his dinner jacket, and Aliki (who was always magnificently dressed) would send a collection of evening dresses from which Joan could choose. When I protested that he and I were neither the same size nor shape, he suggested that if I preferred, I should enlist the help of one of the waiters in the hotel, who might know where I could hire formal evening clothes. It turned out that in those days there was no tailoring outfitter in Rome which did that kind of thing. In the end I bought a white silk shirt and a black tie, and borrowed from a waiter as near a fit of trousers and jacket as he could find among his colleagues. Joan had the choice of four or five evening dresses, all grander than anything she owned. The dinner was splendid, and we could not have enjoyed the evening more, although when dancing at the Embassy I had to keep hitching up my borrowed trousers.

The Russells always entertained lavishly. Many years later, I was with Lord Mountbatten on an official visit to Ethiopia, where John was now the British Ambassador. We were invited to a small dinner party that Aliki had arranged for the Emperor on the occasion of his birthday. The Russells' house in Addis Ababa was far from large, and the dinner was a modest affair by comparison with some of their other parties. But even this one had its grand moment. At about midnight the door of the drawing room opened, and in came four little Ethiopian boys dressed like pages at the court of Louis XIV – gilded turbans, white silk breeches, and coats embroidered with gold – each holding the handle of a small palanquin on which was a vast cake illuminated with candles. The Emperor clapped his hands with joy, and we were all given presents. Mine was the skull of an adult male Gelada baboon.

After the Russells' Rome party and only a few hours' sleep, we flew into the small prewar airport which in those days still served Palermo. Either the Foreign Office or our Embassy in Rome must have sent a message to the British Consul, because he was waiting to greet us when we arrived. But Braybrook had also arranged for a Shell representative to provide us with a car, as had the Sicilian Governor, whom the Shell people had presumably told about my wish to discuss sulphur. When we emerged from the aircraft, we did not know to which of the three unexpected welcoming parties to turn first. They seemed equally confused, each apparently having assumed that they were going to be the only one. Joan was overcome by the profusion of bouquets. The Governor was a rich landowner whom I had met in 1943 when we invaded Sicily. After some fulsome courtesies we were driven in the Shell car to our hotel, followed by the Consul, who had been as disconcerted by the other two unexpected reception committees as we had been embarrassed.

Believing that I was travelling in a diplomatic role, and not realizing that we were on a private holiday with only the limited amount of sterling then allowed to British tourists, the Consul had changed a modest booking that I had made for the most expensive suite in the hotel, the one which, he proudly told us, had been used by King Edward VII. He was surprised, too, when he learnt that no itinerary had been arranged for me, and that I proposed 'playing everything by ear'. He then asked whether I had visiting cards. When I said no, he said he would have some prepared immediately – I couldn't possibly go around Sicily without a visiting card, particularly in view of my connection with the Lord President's office! I was dismayed by his intervention, and as soon as he left went down to the lobby and tactfully asked how much our suite cost. It turned out that if we were to retain the booking, the money we had would not last more than two or three days. When I explained the situation to the Consul on the following day, he offered to lend me whatever we needed. He was a nice man, a bachelor, whose hobby was collecting penny stamps and selling those with irregularities on behalf of a charity to which he was devoted. Our money problems solved, we breathed a sigh of relief, and settled down to enjoy ourselves.

We visited the Palazzo Spadeforo, which had been my HQ in 1943, and called on the Sicilian Governor, where I heard how the government in Rome was about to destroy the natural order by expropriating landowners like himself. Sicily, he said, should be allowed to secede from Italy and become part of the British Empire. Accompanied by the Shell representative, I visited a sulphur mine near the centre of the island.

The mine was beautiful and incredible. We descended in a rickety cage into the glistening yellow bowels of the earth, where naked and barefoot miners cut sulphur from the walls of narrow galleries. It was like a mediaeval woodcut. A day or two later we drove south, past the ruins of Greek temples that I had first seen during the war, to Porto Empedocle on the coast, where men were carrying slabs of sulphur to shallow-draught lighters which then ferried them to ships in deeper water. It so happened that at the time we arrived, the two lines of porters who were moving to and from the lighters, were being continually crossed by a circle of men, women and children, led by a local priest carrying an effigy of the Virgin and child. I was told that this had been going on for days, and that it was a concerted Mafia effort to slow down the work in the quest for higher pay for the porters. We were then entertained to lunch by the Mayor of nearby Agrigentum, after which we were his guests at an open-air recital by an attractive soprano. There was a strong sea-breeze, and she was as much concerned to prevent her light dress from billowing around her waist as she was about the pitch of her notes. The Mayor and the rest of us in the front row were much pleased when she occasionally lost the battle.

From Agrigentum we drove in a leisurely way along the coast, through Catania to Bronte, where we spent the night with Lord Bridport, a retired naval officer whom I had met during the war, and one of whose forebears had inherited, through Nelson's niece, the Dukedom of Bronte. This Dukedom had been granted to Nelson at the end of the eighteenth century by the King of Naples in gratitude for the defeat of the French at Aboukir Bay. Bridport took me to the spot south of Bronte where in August 1943 I had been made to turn back at the point where the 8th Army was then being halted in its fight to enter the town. Then, after a few nights in Taormina, Joan and I flew back to England.

A few years later, Continental sulphur once again came into my life. It did so through the agency of Paul Willert, whom I had first met in 1944 when he was the Air Attaché in our reopened Embassy in Paris. The elegant flat that Paul had leased before the war in one of the old houses in the Ile St Louis had somehow or other been spared the attentions of the Germans during the Occupation, so that when he returned to Paris his apartment was intact, with a magnificent Picasso still in the place of honour in his sitting room. Paul, who now had business interests in France, introduced me to two Frenchmen who had news of rich gas fields at Lacq just north of the Pyrenees. These had been opened by the Germans when searching for oil during the war, and the gas was rich in sulphur. The French authorities hoped that they would in consequence be able to break the world monopoly of natural sulphur which the Americans then enjoyed by virtue of their possession of sulphur 'domes' in the Gulf of Mexico, and from which sulphur was steamed in vast quantities. Would the UK be interested? Willert produced a paper for the Natural Resources Committee, but at the time nothing came of this lead. The Lacq deposits are still exploited, both for the gas which is piped to all parts of France, and for its sulphur, much of which is exported, a considerable amount to the UK.

But there was an unexpected follow-up, which in due course was to have an enormous impact on the British economy. Extensive gas deposits were also discovered in Walcheren in the Netherlands, extending into the bed of the North Sea. Our Geological Survey knew about this several years before drilling was started some miles from the North Norfolk coast. What was even more astonishing was that in the early thirties, in the search for oil, a 'dry' bore-hole had been drilled some four miles from the north coast of Norfolk to a depth of about 3000 feet. I never did discover what clue or hint had led the company concerned to that spot, so close to what were to turn out to be the richest oil and gas fields of Europe.

It used to be said that the health of manufacturing industry could be gauged by the amount of sulphuric acid that a country consumed. The shortage of sulphur thus soon became a major national issue. Ministers became involved, and it was in this way that Harold Wilson, who had been appointed President of the Board of Trade in 1947, came into my life for a second time.* His department was responsible for issuing import licences for raw materials, and two of his officials were members of my committee. He turned his mind energetically to the sulphur problem, and appointed an even more senior official as a kind of sulphur czar. He also dealt with the consortium that Wildman-Lushington and Richard had set up, with the result that the Government joined with the companies concerned in a major venture to build a new anhydrite plant. It was the right thing to do at the time, even though the new plant did become a white elephant after some years – as ICI's Billingham anhydrite works were also to become. New technological developments, the oil and natural gas industries, and affordable imports, were to make the anhydrite process uneconomic.

Since the existence of the Natural Resources Committee was public knowledge, and since most of its members represented government departments, it was not at all surprising that every kind of shortage was drawn to our attention. The officials on the committee were usually interested only in those matters that impinged on their departments' areas of responsibility. I, however, became interested in almost everything – from steel to carbon-black, from synthetic wool to tanning materials. Shortages of copper, tin and zinc, were then a real headache. I found the subject of non-ferrous minerals fascinating, and pursued it with the help of G.L. Bailey, the Director of the Non-Ferrous Metals Research Association. From him I learnt about the history of the Cornish mining industry – almost to the end of the nineteenth century the world's largest source of copper – and about the wasteful use of chrome, nickel and even silver, by the plating industry which, according to Bailey, was pouring into the sewers of Birmingham – a centre of the industry – as much of these metals as it managed to deposit on the metal surfaces that were being plated. I put this point to Ivan Shortt,

*The Board of Trade is known today as the Department of Trade and Industry.

since he was one of the city's leading silver-platers, only to be told that the educational level of his employees allowed of no more advanced technological methods than the early Victorian ones that made his factory such a joy to visit. 'It's not only silver that goes down the drains,' he said, pointing to one of many tanks in which silver was being electrolytically deposited on to copper candlesticks. 'It's all that cyanide, too.'

I visited Cornwall on a tour organized by an association of mine owners who wanted government help to resurrect their industry, and who urged me to recognize that, despite the geological ravages that had resulted from the uncoordinated mining operations that had started in the middle of the eighteenth century, Cornwall was still the richest non-ferrous metalliferous area in the world. I seem to remember that at the time of my visit, only two tin mines were still working, Geevor and South Crofty. I went down Geevor in a cage which seemed to me little better than the ancient ones from whose open platforms 'Jack' (it was said that Cornish miners were always called Jack) would leap as a working level was passed. Until very recently, Geevor had always been profitable. When I visited it in 1950, two small 'pirate' or 'parasite' groups of men were extracting tin from the 'tailings', fluid which poured from the mine over the cliff into the sea. I visited the Cornish School of Mines at Truro and heard what they had to say.

Cornwall was not the only part of Britain which it was claimed was still rich in non-ferrous ore bodies. On another occasion, when on a visit to Wales to discuss possible ways of making small hill farms more productive than they were, I spotted the entrance to an abandoned tin mine. The hill-farming enthusiast who was showing me round was taken aback when I suddenly left him and rushed to the adit of the mine. When he realized that my thoughts had drifted from the possible value of the sparse pasture where only a few sheep grazed, to that of the ore-body within the hill where we stood, he started to impress on me that in addition to sheep, the hills nourished the free spirit of man.

In the end, our enquiries into non-ferrous metals did no more than provide the material for a report that vainly urged the Government to help resurrect the industry. It was many years before help was given, but in the intervening time, a new consideration had become part of the picture – the need to reconcile measures of environmental protection with mining operations. Long after I had retired from government service, I chaired a commission that looked into this problem. Although sponsored by a number of large mining companies, we carried out the exercise with a strong environmental bias, and were able to show that it is possible to pursue both goals without either suffering any serious penalty.[3]

In retrospect I judge that the only area where the Natural Resources Committee did help significantly was in forestry and agriculture. When I first became involved in the grasslands campaign, I knew little about the place of agriculture in the national economy. No-one had told me that before the war we imported well over half the food we ate. Nor had I realized that it was largely because of the need to economize in shipping that the goal of our domestic agricultural policy during the war years had been the maximum production of foodstuffs for direct human consumption. Hill farms and upland rearing areas that had been neglected during the years of fighting now had to be reclaimed. The economic use of marginal land and the associated problem of increasing the domestic production of timber and wood products – of which about nine-tenths were then being bought abroad – were equally important. When the Natural Resources Committee started, it was not surprising that the Treasury, the Board of Trade, and the Ministry of Agriculture encouraged it to study the integration of all parts of what was essentially a single problem.

In 1957 we published a lengthy and detailed report on 'Forestry, Agriculture and Marginal Land'.[4] It became the subject of a debate in the House of Lords, and was followed by two other reports, one on the economics of the sheep industry,[5] and a third, in 1961, on the scale of enterprise in farming.[6] Our enquiries became so specialized that I appointed an agricultural subcommittee, with subsidiary working parties. We took advice wherever it could be found. Officials in different departments were unsparing in the help they gave, as were landowner and farmer friends up and down the country. Landowners were hesitant about tying up capital in costly schemes of afforestation, and wanted government help as much as did the small upland farmers who needed money to pay next day's bills. Tales of woe were plentiful. I had to learn fast, particularly when the volume of food supplies entering world trade once again started to increase, so making it possible to relax import controls. Not unexpectedly, the sense of urgency about domestic food production then started to decline. The environment of scarcity in which the Natural Resources Committee had begun its work could not have been more different than that of the plenty with which the Common Market now struggles in its efforts to deal with gluts of cereals and with butter mountains.

My name has been associated over the years with several governmental reports, but none was better received than the one that dealt with forestry and marginal land. I found myself being turned to as an authority who could talk about farming and forestry in a way that the ordinary person understood. On one occasion I was invited to take the chair at a session of a high-powered three-day meeting on 'Agriculture in the British Economy'.[7] On another I lectured in Cambridge in a course to which Enoch Powell and Lord Parker, then the Lord Chief Justice, also contributed. The theme of my address was the exploitation of Britain's natural resources in relation to the conservation of the countryside.[8] I began by reminding my audience that natural resources achieved 'value' only when they became part of a cycle of change that ended in consumption, and that the capital and technological knowledge necessary to turn natural resources into raw materials – including foodstuffs – were usually far more valuable than were the natural resources themselves. I went on to discuss the pattern of land-use and the social problems posed by economically marginal farms, of which a significant number were then being abandoned every year, so leading to what was a worldwide problem – rural depopulation. I spoke of the relative financial unprofitability of forestry, and of the benefit that could derive from the effective integration of forestry and agriculture in marginal and outlying areas.

I have reread this lecture, which was delivered in 1958, first because it turned out to have been a synthesis of much that I had learnt about the meaning of natural resources, and second because it touched upon two related topics – the growth of population and the protection of the environment. When the Imports Substitution Panel started its work, it made economic sense to do whatever possible to produce at home what we might otherwise have had to buy abroad – given that we had the money to pay for what we wanted, and given, too, that what we needed was there to buy. But we had been bankrupted by the war, and the United States, now the great provider, had to spread its benefice to help resurrect not just the United Kingdom, but the whole of destroyed Western Europe. As the fifties drew to a close, emphasis was increasingly placed on our ability to compete with other exporting countries in order to pay for our imports with our foreign earnings. Resources could not be spared to encourage uneconomic imports-substitution. In purely economic terms the merits of applying financial and technological resources to cultivate our own soil or to exploit scarce mineral deposits had to be judged relative to the returns that the same resources might generate if directed to industry – given that our manufacturers had the ideas and the necessary skills to use the resources competitively. The cultivation of Britain's own garden, therefore, had to find its place in a vast list of national priorities. Moreover, while in wartime everyone benefited from what the soil produced, in peacetime the premium with which the Exchequer could afford to subsidize home-produced food, when it could be bought more cheaply abroad, usually benefited only a section of the community.

But what worried me more and more whenever I was invited to speak publicly about the problem of natural resources was that dispassionate economic analyses of the amount of support that should be provided agriculture or forestry or mining inevitably left out of account the environmental factor. As I put it in the lecture that I delivered in Cambridge, 'A bare countryside of untended scrub, thickly traversed by vast concrete roads linking industrial towns, might emerge from such an analysis as the preferable economic alternative' to subsidizing home-grown food and timber. But, I went on to say, 'our successors of tomorrow are not likely to forgive this generation if we sit back and allow more and more of the countryside to become derelict because of what we are inclined to call the play of economic forces – by which, in this context, one can, however, only mean the balance of immediate financial advantage'. Apart from the question of amenity, there were other long-term considerations that kept worrying me, even though they were unquantifiable economically: the conservation of natural resources, the stability of investment, and the possibility that as the world's population grew, and as shortages of food developed in world markets, we might once again find ourselves going hungry.

In another address, with which I was invited to open the Twelfth Oxford Farming Conference of 1958, I focused on the problem of the small farmer – but at the same time made it clear that I fully recognized the economic argument that what mattered to the Treasury was agricultural output per unit of resources employed, that is to say, the ability of farmers to compete with the price of imported food.[9] As I saw it, this was an all but impossible task for most farmers. In the immediate postwar years, a large proportion of some 100,000 British small farmers lived on poor land in a literally bankrupt state, even though they produced a large proportion of our milk, pigs and poultry. When full account was taken of the subsidies he received, a small farmer's net profit was less than the wage of a farm labourer.

On the occasion of that address I had a feeling that I was making a plea that should have been made by the Ministry of Agriculture itself. As things were, I insisted that it was the bigger and more successful farmers who benefited most from subsidies, even if they did so because the subsidies were needed for their less fortunate brethren. There was no parallel for this in industry. One could not conceive of big successful companies in the chemical industry being allowed to benefit from subsidies that would be needed to keep in business small chemical plants whose product was not wanted.

I was not speaking from a prepared text at this meeting, and it became clear from the ensuing discussion that I had not pleased a part of a large audience that consisted mainly of successful farmers. Thirty years after that particular meeting I still occasionally run into someone who was in my audience, and who tells me that he remembers all I said. But I find myself smiling somewhat ruefully, I fear, when I reread the final words of the speech as it later appeared in print.

> What we need to do – what should be the basis of policy – is to transform conditions in such a way that self-sufficiency and efficient farming would become possible on a national scale. We are not the only ones in the boat here – I do not know of a single country in the world that has not got a 'small-farmer problem'. It is a paradox that agriculture all over the world – whether you are an over-producer or an under-producer – is a problem.

The problem is still with us nearly thirty years later. How much the individual member-states of the European Community should contribute to the fund which supports 'uneconomic' European farmers through the Common Agricultural Policy, is a constant bone of contention, which sometimes even threatens to destroy the young Community itself. Support for the farmer is also an annual headache to the American administration. Selling, of necessity, Western 'butter mountains' and hundreds of thousands of tons of grain to the USSR at below subsidized costs is held by many to be contrary to the strategic interests of the West and to the economies of some of its members. Yet people in vast areas of the world still starve. Maybe the solution to the farmers' problem is merely part of the dream of 'one world'.

The international dimension of the whole problem of natural resources had become acutely obvious at the time of the Korean War, when the US started stockpiling scarce materials.* In the UK the Government found itself riven by a 'guns or butter' dispute, with Nye Bevan, now Minister of Labour, violently opposing Hugh Gaitskell, the Chancellor, both about the size of Hugh's defence budget, which Nye said could never be spent for lack of materials and labour, and about Hugh's proposal to cut a relatively trivial amount from the budget of the NHS. Early in 1951, Nye telephoned to say that he proposed to write a paper on the priority that should be accorded to the exploitation of the UK's natural resources. Would I help brief two of his officials on the subject! This I did, but I heard no more about the matter. It was only a few weeks later that Nye, Harold Wilson, and John Freeman resigned from the Government, all of them strenuously against what Hugh was proposing.

About a year after the Government had changed, Nye published a small book titled *In Place of Fear*.[10] He had sent me for comment a draft chapter entitled 'Raw Materials, Scarcities, and Priorities', but I do not think that what I read in typescript bore much relation to his final text, which is a very wide-ranging analysis of a whole complex of social and economic priorities. Nye referred to the dominance of America in the purchase of the world's raw materials, which would lead to 'all the world, outside the Soviet-dominated Bloc' becoming 'geared to the economy of the United States'.

Not long after Nye's book was published, a lengthy pamphlet appeared under the title *In Place of Dollars*.[11] Its author was Harold Wilson, and its sweep as wide as was that of *In Place of Fear*. In it Wilson referred specifically to the sulphur crisis with which he, as President of

*In 1949 the young United Nations Organization convened an international five-day conference on the subject at Lake Success, Long Island. I was a member of a large British delegation and, as Chairman of the Natural Resources Committee, was called upon to chair one of the plenary sessions.

the Board of Trade, had had to deal, and to the impact which the arms race and the American demand for raw materials were having on our own and other economies. I did not know of this publication until recently, but I have reread the opening paragraph more than once because of the message Harold Wilson was trying to convey.

> The first aim of Britain's economic policy must be to achieve independence of aid from abroad as soon as possible. Without that freedom there can be no independent foreign policy for, more and more, American aid is being voted on conditions which involve British acceptance of American strategic decisions, and control not even by Congress, but by the Pentagon, headquarters of the United States chiefs of staff.

I find these words odd in relation to the policies which the realities of politics forced on its author when he became Prime Minister some twenty years later.

Poisons, Pollution and Population

Soon after Hugh Gaitskell was appointed Minister of Fuel and Power in Attlee's Government, he invited me to become the Department's Chief Scientific Adviser. I said no. Hugh knew that my interests were wide, and that I was easily intrigued by new ideas, but he was wrong in believing that because I had had an eventful career as a researcher and 'planner' during the war, I could repeat the performance in the formulation of energy policy. By this time, too, I had embarked on my new life in Birmingham, and there was no question of my leaving the University for any other occupation, however glamorous. A much more suitable candidate was soon found in Harold Roxbee Cox,* an engineer who at the time was working in the government's Gas-Turbine Establishment.

I did, however, accept Hugh's invitation to become a member of his department's Scientific Advisory Council, on the clear understanding that the ACSP and the Committee on Industrial Productivity came first in my Whitehall interests, and that if it became apparent that I was filling a place that could be better occupied by someone with more time and experience, I would resign. Within two years I offered to do this, but Philip Noel-Baker, who had taken Hugh's place – Hugh having moved to the Treasury – asked me to stay on. So did his successor, Geoffrey Lloyd, who became the Minister of Fuel and Power in the Conservative Government that replaced Labour in 1951. Geoffrey Lloyd accepted my resignation in 1952, but only to ask me to return to the Council in the following year, in his letter referring to my concern about atmospheric pollution. I agreed to do as he asked, but again with qualifications. At the end of 1955 I completely severed my connection with the Council.

*Now Lord Kings-Norton.

I had become worried about air pollution in a very indirect way. Early in 1950 I had written to Roxbee Cox to say that very little was being done to recover sulphur from the flue gases of coke ovens and power stations – naming a figure of nearly 360,000 tons as an indication of what was being poured into the atmosphere. I also wanted him to consider how sulphur could be recovered from the new oil refineries that were being built. My interest then was in the shortage of sulphur. Roxbee Cox did not, however, feel that this was a significant way of overcoming the shortage.

By 1954, however, the question of atmospheric pollution was becoming every bit as important politically as was the cost of importing sulphur. We were still living in the era of the notorious London smogs. There had been a disastrous one in December 1952 when three days of heavy fog caused the premature deaths of some 4000 elderly people. I therefore prepared a paper on the subject, which I put to the Ministry's Advisory Council. Roxbee Cox had by then been succeeded by Kelvin Spencer, who tabled it together with one of his own. I forget whether I expected much to follow, but if I did, I was to be sadly disappointed. I wrote to Spencer saying that, contrary to what had been claimed when our two papers had been discussed, I still believed that the researches on pollution of the Fuel Research Station, the National Coal Board, and the National Gas Board were getting nowhere.

Not long after, John Maud,* then the Permanent Secretary of the Ministry, came to tell me that his Minister wanted me to chair a committee to deal with air pollution. John and I had known each other in the mid-thirties in Oxford, and even though my letter to Spencer clearly indicated that I had learnt something about the ways of Whitehall, John was a little taken aback when I replied that he should tell his Minister that what ought to be done was obvious without setting up a committee – committees were a way of delaying action. Just as he was about to leave my room, I said, 'John, I tell you what. I'll run a committee, provided you let me try my hand at formulating an energy policy for the country.' He laughed at this brash remark, saying, 'We can't do that even with all the resources available to the Ministry.' 'In that case,' I said, 'no committee.' A year later, my third try at resigning

*Later Lord Redcliffe Maud.

from the Council was accepted in a generous letter, which John signed, thanking me in particular for my contributions to the discussion of atmospheric pollution. There was a postscript inviting me to reconsider my decision to leave.

A year later, in July 1956, Parliament passed a Clean Air Act that forbade the burning of soft coal in open grates – the main source of the smogs that plagued our cities. Public opinion could no longer be disregarded. It is possible that my bleatings had helped make officials aware of the urgency of the problem, and that another factor was the idea that the costs might be partially offset by extracting sulphur from flue gases. Today there is still sulphur dioxide in the upper atmosphere. It is part of the acid rain story.

As his deputy chairman, Tizard usually turned to me when some specific matter was referred to him. Two that related to another aspect of pollution proved very interesting – the protection of the environment and population growth – remaining a matter of continuing interest to me long after the ACSP was dissolved in 1964.

The first surfaced when the Advisory Council was asked to examine inter-departmental arrangements for controlling the use of potentially toxic substances or processes in the preparation of consumer goods. The subcommittee on the subject, which Tizard asked me to chair, did not take long to report.[1] Then, in July 1950, I was asked by the Minister of Agriculture and Fisheries to chair a committee to consider the prevailing governmental regulations that concerned the safety of farm labourers who, in the course of their work, had to use toxic substances. The problem was obvious. Nerve-gas chemicals known as organophosphorus compounds were being used as pesticides, and it was known that they had caused accidental deaths. There was one very dramatic story. Some farm labourers had come in from the fields to a local pub and ordered their usual pints of beer. One of them wiped his mouth with the back of his hand, and within a few minutes had fallen to the floor, dead. In those days farm workers did not as a rule wear protective clothing, and the man's hands had been contaminated with the chemical he had been using.

I was so impressed by this and similar stories that in opening my first meeting – the committee mainly comprised officials from the departments concerned – I suggested that since we were dealing with a cut-

and-dried problem, we should not waste time on unnecessary enquiry. All that was needed was evidence from the Farm Workers Union, the National Farmers Union, and the agrochemical industry. If at all possible we should make our recommendations within three months. In fact it took five, but we had the satisfaction of seeing our proposals for protective action translated into legislation with little delay.[2] The administrative arrangements that were then made to control the use of new toxic substances for agricultural use are substantially those that apply today.

The powers-that-be must have been impressed by our speedy action, for I was then asked by the Ministers of Agriculture and Health, and the Secretary of State for Scotland, to chair a reconstituted committee to consider whether consumers face any risks from eating food that contains agricultural products that have been treated with toxic chemicals, or which have been used in food processing and storage. Since many interests were concerned in this enquiry, and because we had to hear evidence from many more organizations, it took two years for the work to be completed.[3] Our main recommendation was that an inter-departmental expert committee should be set up to advise generally on problems relating to risks to the consumer, to liaise on a confidential basis with the manufacturers, and to guide departments in the investigations which manufacturers would be obliged to make before new chemical products were licensed. We had several discussions about the desirability of compulsory and statutory controls, but in the end decided that a voluntary arrangement with the industries concerned was the best that was then possible. And so it remained until October 1986, when the controls became statutory. But the Government has never had the resources that would be needed to set up as elaborate a system as the one that operates in the United States.

No sooner were the results of this second enquiry reported than I was asked by the Minister of Agriculture and the Secretary of State for Scotland to reconstitute my committee once again in order to investigate the dangers to which wild animals and plants are subjected through the use of toxic chemicals in agriculture. We reported after about two years, by when it had become plain that with the resources at our disposal, we could not obtain specific information about the inadvertent environmental dangers we were being asked to consider.

As we had no basis for recommending new legislation, all we could do was propose that the terms of reference of the inter-departmental committee that had been set up following our second report, should be widened to include the risks to wildlife, and that further research should be done.[4]

This abortive enquiry taught me a lot. I shared all the concern there was about the hazards to the countryside that resulted from the use of the new chemicals that were being introduced to improve agricultural productivity. But without hard facts, it was impossible to propose effective measures to offset the dangers. The trouble was that while the profitability of modern agricultural practices could be assessed in monetary terms, the costs of the damage they brought to the countryside could not. Protecting the environment was a 'social good', and had to find its place in a long list of others.

My early and active involvement in the environmental movement was to a large extent a consequence of enquiries that were carried out by the Natural Resources Committee. My interests in the related problem of population growth had a much longer history, deriving as it did from my academic studies of reproductive physiology. As a member of the PEP group that was then preparing a report on the growth of world population, I had been invited to join the British delegation to the first United Nations Population Conference.[5] It took place in Rome in 1954, and while I do not recall that it revealed any new aspect of the problem, I do remember that the weather was fine, and that a number of us were addressed in St Peter's by Pius XII. The Pope, a very elegant figure in white, was borne in on a palanquin by his Swiss Guards. My Italian, learnt in Sicily during the war, was just about adequate to follow the short speech he made, and I leaned forward when I understood him to say how seriously he viewed the problem of the unrestricted growth of population, and that he had given instructions to the Vatican to seek ways by which it could be curbed. But then came the words, 'but within the framework of the Christian faith'. We were brought back to earth with a bump. For it had become clear in the course of the PEP enquiry that without active measures of birth-control, and without the support of the Church, there was little hope that the growth of world population – and particularly that of South America – was likely to slow down. The Pope made a graceful exit, high on the shoulders of his bearers, elegantly and slowly waving a hand to his audience and to the worshippers and tourists in the cathedral.

My researches into the physiological control of the reproductive cycle and into the formation of ovarian egg-cells had laid part of the foundation of knowledge on which Gregory Pincus, an American colleague, was working to devise a contraceptive pill that would be acceptable in societies that were largely illiterate. Pincus kept me in touch with all that he was doing, and my interest in the subject was also constantly reinforced by Fairfield Osborn, who had recruited to his staff Robert G. Snider. Bob, who had held the rank of captain in the US Navy, had immense energy, and soon became totally immersed in the problems of population growth in the Caribbean. He made sure that these also became one of my concerns.

I raised the subject at one of the early meetings of the ACSP, in a discussion about the possibilities of improving food supplies in the 'colonies'. I brought it up again in 1953, but to no avail, even though the importance of birth-control in its relation to over-population in the West Indies had by now become an urgent political issue, to which my attention was also being drawn by Ronald Tree, an ex-MP of considerable wealth who then lived for part of the year in Barbados (and for the remainder in the USA where he had been born). Ronnie's English country house, Ditchley Park, was one of the wartime retreats used by Winston Churchill. Today it is a luxurious conference centre. Ronnie was friendly with most of the political leaders of the Caribbean islands, and had become very knowledgeable about their social and economic problems.

Towards the end of 1955, Bob decided to launch an 'enquiry' into population growth in Jamaica. He had discussed the matter with Norman Manley, then the island's Chief Minister, and also with the Governor, Sir Hugh Foot,* both of whom were acutely aware of the fact that developments in local agriculture and industry were insufficient to absorb the island's ever-growing labour-force – this, of course, was well before the start of the large-scale emigration of West Indians to the United Kingdom. The trouble was that birth-control was a sensitive issue, and while the Jamaican Government wanted to encour-

*Later Lord Caradon.

age any research that could lead to action, they could not give any official or overt support to what was being proposed.

In the way these things are done, Bob arranged that Sir Hugh Foot should send him a formal letter explaining the situation, on the understanding that a copy would also go to the Colonial Office, with a suggestion that another should be passed to me. The message was clear. While both the Governor and the Chief Minister were anxious to find a means of slowing the growth of the island's population, the issue of birth-control was too political for them to help positively in the enquiry that Bob wanted to launch – nonetheless they would give it whatever encouragement they could.

Philip Rogers was then the Colonial Office official whose responsibilities included the West Indies (some years later, we became close colleagues in the Cabinet Office). He, too, knew that the UK Government would be treading on dangerous ground were it to provide financial support to a campaign to promote birth-control in one of its colonies, and one which it was hoped would shortly become part of a self-governing federation. He came to see me with some of his colleagues to discuss whether help could be given indirectly. We decided that I should raise the issue yet again at the ACSP, and at the same time make an approach to the Nuffield Foundation which, as a private charitable British institution, could support work on birth-control in a British colony. Since Alex Todd was both the Chairman of the ACSP and a trustee of the Foundation, I had kept him informed about what was going on, and had gained his support. He agreed that an entire meeting of the Council should be devoted to the subject, and that a number of papers should be prepared as background information for circulation up and down Whitehall. The aim of the paper that I undertook to write was to provide 'a general picture of the world situation'. The enthusiasm I had worked up for the subject was well illustrated in my next letter to Bob, in which I said:

> The prairie's on fire! I have seen both Lord Salisbury (the Lord President of the Council) and Lord Lloyd (who is the Parliamentary Under-Secretary for the Colonies), and have coordinated my efforts with those of the latter. He is immensely enthusiastic about the problem, and I think that as a result of our joint endeavours, support at least for research projects will be

forthcoming. I think there may be more. The London *Times* is also giving me space for a leader article, of which I enclose a copy. I have prepared another article for the journal *Progress*, and after the lapse of a couple of weeks, my intention is to ventilate the subject in the columns of our most respectable Sunday newspaper.[6]

Some two months later Norman Manley was in London, and Philip Rogers arranged a small meeting in order to get an assurance that the Jamaican Government would support Bob's research project if it could be launched. Manley called on me privately to explain once again that with its considerable Catholic population, birth-control was a sensitive subject in the Caribbean. I therefore arranged that he should meet Alex Todd and the Director of the Nuffield Foundation so as to allay any fears that they might entertain on the score of local support. The meeting with the Foundation proved satisfactory, and before long Bob's project was launched, with money from both the Nuffield in the UK and the Conservation Foundation in New York.

My hope that the UK Government would do more to encourage the practice of birth-control was, however, never realized. As Lord Lloyd, only a junior Minister, put it, Alan Lennox-Boyd,* the Colonial Secretary, felt that he could never get such a move 'past the bishops'. However, in order to keep the issue alive, we arranged that the ACSP should discuss the specific matter of research into methods of birth-control, in the hope that the Medical Research Council could be encouraged to increase the trivial amount of money it then allocated to studies of reproduction. Appropriate noises were made at the two meetings at which the matter was debated, but again I do not recall that the MRC was spurred into any vigorous action.

At the time a new population-control organization was being set up in Washington DC with support from a variety of institutions. Its director was Dr M.C. Shelesnyak, who was one of the early group of American scientists who had devoted themselves to the study of reproductive physiology. 'Shelley' had also spent a year working with me in Birmingham, and he soon got me interested in the efforts he was making to reinforce the activities of all institutions that had the same

*Later Lord Boyd of Merton.

purpose in mind. He had made arrangements for a group of American enthusiasts, led by Margaret Sanger, then the undisputed queen of the birth-control movement, to attend a conference on the subject in Japan in the autumn of 1955, and had extracted a promise from me that I would attend and deliver a paper.

I travelled to the Tokyo meeting by way of the United States, and disliked almost every minute of the subsequent conference. I did not find the company of middle-aged female evangelists, with a handful of male consorts, to my taste. They seemed to believe that their constantly expressed convictions about the need for birth-control would result in some kind of world revolution. Nor did I find it easy to tolerate one or two sightseeing trips by bus, which the American party felt impelled to transform into singsongs. Shelley, who knew my ways, explained to all and sundry that my failure to join in was due to a perpetual migraine.

The only pleasant memento of that trip are two small pieces of ancient Japanese porcelain that I bought. There is also the memory of a remarkable surgeon, Komei Nakayama, with whom a friend suggested I should get in touch. In those days cancer of the stomach was very common in Japan, and American surgeons had become aware of Nakayama because of his ability to whip out a cancerous stomach and, if needs be, the adjacent spleen, in the space of about half an hour, and within that short time to sew the end of the severed oesophagus (the gullet) to the bit of the intestine that leads from the other end of the stomach. Nakayama, who spoke fairly good American English, invited me to see him at work. I was ushered into an operating-theatre with little regard for modern standards of sterilization. All that I had heard of his working methods turned out to be true.

He then gave me a simple lunch in his small room, during the course of which I learnt that the reason why he had perfected so rapid an operation was that Japan was then too poor either to afford lavish and lengthy anaesthesia, or antibiotics to avert subsequent infection. The less time the patient spent on the operating-table, the better his chances of survival, and the shorter his stay in hospital. When I asked whether many survived, he gave some instructions to an attendant, and said, 'I'll show you.' In the corridor outside his room was a line of a dozen or so elderly patients in chairs, mostly men, all of whom had been operated on – so he told me – during the preceding ten days. Each patient had with him his nursing staff, which consisted of one or two

139

members of his own family. As we walked down the row, Nakayama said a word or two to each patient – a few of whom literally kissed the hem of his white coat. I was so impressed that when I got back to Birmingham I encouraged my surgical colleague, Professor Stammers, to invite Nakayama to deliver a lecture at our own Medical School. Unfortunately it turned out that Birmingham ears were not attuned to his particular variety of English.

In its annual report for 1955–6, the ACSP noted that:

> An international conference, which was organized in Tokyo in October 1955 by the Planned Parenthood Federation, provided an up-to-date assessment of the stage reached by current physiological research into methods of limiting births. So far as this country is concerned, the Council hopes that the Medical Research Council will proceed as fast as possible with its researches into fertility and infertility and the factors affecting these. Up to now it has been difficult to persuade sufficient scientists to take up this type of work and it is important to try to attract more.[7]

So far as the ACSP was concerned, that was the end of the matter. I cannot find any further reference to population control in any of its later reports.

Very soon after my return, the influential Sunday newspaper, the *Observer*, carried an article by W.A. Lewis, the economist who had taken part in one of my Lunar Society of the Air programmes.* His message was that the problems caused by population pressure in India could not be solved unless all countries emulated the success that had been achieved by Japan in raising food production during the forty years before 1914. For this to happen, the resources available for development would need to be doubled, and an effective programme of family limitation imposed.

I decided to send the newspaper my own impression of the problem, and in the opening sentence of my article, I observed that in Europe and the United States the topic of world population and resources was 'usually treated as something that lies in the future, related mainly to

*Now Sir Arthur Lewis of the Woodrow Wilson School at Princeton.

the eventual exhaustion of the riches of the earth's crust'.[8] But, I went on, 'In the so-called "under-developed" areas of the world, the debate is being waged not in words but in facts – in the squalor and aspirations of millions of people who by our standards of living are on the edge of starvation.' The rest of my article was based on the deep impression that had been made on me by what I had seen and learnt during my brief glimpse of India, where my plane had touched down on the flight back from Tokyo. Having referred to the small size of the Japanese homeland, and to the low standard of living of her enormous population – then 90 million – I pointed out that Japan was importing a quarter of the food which it consumed, and nearly 80 per cent of its raw materials. With her population growing as it was, so I wrote, Japan was living in a state of 'precarious balance'. All her efforts to improve her trading position and to promote birth-control might not prove sufficient to prevent mass unemployment and poverty. I could not have been more wrong. Japan is now almost the world leader in international commerce, and is rich enough to sustain a population of almost 120 million. Education and tough national policies can work miracles.

But in most of the rest of the Third World – the world out of which Japan made so spectacular a leap – the situation is as it was when I wrote the article. No miraculous measures of birth-control have yet been discovered. Nor have ways been found to eradicate poverty, malnutrition and starvation. Sadly, too, and contrary to what Professor Lewis hoped, the history of Japan has not proved a model for the rest of the world.

There was another overseas conference on population that has stuck in my memory. Early in 1957, that is to say about a year after I had succeeded in arranging Bob Snider's Jamaican project, I received an official invitation to attend a meeting in Trinidad of what was known as the Caribbean Commission, at which representatives of all the West Indian islands – British, French, Dutch and American – were to meet to discuss their common problem of adjusting the growth of population to that of resources. The invitation must have been inspired either by Mr Manley or by Ronnie Tree. When I informed the Colonial Office, they said that they would like me to go, but circumstances precluded them from being officially represented. I decided not to go.

The reluctance of both the Colonial Office and the Commonwealth Relations Office to be represented was at least partly due to the fact that the United Kingdom was about to surrender its colonial power to what proved to be a very short-lived 'Federation of the West Indies'. The two departments also knew that the meeting would be attended by delegates from all the major British Caribbean islands. In July, barely a month before the conference was due to open, I received an urgent message asking if I could rearrange my affairs and represent the UK. The message could not have come at a worse moment. Joan was about to go into hospital for a serious operation, and we had rapidly to arrange for the two children to stay in Lincolnshire with our friends, the Jarvises. June was also the month for University examinations – the one administration chore that I had never wanted to delegate. Finally I did manage to get things sorted out and went, having been assured that the trip would be made as comfortable as possible.

If it did not turn out to be that, it certainly proved an extraordinary experience. Having learnt that Trinidad was very hot, I telephoned my tailor to tell him that he had a week in which to run up a light suit, on the understanding that he chose the material and that I could have any fittings that might prove necessary on my return. Having picked up the suit at London airport, I flew out overnight, touching down in Bermuda, where I was met by two local dignitaries, I presumed officials, who seemed both surprised and disdainful at having to meet someone of whom they had never before heard, yet with instructions to treat him with respect before putting him on another plane for Trinidad. Tired as I was, I agreed to a short drive before being given lunch in a somewhat grand club, after which I tried to get a few hours' sleep. I re-embarked that evening, and arrived in Trinidad at about midnight, where I was met and taken to a hotel. It was terribly hot.

Next morning I was driven to the conference centre, a vast tent-like building and, as I remember it, open on all sides. It needed to be. There was a large gathering of delegates from all the countries concerned. The majority of the representatives of the British colonies were members of their respective governments, and to my consternation I found myself being treated as their leader. I had no brief, and my 'tropical' suit, which turned out to have been made of a thin tweed, was far too heavy. Many members of the other delegations wore open-necked shirts without jackets, but I decided not to remove mine since my black British colleagues, most of whom wore starched white collars, showed no sign of removing theirs. Bob Snider was about the only person I knew in the whole assembly. On the first day I religiously did what seemed to be expected of me, but in the afternoon of the second, Bob took me to the Officers' Club at the American naval base on the island, where we bathed and drank. His rank as reserve captain USN had never been put to such pleasurable use. Since my absence that afternoon did not provoke any sour looks from the rest of the British delegation when I arrived at the meeting next morning, from then until the conference ended nine days later, I put in only an occasional appearance. The rest of the Commonwealth team behaved to the last day with the decorum they felt the occasion demanded. I attended the final plenary session, where I learnt much that was interesting about population growth, economic development, the need for education, and the possibilities of emigration.

As soon as I realized that there was no need for me to make more than an occasional appearance, I decided to get myself some clothes better suited to the climate. A local tailor quickly made me a pair of slacks and an ill-fitting suit out of a very lightweight material. The only time the suit was ever worn was at the final plenary session.

I got in touch with Geoffrey Herklots, the Director of the Imperial College of Tropical Agriculture, an institute which today is a centrepiece of the University of the West Indies. Herklots introduced me to a young Trinidadian zoologist, a local expert on the island's reptiles and amphibians, who took me on an excursion into the tropical forest, where I was shown creatures I had never heard of before, or some, like tree-frogs, which I had only seen in captivity. On my return to England I arranged for my young Trinidadian to spend a year in England as a research scholar.

One day, Hugh Fraser (p. 42) turned up to join me, in theory to attend the conference as a UK parliamentarian. In fact he spent most of his time with Bob and me in the water at the US Officers' Club. On my return to the UK I duly sent the Colonial Office a report of my impressions of the conference. Bob provided some of my material. Joan's memory of the occasion is that on my return I did not want to hear about her operation, but called for her sympathy because I had been badly bitten by mosquitoes.

Not long after this, I accepted an invitation to deliver a series of public lectures on population at the University of Birmingham. It was a flattering invitation. The Mason Lectures, which commemorated the founder of the mid-nineteenth-century college that had formed the nucleus of the University, were usually delivered by a scholar from another university and, even though one of its own professors, I had already delivered the only other two special lectures that were then named in the University calendar – the William Withering and the Ingleby.

I gave eight lectures. In my first I discussed the factors that determine fluctuations in the size of populations in the animal world. I then moved on, through a discussion of the physiology of reproduction, to the possibilities of devising effective methods of birth-control. I dealt with demographic projections, and ended with a discourse on the economic problems of the Third World. In my effort to set the population problem into a broad, almost evolutionary framework, I had ranged widely, and it pleased me that my large audience never dwindled. I am sorry now that I was then so tied up with other matters that I was unable to fulfil an undertaking to publish the lectures in book form. A pile of typescript on a table in my study keeps reminding me of the promise I never kept.

I did, however, publish a few articles that dealt with the growth of population in relation to resources, being careful to avoid any forebodings of disaster. I disliked the grim warnings of what a later generation of writers called a 'population explosion'. As I wrote in a postscript that I contributed to a book edited by Harrison Brown, estimates of the numbers of people who will be alive in the year 2000 are simply speculations 'about the reproductive habits of men and women not yet born', while forecasts about population growth 'are no more than assessments of relative probabilities'.[9]

Forecasts of the size of Britain's population were to become one of my official concerns when, some years later, I became the Government's Chief Scientific Adviser.

MILITARY AFFAIRS

16

Rifles and Mine-Dogs

Until the end of the fifties relatively little of the time that I devoted to non-academic matters was spent on questions relating to defence. I had, however, found it impossible to divorce myself completely from the military world. The British Bombing Survey Unit (BBSU) was not formally disbanded until September 1946, and when Claude Pelly, the unit's administrative chief, left to become head of the procurement side of the Air Ministry, it took me, the Scientific Director, a few more months to complete our overall report.[1] Some senior members of the Air Staff would have liked to have had it suppressed, since the story of the operations of Bomber Command had by then become very sensitive politically. The report questioned the value of the presumed economic consequences of the Command's bombing offensive against German cities and, now that we had analysed the German records, I had also re-emphasized the view that it would have been far better policy to have focused our bombing effort earlier and more consistently on the enemy's communications network. If Lord Tedder, who had promoted the latter policy when Deputy Supreme Commander to Eisenhower, had not become Lord Portal's successor as Chief of the Air Staff, it is possible that the report would not have been accorded even the limited and confidential circulation that it was allowed at the time.

Tedder had wanted me to join him as full-time Scientific Adviser to the Air Ministry. Much as I had enjoyed working with him during the war, I declined the invitation. The appointment, as offered, would initially have meant a two to three year contractual extension of 'national service', and Tizard, who came to see me formally about the invitation, warned me that were I to accept, the likelihood was that the rest of my working life would be spent in government service. One reason I gave for declining was that I wanted to be assured there and then that the policies of the three Armed Services were going to be integrated. That, alas, was something that no-one could promise. But my main reason for saying no was that I was determined to carry on with academic life.

Before I had completed the final Bombing Survey report, I was asked to prepare for the official war history a summary account of the researches on wound-ballistics that my Oxford Unit had carried out. This done, I was then asked to prepare a much more detailed and lengthier report on 'The vulnerability of human targets to fragmenting and blast weapons' for a *Textbook of Air Armament*.[2] This proved to be a tiresome job, and I resented the time it took from my more immediate academic interests. The chapter that I wrote for the Medical Research Council history appeared in 1953,[3] but although the one for the *Textbook* was printed a year earlier, it was not declassified until 1969. I believe that it is still regarded as a definitive text on its gruesome subject.

In the first year or two after the war I also occasionally attended meetings of a few wartime service committees that had not yet been wound up, and of which I was a member. I was, however, flattered when the Ordnance Board, that fifteenth-century institution whose main function today is to approve new munitions, made me one of its Associate Members – a category of membership that has since lapsed. The few surviving members are now styled Associate Members (Emeritus).

From time to time I saw Tedder. One day he asked Claude Pelly to arrange a meeting with me to discuss 'a very secret matter'. It was Barnes Wallis's idea, then code-named Swallow, for what has since become a practicality – a swing-wing supersonic aircraft. Barnes Wallis was a legendary figure in the aviation world. He had devised the lattice framework of the wartime Wellington bomber, and was even more revered as the inventor of the bouncing bombs that had been used in the daring RAF raid that had destroyed the Moehne Dam. The idea of swing-wing intrigued me, but obviously I had nothing to offer in the way of practical advice. I did, however, wonder whether Tedder had asked Claude for my views in order to keep my interest in RAF matters warm.

Occasionally I lectured at the RAF Staff College and at what was then called the Imperial Defence College – today it is more appropriately styled the Royal College of Defence Studies – my subject being either the lessons of the air war or operational research. One of the first took place only three weeks after VE Day at the RAF's Empire Air

Armaments School at Manby in Lincolnshire, before an audience that included many senior RAF officers – most of whom were there, I suspect, because the lecture had been arranged to coincide with one of the first grand postwar mess dinners.

I had flown up with Air Chief Marshal Sir Douglas Evill, Vice Chief of the Air Staff, and on the following morning, after a wild party that followed the dinner, I returned to London with him. When we reached Northolt, the small RAF airfield near London, the pilot, a squadron leader, overshot the runway, and had to apply full throttle to avoid a hangar. He made another circuit, came in to land, and did exactly the same thing. I had a feeling that he was nervous because of his cargo of 'top brass'. It was all very scary. As soon as we were again airborne, he handed over to his co-pilot and came to apologize to Evill, next to whom I was sitting, saying that we would now have to circle since the control tower had told him that other aircraft would have to be allowed to land before us. No sooner had he returned to the cockpit than an elegant and clearly worried air commodore, who had been sitting behind us, came up and suggested to Evill that he order the pilot to land at another RAF field. Evill merely pointed to a notice which said that 'the pilot is captain of the aircraft'.

A year later I was again at Manby, as one of a party of 'eminent scientists' who were being given a tour of a number of RAF establishments. Barnes Wallis was also a member of the group and, on the day we arrived, he invited me to go walking with him. Even though it was drizzling, I said yes, looking forward to a talk with the great man. We set off at a brisk pace, but after a few minutes he said that he never talked when on a walk. I kept up with him for about a quarter of a mile, and then turned back to the warmth of the mess building, leaving him to disappear into the mist. Wallis was an extraordinarily single-minded man, dying in his nineties while still at work designing what he hoped would be a civil transport aircraft that could fly at something like 3000 mph.

Keeping in touch with men with whom I had worked during the war was really part of the ever-widening and stimulating postwar social life that Joan and I were enjoying in Birmingham and London. Soon, however, I found myself being consulted about new military matters. Early in the war I had tried, but with only limited success, to persuade the wartime American central organization that went by the name of the Office of Scientific Research and Development (the OSRD), to take up the study of wound ballistics. Both Lewis Weed, who was head of the National Research Council's Division of Medical Sciences and also Vice-Chairman of the OSRD's Medical Research Section, and John Fulton, my Yale colleague of the early thirties, were keen on the idea. They had been among the many anglophile American scientists who, in the early part of the war, had come to see the work on which we were engaged in Oxford. But during the three and a half years in which America was in the war, the OSRD had not attempted to set up a wound-ballistics laboratory comparable to my own. Instead they had sponsored a small amount of experimental research on the subject in two university laboratories. When the fighting stopped, a wound-ballistics laboratory was established at Edgewood Arsenal, the vast Chemical Defense Research Establishment to the northeast of Baltimore.

The scientist who was appointed as its first director was C.M. Herget, to whom I had been introduced during the course of a visit to Washington in May 1946 (p. 165), and who I tried to make time to see in later years whenever I was there. In 1950 I agreed that Peter Krohn should spend a few months with him to help in the planning of his new laboratory and that, as 'honorary adviser', Peter should return from time to time to see how the work was progressing.

One of our more significant findings had concerned the wounding 'economics' of bombs and grenades. When compared on a cumulative weight-for-weight basis, the vastly greater number of minute metal fragments that result from a burst caused many more casualties than did the more impressive, but far fewer, larger pieces. It had also become clear that the severity of a wound could in general be related to a fragment's momentum when it struck the body. The greater the momentum, the more the damage that was caused as the piece of metal forced tissues away from its path. We had also noted that most men who became battle-casualties had been hit at close range, and from our analyses of the wounded who had been evacuated from Dunkirk in 1940, and later from the Dieppe raid of 1942, it was also clear that under normal conditions of combat, bullets and fragments struck the body at random. This had made me ask why smaller calibre rifle and machine-gun bullets rather than the regular and heavier ·303 of those days were not standard issue. It was true that the bigger bullet was more stable in flight, and therefore better from the point of view of long-range marksmen, sharpshooters and snipers, that is to say for the kind of long-range rifle-fire exchanges of the Boer War. But conditions were now totally different.

The idea was taken up, and before the war ended, Brigadier J.A. Barlow of the War Office had started to design a rifle of smaller calibre. Herget was much interested in this work, and I gained the impression that he would support the British initiative.

This was in 1950. NATO had just been formed, and it seemed only logical to suppose that all its constituent forces would want to use the same small-arms ammunition. I was wrong. Brigadier Barlow's success in developing a ·280 calibre rifle proved pointless when it came to deciding whether his weapon was to be preferred to a ·300 weapon which the Americans had then designed. I was kept informed and consulted about what was going on on our side of the Atlantic, while Herget was on his.

In the summer of 1952, two senior officers came up to Norfolk from London to urge me to sacrifice a few days of my holiday in order to attend a conference in Washington at which the comparative merits of the two prototype rifles were to be decided. I agreed, having been promised a quick return. On the way over I slept remarkably well, and was fully alert when I was met in Washington by a brigadier who whisked me from the airport straight into a meeting at the Pentagon. The three-star general who was presiding greeted me coldly, but the entry of a British 'expert' who, rumour had it, had 'invented' the subject of wound-ballistics seemed to impress the others, including Herget. But whether or not they were impressed, my visit was pointless. The American ·300 calibre rifle won, and I left the meeting surprised that Herget had been so overawed by the American generals and colonels that he had not opened his mouth. Shortly after my return, I received a letter from Dr Wansbrough-Jones, the Principal Director of Scientific Research (Defence) at the Ministry of Supply.[4] It summed up what we all felt:

> I find this very depressing. It seems to me that almost what one feared is tending to happen; wartime results, experience and past work are being overlooked, rather bad experiments with insufficient controls are being conducted, and I fear even that the

scientific group are either being used to rationalize some staff decisions or, what is worse, are using themselves to try to rationalize some of their own hunches.

That early and futile attempt at the standardization of NATO equipment was to prove a pointer to almost all that has happened since. Effort after effort to agree the requirements for forces which in the event of war would be fighting side by side, have failed because of national industrial competition. So far as the rifle is concerned, NATO first standardized on 7·62mm,* and then in 1982 agreed on the even smaller US Armalite 5·56mm. In a competition that year we again lost with our even smaller 4·85mm. I suppose it is only to be expected that American companies will usually win in the battle for standardization. That is the way part of the arms race goes.

Then there was body armour. In the Korean war, the Americans had arranged an elaborate field-trial of body armour, of which sixteen hundred 'suits' were issued to the British Commonwealth Division which was fighting alongside US forces under the United Nations flag. Nothing decisive emerged from this expensive exercise but, because of the arguments which the subject had generated, it was decided to resume British work on wound-ballistics. I agreed to serve as chairman of a small War Office committee, and also as honorary adviser to the men who were to carry out the work. This was a chore I could hardly refuse, but I firmly opposed a suggestion that I re-establish in Birmingham the kind of laboratory that I had built up in Oxford during the war years. Without Peter Krohn's help, I could not have gone on doing even the little I was prepared to do.

In early 1948 I was also asked to look into the problem of detecting non-metallic anti-personnel mines. Effective measures to locate and deal with buried metal-cased anti-tank or anti-personnel mines had been devised well before the start of the Second World War, but when the enemy started to use plastic-covered mines, the problem became very difficult. For want of a better idea, so-called mine-dogs were being used in Korea, but without anyone being confident that they really were effective 'pointers' in minefields. What was needed was an experiment that would yield a clear answer to the question whether dogs really can detect buried non-metallic objects as they do buried bones and, if they

---

*A calibre about a third smaller in diameter than the obsolete '303'.

can, how they do it. If the story were true, the mine experts were going to try to produce an instrument which could replace the dog!

No-one appeared to have studied the way dogs find the bones they bury, and the military authorities must have assumed that one biologist was as good as another when it came to investigating their problem. It was obviously thrown at me because I was regarded not only as a willing horse, but also as someone who had had some success during the war years in applying scientific method to the analysis of a variety of novel problems. The investigation turned out to be fascinating although, so far as I am aware, what we discovered had little practical value – except that sniffer-dogs have since become commonplace in detecting explosives in the effort to deal with terrorism, and also in detecting drugs brought in by smugglers.

A mine-dog demonstration was laid on for me at an army establishment where tracker and guard dogs were trained and, because of the unusual nature of the test, several senior officials and staff officers came along to enjoy the fun. Handlers led trained dogs along three strips of ground in which mines had been superficially buried. When a dog stopped and pointed at one of the disturbed spots of ground, it was rewarded with a piece of meat. The trial was utterly unconvincing. Its high-point came when a senior and learned official crawled along on hands and knees to see if he too could discern where the mines had been buried. He turned out to be as successful as any of the dogs. A demonstration of tracker-dogs at work was much more striking.

When I got back to Birmingham I described what I had seen to John Eayrs and Eric Ashton (pp. 18, 27), and both agreed to take part in an enquiry which I proposed we should undertake. I did not realize that I was also helping them to take a step that was to lead them irrevocably from the conventional career of a medical student. Facilities for our work were provided at the military establishment where the demonstration had been laid on. We began by training dogs – mongrels that we had selected from Birmingham City's dog-pound – to move along parallel paths that led to three identical rectangular pits which we had lined with breeze-blocks, and into one of which a piece of meat had been dropped. All the pits, which were about nine inches deep, were covered with hessian cloth. The dog that stopped and sniffed at the baited pit was rewarded. In the next lesson, we placed a plastic mine-case in the pit, and a piece of meat on the hessian cover. This was obviously no problem for the dogs. The next step was to put the meat into the pit together with a mine-case. Again this was no problem for the dogs. They were next trained to sniff and choose the pit that contained only a mine-case, being rewarded only when they made the right choice. It was not long before all our animals were a hundred per cent successful in this exercise. We now had a clear indication that dogs could detect mines that they could not see.

In the next stage of training, we tried to exclude the possibility that the dog was responding to a difference between the smell of a plastic cover and that of the breeze-block with which the pits were lined. We did this by dropping into the 'positive' pit not a mine-case but a piece of building block. To our surprise this also proved no problem for the dogs. This result raised the possibility that the dogs chose the pit that contained something which, having been handled, bore a human smell. Instead of a mine-case or a piece of breeze-block, we therefore used as bait a glass dish that had been sterilized in boiling water and handled only with tongs. To our ever-growing amazement the dogs still learnt to make the right choice. Now the implication was that the dogs were reacting to something that had diffused from the surface of sterilized glass. There was, of course, the remote possibility that the presence of an object changed the resonance of the pit as the dogs sniffed at the hessian. But smell seemed to be the best bet for further study.

At this point I arranged for the work to be transferred to a laboratory in Birmingham. In a carefully designed experiment, Ashton was able to show that a dog could discriminate the different smells of infinitesimally small amounts of related organic acidic compounds. Eayrs in turn tried to find out how effective dogs really were at identifying disturbed earth. This part of the enquiry was carried out on a protected beach belonging to one of our coastal military establishments. Mines were buried between the high- and low-water marks, and dogs, which had first been trained to react to the disturbed sand, were then tested and re-tested after the tide had washed over the beach a few times. In general they failed this test.

A summarized account of the work was published in 1970.[5] It ended with the discouraging conclusion that, whatever else it could do, the dog could not be regarded as having much value as a detector of buried mines, 'except in circumstances where the stimulus is large or the zone of detection circumscribed'. For all practical purposes that meant open grassland during only a short period after mines had been planted.

Our work was wound up in 1956. But the need to find ways of detecting non-metallic mines did not disappear, and the Americans were equally concerned. On a visit to the States two years after we had started our own enquiry, I was asked to meet, first, a team that was about to start working on the same subject at the recently-established Stanford Research Institute and, second, Joseph Rhine, a Duke University parapsychologist, who was already internationally known as a scientist who had become converted to a belief in the reality of extrasensory perception. Rhine was the man who coined the term ESP. I learnt nothing at Stanford, where the people concerned had not even decided how to set about the problem. Two scientists from the Pentagon had flown in for the meeting, but it was the era of the McCarthy witch-hunt, and no 'classified' paper could be removed from any government office. So we just sat around while I told them about the progress that we had made. Whether the Stanford team ever got any further than we had, I do not know. My visit to Rhine proved the more interesting. He had a Pentagon contract to enquire into the possibility of training homing pigeons, through the medium of ESP, to alight on buried mines! I had a vision of fields dotted with white birds sitting patiently over mines waiting for sappers to clear them. Rhine was absolutely genuine in his belief in ESP, which remained unshaken to the end, even though the price he paid for his conviction was virtual excommunication from conventional academic circles.

I never expected to hear again about mine-dogs. But then came the Falklands War and, after the surrender of the Argentine forces, our troops had the problem of trying to find and destroy a very large number of non-metallic anti-personnel mines that the Argentinians had laid, apparently with inadequate mapping. Many British soldiers were wounded when trying to clear the island, as were considerable numbers of cattle and sheep. Once again dogs were brought in, but apparently to no avail. I wrote a short article on the subject for *The Times*,[6] and soon afterwards the London-based staff officer who was coordinating the work of mine-clearance came to see me to discover whether our experimental work had revealed more than had already been published. Alas – I could remember nothing, nor could Eayrs or Ashton. How much use, if any, mine-dogs were in the Falklands will no doubt be revealed one day.

R&D – Control and Cooperation

During the course of a visit to Washington in 1946, I had met Julius Edelstein, a man who had served in the US Navy in the Pacific during the war, and who at the time was working in the State Department as an adviser on reparations. He was a friend of some of the senior advisers whom President Truman had inherited on the death of President Roosevelt, and was always full of interesting, if at times disturbing, information. I wrote to him later, soon after the Czech coup, saying that I did not believe that an America armed with atomic bombs, even at a time when the Soviet Union was presumed to have none, had the power to reverse what the Russians had done. Even if one assumed that our political leaders were 'fully aware of what is involved in the idea of military sanctions, they would hesitate in coming to hot-headed conclusions' given they considered their own spheres of political interest. 'We are', I said, 'so close to the bitter fruits of our last victory that only a lunatic could suppose that a reopening of the shooting war will do anything but increase our load of misery. I am not arguing here whether or not armed conflict is a means of opposing Communism and of spreading Western ideas of democracy. That point would have to be argued on its own. I am merely saying that even if one conceded this issue, there is no evidence that armed conflict would get us to our immediate goal.'

When I returned to England, I wrote to my 1944 RAF colleague, Air Vice Marshal Kingston-McCloughry,[1] saying that 'the general atmosphere in the States was very militant and frightening. I thought we had done with wars for the moment.' I was wrong. In England, as in America, there were people who saw a new war looming. Because of my wartime operational experience, I was invited to join a small informal body that had been convened by Leo Amery to consider whether the Army League should be resurrected. Amery had been a member of several prewar Conservative Governments.

The ten or so members of his group consisted of ex-cabinet ministers and retired senior military men. Julian Amery, Leo's son, who in due course was himself to become a member of both Macmillan's and Heath's Governments, kept the notes. The only contribution that I can remember making was in reply to a request from Leo Amery – which he prefaced by saying that I was a young man who had had a 'successful war' and who was informed about new military developments (which was hardly the case) – to comment on some critical observations that had just been made by a recently retired head of army intelligence about the way the British defence Chiefs were going about their business. It was winter, and we were sitting in a semi-circle round the fire. Without hesitating, I replied that it was extraordinary how easy it was to criticize those who now occupied the seats which the critics had only recently vacated, and when we lacked the up-to-date intelligence which our successors now possessed. I left the gathering shortly afterwards, followed by General Sir Frederick Morgan, never to return. 'Well spoken,' he said. He had every reason to agree. He had been responsible for planning the Overlord invasion of Europe during the two years or so before Montgomery arrived from the Mediterranean theatre, and had had to suffer the humiliation of seeing his plans decried by a man who had only just been brought in to command the British forces.[2]

Inevitably the formation of NATO in 1949 began to affect my life, particularly as more and more American friends were posted to NATO's Paris headquarters. Larry Norstad, who in 1951 was appointed C-in-C of the Allied Air Forces Central Europe, as well as C-in-C of all the US Air Forces in Europe, had as a part-time scientific adviser Bob Robertson, whom I had got to know during the war, and with whom I had kept in touch afterwards. Theodore von Karman, America's most distinguished aerodynamicist, had also been brought over, to direct an Advisory Group for Aeronautical Research and Development (AGARD) which had been set up to help the USA's NATO allies. I had met von Karman immediately after the war, and had looked after him in 1946 on the occasion when he had signed the Charter Book of the Royal Society on his admission as a Foreign Member.

Then in October 1957, the Soviet Union surprised the world by launching Sputnik 1, and a month later Sputnik 2, with a dog as passenger. This was regarded as a clear challenge to the West, and within a few months, the United States responded by launching the first of its Explorer series of satellites. Another immediate reaction was an effort to strengthen the scientific resources of the Western alliance.

The NATO Council had already appointed a committee to advise, among other things, how scientific and technical cooperation could be encouraged between the member states. Later, in June 1957, it had appointed a task force on Scientific and Technical Cooperation to make specific recommendations. The USA was much keener on this move than was the UK, where the official line was that NATO should concern itself only with scientific matters that were specifically military, leaving the broad subject of scientific cooperation to such non-military institutions as the Organization for European Economic Cooperation – the OEEC. The NATO Council nonetheless went ahead, appointing as Chairman of the task force Joseph B. Koepfli, a Professor of Chemistry at the California Institute of Technology and a 'science adviser' to Dean Acheson when the latter was Secretary of State. I was appointed to represent the UK, with Dr B.K. Blount, a specialist in military technical intelligence, as my 'alternate', or stand-in. Belgium, Canada, France, Germany and Italy each appointed one representative.

Contrary to Whitehall opinion, the task force took the view that NATO was in a better position than any other international organization to influence member governments 'to implement existing, and if needs be, expanded national programmes for the development of scientific and technical resources'.[3] We therefore advised that a NATO scientific committee should be appointed, and that its chairman should also serve as full-time scientific adviser to the Secretary-General and the NATO Council.

Our recommendation was accepted, and in December 1957, a Science Committee and a Science Adviser were formally appointed at a meeting of NATO 'heads of government', which was attended, among others, by President Eisenhower and Harold Macmillan, then the British Prime Minister. Soon after this, I was appointed to represent the UK on the committee, which I continued to do until 1967. The first Chairman was Norman Ramsey, a distinguished

American nuclear physicist who had worked on 'the bomb'. Because of the Congressional Act which precluded any exchanges on nuclear matters with other countries, for many years only US scientists who had the necessary 'clearances' could be chairmen.

I remember the first meeting of the committee, which took place in March 1958, mainly because that was when I first met Isidor Rabi, the American delegate, a man from whom I was to learn a great deal and with whom I remained on the closest terms until his death in January 1988. We were milling around waiting for the meeting to begin, when Bob Robertson, who was Rabi's alternate, introduced me to his senior colleague. Rabi slowly looked me up and down, and then said, 'So, you're the redoubtable Solly Zuckerman.' I found the word 'redoubtable' amusing, for Rabi, a physicist who had played a critical part in the development of his particular field of science, was the most influential man in the room. He was not only a Nobel Laureate, but had also seen a few of his disciples follow him to the same honour. I knew that he had been the scientific genius behind many of the achievements of the famous wartime MIT Radiation Laboratory, and a main consultant to Robert Oppenheimer, the scientific head of the Los Alamos atomic bomb establishment. He had been a key figure in bringing about the 1955 International Conference on the Peaceful Uses of Atomic Energy, and from 1956 to 1957, Chairman of President Eisenhower's Science Advisory Committee. I would not have suspected that he had ever heard of me.

The other members of the committee seemed to know that the two of us had been closely, even if separately, involved in governmental matters. We were both members of national bodies that dealt with scientific policy, and were also the representatives of the two nuclear powers – the USA and the UK – which then dominated the NATO alliance. The UK was bound to the USA by some undefined 'special relationship', and was still the head of a Commonwealth of Nations. Rabi and I realized that we would have to move warily if the other members of the committee were not to feel that they were being pushed around. At that time our two countries were devoting about three per cent of their respective GDPs to the advancement and exploitation of science. The corresponding figure in the other NATO countries was barely one per cent. Our first task, therefore, was to reach agreement about what percentage figure should be a common national 'target'.

After some debate, we settled arbitrarily on two per cent, a figure which was no problem for either the USA or the UK, but one which we thought the other members of the committee might have difficulty in negotiating with their respective governments. Since each national delegate was accompanied at the meetings by at least one of his country's officials, the message was, however, transmitted to the right quarters straight away. I seem to remember that it did not take more than a few years for all the NATO countries to reach the target.

Norman Ramsey was an excellent chairman, but because both Rabi and I had more to say – or said more – than the others, and because it must sometimes have appeared as if we were in collusion, we soon developed a technique of seeming to oppose each other. On occasion we even rehearsed our arguments, which we used first in the discussions that led to the establishment of a series of NATO Summer Study Schools. This idea had been spelt out in the report of the NATO Parliamentarians, and was based upon what was already fairly common practice in the United States. The project necessitated the establishment of a common fund that would provide for the cost of setting up a temporary school or 'institute' – in reality a lengthy symposium – given that its sponsor had the requisite standing, and the topic adequate merit. A NATO fund for scientific grants was also established.

At no time do I recall any hesitation on the part of the USA in providing whatever was to be its share of the money that was called for. After some delay, the other members, the UK included, always followed suit, but in proportion to their overall contributions to the Treaty Organization, it being implicitly understood that each would take out from the NATO fund for summer schools and research grants approximately what it had contributed – given no serious relaxation of standards. At the beginning, of course, this did not help the weaker members of NATO, who benefited far more from a Science Fellowship programme, which we also managed to launch. Overall, however, all member countries benefited, and particularly from the Summer Study Institute programme, which I have heard described as the most rewarding international scientific enterprise ever mounted. By the time the twenty-fifth anniversary of the NATO committee was celebrated, scores of volumes which recorded the proceedings of 'Institutes' had been published.

Military matters were never discussed. Indeed, there was a wide gulf between the committee as such and other scientific bodies within the NATO organization. Larry Norstad, now Supreme Commander, already had his own full-time science adviser, an American by name of Kenneth Davidson who, in those early days of the nuclear era, was certainly needed. Dr Davidson's deputy was an Englishman, Tony Sargeaunt, who had been seconded from the War Office, but who was not privy to nuclear matters. Theodore von Karman's AGARD was also very active in helping, with American money, European aeronautical designers to get back on their feet. Larry had great faith in von Karman, and had encouraged the development of AGARD when he first came to Paris in 1951.

There were other international scientific projects to whose implementation I unsuccessfully turned my energies. The most important was the idea of creating a major European technological university.[4] This proposal was one of the recommendations of a small but powerful study group that was set up in the 1950s under the chairmanship of Louis Armand, President of the Council of the Ecole Polytechnique and a former head of the European nuclear organization, EURATOM. Armand had been in charge of the reconstruction of the French railways after the war, and I found it odd to think that I, the author of the bombing plan that had torn them apart in 1944, should be a member of his committee. I gave him a copy of an article that I had published in 1948 about the rebuilding of the French railways[5] and also, I seem to remember, a brief statement of the bombing plan itself. The other UK member of Armand's committee was John Cockcroft. Our recommendation that an International Technological Institute should be established was then examined by an even smaller *ad hoc* committee under the chairmanship of James Killian, previously the President of MIT and Science Adviser to President Eisenhower. John Cockcroft represented the UK on this body. Its endorsement of the idea could not have been stronger.

> . . . an International Institute of Science and Technology would be a symbol and a precedent of significance transcending its direct contributions to education and research. The successful launching of an international educational establishment could be a fillip for Western morale, and a dramatic demonstration of the intellectual strength, vigour, and unity of Western nations

working together. It offers an opportunity to demonstrate that only in the Free World is it possible to achieve a truly international educational institution attractive to first-rate scholars from all countries.[6]

I was immensely impressed by the vision that lay behind what was being proposed, and since the UK was the only member of NATO which at the time could have provided a home, I tried hard to have the idea taken up by the UK authorities. But it all came to nothing. At meetings with officials of the Foreign Office and of senior scientists, only John Cockcroft – who had then become Master of Churchill College in Cambridge – and I supported the proposal, and in the face of the opposition even John's enthusiasm was short-lived. The University Grants Committee and the Committee of Vice Chancellors, as well as most members of the ACSP, shared what to me was the same short-sighted view – that if the UK were to contribute to a cooperative European scientific venture, it could only be to the detriment of our own national interests. I went so far as to make some private soundings, and discovered that the directors of both the National Physical Laboratory at Teddington and its neighbour the National Chemical Laboratory – which no longer exists – were not only interested, but ready to consider the transformation of their fairly big institutions into the nucleus of a much more extensive European technological complex. But without support at the centre, the idea got nowhere. Neither did a proposal that I put forward to transform the UK's Colonial Research Service, which was being run down, into a contract advisory body that could be called upon by what are now called Third World countries, as well as by the United Nations and other international organizations. For years afterwards I used to bemoan the fact that of the major European countries, the UK was alone in not providing a home for an important international organization.

But if the Government was reluctant to engage in long-term international cooperation in science and technology, it became increasingly concerned about the lack of standardization in the Western rearmament programme. For years, too, there had been mounting concern, both in and out of Parliament, about the way the demand for additional resources for R&D continued to increase, particularly in the Service departments, whose programmes, it was felt, were neither adequately coordinated nor monitored. In his capacity as Lord President of the Council and as Minister for Science, Lord Hailsham therefore set up a committee in May 1958, with Claude Gibb as Chairman, to enquire into the management and control of the research and development that was carried out by government departments and the Research Councils. The main reason why the task was not assigned to the ACSP was that the Council, despite its high-sounding title, had no authority to enquire into the way the Research Councils or government departments discharged their responsibilities. A more immediate reason was that it was the Treasury that had instigated the enquiry.

A preliminary and hurried examination had already been carried out by Sir Alan Wilson FRS, then Chairman of one of our larger pharmaceutical companies, but his report was judged by the Treasury to be far too anodyne. Apart from himself, Claude Gibb's committee comprised only four members. One was a senior civil servant, Antony Part, then Under-Secretary in the Ministry of Education.* The others were Sir Patrick Linstead FRS, then Rector of Imperial College in London (and my mentor in the late forties in the search for nitrogenous fertilizer and sulphur), Sir Willis Jackson FRS, at the time on the board of Associated Electrical Industries, and previously Professor of Electrotechnics at Manchester University, and myself.

Sadly, and only a few months after we had started work, Claude Gibb had a fatal heart attack while waiting to board an aircraft in New York. I was asked to take his place as Chairman, and Sir George Edwards† was appointed to the committee. George was one of the best aircraft designers in the country, and at the time was responsible for the highly controversial and costly advanced military aircraft known as the TSR2. He knew the ways of the then Ministry of Supply, and although dependent on government support, was highly critical of the 'bureaucracy'. I do not know who suggested his name, but whoever it was, his appointment was a stroke of genius from the point of view of the work of the committee. Served by an excellent secretary, we settled down as an intimate and single-minded body, determined to assemble all the facts we could, and to suggest what improvements could be

*He retired from the service in 1976 as Sir Antony Part, GCB.
†Now OM, FRS.

made in the manner by which government departments controlled their R&D expenditures, and in the way the Research Councils – with which Linstead, Jackson and I were separately familiar – operated.

My own knowledge of the Councils derived partly from the fact that the MRC supported much of my university research, and partly from my familiarity with the Agricultural Research Council, of which I had been a member for ten years – all but one of them under the chairmanship of Lord Rothschild. Victor Rothschild was an assiduous but autocratic chairman, who never disguised his dislikes, which were not always shared. On one occasion they focused on the highly respected director of one of the ARC's institutes. A concerted effort had to be made to frustrate Victor in his manoeuvres to remove the man from his post. Victor was also so diligent in seeing that the Council discharged its duties that we sometimes found ourselves cutting across those of Bill Slater, who had joined the Council as Secretary when he retired from his post as Chief Scientific Adviser to the Ministry of Agriculture. As a full-time official, Bill was both the Council's chief executive and the 'accounting officer' responsible to Parliament for the way the Agricultural Research Council spent the money allocated to it.

We pooled our knowledge about the way the Research Councils discharged their responsibilities, and also took additional evidence, both verbal and written, from those who might be affected by our recommendations. This part of our enquiry ended with the harmless observation that basic or fundamental research is best carried out in the environment of a university rather than in that of a government research establishment. There were those who took this as implying that we questioned the purpose of some of the work that was being encouraged by the Research Councils in their institutes. My own view was that we did not go far enough. As I have already said (p. 105), I had come to believe that it would have been a far better arrangement if the ARC, for example, had become the advisory body of the Ministry of Agriculture, so that its staff and those whose work it supported were continuously informed about what mattered in the farming world.

Most of our discussions concerned defence research. Here the basic trouble was that the ultimate cost of major projects bore little relation to what was estimated when they were started, and that those that were not cancelled usually took far longer to complete than had been originally promised. Our task therefore was to try to formulate management procedures that could help the Government to get better value than it did for the relatively enormous sums that went to the development of hardware – military aircraft and other weapon systems. We took a great deal of evidence, and found much to criticize. The outcome was a proposal to institute a precise and phased set of procedures, starting with the definition of an 'operational requirement' and leading to the monitoring of the final manufacturing process. We criticized the Service Chiefs and the DRPC for their failure to coordinate the requests that were made by the three Services for new weapons, or for improvements in old ones, and we emphasized the need for standardization with our NATO allies. We also suggested that the senior staff officers who were responsible for putting forward operational requirements should have an 'experience of scientific and technical as well as operational matters'. But while we all felt that our proposed procedures would help bring as great a measure of certainty as could be secured in a very uncertain field, we were insistent that there were times when the Government had to 'cancel projects even when a great deal of time, money and effort' had been devoted to them. In these cases, so we wrote, 'it is always tempting – because cancellations may be thought to argue incompetence – to go on in the hope that the effort already spent will in the end not be wasted. But the truth is that, however much money and effort may have been spent on a project, it is not worth spending more unless the development when finished will meet a real need in an effective way.'[7]

There was a hiccough before our report could be submitted to Lord Hailsham. I had become Chief Scientific Adviser to the Ministry of Defence the year before, and as such could no longer be regarded as 'independent'. What is more I was now Chairman of the DRPC, a body that my committee had seriously criticized. We had also been critical of the Ministry of Aviation (Supply), which was the main target that the Treasury had in mind when it instigated the enquiry, and which, during the course of our exchanges, had already started to tighten its procedures. However, William Strath, who had become its Permanent Secretary, felt that some of our sentences were too harsh, and he had called in Sir Burke Trend, then deputy to Sir Norman Brook, the Secretary of the Cabinet, to mediate between us. After consulting the other members of my committee, I made what textual changes seemed reasonable, and in its softened form the report was duly presented and published in July 1961. In subsequent exchanges in Parliament, a member of the Opposition commented that while we had used 'moderate language', the 'Zuckerman Report' implied devastating criticisms. This led Harold Watkinson, the Minister of Defence, to point out that the Zuckerman referred to was now his Chief Scientific Adviser.

When I think of the long list of abandoned projects on which hundreds of millions of pounds have since been spent, I wonder whether the 'new Zuckerman procedures', as they were called, really did much good, any more than have subsequent attempted reforms. Millions of pounds are still being wasted. The fact is that efficient financial management of military R&D matters far less than choosing the right projects on which to work, and the right people to do the job.

Nuclear Ignorance

In September 1945, the British Government had formally proposed to the American authorities that a British team, consisting mainly of members of the Research and Experiments Department of the Ministry of Home Security, should go to Japan to cooperate with the Americans in a detailed damage and casualty survey of Hiroshima and Nagasaki. Despite my ignorance of the general effects of radiation, the intention was that I should direct the casualty studies, since it was then incorrectly believed in London that casualties due to radiation would be relatively few. As Sir Reginald Stradling, the Chief Scientist at the Ministry, had put it, whatever the effects of radiation, it was necessary to distinguish them from casualties due to blast and fire – and that was where I had to come in. The American Congress was already considering a Bill that was to foreclose any US cooperation with the UK in the nuclear field.

The American authorities did, however, agree in May 1946 to my visiting Washington in order to be told what they had already discovered about atom-bomb casualties. My contact was Dr Shields Warren, the Chief Medical Officer and radiological expert on the staff of General Groves, the director of the Manhattan Project, the name of the secret organization that had developed the bomb. Shields Warren told me what little he knew, and sent me on to some young pathologists who were studying tissues removed from victims of Hiroshima. They knew nothing about the kind of lesions caused by 'conventional' blast, and were keen to discover whether what they could see down the microscope differed from what might be expected in the victim of an ordinary bomb explosion. There were no differences. I remember the occasion less for its scientific interest than for the fact that no sooner had I started to look down the microscope than one of the pathologists was called to the telephone. It was General Groves himself, telephoning to say that no nuclear secrets were to be revealed to me. But, as the pathologist said, since he had no secrets to disclose, and as he wanted to learn from my experience, he'd pay no attention to the call.

It was only many years later that I learnt about Groves's preoccupation with security, and about the total ban that he had imposed only a few weeks after the bombing of Japan on the passage of 'atomic' information to the nationals of any foreign country. But what amazed me at the time was that his office knew where I was and what I was doing in Washington. While our wartime allies had agreed to allow a small British team to make a rapid and preliminary field study of the physical destruction which the two atomic bombs had caused, the American authorities were no longer willing even to discuss casualties, and in particular radiological hazards. The refusal of the American Government to countenance a detailed British survey of the two Japanese cities came as a relief to me. I was busy enough without that.

Four years later, in 1950, the year after the Russians exploded their first atom bomb, President Truman decreed that the American Atomic Energy Commission should work 'on all forms of atomic weapons, including the so-called hydrogen or super bomb'. 'All forms of atomic weapons' included nuclear bombs for battlefield use, despite the fact that there was then little military interest and no operational requirement for such weapons. It was, however, widely felt that it would be useful to learn something about the lethal power of 'small' atomic charges so as to decide whether they could have any military utility in field warfare.

That is how I first became involved in the practical problems of nuclear weaponry. Through what are called 'official channels', and despite the 1946 McMahon Act, I was invited in August 1951 by Dr W. Randolph ('Randy') Lovelace, the Chairman of the US Armed Forces Medical Policy Council, to advise on the design of a programme of experiments to discover how the blast-wave from a nuclear explosion exercises its effects on the body. Randy Lovelace turned out to be the nicest of men. By profession a surgeon, he was enamoured of all things aeronautical. He was an experienced pilot, and for a time held the world altitude record for a parachute jump, which he had made in order to demonstrate to aviators that it was possible to survive a jump from the rarefied atmosphere of 40,000 feet without an oxygen mask. Together with his uncle, also a medical practitioner, he had established in Albuquerque, New Mexico, the Lovelace Clinic and Medical Foundation.

Quite apart from his interest in all matters military, and his friendship with a number of senior officers (almost all the American Air Force generals used to go to Randy's clinic for their annual medical check-up), Randy's interest in nuclear weaponry stemmed from the fact that the hospital complex which he had built was little more than a mile from the perimeter of the Sandia Corporation, the vast weapons complex that the American Atomic Energy Commission had established to complement their Los Alamos and Livermore weapon research laboratories.* The Lovelace Foundation was new, and research contracts from the Pentagon were welcomed. By coincidence the member of his staff to whom Randy intended to entrust the programme of blast research was Dr Clayton S. ('Sam') White who, as a Rhodes Scholar from Colorado, had attended my lectures in Oxford in the thirties.

In view of the McMahon Act, the invitation was strange. William Penney,† who had worked at Los Alamos in the last year or so of the war, was, to the best of my knowledge, the only exception the Americans had made to the provisions of the Act. He had been invited to participate in the Bikini test of 1946, on the grounds that his presence was needed 'in the interests of the defense of the United States'.[1] I told Tizard about the invitation that had been sent me, and he suggested that I should accept. But he also advised me to consult Sir Harold Parker, then the Permanent Secretary at the new Ministry of Defence. Parker encouraged me to go, but made the condition that the Americans should accept my British 'security clearances' – not that I knew what they were – as equal to their own, which they did. I did not then know that Tizard believed it unwise for the UK to embark on a nuclear weapons programme, and that he had advised the Attlee Government against doing so.

A year passed before I could find the time to visit Albuquerque. Colonel Gagge, a tall and powerfully built air-force officer, flew over to make the arrangements, and it fell to me to take him to dinner. I chose Au Jardin des Gourmets, a well-known Soho restaurant and, seeing

---

*Los Alamos was to the north-east of Albuquerque, and Livermore to the west of San Francisco.
†Now Lord Penney OM.

that grouse was on the menu, suggested that we made that our main dish. After a customary first course, we each had a grouse. His went down very quickly, and with such evident pleasure that I innocently asked if he would like a second. He eagerly accepted. That is the only occasion in my life that I have eaten two grouse at a sitting, washed down by two bottles of an excellent claret, the first having disappeared as quickly as had Gagge's first bird. I made a mental note that the next time I entertained him it would be at a cheaper restaurant.

In 1952 I flew to the States by way of Paris in the 'Blue Plate Special', a Constellation aircraft of the US Military Air Transport Service, which in those days claimed to be the biggest airline in the world. I had been accorded a high flight priority, and was seated in one of the two most roomy seats in the plane, next to a two-star air-force general, who was the 'ranking officer' aboard. It was an eventful journey.

We took off in the evening for the Azores, where we were due to refuel. After a few polite exchanges with my neighbour, I settled down to read, and before long the general was invited to the cockpit. I continued reading, and forgot all about him until he returned after what must have been well over an hour. He was grim-faced and clearly wanted to talk. He began by asking whether I had noticed that number one port engine had cut out, and that number one starboard was about to go. I'd noticed nothing, nor could I detect any difference in the sound of the engines even when I tried. 'A third engine is also giving trouble,' he continued, 'and we have passed "the point of no return". A back-up plane is following hard after us, and aircraft are coming out from the Azores.' I foolishly asked whether the other passengers were going to be told. 'No, what's the point?' he replied.

I tried to concentrate again on my book, saying to myself that if the general was bravely facing the prospect of coming down in the sea (I remember thinking that at least it would be warm), I, as a non-American civilian, proposed to face the prospect of drowning at least as stoically. I could not see what use back-up aircraft, let alone alerted ships, could be in the dark. After a while he again broke the silence. 'As I'm probably not going to be able to speak to the President, I might as well tell you.' And he started to unburden himself. Now that the Russians had the bomb, he had been thinking hard and, unlike his colleagues, he no longer believed that Europe could be defended against Soviet invasion by means of nuclear weapons. Millions would die in a nuclear exchange, and the devastation of the last war, only a small part of which had yet been repaired, would be multiplied a thousand-fold. There could never be any recovery. He had been given permission by his C-in-C to make his views known to the White House, and now it seemed that his message would never be delivered. He spoke quietly and with enormous sincerity. There was no comment I could make, and he then lapsed into silence, while I read fitfully and waited for whatever might happen. At no moment did the general ask why I was on the plane, nor did I tell him.

With only two of the four engines working, we landed near midnight in the Azores, on an airfield ablaze with light, its fire engines and 'meat wagons', as they were called, waiting for the expected crash. Only then were the rest of the passengers told about our troubles. Celebratory drinking followed in the officers' mess; there was much milling around the slot machines, and most of us bought huge bottles of Portuguese brandy. After some hours we took off again in the back-up plane, arriving next morning at Andrews military airbase outside Washington. The general and I did not return to the subject of his conversation. I never knew his name or what happened to him, and I did not manage to get rid of my bottle of brandy until I got to Albuquerque three days later. In its wooden case, it looked like a baby's coffin.

I was very busy during my short stay in Washington, where I discussed my assignment with Shields Warren. I also saw several friends who had joined the growing army of government scientists. They were concerned to learn about the developments that were taking place in the central organization of British science. There had been a hold-up in establishing the National Science Foundation, which had been proposed to the President by Vannevar Bush, the head of the OSRD, before that organization was wound up.

New Mexico, where I spent nearly three weeks, was a new world to me. After the fuss in arranging the visit, and my busy time in Washington, there seemed nothing to do. Randy Lovelace had the contract to carry out the work, but there were no papers or proposals for me to examine, and nothing to discuss. The planning meeting which I had assumed would take place straight away was put off from day to day. I didn't mind. I could do with a holiday.

Albuquerque, which is set on a high plateau ringed by distant mountains, had grown during the war from a town of a few tens to one of more than a hundred thousand inhabitants. There was much to see and the weather was perfect. Opposite my delightfully old-fashioned hotel, close to the station of the famous Santa Fe railway, was a tattooist who was constantly at work in his small parlour. Next door was an equally busy gunshop. Indians – Pueblos and Navajos – thronged the streets. I had never seen any before. I bought simple gifts for Joan and the children from shops which were lavishly stocked compared with those of still austere England. Randy took me to the races, and also flew me in a small plane to a vast ranch in the country. All the landowners and race-horse owners in New Mexico seemed to be both his friends and patrons of his clinic. He drove me to Santa Fe, on a kind of D.H. Lawrence pilgrimage, although I doubt that he had ever read any of Lawrence's novels. His clinic provided a medical service for the Navajos, who in those days were prone to tuberculosis, and I spent a couple of nights with two of the clinic's doctors at Fort Winslow, the capital of the vast reservation that lies some 200 miles from Albuquerque. I bought Navajo jewellery in a pawn shop not far from the main gate of the reservation, which I was told was the only place to buy the 'real stuff'. It was there that the Indians pawned their turquoise-studded silver bracelets, brooches, necklaces and rings for money to buy drink in the neighbouring town. No alcohol was allowed on the reservation.

While I waited to get down to the serious business for which I had come, there was also time to make use of what to me was a novel piece of X-ray equipment, with which Dr Grossman, the clinic's radiologist, took pictures at different planes through the body. He joined me in a study which I suggested we could make of the changes that take place in the base of the skull as a child grows – a small piece of research, the results of which we subsequently published. Far more sophisticated apparatus of the same kind is commonplace today.

When I realized that nothing had been decided except that the problem of the effects of blast on human beings should be studied, I sat down and wrote a paper in which I laid out the problem as I saw it, and an outline of the kind of experiments that I felt it would be worth doing.

Some two weeks after my arrival, Colonel Gagge and a representative of the Atomic Energy Commission turned up from Washington.

An MIT graduate, Lawrence Levy, who had studied the damage suffered by parked aircraft in an atomic test explosion, and who Randy thought might be useful, came with them. Together with some six representatives from the nearby Sandia Corporation, we gathered for our first meeting to discuss my paper – there was no other. The US official report, *The Effects of Atomic Weapons,** together with published accounts of the destruction and casualties of Hiroshima and Nagasaki, were all that I had needed to fit into a nuclear frame what I knew about the wounding mechanisms of conventional bombs. There was no point in studying what happened in the extensive central zone of a nuclear burst, where people would be blown to smithereens, burnt to cinders and hopelessly irradiated. I therefore advised that the only thing worth doing was to see what happened at greater distances, where the shock wave would be somewhat different from that of a conventional explosion, and where the blast pressure would have fallen to low levels that could be simulated by means of a shock-tube.† What also needed to be considered were the fatal and non-fatal injuries which would be expected to have occurred at a distance from the centre of the explosion, where people would still be violently thrown, or hit by bits of flying masonry and other secondary missiles. I painted a picture of huge panels and blocks from skyscrapers being hurled for hundreds and hundreds of yards leaving a trail of destruction in their wake. Using the methods that we had developed in the casualty surveys that we had carried out in the UK during the war, it was possible to devise an estimate of the numbers and nature of the casualties that might be caused by the blast from nuclear explosions of different yield. There was, in fact, little to discuss, and I had a sneaking feeling that, with the possible exception of small anti-personnel nuclear weapons about which hints were being dropped, the project was all but a waste of time and money. But what I had laid out in my paper was accepted as a

*This report[2] was based on that of Professor Smyth of Princeton, which had been published by the American Government in 1945,[3] it is said against the advice of British Intelligence. The information which it embodied related to a 'nominal bomb' with an energy release of 20 kilotons of TNT. In order to take account of explosions of hydrogen bombs with yields of up to 20 megatons, that is to say, up to a thousand times greater, it was reissued in 1957.[4]
†A wide tube into one end of which air is pumped under pressure until a thin metal diaphragm, which closes the other end, bursts.

practical programme, and at later meetings we went on to consider the design of the experiments which might provide answers to the questions I had posed.

The following year I returned to Albuquerque to learn what progress had been made in implementing the research programme. The answer was, very little. This second visit stands out because it coincided with a gathering of space scientists that had been convened by Randy, who was still leading the American effort in aerospace medicine. One of those present was Wernher von Braun, the German rocket expert who, as the Director of the Peenemunde establishment, had developed the V2 ballistic missile, the 'secret weapon' that had been launched against London towards the end of the war. They were a very single-minded bunch of people. At a cocktail party I asked von Braun whether, with so much devastation of the war still to be made good, he really thought that rocketry deserved all the resources the space lobby was demanding. He thought it did, even the resources necessary to launch into space something as big as the Empire State Building.

At the end of this visit, I flew on to Los Angeles, having accepted Bob Robertson's invitation to spend a few days with him at Caltech, of whose staff he was a leading member. I was delighted to go as it meant that there would be more to talk about than at Albuquerque, and because I would once again be able to stay with Ira and Lee Gershwin, and call on Alfred and Alma Hitchcock and Charles and Elsa Laughton, who had now made Hollywood their home. One night Bob laid on a big party for me. The occasion stands out because he and Robert Bacher and Charles Lauritsen, two senior Caltech physicists who had played a major part in the Manhattan Project and who were still closely connected with the Atomic Energy Commission, in turn drew me into the quiet of the garden to try and make me understand that now that the Soviet Union was well ahead with the bomb, it would be better if the UK, even though it had just tested its first warhead, did not enter the nuclear arms race. All three spoke earnestly, urging me to tell Tizard and anyone else of influence in the UK, that the abandonment of the British nuclear weapons programme would make the world a safer place than it would otherwise become. In their view it was bad enough that the USA and the Soviet Union were now embarking on a nuclear arms race. It would be worse if more countries joined in. At best – and a pretty poor best it was – mankind might survive a 'bi-polar' nuclear world, with the two major powers deterring each other with the reciprocal threat of nuclear annihilation. I found it all very depressing.

At about eleven o'clock I asked Bob, who had certainly over-estimated the influence I had in these matters, to call a taxi to take me from Pasadena to Beverly Hills, where I was staying with the Gershwins. He offered to drive me himself, especially when he learned that I proposed to stop *en route* to call on Charles Laughton and Elsa Lanchester. Bob was as thrilled as any teenage fan at the prospect of meeting the Laughtons and the Gershwins. I did not get to bed before about three in the morning, leaving Ira, whose normal regime was to turn night into day, still talking to Bob.

Two years passed before I next returned to Albuquerque. In the intervening time, Sam White had also been called upon to investigate the effects of blast on animals exposed to atomic bomb tests in the Nevada desert, mainly to see whether there was any value in simple nuclear bomb shelters. In spite of the fact that I had laid out the programme of the work on which he was engaged, he had now been instructed not to give me any details about the field tests. We kept in touch after this third visit, but it was not until 1960, after I had become Chief Scientific Adviser to the Ministry of Defence, that I was next in New Mexico.

Because we were denied American information, the UK started to carry out its own 'nuclear effects studies', and limited though it was, the information which I had gained during my Albuquerque visits nonetheless proved useful, particularly when I was asked to embark on a programme of work similar to the one that I had laid out at the Lovelace institution. Once again I felt bound to agree, since the basis for any new UK enquiry would inevitably be the knowledge that my Oxford Unit had gained during the war years. Unfortunately for me, the example set by the US after the war in establishing Herget's wound-ballistics laboratory had not been followed in the UK, and here I was, being asked to undertake a chore that had little or no intellectual interest – far less, indeed, than had the enquiry into the presumed ability of a dog to detect non-metallic mines.

With the help of Peter Krohn, however, I made a few preliminary experiments at a Service establishment which, to make matters difficult, was some miles to the east of London. It was the only place that had the shock-tubes that we needed. What we wanted to check was whether the blast-wave from a nuclear explosion, by the time it has travelled far enough from the burst for its pressure to have fallen to the level of a blast-wave close to the burst of an ordinary bomb, would have the same wounding effect – the need for an answer to this question being the difference in the physical characteristics of the shock-waves generated by the two kinds of explosion. Today the question seems academic. Indeed, it was academic in the 1950s. I have a note that I penned after my 1955 visit to Albuquerque in which I wrote that, if blast pressures as high as those that had been found to be the threshold for casualties in the case of conventional bombs were to prove correspondingly dangerous after a nuclear explosion, the number of people who would be exposed to risk, whether they were troops in the field or civilians in towns or in the countryside, would be enormous. Depending on its yield, pressures of this magnitude would be experienced miles from the burst of a hydrogen bomb. I failed to see how the information which our experiments might provide could have any practical value since, whatever was done, hundreds of thousands, even millions, of people would be killed. But dreary though the problem was scientifically, it had to be investigated for, in those innocent days, the authorities were thinking seriously about building shelters to protect against a nuclear onslaught, at the same time as soldiers and sailors were conjuring up theoretical battles in which nuclear weapons were used. Something more than what had been published about Hiroshima and Nagasaki seemed essential if any sense was to be made of proposals for a shelter policy, or of the use of nuclear weapons in warfare. Since the Americans were barred by law from telling us, we had to find out for ourselves.

Three government departments – the War Office, the now-defunct Ministry of Supply, and the Home Office, which has always been responsible for civil defence – were urging me to take on this additional work. Our studies of mine-detection by dogs were being pursued some fifty miles to the east of Birmingham, and many more miles away on the south coast. Our preliminary work on blast was being carried out, as I have said, to the east of London. It was all too much of a good thing, particularly since the researches of my department had progressed so fast that we were already submitting for publication in scientific journals some forty papers every year. The military authorities therefore proposed that, were I to agree to continue with the work which they wanted done, I could recruit for the purpose a full-time research student, build our own shock-tube, and concentrate as much of our 'war work' as possible in part of a disused military camp not too far from Birmingham.

Official agreement was one thing; action another. I recruited an excellent young research student – James McGregor. Bill Penney, then the Director of the Atomic Weapons Research Establishment at Aldermaston, helped us design our shock-tube, and a site was selected for the new laboratories, with money allocated for the necessary conversion of existing army huts. But that is where the effort to pull together all our military work ended. Just about the time when the money for the necessary conversions was starting to run out, and with much still left to be done, I had to start considering the practical implications of our participation in what turned out to be the last series of British atmospheric nuclear tests, codenamed Buffalo.

These were due to take place at Maralinga in Australia in 1956. The first request for my participation had come at the end of 1953. I was asked to investigate the effects of nuclear blast on human beings, using laboratory animals and dummy figures of men as test objects. The request was put to me at the start of our shock-tube experiments – the authorities also being aware that I was involved in the investigation of these same problems in New Mexico. An extensive series of tests of the effects of an atomic bomb explosion on a wide variety of 'targets', (e.g. tanks, concrete shelters, and so on) was being precisely planned down to the last detail, and a vast army of experts of one kind and another was involved.

Even though our own job was little more than a walk-on part, it consumed a fair amount of my time, more of Peter Krohn's – whom I had already introduced to the Albuquerque team – and all of McGregor's. At first only the three of us were slated to go to Australia, but when I realized how much needed to be done, I called in Sandy Thomson (p. 12). In the end, I had to drop out. Until we were at Maralinga no-one could tell us the exact date of the shot for which our work was planned – all depended on weather and various other factors. I simply did not have the time to hang around in Australia. Apart from my work in Birmingham and Whitehall, I had also arranged to be in America for some scientific meetings, the dates of which could not be adjusted to the variable one of the test in Australia. Nothing was lost by my not going. What Peter and the others learnt from the experiments that we had planned added little to what we already knew – except that we were now better able to fit our understanding of the primary and secondary effects of blast into the wider context of nuclear destruction.

There was, however, some useful 'fall-out' from our participation in the Buffalo trials. The little we had learnt made it clear that there would be no point in continuing with our shock-tube experiments. So, in agreement with Patrick Johnson, who had become Scientific Adviser to the Army Council, I decided to call a halt to the conversions in the army camp. Johnson and I had known each other in Oxford before the war, when he was a chemistry don. He had joined the forces at the outbreak of war, and I had run into him on my first visit to the Western Desert at the beginning of 1943. Like Wansbrough-Jones, he had decided to remain in military service after the war. But being an understanding academic, he took steps to see that McGregor was not left high and dry now that I had decided to abandon the work for which he had been recruited. So far as I was concerned, the end of our experiments on blast came as a blessed relief, and this despite the fact that I had already been drawn by the RAF into theoretical discussions of higher nuclear policy.

PART IV

A Professional in Whitehall

Recruitment, or the Defence Adviser

A few days after the world learnt that Hiroshima and Nagasaki had been destroyed, Cyril Connolly asked me to write an article on the atomic bomb for *Horizon*, the small highbrow monthly that he had managed to keep alive during the war. I sent him a hurriedly written piece, but by September so much had already appeared in the daily and weekly press that Connolly decided that my article would hardly be topical by the time he could publish. He therefore sent what I had written to a journal called *World Review*, from which I then withdrew it, giving as reason that during the two months that had elapsed since I had written my piece, the points that I had made, while perhaps worth making in the week after the bombs had been dropped, had become all too obvious. My text makes strange reading today.[1] One view that I expressed was that it was silly to imagine that 'the use of the bomb, or of some future atomic missile', could be prohibited. 'One cannot', I wrote, 'start applying the ethical argument at an arbitrary point in the scale of destruction.' I was also naive enough to suggest that decisions about the future of 'the atom' should be left to an international body of scientists who understood what the real issues were. 'It would be a pity', I said, if the world 'blew up now as a result of the fumbling of some national scientist working in secrecy to improve the present explosive.'

There had been little argument about the ethics of bombing during the war years. Ever bigger bombs had then been the order of the day, despite the fact that it had become clear from analyses of the actual results of bombing – including my own on air-raid casualties – that *in general* more damage was being caused by a load of smaller bombs, including small incendiaries, than by an equivalent load either of a few bombs or of only a single bigger bomb. The Civil Defence Research Committee, of which I was a member, had been asked in 1944 to give its views about the likely effects of the shock-wave from what we were told would be a vastly more powerful explosive than the kind with which we had been dealing – presumably what was implied was an atomic bomb. The task was passed to the R&D department of the wartime Ministry of Home Security. Since nothing was then known about the likely yield of an atom bomb, our estimates were based on the arbitrary and, as it turned out, ridiculous under-estimate that an atom bomb would yield, when detonated, only a hundred times more destructive energy than one would expect from the same weight of conventional explosive – not a fifteen to twenty thousand times increase as proved to be the case with the bombs that destroyed the two Japanese cities.

I had been somewhat offhand, too, in the reference I made to the atom bomb in my final paragraphs of the British Bombing Survey Unit's Overall Report (p. 145).[2] The peculiarity of atomic bombs, so I wrote, 'lies not so much in the amount of physical destruction that can be encompassed at a single stroke, as in the fact that they represent the most devastating anti-personnel weapons that have yet been produced. Atomic bombs are not weapons that could be economically used in the elimination of dispersed industrial plants, nor, as we know them today, are they weapons of choice in the destruction of railway or power facilities, although they might prove very effective in the devastation of such targets as the surface industrial complex associated with mining operations. Unless, therefore, atomic bombs become available in sufficient quantity for use against such specific targets as large railway centres, or concentrated industrial areas, their application will be limited to the heterogeneous extended type of target that is constituted by large cities' . . . and by 'human beings in the mass.' I had become so inured to the study of death and destruction that I am sure that I was unconscious of the insensitivity of my words. A few years were to pass before I asked myself whether, given that both sides had nuclear weapons, so-called strategic bombing had any relevance in an East–West conflict.

Since we were both members of Alan Barlow's committee on scientific policy and manpower, I saw Patrick Blackett frequently during the first two postwar years. When we had first met in the thirties, Patrick was on the scientific subcommittee of the Committee of Imperial Defence, and had sided with Sir Henry Tizard in his arguments with Lord Cherwell. After Hiroshima, Patrick had been in touch with some of the American physicists who had been involved in the development of the atomic bomb, but who, as the Manhattan Project approached its climactic end, had warned the American Government about the disruptive political consequences that would follow if the bomb were ever used. Now that it had been, Patrick tried to convey the same message to the British Government.

Despite the fact that he was Deputy Prime Minister in the War Cabinet, Attlee did not know that Churchill and President Roosevelt had agreed in Quebec in 1943, and a year later at Roosevelt's Hudson Valley house, that the United States and the UK would continue to cooperate in the exploitation of nuclear energy when the war ended, both in the civil and military fields. It was not until he became Prime Minister on 27 July 1945, and had taken Winston Churchill's place at the Potsdam conference, that he learnt for the first time about the 'bomb'. On 16 July, during the course of that meeting, President Truman had received the news that an atomic bomb had been successfully tested at Alamogordo in New Mexico. When he joined the conference some twelve days later, Attlee was informed in writing about the test, but he clearly did not appreciate its significance. Stalin, who was also told, did. The Potsdam meeting ended on 2 August, and Truman went straight back to Washington.

The destruction of Hiroshima by a single bomb on 6 August, only four days later, came as a considerable shock to Attlee. Before Nagasaki was effaced in the same way three days later, he sent a telegram to Truman in which he referred to the 'widespread anxiety as to whether the new power will be used to serve or to destroy civilization'.[3] Attlee went on to urge the President to join him in making an immediate declaration that the UK and the USA would be prepared to become 'trustees [of the atom] for humanity in the interests of all peoples in order to promote peace and justice in the world'. Truman, however, was also in the dark about the Quebec agreement and was not prepared to enter into any bilateral arrangement with the UK, particularly as Senator Brien McMahon had already* introduced his Bill calling for the exclusive American control of atomic energy.†

*Soon after Japan's formal surrender on 2 September 1945.
†Truman was equally unaware of the 'understanding' between Roosevelt and Churchill which was recorded in an *aide-mémoire* that the two had signed at Hyde Park. As was to transpire some years later, the American note of the meeting had got mixed up with

Anticipating that the Bill would be passed, Attlee had sanctioned the building in the UK of a nuclear reactor to make fissionable material, and had encouraged the British Chiefs of Staff to provide an estimate of the number of bombs they would like. The formal decision that the UK would go ahead was taken secretly in October 1946, and as secretly ratified in January 1947 by a handful of Attlee's Cabinet colleagues, amongst whom the voice of Ernest Bevin, the Foreign Secretary, was decisive.[4] In his view, without the bomb, the UK would become subservient to America. The consideration that weighed heavily with Attlee was the possibility that America would 'go isolationist', with the UK being left on its own to withstand pressure from the USSR.

During all this time, Patrick Blackett had been advising Attlee that the UK should not develop its own nuclear arsenal. In September 1945, soon after the fighting stopped, he had also taken the lead in organizing a meeting to consider 'the social implications of the atomic bomb'. Most of the physicists who spoke (a few of whom had been involved in the development of the bomb in the US) shared his views.

I found the discussion both impressive and puzzling, for it left me with the feeling that somehow or other scientists were going to be blamed for all the ills of mankind. In a note which I penned after the meeting I wrote:

> It is political differences which make war, and wars will occur until these differences are ironed out. If humanity is ever again so ill advised as to go to war undoubtedly atomic bombs will be used, whatever the views of scientists. It is conceivable, but highly improbable, that all scientists might make a resolve to stand out from a war and to act as an international body of conscientious objectors. If they did this, and did it in a proper way, they could constitute a brake on social disaster. It is however too much to ask that such a change could occur out of phase with the moral state of the rest of the world. It is far more likely that, if a war does

---

some other papers, and so mislaid. Truman was being advised by General Groves, among others. The McMahon Act became law in August 1946 and, until it was amended in 1958, it foreclosed any kind of British cooperation with the USA on either the military or the civil applications of the 'atom'.

break out, the majority of scientists in all countries will once again find themselves involved in the conflict.

'The problem,' I concluded, 'is not to stop the atomic bomb but to stop wars.'

Despite his heterodox views, Patrick was a member of the official advisory committee on atomic energy that Attlee set up in August 1945, and which was disbanded some two and a half years later; that is to say, after the decision had been taken that the UK would become an independent nuclear power. Patrick then decided to write a book explaining the strategic situation as he saw it.[5] I was one of those to whom he sent his text for comment, and my memory is that he accepted most of my suggestions, which were directed mainly at his denigration of so-called 'strategic' bombing. I have reread the book, and in retrospect I find it surprising that at the time I was much less interested in Patrick's strategic vision and political arguments than I was in toning down his more extreme assertions about the futility of all bombing operations.

Patrick was not the only prominent British scientist who was making his views known, both publicly and privately, in opposition to what was clearly becoming government nuclear policy. Another was my new colleague at Birmingham University, Mark Oliphant.

Early in 1947 Mark asked me to comment on a short paper that he had written on 'military policy'.[6] It concluded with the statement that 'if a policy of strict disarmament and neutrality is incompatible with the global interests of UK', the right thing to do was to produce nuclear weapons in cooperation with 'the Commonwealth'. His reason for bringing in the Commonwealth was that any nuclear attack by an aggressor on the UK could wipe out the 'motherland' at a stroke. And, as Mark put it, if the new United Nations Organization failed in its peace-keeping responsibilities:

> Britain has a finite chance of avoiding attack . . . in only two ways. She can be strictly neutral, in peace as in war, or she can arm herself in such a way as to be able to inflict deadly reprisal upon Europe if she is attacked. This last policy might be a deterrent to the outbreak of war, but it could never save the UK from destruction if she becomes involved in the war.

I was more inclined to agree with Mark than with Patrick about the right policy for the UK, and at his request I therefore approached Tizard, and asked him to see Mark, who, a week or so later, sent me a note saying that he had now spoken to Tizard, who had assured him that they 'have the matter in hand and know all the answers'.[7] Mark, however, was doubtful. He did not know 'who among them has any real knowledge of AE [atomic energy], but,' as he wrote, 'perhaps this does not matter'. Tizard gave Mark an opportunity to ventilate his views by appointing him to a committee set up to consider the implications of atomic energy for defence policy. I doubt whether this helped anyone, or influenced the course of events.

As Tizard's deputy in running the ACSP, it was widely assumed that I was also concerned with nuclear matters. Consequently I often had to confess to my total ignorance of what UK policy was in this field – and in retrospect it is remarkable how ignorant were many of those who carried major political responsibility. For example, at the time of the 1948 Communist coup in Czechoslovakia, Nye Bevan, a major figure in Attlee's Cabinet, asked me to find out whether it would be feasible to prevent any further encroachment of Soviet power by laying a belt of 'atomic mines' across Europe – as though these could be turned out overnight like ordinary mines. I had to confess that I did not know whether nuclear mines existed, and that anyhow, if they did, the idea was nonsense since paratroopers could cross any belt of mines.

Even senior military people were totally in the dark about the nature and effects of nuclear explosions. In the early fifties, arrangements were being made for what was to be the first test of a British atomic weapon – at Monte Bello in the Pacific in October 1952. Dickie Mountbatten had returned from his Vice-Regal post in India and was now Fourth Sea Lord. At a party given in Admiralty House in 1951 by Lord Pakenham,* the Minister in charge of the Navy, Dickie pulled me into a corner to talk about rumours that the Americans were also about to test, but something called a hydrogen bomb. He was very worried. Couldn't a nuclear explosion at sea cause a chain reaction and blow up the whole ocean? Having reminded him that I was not a nuclear physicist, I said that I was sure that the scientists who were involved would not be so mad as to risk blowing up the whole globe.

*Later the Earl of Longford.

In 1954, during the course of a visit to Paris, I had called on Larry Norstad, who by now was Air Deputy to the Supreme Commander. We lunched alone in a private dining room in the NATO HQ building, and had a wide-ranging conversation about NATO policy. Suddenly he suggested that we slipped along the corridor to sneak a look at a party of German generals who were about to be shown into the Supreme Commander's, General 'Al' Gruenther's,* office. Arrangements were being made for West Germany's entrance into NATO in the following year, and Larry wanted to see General Steinhoff, the famous German fighter-pilot, in the flesh. It was a curious moment. Two years later Larry himself was Supreme Commander, and, soon after, I received an invitation to give the opening address at a NATO conference on Operational Research. This was held in Paris in the spring of 1957. The way Larry introduced me must have bewildered his audience. We still argued, he said, whether he, the Supreme Commander, or I, a Professor of Anatomy, had won the war.

The fact that I was clearly on close terms with the Supreme Commander added to the attention that was given to my speech. By then, too, my views about the military and political significance of nuclear weaponry were becoming both clearer and unconventional, largely as a consequence of my association with the programme of work that I had designed for Randy Lovelace in Albuquerque. Rereading my

*Al Gruenther, whom I had met in the Mediterranean theatre during the course of the Second World War, succeeded General Ridgway as Supreme Commander NATO in May 1953. When Joan and I were in Washington in 1949, soon after the Russian imposition of the blockade of Berlin, we accepted the Norstads' invitation to dine on an evening when the Science Counsellor at the British Embassy had thrown a cocktail party in our honour. Both our hosts were confident that we could manage the two engagements. The Norstads were then living in Fort Mayer, the enclave for senior Air Force officers, where Spaatz had been living when I dined with him in 1946.[8] It was late when we left the Counsellor's party, and I soon realized that our chauffeur did not know the way. After a fairly long drive we entered a military residential compound which I could see at once was not Fort Mayer. I asked the driver to pull up at one of a row of grand colonial-style houses – one with a portico that covered two floors – and to ask if General Norstad lived anywhere nearby. We could see the driver standing in the hall chatting to someone for a couple of minutes. When he returned he had a wry look on his face. 'What do you know,' he said. 'You were right. That was General Gruenther. He was on the telephone to your general, who had just told him that his two English guests must have got lost. I now know the way.' He had driven us to the wrong fort, and we were nearly an hour late. Larry and I spent some minutes marvelling at the coincidence of the timing of his telephone call. We did not know then that fate was to throw us together again in debates about strategic policy.

address, I find it interesting that one of the points which I made – that technical developments might become a hindrance to clear military thinking – was later to become a dominating theme in my approach to military matters. To illustrate the point, I observed that

> if all-out nuclear warfare really does mean mutual suicide, and if it were ever to break out, those who survive, or their descendants – such as they might be – might well judge that technical developments of the 1940s had led to somewhat disastrous national and military policies and strategies. This, rather bluntly, is what I mean by the danger of technological developments forming strategies which may be incompatible with presumed national interests. Equally, these nuclear developments might prove quite ineffective for dealing with localized military situations which are perfectly reasonable in their strategic aims. The critical problem here would be not the usefulness of, say, nuclear weapons, but the difficulty of restricting their use either by limiting the size of weapons or by confining the geographical area in which they are used, through a policy of graduated deterrence. The trouble is that nobody has yet agreed on a set of rules for the Atomic Age.[9]

The RAF did not wait to hear whether Attlee's inner Cabinet had ratified the decision that the UK would 'go nuclear', before it started to lay plans to build aircraft as 'delivery vehicles' for nuclear bombs. As a result, three new V-bombers were being readied for deployment by the end of the 1950s. By then, however, the scene had been transformed by two critical developments. First, the era of the nuclear ballistic missile had dawned. In 1957 the UK accordingly embarked upon the construction of a liquid-fuelled nuclear ballistic missile called Blue Streak. Second, the Soviet Union had started deploying air defences which made it highly unlikely that our V-bombers could safely penetrate Soviet airspace. In parallel with Blue Streak, we had consequently started to develop a nuclear glide-missile called Blue Steel, which the V-bombers could launch from outside Soviet airspace. In effect it was a 'cruise' missile which, while it did not have the range to threaten Moscow, was able to reach Leningrad.

To this day I do not know what technical considerations had led the

Government to choose Blue Streak, based as it was on an early American missile, as the linchpin of British defence policy. In 1957, Duncan Sandys, the Minister of Defence, announced that the basis of future UK defence policy was 'the power to threaten retaliation with nuclear weapons'.[10] At the same time he warned that the United Kingdom could not be defended against a nuclear assault. The Government's new plans immediately came under attack, both in Parliament and in the press.[11] The RAF was also little pleased by the Government's decision. They were committed to their manned V-bombers.

Early in 1958, Air Chief Marshal Sir Dermot Boyle, the Chief of the Air Staff, and Sir Maurice Dean, then the Air Ministry's Permanent Secretary, both of whom I knew from the war years, asked me to chair what they called an Air Ministry Scientific Policy Committee. I was, however, so busy with other work when the invitation came that I had to tell them that since I could not put 'the right amount of drive into the job' until the end of the year, the Ministry should look elsewhere for a chairman. The answer was that they would prefer to wait until I was ready. In consequence, the new committee did not have its first meeting until six months after I had been approached. The other members were Sir William Cook, then Deputy Director of the Aldermaston nuclear-weapons laboratory, a post to which he had been appointed after more than twenty years' experience of government defence science; William Hawthorne, then Professor of Applied Thermodynamics in Cambridge; and James Lighthill, at the time Professor of Applied Mathematics in Manchester. I had met Cook in connection with our shock-tube work, but the others were new to me.

After some months we submitted an interim report that dealt with the concept of nuclear deterrence in the light of the UK's actual military commitments. We began by pointing out that it was illogical to talk about assuring national security by way of a policy of deterrence if that meant that nuclear weapons would actually be used in a 'first strike', and if the United Kingdom were consequently destroyed by a retaliatory blow. We were therefore worried by the confused way in which the term 'credibility' had started to be used in discussions of nuclear weaponry. Some used it in a political sense to imply that, come what may, the Government meant what it said when it declared that, if attacked, the UK would retaliate with nuclear weapons. By others the term was being employed as though it had to do with the weapon itself, to imply that nuclear weapon systems had to be both reliable technically, and also invulnerable to attack. Our view was that Great Britain was too small geographically for it to be sensible to deploy a mobile system of nuclear launchers. On the other hand, we were not at one in our views about the question of whether Blue Streak could be regarded as an effective deterrent even if the missiles were buried in underground silos. For that reason we suggested that the time was ripe to start considering what its successor system should be. The only sensible alternatives that could then be envisaged were either a force of long-endurance aircraft armed with 'stand-off' (i.e. cruise) weapons, or missile-firing nuclear-powered submarines.

The reasoning that led to these obvious conclusions is so commonplace today that I find it difficult to believe that at the time – thirty years ago – our discussions seemed to partake of the quality of an intellectual debate. Much of our thinking was based on guesswork. But what in retrospect strikes me most is the fact that during the whole time that my committee was at work, we were never properly informed about the technical talks that were then going on in Geneva regarding a possible test-ban. It was as though these matters were being dealt with by a section of the Foreign Office that was not involved in discussions of military policy.

By the time I was ready to send Dermot Boyle a second report on the 'deterrent', my position in the world of defence was about to undergo an abrupt change. I had been invited by Lee duBridge, then the President of Caltech, to spend the months of May and June 1959 as a visiting professor in Pasadena, and to deliver the Commencement Address on the occasion of the annual degree-giving ceremony. Needless to say, when the time came to leave for the United States, I had so much work on my hands, both academic and 'extracurricular', that I was reluctant to go. On the other hand I had just emerged from my gruelling encounter with the Zoo rebels (p.61). I could do with a change and a holiday. My friends in Caltech and Hollywood beckoned, and I had no fears that my absence would disrupt the progress of my thriving department in Birmingham.

I was not disappointed. Joe Koepfli, who had chaired the NATO Task Force of which I had been a member, had few duties and considerable means. He gave me the free run of his luxurious house in Pasadena, which was looked after by a well-trained Philippino. Joe was seldom there, but on occasion I stayed with him in Santa Barbara at another of his houses. Bob Robertson and other faculty colleagues entertained me often and well, and whenever I had the time, I was driven to Beverly Hills to spend a day or two with the Gershwins, or with Alfred and Alma Hitchcock. My only 'work' comprised a few seminars with students in the biology school. When on campus, I therefore spent most of my time in the library, reading widely on the subject of 'liberty'. I had decided to take as the theme of my address 'liberty in an age of science', treating science as a process that enriches our lives through the growth and exploitation of knowledge, at the same time as the way we spend our lives is determined and circumscribed by its very exploitation.

Joan and I exchanged letters frequently, and I had also arranged to be kept informed about what was going on in my department and in the Zoological Society. Papers were also sent by the secretaries of my Air Ministry Policy Committee. Then one day came a letter from Sir Richard Powell, the Permanent Secretary of Defence, which disturbed me greatly. He wanted to know whether I would consider taking on the post of chief scientist to the Ministry in succession to Sir Frederick Brundrett, who was due to retire at the end of the year. I delayed more than a week before replying. My academic appointments had been of my own choosing, and during the five years of war I had also 'done my own thing' without waiting to be told what to do by my scientific elders. In the postwar years I had engaged in committee work in Whitehall because it was stimulating and because it provided an opportunity to learn about 'public science'. But now I was being asked to become a full-time civil servant.

There was no one around to help in my cogitations, and for days I wondered how to reply. In the end I wrote to say that I would consider the proposal, on the understanding that I did so 'in principle' only. The letter was still on my mind when, surrounded by members of the faculty and bedecked in heavy academic robes, I stood in the full heat of the Californian sun on an open-air dais in front of a vast crowd of students and parents. I soon realized that my Commencement Address was of no interest to an audience of parents who were there to see their offspring being handed their diplomas. I even wondered whether the members of faculty on the platform were interested in the message that I was trying to convey. When, some time later, the paper appeared in print, it attracted far more attention than it ever did on that hot day.[12]

On my return to London I explained my misgivings to Sir Richard Powell. I then saw Eddie Playfair, now the Permanent Under Secretary of State in the War Office who, with Maurice Dean of the Air Ministry, had conceived the idea that I should be recruited rather than have Brundrett replaced by another professional 'defence scientist'. Duncan Sandys, the Minister of Defence, simply could not understand that I was unprepared to consider the post if it meant that I would have to abandon my academic work and resign from the secretaryship of the Zoo.

With everything still in the air I returned to the United States to take part in an international symposium on population growth. It was a fascinating meeting – held at the military academy of West Point during vacation time – and at its end I was called upon to sum up several days of discussion in an hour-long after-dinner speech. When we disbanded, a few of us were invited to spend a few more days at the Rockefeller Institute in New York in order to prepare the text of a book for immediate publication. By the end of the allotted time, however, my after-dinner speech was the only contribution that was ready for the press. It was published in the American journal *Science*.[13]

But I was not allowed to put Powell's proposal out of my mind during the course of the meeting. First came a message from Joan telling me that Chapman Pincher had published a piece in the *Daily Express*, not only saying that I had been approached to take over from Brundrett, but implying that I was behaving as though the job was beneath me. Eddie Playfair had asked Joan to telephone to warn me to say nothing if any reporters approached me before my return. Our Washington Embassy then telephoned with a similar message. A third call was the more interesting. As the chairman of the main scientific advisory board to the Pentagon, Bob Robertson had been told about the invitation and about my reluctance to commit myself. He telephoned from Washington to say that my American friends hoped that I would accept, and that if I did, there was no help which they could provide that would be denied me. If any single thing finally tipped the scales, it was that.

When I returned, the summer holiday season was in full swing, but before joining Joan and the children in Birmingham, I decided to see

Brundrett again, so as to learn something about the job. Since I was still hesitating, he suggested that he could try to arrange to carry on for a further year – making it plain that he himself was in no hurry to go. I discussed the matter with Sir Robert Aitken, the Vice Chancellor of Birmingham University, to see whether he would allow me to retain full responsibility, but without pay, for my department, were I to get Duncan Sandys to agree that I could take up the Defence post on that condition. Knowing that I would not have suggested such an arrangement if it meant that the department would suffer, Rob readily undertook to obtain formal assent for so strange a precedent. That done, Joan and I, plus children, went off to Burnham Thorpe in Norfolk for our usual summer holiday near the sea.

By the time I was next in London, Dickie Mountbatten had been transferred from his post as First Sea Lord to that of Chief of the Defence Staff. He asked me to dine to talk the matter over, but because I had arranged to meet my Air Ministry Scientific Policy Committee on the evening he suggested, I said that I would drop in after dinner. Dickie and Edwina, his wife, were alone when I arrived at their house. When Edwina learnt that I had eaten only a few sandwiches, she went in search of food, returning a few minutes later with a wing of cold chicken – all there was, she said apologetically. We went over my reservations for more than an hour before I said that it was time for me to leave. Both of them came to the door and followed me on to the pavement, with Dickie holding one hand saying that I had to accept, and Edwina the other, declaring that if Dickie was to make a success of his new job it was essential that I worked with him. Years later Dickie used to tell the story – once, I remember, in a speech at a public luncheon – embellishing it by saying that it was only when he and Edwina had all but wrenched my arms off that I had said 'yes'. In fact, Duncan Sandys had not yet agreed my terms – that I would not have to resign either my chair in Birmingham or the secretaryship of the Zoo. This he did a few days later, smiling wryly as he repeated that he couldn't understand why I wouldn't resign from the Zoo. In the light of all the trouble which that association was to go on causing me, I sometimes wish I had heeded his words.

After all the agonizing of the previous six months, the decision was an enormous relief. As I look back I can also see that I was far wiser than I knew when, years before, I decided not to be lured into full-time government service either by Lord Tedder or by Hugh Gaitskell. Hugh often said that when he became Prime Minister he would want me in the Cabinet Office as some kind of scientific and military adviser.[14] He never did become Prime Minister, but before his death I had become a full-time government servant.

I accepted the post of Chief Scientific Adviser to the Ministry of Defence, not only on my own terms, but fortified by a fairly considerable knowledge of the ways of Whitehall learnt as an 'independent' adviser. The two to three days a week that I used to spend in Whitehall had been a continuing and stimulating tutorial, helped and guided as I was by many civil service friends.

On 1 January 1960, I ceased to be a salaried professor. My Birmingham academic life otherwise remained unchanged. My department was already working a seven-day week, and becoming Chief Scientific Adviser to the Ministry of Defence merely meant that weekends became a bit more hectic than they already were. My responsibilities to the Zoological Society remained unchanged. I was also still Deputy Chairman of the Advisory Council on Scientific Policy as well as Chairman of both the Scientific Manpower Committee and the Committee on Natural Resources. Within days of taking over from Brundrett, I began to realize just how much information of a 'non-sensitive' kind, which would have been invaluable to the ACSP, had been denied them because of the barrier between civil and defence affairs. The only body from which I formally resigned was my Air Ministry committee, which I did when I submitted a report on air defences to Air Chief Marshal Sir Thomas Pike, who by then had succeeded Dermot Boyle as Chief of the Air Staff. It was plain that I could not continue as a member of a committee on whose recommendations I might, in another capacity, have to comment.

Bob Robertson was not the only one of my American scientist friends who had been interested in my move to the Ministry of Defence. After my appointment was announced in October 1959, a group, which included Bob and Rabi, came to London after attending a meeting at the NATO HQ in Paris. I was invited to lunch, mainly so that I could be introduced to George Kistiakowsky and Herbert York. Kistiakowsky, a tall and impressive-looking man, had recently succeeded James Killian as President Eisenhower's science adviser in the White House. He was a Russian emigré who in 1917 had fought in the

White Army against the Bolsheviks. He had then made his way to the United States where he began his brilliant academic career as a chemist. During the Second World War George was a leading member of the community of Los Alamos scientists who were producing 'the bomb', he himself being head of the team that designed the chemical implosive jacket for the nuclear fissile core. He had been given leave from his Chair of Chemistry at Harvard to become the President's science adviser.

Herb York, a nuclear physicist, was a much younger man, not quite as tall as George, but powerful-looking and stocky. He had been the director of the Livermore nuclear-weapons laboratory – under the shadow of Edward Teller – before becoming the Defense Department's first Director of Defense Research and Engineering, a post which in those days ranked third, so I was told, in the Defense Secretary's vast and complicated hierarchy. I must have seemed a strange animal to them, a biologist who knew nothing about military hardware, but who nevertheless had the reputation of knowing something about the facts of war. We got along famously, and at the end of lunch Rabi declared that, now that I had been fool enough to get myself trapped into a paid governmental job, he was sure that I would not be able to endure the post for even a year. As it was to turn out, I outlasted all of them in service to our respective governments.

Before returning to the United States, Herb York let me know through Bob Robertson that he thought it might be useful if he spent a day with me in Birmingham – he obviously wanted to size me up more carefully than had been possible in London with others around. Since the United Kingdom was the second most important power in the Western Alliance, I was in a sense his opposite number. The friendship we established then has continued unbroken to this day.

20

The Burdens of R&D

Duncan Sandys had been moved in October 1959 from the Ministry of Defence to that of Aviation, and Harold Watkinson, until then Minister of Transport and Civil Aviation, had been appointed in his place. I was introduced to him by Richard Powell, and it was Harold Watkinson who, in effect, formally approved my appointment as his Chief Scientific Adviser. Brundrett had always been listed in the official directory of civil servants as the Ministry's 'Chief Scientist'. I felt that the title was inappropriate for someone who knew as little as I did about the 'hardware' side of the military scene, and whose main interest was defence policy. Chief Scientific Adviser (CSA) seemed a more appropriate title. Not long after I took over, I was called to Number 10. Harold Macmillan wanted to wish me well, and to warn me that defence R&D was difficult to control. Projects begin, so he said, as small-fry, and then, continuing the piscatorial analogy, grow into sprats, and the sprats into herrings. If they are likely to be cancelled, kill them when they are no bigger than sprats, he advised. They are more difficult to get rid of when they are the size of a herring. Sir Norman Brook, the Cabinet Secretary, had already told me that in addition to being the Defence CSA, which was my public appointment, I was to be the Prime Minister's scientific adviser on defence policy and disarmament. That part was secret. And so it remained until Harold Wilson became Prime Minister in 1964.

In those days the home of the small Ministry of Defence was the wing of the Treasury Building that overlooks St James's Park, and in the sub-basement of which the War Cabinet and Defence Committee used to meet during the war years, and where Winston Churchill had spent many nights as well as days. I had first seen my office when it was Sir Henry Tizard's. It was large, ornate, oak-panelled, and lined with empty glass-fronted bookshelves. The room had started life as the library of what in the early years of the century was called the Office of Works. The empty shelves gave the room a dismal look, and a few months after I had settled in, I asked for them to be removed, threatening that if they were not, I would fill the cases with jars of anatomical specimens. When I returned from my summer holiday that first year, the shelves were gone, and the room had been redecorated.

The many years that I had spent as an amateur 'Whitehall warrior' had certainly not prepared me for the life of a full-time civil servant. Since business had to go on as usual, files, which before would have been immediately disposed of by Brundrett, piled up on my desk. Miss Connolly, a serious, tall thin woman, who had been Brundrett's personal secretary, and who became mine for seven years, did not know what to do as I pushed the files aside after a cursory reading. Brundrett would have added a paragraph or page to each. Weeks must have passed before I contributed anything in writing to a document, or verbally at the many meetings to which I was summoned almost daily.

Members of the small staff that I had inherited introduced themselves. By a happy chance I knew the most senior of them, E.C. ('Bill') Williams, a radar specialist who, on my return to the UK from the Mediterranean at the end of 1943, had taken over the direction of the Bombing Survey Unit that I had established there. There was Robert ('Bob') Press, another scientific civil servant, who served as a liaison officer between my office, the Foreign Office, and the Atomic Energy Authority, and who continued to serve on my staff until my retirement from government service twelve years later. There were also three 'one-star' officers, one from each of the Services, who served as my link with the Deputy Chiefs of their respective Service boards who were in charge of procurement. From time to time Dickie Mountbatten poked his head round the door to smile at my bewildered face. And I met Richard Chilver, Deputy Secretary to Richard Powell, who soon became one of my most treasured Whitehall tutors. There was a relentless clarity about his mind, and his questions about scientific or technical matters were always searching. His fault, if it is a fault, was that he had little patience with those who did not live up to his rigorous standards, nor did he disguise his disdain for those who failed to meet them, be they fellow civil servants, military chiefs, or Ministers.

Brundrett had spent his life in the Naval scientific service, and knew whom to approach in R&D establishments when he needed specific information. I didn't, and it happened that Bill Williams, on whom I had hoped to rely, was soon posted to the directorship of one of the NATO R&D establishments on the Continent. I was, however, fortunate in my choice of Clifford Cornford, another senior defence scientist, as his replacement. Cliff had spent his working life at the Royal Aircraft Establishment, and he came reluctantly, being suspicious of Whitehall. But he never returned to Farnborough. Cliff was the first, and one of the very few, scientists to become a Whitehall 'mandarin', his public career ending nearly twenty years later when, as Sir Clifford Cornford KCB, he retired from the post of Chief of Defence Procurement. Because I also needed help in my enquiries into defence policy, authority was given for the establishment of an addition to my staff, and I was joined by an experimental nuclear physicist, B.T. ('Terry') Price. For want of better designation, his post was called 'studies'. Terry Price has a quick, brilliant, and independent mind, and it was a joy to work with him once I managed to stop him giving me tutorials on the splendid research on nuclear fusion that was going on in the Culham Laboratory. He got on well with the military staff of the Ministry. One of the first things he did for me was choose as my principal private secretary a young Admiralty mathematician, Glyn Owen who, with a slight break, remained with me until my retirement from government service.

I also induced John Kendrew to join me in a part-time capacity, which was the most he was prepared to do.* John was one of the band of molecular biologists who had been set on their paths to greatness by Desmond Bernal. He was on the point of completing his analysis of the molecular structure of the complicated blood protein, haemoglobin, a piece of work that earned him a Nobel prize. He simply would not listen to me when I somewhat cynically gave him as my opinion that after so laborious and penetrating a study, he was very unlikely to turn his energies to the analysis of an even more complicated molecule. I was right. John never did go back to laboratory work. After becoming the first Director General of the European Molecular Biology Organization, whose foundation owed everything to his efforts, he became President of St John's College, Oxford.

Within days of my taking over from Brundrett, I had to chair the

*Now Sir John Kendrew FRS.

Defence Research Policy Committee (the DRPC), the now-defunct body that had been set up in 1946 in parallel with the Advisory Council on Scientific Policy. The committee then comprised the Deputy Chiefs of the Naval, Army and Air Staffs, each of whom had the responsibility for dealing with the operational requirements and procurement for his own Service. The chief scientists of the three Services were also members, as was the chief scientist of the Ministry of Aviation. A senior Treasury official sat in as silent observer, as did Richard Chilver. After a while I saw to it that both the latter spoke up as members in their own right.

It did not take long to discover that, despite its name, the committee had little to do with policy of any kind. Its essential function appeared to be that of setting an order of financial priority for the R&D needed to satisfy 'operational requirements' which the Services put up separately – ostensibly in the implementation of a coherent defence policy. The committee's recommendations went up to the Service Ministers and, more important, to the Minister of Defence. The budget that came under its purview when I took over was, at present day values, about £10,000 million (somewhat more than half of the total amount that the UK was then spending on all R&D). The bulk was always committed, mainly to the industrial firms that had been given contracts for the development of major equipment (i.e. missiles and aircraft). In effect, therefore, the committee was a gentlemanly forum in which the Services competed with each other for a share of the trivial amount of new money for 'research and development' that became available each year. It also had the notional responsibility of keeping under review the progress of all projects under development, while another bit of theory was that it advised about the merits and cost of allowing changes to be made in original specifications.

I was no innocent when I took over the DRPC. My committee on 'The Management and Control of Research and Development', which was still in being, had taken evidence from all the departments that were directly responsible for R&D which was financed by public money. Many of my Whitehall friends had hoped that, since the chairman of what in effect had been a disciplinary committee had now become chairman of the DRPC, defence R&D projects would never again be launched in the expectation that they would cost a fraction of what they eventually did or, what was worse, with the project being

197

abandoned before it even reached prototype stage. The parliamentary debate on the report echoed the same hope. The reality proved to be very different.

It was as plain to me as it was to Harold Watkinson, my Minister, that the total defence R&D programme was hopelessly overloaded, and that a few major items were responsible for most of the strain. When the war ended in 1945, the Ministry of Supply was promoting scores of weapon-development projects, many of which were still in being in 1960. The decision that Britain should become an independent nuclear power was taken in January 1947, with our first bomb being tested in 1952, and, as I have said, with the RAF having begun to plan for an operational nuclear bomber force as early as 1946. The Valiant and the Vulcan entered squadron service in 1955 and 1957 respectively, and the Victor in 1958. The Valiant was withdrawn in 1965, while the Victor was adapted as an air-to-air refuelling tanker. The Vulcan was still flying in 1982, when it was used during the Falklands war. In addition, a medium bomber, the Canberra, was also coming into service at the start of the fifties, and four fighters, which were later cancelled, were in various stages of development. There were other important aviation projects in the pipeline. The Royal Navy was developing its own fighter-bomber, the Buccaneer. The RAF was designing the TSR2 as a replacement for the subsonic Canberra which, although due to be withdrawn in 1965, was still operational in 1985. There was the P1127, a vertical take-off ground support machine, and a military transport, the HS681. Finally, there was the supersonic Concorde. The industry was also producing subsonic civil aircraft, of which the Viscount, a propeller-driven machine, was outstandingly successful, in contrast to the Comet, Britain's first jet passenger-aircraft.

The Services had clearly been operating as though the country could afford almost anything. The reality was utterly different. Defence had to be fitted into a new set of national priorities. It had proved impossible to spend the money that Hugh Gaitskell had allocated to defence in his final budget, and it was for that reason, not to prove that Nye Bevan had been right, that the figure was reduced by Winston Churchill when he became Prime Minister in 1951. We had also become part of the Western Alliance, in which our influence, however much we tried to magnify it, was small in relation to that of the US. If our efforts in defence R&D were to become rational and effective, it seemed essential to me that they had to be coordinated with those of the US and, wherever possible, with those of our other allies.

In the early summer of 1960 I flew to Washington for talks with Herb York. My visit happened to coincide with one which Dickie Mountbatten was making to the American Chiefs of Staff, and our Ambassador, Sir Harold Caccia,* arranged a dinner to entertain the various dignitaries with whom we were conferring. It was a warm evening, and I had first called on some friends, so that when I arrived, I found the rest of the Ambassador's guests having drinks on the terrace. As I moved to greet my host, Dickie leapt towards me, saying, 'Now you've let me down. The black dinner jackets outnumber the white. I could have sworn you'd wear a white one.' I waved to Harold Caccia, and so as to stop Dickie's badinage, said, 'There's George Kistiakowsky. Let's call him over.'

George joined us, and I congratulated him warmly, suggesting to Dickie that he should do the same. 'Tell me why,' he said, just as Herb York joined us. 'Because he's been elected a Foreign Member of our Royal Society,' I replied. Dickie offered his congratulations, and then added that his brother-in-law had also just been elected an FRS. 'What does your brother-in-law do?' asked Herb. 'What's his science? Physics, botany, or what?' Dickie hesitated a moment before saying, 'Oh, he's King of Sweden.' The look of amazement on the two American faces was understandable.

At dinner Harold Caccia sat at one end of his long table, with Dickie at the other. Herb was on Dickie's left. Between Herb and me was John McCone, then the head of the Atomic Energy Commission. I was in deep conversation with him about the moratorium on nuclear tests which the Russians had started unilaterally at the end of March 1958, when Herb reached his long arm across the front of McCone, and tugged at my lapel. 'Now he's talking about his son-in-law,' he said. 'If he imagines I'm going to ask who he is, he can think again!' It was an opportune moment to interrupt my conversation with McCone, who was trying to persuade me that the moratorium was a bad thing for the Alliance, and that I should try to persuade Harold Macmillan to agree that the US should break it.

*Now Lord Caccia.

The more formal talks that I had on that visit to Washington were rewarding. Those with George Kistiakowsky concerned the test-ban negotiations that were in progress between the US, the USSR and the UK, and a suggestion of mine that we should examine the NATO doctrine that nuclear weapons could be used as weapons in field warfare.

My meeting with Herb York had a far more immediate purpose. I was absolutely convinced that the UK could not continue to engage in every manner of defence R&D. TSR2 may have been the most prominent R&D project at the time, but there was also the P1127, on which the Hawker aircraft and the Bristol Siddeley engine companies had started work with help from the US Mutual Weapons Development Program (the MWDP), but in which, at the time, the RAF had no interest. Bristol Siddeley was running into difficulties with the vectored-thrust engine it was designing for the P1127, and was also overstretched with the Olympus engine which it was building for the TSR2, at the same time as it was modifying it – in fact redesigning it – for Concorde. Rolls-Royce, which I had regarded as the very symbol of all that was solid in British industry, was also in trouble. I learnt this shortly after I joined the Ministry of Defence. Sir Denning ('Jim') Pearson, the Managing Director of the vast engine factory in Derby, telephoned to ask if he could drive over to Birmingham to see me. I thought that it was a courtesy call, but it turned out that its purpose was to make me understand that Rolls-Royce, whose engines he told me were then powering more than half the aircraft that were flying in the world, was becoming swamped by the big American engine companies. As larger civil aircraft were coming into service, engines were increasing in size. Rolls-Royce had to be in the big league, and for this it needed help. Joining either of the two major American engine manufacturers – Pratt & Whitney and the General Electric Company – would not do. Neither had anything to gain from merging with Rolls-Royce, whereas the only American company that was likely to benefit was too small to make any difference to Rolls's fortunes. Pearson scoffed at the idea of getting together with SNECMA, the big French engine company. No – Rolls had to get into the American market on its own.

It was not only the British aircraft industry that was making inordinate claims on the public purse. The Air Force had its ground-to-air anti-aircraft missile, the Bloodhound (it is still operational!); but the Army had started to develop a different one, called the Thunderbird, which was withdrawn from service very soon after it was deployed. The Navy wanted new ships, and the Army new tanks. Weapon-systems standardization in NATO was getting nowhere. Every one of the member countries with an armaments industry put national interests first – the USA and the UK with their factories intact, and the French and the West Germans, and even smaller countries like the Netherlands, which were in the process of rebuilding what the war had destroyed.

While not as sanguine as I was about the possible outcome, Harold Watkinson had agreed that I should try to make whatever arrangements I could with Herb York that would help spread the R&D burden, and Herb was ready to try. So was Tom Gates, President Eisenhower's Secretary of Defense, to whom Herb reported. As Director of Defense Research and Engineering (DDR&E) in the Pentagon, Herb was nominally in control of some five times the amount of R&D money that came under my general purview, and the MWDP was also his responsibility. But as he saw it, a dollar bought much more R&D in the UK than it did in the United States. After the necessary allowances had been made, we agreed that the UK disposed of enough R&D resources to assume the prime responsibility for one-third of the spectrum of all military R&D, with the USA taking care of the other two-thirds. We parted on that understanding, and I returned to the UK expecting action to follow. None did. Herb may have been the supreme chief of all US defence R&D, but below him were directors of research in each of the three Services, as well as the directors of a number of other R&D defence agencies. Whenever an opportunity arose for the UK to cater for American as well as our own interests, it turned out that someone or other in the States had already committed funds for a corresponding project. There was also a deep reluctance on the part of the Americans to depend on any overseas source, however friendly, for the satisfaction of a defence requirement.

Very early in 1961 Herb, still in his thirties, suffered a heart attack, and after recovering, he resumed his academic career, interspersed with spells of government work. His place in the Pentagon was taken by Harold Brown, an even younger man, who had previously succeeded him as Director of the Livermore Laboratory. That was where I had first met him. Harold, who some fifteen years later became Secretary of Defense in the Carter Administration, was keen on reaching a better UK–US R&D agreement than the one that had proved abortive. At a preliminary meeting we devised a draft plan for the setting up of a joint pump-priming R&D fund, to which, if I remember correctly, the UK was to contribute £5 million at the start.

Our idea was that when the US and UK military had an interest in some new R&D project, both would bid for the work and for money from the fund. In April of 1961 Harold Watkinson visited Washington with a team of advisers, of whom I was one, for talks with Robert McNamara, the Defense Secretary in the Kennedy Administration. Harold records that the visit was not as relaxed as the one we had made the previous year to Tom Gates, but after 'a wide range of businesslike talks', he and Bob McNamara 'signed a formal undertaking, covering a policy for greater interdependence'.[1]

Once this had been agreed at ministerial level, Harold Brown and I decided that it would help if I sent a personal representative to Washington to keep up the pressure for cooperation. I chose as 'my man in the Pentagon' Will Hawthorne, (see p.187) who, as it happened, always spent part of the year in the States. The authorities in London agreed the necessary administrative costs, and also posted J.R. Christie, an Assistant Secretary from the Ministry of Aviation, to help Will.

On our return to London, Harold sent the Prime Minister a minute in which he told him about the Memorandum of Understanding that he had signed, and about talks regarding its implementation which I was due to start with John Rubel, one of Harold Brown's deputies. He warned that:

> . . . not everyone realizes that though the Americans can be self-sufficient if they choose, we shall increasingly find, as weapons become more and more complex, that we have to buy more equipment abroad or do without. What we are hoping from these discussions is to make matters less one-sided than they would otherwise be, and to reduce competition between the Americans and ourselves in Europe. In this situation we must have regard to politics as well as to commercial and financial considerations in the package deal with the Americans. I made it plain to the

Americans in Washington that this exercise must be a genuine 'two-way trade' if it is to be defensible in this country. It is on this basis that I have directed that the exercise shall start.

The only American proposal that I can recall ever having been put to me came from John Foster, Harold Brown's deputy, whom he succeeded in 1965 when Harold was appointed Secretary for the Air Force. Foster seriously suggested that the UK should set about designing a reusable space-launcher – this some twenty years before the Americans, after an expenditure of billions of dollars, first launched their Space-Shuttle! Johnny, to whom the improbable was always possible, was a Canadian by birth. Maybe he still saw the United Kingdom as the powerful Great Britain of his forebears when he put his proposal to me.

Harold Watkinson rightly says that the failure of the agreement to yield any material results was due to the pressure 'of the American arms lobbies and a desire on the part of the Kennedy Administration to recover a large share of the cost of policing the world by selling Americans arms and equipment'. A year later he again warned the Prime Minister that 'any arrangement with the Americans is unlikely to be successful because of the inability of the Administration, however willing they may be, to stand up to the pressures from the armament manufacturing industries in America. After all, they have never succeeded in controlling them in the past and it is difficult to see why they should now be more successful in the future.'

Despite the stillbirth of the scheme for general cooperation that Harold Brown and I had launched, Bob Robertson, true to his promise, did all that he could to help my small efforts to make sense prevail in the R&D field. Jim Pearson had suggested that since I had good friends in the Pentagon, I should arrange for one to visit the Rolls-Royce works in Derby so as to be persuaded that the company's Spey engine could power the American Phantom fighter-bomber, of which the production order had just been greatly increased. I did as he asked, and invited John Rubel.

John was a graduate of Caltech, and had had nearly twenty years of experience in a variety of R&D posts in industry. He was a cultivated and widely-read man, and we were both to become involved in the ill-fated Skybolt venture, about which more later. Late in 1961 he flew over to spend a weekend, the first of a series that happily has not yet ended. We drove to Derby, where the red carpet had been rolled out for him. Jim Pearson did everything to impress his visitor, and John was indeed impressed – but not enough. He said nothing to discourage the Rolls-Royce team, but when we got back to Birmingham he confessed that he would be hard pressed to persuade his colleagues that Rolls was as well geared to power the Phantom as was either Pratt and Whitney or GEC.

Some months later I visited the McDonnell plant, today McDonnell–Douglas, which was then producing the Phantom. This gave me a sense of the difference between British and American aircraft companies. Mr McDonnell was then turning out some twenty Phantoms a month, but he had agreed to double (maybe it was triple) the number. His twenty-aircraft production line was in full swing, and I innocently asked how it was going to be extended to increase its output. 'Oh,' said Mr McDonnell, pointing to a vast new building some distance away, 'a new line is being assembled there. It'll be ready soon and in production right after that. And then,' pointing to the enormous assembly-line where we were standing, 'all this will be swept away.' It was a dramatic indication of the difference between British and American production methods. In those days American companies, given that their products had defence labels, could count on the Federal Government to provide apparently limitless financial help.

I learnt a great deal from my frustrations in dealing with defence R&D. It had taken little intelligence to appreciate that the chaotic nature of the pattern of R&D projects that were before the DRPC was in part a legacy of past commitments, in part a result of cancellations, and in part a measure of the consequences of interService rivalry – a process to which I had been no stranger during the war years. What was equally clear was that the pattern was no more nor less irrational than what went by the name of defence policy. Both had undergone kaleidoscopic changes during the postwar years, and there seemed little doubt that more changes were to come. Moreover, their timing, whether because of political changes or financial stringency, was always unpredictable. Foreign and defence policy always reflects commitments made in, and to, the past, and is a patchwork whereby these are fitted to the realities of the present.

Obviously, too, those whose business it is to design new military

equipment always try to incorporate in their product the latest technological promises. Failure to surmount a technological obstacle is
frequent and results in unpredictable delays and increases in costs.
The situation becomes complicated by competition in weapons sales,
which, in turn, encourage small wars, uprisings, terrorism, wars of
national liberation – call them what we will – all of which then threaten
the stability of the relations between East and West, and by so doing
add momentum to the arms race.

The process was self-destroying. Like every other nation that
maintained military forces, we were involved in an arms race that
became ever more demanding and ever more costly. When I moved
into Brundrett's seat in 1960, we were still trying not only to outbid the

*'British scientists, madam, are
second to none, and if only the
Government would produce
adequate funds for research we
could produce a weapon that
would be just as obsolete as the
Americans' in half the time!'*

Osbert Lancaster
19/12/63

armament industries of the Warsaw Pact powers, but also those of the USA and of France. Our three Services were bidding against each other as well. Opposing national industrial interests prevented weapons standardization in NATO, where my first lesson had been the way the competition between the UK and the US to design a small-calibre rifle for NATO had ended (p.149). No wonder that when I urged the merits of R&D cooperation with our allies, members of my staff would tell me that it would cost more, in time as well as money, to embark on a defence project with a partner than to do it on our own.

For me the essential trouble was that our prevailing pattern of R&D, which in theory the DRPC controlled, had never been designed in accordance with a rational overall plan of defence needs. Polite though our deliberations were, the Admiral, General and Air Marshal who represented the three Services on the DRPC, were concerned to fight their own corners. What I found even more odd was that the assumed cornerstone of British defence policy, the 'nuclear deterrent', did not fall within the scope of the committee's responsibilities.

In one of the Lees Knowles Lectures that I delivered in 1965 in Cambridge, to the general theme of 'scientists and war', I described what I had learnt in my efforts to apply the recommendations of my Committee on the Management and Control of Research and Development. Richard Chilver had helped me formulate in strict logical terms what I had called an 'inexorable law of R&D'. This 'law' states that, because of the increasing technical complexity of modern weapons, the cost of the underlying R&D increases so rapidly that, with few exceptions, each new generation of equipment that emerges in the arms race between the powers costs much more than the one it replaces, not only in money but also in trained manpower. Moreover, because the cost of developing a weapon system of a given degree of sophistication is much the same in all advanced industrialized countries, the absolute size of the economy usually determines the outcome. 'The greater the "buy" over which these costs can be spread, the lower the resultant unit cost. For this reason alone, the United States and the Soviet Union by their very size can, therefore, always expect to produce sophisticated weapon systems more cheaply than we can in Britain.'

If, I went on to argue, our Gross National Product were to rise as a result of greater productivity, with the same proportion – taking inflation into account – always being devoted to defence, the absolute increase in purchasing power would not mean 'more defence'. Unless we were prepared to spend a larger proportion of our Gross National Product on defence, increasingly expensive re-equipment could be afforded only if we were prepared to reduce the manpower cost, in other words the size of our forces. Alternatively we could, of course, 'buy from the cheapest shelf' abroad, a measure that was usually regarded as unpatriotic.

But, I insisted, in the end all such measures are no more than palliatives. If Britain wanted to be efficient in defence, our equipment could not be allowed to become obsolete. Equally, we could not assume that a rising share of the Gross National Product would be allotted to defence during peacetime. 'Therefore, the alternatives between which we are forced to choose are to plan on altering our tasks (i.e. commitments) so as to avoid the need to introduce some of the most expensive new weapon systems; or to make our forces smaller; or a combination of both these measures.'

I have thought hard about these propositions since I formulated them more than twenty years ago, and I believe that they are even more relevant today – not only to the UK but to all who are caught up in the arms race between East and West. There is no finishing post to the race unless, of course, it were stopped by the ultimate disaster of an East–West war. The cost of rearmament or 'modernization' – as some now term the process to make it sound more palatable politically – cannot but go on rising at a rate greater than the rate of increase in the fund of resources that can be devoted to all public expenditure. This conclusion applies as much to the USA, and presumably to the USSR, as it does to Britain. The economic burden can on occasion be reduced in the short term by arms sales or by the application to civil industry of some useful technological development made in the course of a piece of defence R&D. That, however, occurs far more rarely than is thought. Japan, which has now all but outstripped the US in hightech industry, has done so by focusing directly on the civil field. It has not waited for spin-offs from defence contracts. As Charles Lamb put it, there is no need to burn down a whole house in order to have roast pork.

It became clear to me soon after I started in the Ministry of Defence that the inexorable law of R&D was already having a major influence on our defence and foreign policies. We could no longer afford to maintain forces in the Far and Middle East. The 'law' has gone on working, even though we no longer have the scattered military commitments which, as a colonial power, we were trying to discharge thirty years ago.

21

Cancellations and Survivals

Every one of the six years that I served as CSA to Defence was associated with a request to trim the R&D budget by 'x' or 'y' millions of pounds. Since most, if not all the money was always committed, the result was that when an urgent new demand surfaced, either additional resources had to be sought – always a matter of lengthy and often fruitless negotiation with the Treasury – or some project that was already in the programme had to be eliminated. The easy way of achieving economies by imposing a small percentage cut all round was pointless, since it was inevitable that the cost of what remained in the R&D programme would go on increasing automatically with each year. That was how the 'inexorable law of R&D' operated.

One of my early lessons in the way the Services worked concerned a ground-to-air defence system known as PT428, which was in competition for resources with a ground-to-ground nuclear missile that went by the name of Blue Water. Both were under development, but one had to be cancelled, and the Treasury did not mind which. PT428 was a highly sophisticated RAF project for an all-weather, day or night, automated anti-aircraft weapon; Blue Water was an army weapon designed for use on a presumed nuclear battlefield. I was warned that it would be impossible to reach a decision if the matter were discussed by the DRPC which, in my innocence, I still thought was where the question should have been debated. Instead I was advised to invite the Deputy Chiefs of the Services, who were responsible for R&D, to my room, and not to let them leave until a clear decision had been agreed. If needs be, I was to provide them with sandwiches and drinks.

The meeting was a lengthy one, and in the end we recommended the cancellation of PT428. My own view, which I made perfectly clear, was that Blue Water should go. While I recognized that PT428 was highly ambitious from a technical point of view, it made more sense to spend such money as was available on a weapon system that had some ostensible military purpose, than on one which I thought had none. For all I knew, the three Deputy Chiefs may well have decided what the recommendation should be before they entered my room. In those days there was a certain amount of mutual back-scratching in these matters, with 'Buggins' knowing that his turn would come.

The 'lead contracts' for both Blue Water and PT428 had been placed with English Electric (the aircraft component of which is now incorporated in British Aerospace). Lord Caldecote, an engineer whose professional career had begun as a lecturer in Cambridge, was in charge of the PT428 project. He was utterly cast down by the decision, and tried to make me understand what it meant in terms of the laying-off of high-grade technical staff. If it would help, he was prepared to relax the PT428 specifications to reduce the cost – for example, to design the missile for operation only in fair weather and in daylight. Total cancellation, he said, would be a disaster.

I could never have anticipated what came next. Little more than two weeks after he had taken over as Minister of Defence in 1962, Peter Thorneycroft cancelled Blue Water without, to the best of my memory, ever having discussed the matter either with me, his new Chief Scientific Adviser, or with anyone on my staff. It may well be that when he moved to Defence there had been some understanding between him and his Cabinet colleagues that defence expenditure would be cut. Since men in uniform cannot be demobilized overnight, or troops withdrawn at a moment's notice from overseas commitments, the only way to achieve immediate economies in defence expenditure is to cancel or slow down contracts for production or R&D. Blue Water was less of a political problem than was TSR2, and was therefore easier to cancel.

Had Peter Thorneycroft asked for my views, I would not have disagreed with his decision. Twenty years later I continue to be surprised when I sometimes hear it said that he was wrong to do what he did; that Blue Water would have been a far better weapon than its American equivalent, which is still deployed by NATO, but which is now likely to be withdrawn. In my view, neither was relevant to any realistic battlefield scenario that relates to NATO Europe.

If I did not anticipate the cancellation of Blue Water, equally I would never have believed that PT428, although cancelled, would live on and

In Ottawa *en route* to Washington for the Skybolt briefing, 1960.
S.Z. (centre, holding briefcase); on his left, Harold Watkinson,
and, on his right, Richard Chilver.

The CSA visits the Royal Aircraft Establishment, Farnborough,
1961. Left to right, S.F. Follet, Clifford Cornford, James
Lighthill, S.Z., Handel Davies.

The Polaris purchasing mission, January 1963. Left to right,
John McNaughton, Admiral Galantin USN, S.Z., Admiral
Varyl Begg RN.

Flight Control of the USN nuclear carrier *Enterprise*.

Badinage at the Kremlin at the start of the Partial Test Ban
Talks, 1963. Khrushchev, Gromyko, Zorin and Tsarapkin face
Averill Harriman, and Lord Hailsham. S.Z. is fifth from right.

The initialling of the Partial Test Ban Treaty in the Spiridonovka
Palace, 1963. Gromyko (partial profile, back to camera, extreme
left), Humphrey Trevelyan, Duncan Wilson, Lord Hailsham,
S.Z. and Frank Long.

Inspecting the rations with General Walker, Director of Army
Operations, Borneo 1965.

Visit to the Federal Republic of Germany, 1965. Left to right,
General Heinz Trettner (Chief of Staff of the Bundeswehr), staff
officer, C.F. McFarlane (UK military supply counsellor), S.Z.

With Joan (holding flowers) when she launched the
submarine *Repulse*, November 1967.

U Thant's Expert Committee on Chemical and Bacteriological
Weapons. On the left, Bob Press, and fourth from right,
Academician Reutov.

At the White House, 1967. Fourth from left, S.Z.; seventh,
Robert McNamara; ninth, Dean Rusk; eleventh, Harold Wilson;
twelfth, President Johnson; fourteenth, Sir Patrick Dean;
sixteenth, Burke Trend; eighteenth, David Bruce, US Ambassador.

AMERICAN FRIENDS

1 Jerome B. Wiesner.
2 George Kistiakowsky.
3 Robert McNamara (centre) and
   Harold Brown (right) with Deputy
   Defense Secretary Roswell Gilpatric.
4 Isidore I. Rabi with Joan at Carpenter
   Road, May 1958.
5 Herbert F. York.

emerge some two years later as a project called ET316, and materialize as the Rapier ground-to-air anti-aircraft weapon it is today. Rapier may not be the 'all-singing, all-dancing' anti-aircraft rocket that PT428 was designed to become, but without the latter's frills, it is a very useful defensive weapon. I have no idea how the development team working on the PT428 was maintained after the project was officially cancelled. The company must have found the money on its own.

Other than nuclear projects, the main burdens on the R&D budget during the time I was Chief Scientific Adviser were in the aerospace field. There were three projects in particular: Concorde, the TSR2 and the P1127. Of Concorde, I shall say no more except that shortly after the election of Harold Wilson's Government in 1964, I was appointed a member of a small Treasury team, presided over by Otto Clark, which was charged to look into costly 'prestige projects'. Having taken evidence from all concerned, we reported that because of insurmountable technological constraints which limited 'payload' and range, it was improbable that Concorde could ever become a success. We were wrong, and it is fortunate that the French, our partner in the venture, frustrated the Government's attempt to cancel the project. Concorde, a magnificent aircraft as all who have flown in her will know, has confounded most of the gloomy prognostications which characterized her birth. Of course, that may be partly because she has no competitor in the supersonic passenger-transport field.

The TSR2 – the T stood for tactical, the S for strike, and the R for reconnaissance – was not so fortunate. The operational requirement for an all-purpose low-level supersonic bomber had been mooted during the heady aeronautical days of the mid-1950s, when it was already being suggested that our V-bombers, which were not yet in squadron service, would be vulnerable to the medium- and high-level missile air-defences that the Soviet Union was then developing. In theory what was therefore wanted was an aircraft that could fly at, say, 200 feet, and so under an enemy's radar screen.* The TSR2 was designed to do just this. So was the Navy's Buccaneer. But the RAF had no interest in an adapted Navy plane.

The American Defense Department was interested in both the

*Much later, the RAF showed that the Vulcan could also fly 'on the deck'.

TSR2 and the Buccaneer, as they were in all new ideas for weaponry that were being suggested by their European allies, and especially by the UK. The Mutual Weapons Development Program, as a division of Herb York's DDR&E, was both a means whereby the United States provided aid to Europe, and a friendly technical intelligence exchange agency for the United States. It was run by a member of Herb's staff, a charming man by name Jack McCauley, and it was his job to ferret out ideas that merited American support, and particularly those which, if helped, were then more likely to be supported by the countries concerned. On paper, the MWDP was also a way of bringing about weapon standardization in NATO. Unfortunately, the resources that it deployed were minuscule compared with those that were disposed of by the rapidly growing and immensely powerful armaments industries of the USA. It had few successes to boast about.

It so happened that the USA also had an operational requirement for a supersonic all-weather reconnaissance and strike aircraft. The MWDP staff were favourably disposed to the Navy's fixed-wing carrier-borne Buccaneer, to whose development they were in fact contributing. But they were not at all impressed by the TSR2's technical specifications, advanced though they were. Herb York and Jack McCauley, as well as other American friends, kept telling me that the TSR2, if completed, would be the last fixed-wing military aircraft of its kind, and, as they put it, they were not in the market to buy dinosaurs. They were determined to build a swing-wing machine.

The concept of swing-wing or 'variable geometry' was developed towards the end of the Second World War by G.T.R. Hill of University College London as a way of compromising between the low take-off and landing speeds needed by an aircraft, and the high speeds it had to achieve in flight. The more closely an aircraft assumes the shape of a bullet – having rotated or 'swept' its wings backwards towards the fuselage – the less 'drag' it generates at height, and the less resistance therefore to its forward movement. Barnes Wallis had demonstrated the practicability of the concept, and had devised a pivot mechanism for the wing of a small prototype – the Swallow project which Claude Pelly had discussed with me years before (p.146). There had been an agreement between the UK and America to cooperate in the exploitation of the principle of variable geometry, but it had lapsed by the end of June 1960, by when the specification for the TSR2 had been circulated to the British aircraft industry. In October of the same year, the Americans commissioned design studies for the swing-wing aircraft that finally emerged in 1966 as the F111 fighter-bomber. The dates are important in the light of the dramatic stories that have been published about the way the Americans let us down or, worse, 'stole' our swing-wing concept.

It was in July 1959 that the then Secretary of State for Air, George Ward,* announced that a contract had been placed with the Vickers and English Electric companies for 'the initial work of project design, planning and programming' of the TSR2 airframe and its associated equipment. The contract for the engine was placed with Bristol Siddeley at the end of the same year, and this was followed in October 1960 by a contract for the development of the airframe. Harold Watkinson writes that it had been a 'tough battle' to get the Government to agree to place the contract, and that it 'was only achieved by putting my total Ministerial and personal influence behind the project'.[1] By then, because of its heavy demands on resources, the TSR2 had already become the subject of much questioning in Parliament. Since it and the Buccaneer seemed to have overlapping characteristics, it was not surprising that Harold Macmillan as well as the Treasury became concerned. In September 1960 he asked Harold Watkinson, to examine the whole project critically. Watkinson in turn asked me to prepare a 'personal review'.

I was wary about becoming embroiled in an inter-Service dispute. One or other member of my staff always seemed to be advising me to do this, and not to do that, not to listen to so-and-so, that this was the true story, and that one false. From the start, too, Dickie Mountbatten had invited me to meetings of the Chiefs of Staff – the day was not far distant when I was accorded what was in effect a regular seat at their meetings. He also always invited me to what he called his 'COSIs', when the three Service Chiefs met with him, minus staff, over a glass of sherry – presumably to consider wider issues of strategy. Dickie was always enamoured of initials and acronyms. COS stood for Chiefs of Staff, and what I first took for a 'Y' denoted the informal nature of the gatherings. I do not recall any arguments breaking out at a COSI. This was before the days when our two names had become associated, as

*Now Lord Ward.

though partners either in crime or the search for power, as 'the Zuckbatten Axis', a term coined by Chapman Pincher.

By the time I started on my TSR2 review I had, however, inadvertently managed to make the Air Staff and its Chief, Tom Pike, highly nervous because of the questions that I had been asking about the military significance of the characteristics that had been written into the specifications of both the RAF's TSR2 and the Navy's Buccaneer. I particularly wanted to know what the tactical advantages of the better performance of the TSR2 were in relation to its extra cost.

Having gathered all the papers that were available to me, I retired to Birmingham, and for a few days did nothing but review the history of the TSR2 project. Answers to my technical questions were provided either by Sir George Gardner, then the Controller of Aircraft in the Ministry of Aviation, on whose dispassionate technical advice I had quickly learned to rely, or were sought on my behalf by Cliff Cornford. Because I knew that the Air Staff were highly suspicious about Dickie Mountbatten's attitude to TSR2, and about his hope of launching a joint RAF–Navy project based upon the Buccaneer, I took good care not to discuss my review with him.

The report that I produced focused mainly on the strategic significance of the operational requirements which the TSR2 was designed to fulfil. Given that the decision to have a fixed-wing machine was technically sound – and I was in no position to question this – it was clear that only an aircraft with the advanced features that had been built into the specifications of the TSR2 could satisfy the Air Staff's operational requirement – the two had been written around each other. To me the question was whether we were being asked to pay too much, to the detriment of other military needs, in order to satisfy requirements that were possibly illusory. The TSR2 was to be an aircraft that could fly very low and fast, but no-one could explain to me how significant it would be to its potential vulnerability if it flew a few miles faster at lower levels than the Buccaneer. The difference meant millions of pounds. Flying at what was hoped would be twice the speed of sound at altitude was obviously a critical 'requirement', but the Buccaneer, while incapable of that speed, was further on in development. Another point that worried me was that a supersonic aircraft was not likely to be used for close-support of troops fighting on the ground. Were a war to erupt on the European mainland, I could hardly imagine that the Russians would wait to find out whether aircraft making deep strikes on targets within their territory were carrying conventional bombs, leaflets or nuclear weapons. If we and the Russians meant what we were saying, the response would most likely be nuclear, in which case one would have to ask, to which bases could those TSR2s return that had not been shot down after penetrating into Warsaw Pact airspace? If nuclear strategy meant anything at all, our bases would by then have been destroyed by a Russian missile counterstrike.

The cost of the R&D for the TSR2 was rising fast. The figure I was given when I became CSA was some £40 million. Within six months it had leapt to £85m. New technical problems were cropping up all the time – in the weight and thrust of the engine, and in the design and development of the complicated radar and computer systems that were needed in an aircraft that had to 'fly blind' at 'tree height' in all weathers. But above all I could not see any strategic sense in the notion that the TSR2 could be operated as a fighter-bomber armed with nuclear bombs for use on a European battlefield. The idea of nuclear field-war was nonsense – a point which I discuss later. In the background was the fear that the Americans were likely to trump our TSR2 with their swing-wing and much lighter version of a fighter-bomber.

Harold Watkinson called a meeting of the Chiefs of Staff to discuss my review. I do not recall that either Dickie Mountbatten, the CDS, or Admiral Sir Caspar John, the First Sea Lord, or General Sir Frank Festing, the Chief of the Imperial General Staff (the title was still in vogue) said much, if indeed anything. But despite the fact that I had concluded my paper by saying that if 'relaxations' could not be made in the operational requirements of the TSR2, then the technical specification had to stand, Tom Pike was indignant that I had dared to offer what to him was a controversial analysis of the RAF's pet project. He was going to have none of it.

The meeting did not change anything, and Harold Watkinson succeeded in persuading the Prime Minister as well as the Treasury that development should proceed. I was neither surprised nor set back. But from that moment, the Air Staff started to spread it around that I was out to 'kill' the TSR2.

On the morning after Watkinson's meeting, and before I left for the Ministry, a messenger brought me a long handwritten screed from

Dickie, commending both my report and the 'defence' I had put up against Tom Pike, and saying that while he had agreed with all that I had said, he had not spoken out because doing so would have prejudiced his position as Chairman of the Chiefs of Staff Committee. He could not take a public stand against one of his colleagues. If, however, I was going to carry on with the debate, I could count on his full support. I acknowledged his note over a cup of coffee when I got to the office. I could understand his reluctance to speak out, although I was not then as aware as I was to become of the extent to which, behind the scenes, he was promoting the Buccaneer as a joint Service project.

A few days later Bob Robertson gave me a lift to Paris, where we both had to attend a meeting at NATO Headquarters. Bob was still Chairman of the Pentagon's Scientific Advisory Board. With us in a small American military transport plane were Jack McCauley of the MWDP, and John Stack, the Assistant Director of Langley Research Center, which was one of the main experimental establishments of NASA and the American Air Force. Stack was a protagonist of swing-wing and the F111 – then called the TFX – and it happened to be his birthday. Bob had brought along a cake bearing a single candle, which was duly lit and then blown out. We were all very relaxed, but in the course of casual conversation I discovered that the Americans knew far more than I suspected about the technical progress of the TSR2 development programme. Stack remarked that he was amazed that the UK was pressing on with the development of an aircraft when its weight had already far exceeded the specified limit. The fuselage of the TSR2 was so full of wires connecting various black boxes, he said, that it would now be impossible to pull even a silk thread through it. He was certain that the project would be cancelled when the all-up weight of the prototype aircraft reached 100,000 lb. The UK was caught in a vicious circle. As the weight of the aircraft increased, more engine power was needed, and therefore bigger fuel tanks, bigger wings, and so on. I asked whether he was prepared to bet on his judgment. So on the back of the flight-information card – which I still have – he solemnly wrote, 'I don't understand how her HMG [sic] can stand the loss of prestige it will have to face in 1970 if it goes ahead and finishes the TSR2.' At that time the F111 project was not as far advanced as was the TSR2, nor were the Americans inviting the UK to join them in their programme. They were, however, far more confident about their eventual success than we were about ours.*

Despite mounting doubts about where it was all going to end, the development of the TSR2 went ahead, and as the months dragged on, I saw more and more of George Edwards, the Managing Director of the British Aircraft Corporation, who was in overall industrial charge of the project. George's loyalties were sorely tried. He had helped formulate, and had given his unqualified support to the recommendations about the control of government R&D that had been put forward by the small committee of which he was a member, and he fully accepted that the procedures we had advocated should be implemented in the case of the TSR2. But time after time when we dined in a small suite in Brown's Hotel, I would have to listen while he bemoaned the reluctance of the Government to arrange a firm contract for the project without further ado, and the fact that the Ministry of Aviation kept interfering in its industrial management.

But the interference did not stop. Costs mounted as new problems arose with the prototype engine, and as changes continued to be made in the various avionic systems with which the aircraft was to be fitted. Worst of all, the take-off weight of the aircraft, which had been specified as 70,000 lb, was fast nearing 100,000. TSR2 had become almost as big as the Vulcan strategic bomber. George appreciated that I would not presume to comment on the technological merits of a design for which he, one of the most distinguished aeronautical engineers in the country, was responsible, but he felt sure that the British aerospace industry would be doomed if the TSR2 did not go ahead, even though he knew full well that not only the United States but other countries as well were then proposing to incorporate the variable geometry principle into a new generation of fighter-bombers. One of George's problems was that Barnes Wallis, who was on his staff, rarely lost an opportunity of showing, in his quiet, superior way, his disdain for those who were still pursuing fixed-wing designs. The two did not get along

---

*Stack withdrew from the F111 project when, at the end of 1962, the main contract was given to General Dynamics. Much later, I bet Jim Leatham, who became the Pentagon's project manager for the F111, that the first F111s would also fail to meet the aircraft's very stringent specifications, as well as its time-schedule. The stake was a case of champagne. I won. Year after year, on his way through London, Leatham would solemnly bring me a bottle.

well. When the operational requirement for the TSR2 was formulated in 1957, George had been among those who judged the swing-wing idea to be premature.*

When I left George after those dinners *à deux*, I used to feel as I might have done if I had been having drinks with a brother officer who, when I had left, would pick up his revolver and blow out his brains.

In the major Cabinet reshuffle that took place in July 1962, Harold Macmillan appointed Peter Thorneycroft in Harold Watkinson's place. Four years earlier, in January 1958, Thorneycroft had resigned the office of Chancellor of the Exchequer in protest against the high level of public spending. He had rejoined the Government in July 1960 as Minister of Aviation, a post which gave him ample opportunity to learn just how great a strain Britain's overloaded aircraft programme was imposing on the public purse. By the time he took over from Watkinson, no firm production orders had been placed for the TSR2 and, what was worse, the estimated production cost of a single aircraft had passed the £2 million mark (equivalent to £15 million now). TSR2, Thorneycroft said to me, was 'an albatross round our necks', and was seriously distorting the entire military procurement programme. I found it ironical that I once had to accompany him to a formal meeting with one of his Treasury ministerial colleagues to plead for the further funds which, if not forthcoming, meant cancellation.

I kept him informed, as I had Watkinson, about what I was learning about the progress of the R&D programme, and I warned that because of increasing technical demands and difficulties, it seemed highly improbable that the aircraft could come into squadron service before the end of the 1960s. I seem to remember that even the main avionics contractor, Ferranti, told us that the aircraft was becoming so complicated, with its forward- and sideways-looking radar and sensor/computer systems, that it would be impossible to fly it 'at tree height' in all weathers at near the speed of sound. On paper it all looked possible, but 'the state of the art' at the time made it improbable. I kept warning that even with its novel swing-wing, the F111 looked more and more

*The idea of designing the TSR2 as a swing-wing aircraft had been considered at the start, but formally rejected at an early stage, the reason being that designing and developing a swing-wing machine would have delayed the date when the TSR2 could be brought into service. Wallis had failed to persuade his employers that the pivot mechanism which he had devised was adequate for the job.

likely to emerge as a less complicated and lighter form of fighter-bomber than the TSR2, with a far greater 'radius of action' – and sooner.

Another difficulty was that there were no buyers for the TSR2. The USA had its F111 project. Our European NATO partners were not in the market. In December 1963 Peter Thorneycroft, in order to spread the cost, had even proposed, but unsuccessfully, that a mixed-manned NATO squadron of TSR2s should be formed. The only likely buyer had been the Australian Air Force. George Edwards had visited Australia to try to make a sale, but some initial encouraging noises came to nothing. In the end, the Australians said they were going to buy the F111.

In one of the many accounts that have been published about the cancellation of the TSR2, Stephen Hastings,* in a book called *The Murder of TSR2*,[2] implies that Dickie Mountbatten and I deliberately discouraged the Australian Chief of Defence Staff from buying the TSR2, Dickie because he wanted to interest him in the Buccaneer, and I because I favoured 'buying American'. The implication is that, whatever its merits, we were both out to sabotage the TSR2. This was total nonsense. The Australian Air Staff could hardly have been ignorant of the controversies about the TSR2, or about how it compared technically and financially with the F111. They probably viewed the TSR2, as did the American aircraft industry, as a symbol of an overloaded and non-competitive aerospace industry.

In October 1964, the Government changed, and Harold Wilson became Prime Minister, with Denis Healey taking office as Secretary of State for Defence. A few weeks after he took over, he asked me, in the same way as had Harold Watkinson, for a personal appreciation of the TSR2 project, of which, when in opposition, he had been highly critical. As a basis, I used the report that I had prepared for Watkinson, amending it in accordance with what I had learnt in the three years that had followed, and consulting only my own files. Healey went over my report line by line, with me at his side, and in my mind's eye I can still see him underlining passages. What influence my paper had I do not know, but what I cannot forget is the determination of the new Government to make major cuts in defence spending. TSR2 was an

*An MP who happened to be a director of an aircraft company.

obvious victim, but the decision to cancel was no easier politically for the Labour Government than it had been for its predecessor.* Too much political capital as well as money had been sunk in it.

I barely knew Denis Healey before his appointment to Defence. Roy Jenkins, who was Minister of Aviation at the time, was the only personal friend I had in the new administration. But neither he, nor anyone else in the Government, could isolate the problem of the TSR2 from that of the aviation industry as a whole. Other projects, civil as well as military (and including Concorde), would also have to be pruned if something like a sensible aircraft programme were to remain. The unrealistic ambitions of the aircraft industry, so Roy informed Parliament, had resulted in a situation in which it had to be supported by a subsidy of, on average, £15 a year from every man, woman and child in the country. Nonetheless, Roy knew that drastic and immediate surgery was impossible. It was not only the RAF but also industry and the unions who were opposed. By April 1965, however, the Government decided that it could wait no longer, and the cancellation of TSR2 was announced. There was more to come.

Deprived of TSR2 the RAF felt naked, and the industry hailed the cancellation as a sentence of death – despite the fact that all concerned knew that the previous Conservative administration had had its worries about the project. The RAF, on the other hand, was temporarily silenced by an undertaking that the Government would purchase F111s from America to fill the gap that the cancellation had made. This undertaking was never fulfilled. More than a decade was to pass before the Air Force got the plane it wanted – the Tornado, an aircraft which weighs about half what the TSR2 would have done.

Before the passing of sentence, I had gone with George Edwards to his Weybridge plant to see parts of the TSR2 airframe being made. I had also been to Bristol to see the TSR2 engine on its test bed. When the announcement of the cancellation was made, and orders given to destroy the jigs, I decided to go to Boscombe Down, the RAF R&D airfield in Wiltshire where one of the prototype TSR2s was being tested. I stopped on the way to see Christopher Soames, who had been Minister of Agriculture in the previous Tory administration, and who was in hospital near Slough recovering from a minor operation. We

*Either Healey himself or someone in his outer office leaked my new paper to the Air Staff, which by that time had certainly realized which way the decision was going to go.

were good friends, and I had with me an offering of wine – not that he needed any further supplies of that commodity, judging by what I saw in his room. After chatting for a while, I told him that I had to be on my way, remarking that I didn't want to miss the only opportunity I would ever have of touching an object that had cost £400 million – my own rough estimate – before it was torn apart and thrown on the scrap heap. Christopher ribbed me more than once about that light-hearted remark.

Contrary to what many have said – and still say – about the cancellation, I believe that the decision was inevitable. TSR2 was a controversial venture from the start. The issue was not merely financial. The first problem was the presence of the Buccaneer, which years later I heard senior RAF officers say the Air Force should have accepted as a joint project. Second, the design was in competition with the American F111 and the French Mirage and, more importantly, it had to face the Russian MiGs; all three were due to enter service within a very few years. The first version of the F111 was in fact in squadron service in 1967 (well before the TSR2 could have been), and at a weight which I was told was considerably under 100,000 lb. I doubt, too, whether we could have continued to improve the TSR2's performance to keep pace with the improvements that have been made over the years in its competitors. Yet I do have a niggling doubt. Despite the statement at the end of the sixties that the US was no longer interested in fixed-wing aircraft, it has not followed the F111 with other swing-wing machines. Why? The Russians have produced a number. We have the Tornado. But new designs are said to favour the delta fixed-wing principle. Have new lightweight materials made swing-wing obsolete?

The resources that went into the TSR2 were not wasted. Many years after its demise I asked Sebastian Ferranti to find out for me how much his company, which was the main contractor for the machine's avionics, had lost by the cancellation. Very little, was the answer. They had been able to use what they had started to develop for the TSR2 in several other contracts, including the Tornado.

By contrast, and despite a development programme that at times looked at least as precarious as that of the TSR2, the P1127 turned out to be a success. It was designed to satisfy a seemingly joint Anglo-American need for a vertical take-off aircraft for the close support of troops engaged in battle. The idea was that by providing a jet engine with nozzles that could be swivelled so that the exhaust gases were directed downwards, the machine would be impelled vertically off the ground like a simple rocket. Once in the air, the nozzles were swivelled back so that the combustion gases shot backwards as in an ordinary jet engine, so driving the machine forwards. The original patent for the P1127 engine was French, and the Americans had arranged through the MWDP that it should be developed by the Bristol Siddeley engine company.* The airframe was designed by Sir Sydney Camm, the celebrated aeronautical engineer to whom the UK owed the wartime Hurricane and several other well-known aircraft, and its weight and size were obviously set by the power of the engine that had to lift it off the ground. The size of the engine also limited the range of the aircraft.

My American friends seemed far more concerned with the progress we were making with this project than was my air-commodore liaison officer, and were worried because the Treasury had not provided money for the building of more than two prototypes. Having taken advice, I became so fascinated that I decided to go and see for myself how much had been achieved by the Hawker and Bristol Siddeley Companies. I encouraged Harold Watkinson's interest, and he persuaded the Treasury to give the P1127 greater support than it was receiving. He also arranged that a tripartite evaluation of the project – by the UK, the US, and the West Germans – should be made on behalf of NATO. But the RAF had little, if any, interest in what to them was a small army-support aircraft, and a subsonic one at that.

The Americans next suggested that I should find out whether or not the principle of variable geometry could be incorporated into the P1127 airframe. If it could, the speed of the aircraft once off the ground would be significantly increased. Sir Arnold Hall, then the Managing Director of the Bristol Siddeley Company, came to discuss the idea with me. Before becoming an industrialist, Arnold had been, first, a professor at Imperial College and then, when still in his thirties, Director of the Royal Aircraft Establishment at Farnborough. I had enormous confidence in his judgment. His answer was that he was having enough trouble in getting the P1127 Pegasus engine, as it was

*Today part of Rolls-Royce.

known, to work properly, without complicating matters by having the as-yet-unproven principle of variable geometry incorporated into the airframe. So far as I can remember, the 'thrust' that had been achieved at that time was no more than about 13,000 lb, and this had to be raised to something nearer 19,000 to reach the specification required for an operational P1127. I followed his advice, and told my American friends that their suggestion simply wasn't on.

With the RAF continuing to show no interest in the P1127, Harold Watkinson called a meeting to discuss what should be done. Both Julian Amery, who had become the Secretary of State for Air, and Tom Pike took the view that if the Ministry of Defence insisted on going ahead with the P1127, the RAF would be prepared to take thirty aircraft, but only on condition that the cost did not come out of the RAF budget. That did not go down very well, but nonetheless the project continued. Harold had become thoroughly impatient about the way it was proceeding. As he records in his autobiography it was 'quite disgraceful that projects that come to Ministers and take up a good deal of time are then apparently allowed to fall back into inaction again'.

About a year later, after Peter Thorneycroft had taken over from him, I returned from an official visit to the United States and was staggered to hear that the RAF had persuaded the new Minister that were a 'jump-jet' aircraft ever to be developed for military service, it had to be supersonic lest it was 'jumped' by a faster fighter. The P1154, as the new theoretical version was designated (54 being twice 27!), needed engines with a thrust in excess of 30,000 lb. I nearly went through the roof. There we were, with the P1127's Pegasus engine still at an experimental stage, with its thrust well below the rating which the specification demanded, and the RAF was asking for a new and novel engine with far more than double the power that had so far been achieved. I sought independent expert advice, and was assured that all engineering experience indicated that the idea was then unrealizable. But I was powerless to do anything now that the decision had been blessed by the PM who, in my absence in America, had been briefed very differently from the advice I would have given. Since the project had the Cabinet's approval, the engine and airframe companies started to produce blueprints for a P1154.

Two years later, after Denis Healey had taken Peter Thorneycroft's place, the P1154 project was cancelled. The abortive attempt to develop a supersonic jump-jet had cost millions, even if it could be claimed that the project had helped to keep some designers and craftsmen in work. But for years I used to pin an invisible ticket marked £40 million on a certain civil servant who I knew was the man who had persuaded Thorneycroft. Twenty years later, and after a great deal of work in the UK and in other countries, the idea of a supersonic vertical-take-off aircraft is still only a dream. The cancellation of the P1154 was associated with that of the short-take-off transport aircraft, the HS681, and of some other projects then under development. The industry was thrown into total disarray.

Contrary to my advice, Healey had also been persuaded that there was no operational future for the P1127, and at first he was determined that it too should be cancelled. Fred Mulley, who was then Minister of Aviation, has told me that he had to use all his influence to keep the project in being. The fact that Healey was opposed is, however, not surprising. Like his predecessors Sandys, Watkinson and Thorneycroft, he was always being urged to reduce defence spending. According to *The Crossman Diaries*, he told his colleagues at a Cabinet Committee meeting on 19 December 1966, that either the P1127 had to be treated as a firm commitment, and paid for outside the defence vote, 'or it ought to be scrapped straightaway. He himself recommended immediate cancellation.'[3] He was supported by Jim Callaghan, the Chancellor, as well as by George Brown, the Foreign Secretary, and by Dick Crossman. Roy Jenkins, who had then become the Home Secretary, Fred Mulley and two or three others wanted the project to continue.

Four days later the matter was due to come up at a full Cabinet meeting, and in my capacity as the Government's Chief Scientific Adviser, I urged the Prime Minister not to cancel. I take up the story as told by Dick Crossman.

This afternoon Solly Zuckerman put his head round the door and said he must have a word. In he came and warned me that I really must take a sensible view about the P1127. I told him I was perfectly content that it should be kept in the programme providing the ceiling was kept down to the agreed figure. It was up to the defence people to decide what they spent their budget on. What I was determined to prevent was the P1127 being paid for as an addition to the maximum defence programme which I thought we could afford. Of course, Solly had been sent from Number 10 to try to seduce me, which proves once again that Harold's choice of people is sometimes very extraordinary.

Dick was right. I had been encouraged by the Prime Minister to see him. What his record of our brief meeting does not include was his remark, 'Why the devil should I follow your advice? Denis surely knows better.'

The Cabinet meeting that followed must have been curious. As Dick records:

> The proceedings started with Denis Healey, who'd obviously been brainwashed by Harold, making the astonishing statement that as Minister of Defence he had brought the issue to Cabinet and as a member of Cabinet he now advised us not to accept the advice of the Minister of Defence. This confirmed my suspicions that he had recommended cancellation not because he wanted the aircraft cancelled but in order to be instructed to produce it without paying for it. So we went through all the formalities once more: Wedgy Benn in support, Michael Stewart against, Callaghan against, and I said again, 'I'm not against the P1127: I'd rather have it than six battalions of troops in Malaya. But I'm not going to see defence spending pushed above the ceiling.' After all this, Cabinet agreed that the cancellation would not take place and that it was still an extra outside the defence budget. As usual Harold got his way.

Until I scanned his diaries, I used to think that I understood Dick, having known him from the beginning of the thirties. He was always opinionated and over-confident, and I was well aware of his quixotic personality. But I found his references to our encounters after he had become a Minister strange. One in 1966 concerned the part the UK was to play in 'space science', of which at the time a rocket project called Black Arrow was a critical part. The Cabinet had decided that it should be cancelled but, as Crossman records:

> I predicted the other day that *Black Arrow* would come back to Cabinet and here it was once again with a new paper by Solly

Zuckerman, who has a great influence on Harold as a scientific adviser and whose paper had encouraged the PM to refuse to sanction the cut which the [Government's] Science and Technology Committee had almost unanimously agreed. The discussion showed how little any of us politicians can really understand these enormously expensive space enterprises. I was in favour of cutting it on the clear evidence of both the Defence Department and DEA. Now Solly comes up with a paper giving a totally different account of what *Black Arrow* is. How can Cabinet come to a sensible decision when none of us have the vaguest idea what these things really are?

That was, and remains, the trouble with governmental decisions about highly technical matters. How, indeed, can Cabinets come to sensible judgments about the political consequences of technological ideas which they do not usually have the time even to try to understand?

Despite the Cabinet's decision, the P1127 might well have followed TSR2, the P1154 and the HS681 onto the scrap-heap had it not been for Lawrence Levy, the MIT graduate whom I had first met in Albuquerque in 1951 (p.170). Larry had become Minister to Mr Finletter, President Kennedy's Ambassador to NATO, and had settled down in Paris. He had heard about the P1127 and thought it was the very aeroplane that the American Marine Corps needed. I encouraged him all I could, and put him in touch with Arnold Hall, who by now had become Managing Director of the Hawker Siddeley Group. Before long Larry resigned his diplomatic post to form a small company with Hawkers to further his idea. He succeeded, but he and Hawkers, as well as the Marines, had to overcome considerable opposition from the Pentagon before 'a sale' was made – one condition of which was that there would not be a direct purchase, but that production of the machine would proceed independently in the USA. Several American companies were interested, and Arnold finally chose McDonnell–Douglas as Hawker's partner, having arranged adequate commercial and work-sharing terms.

The rest of the P1127 story we all know. The Harrier, as the P1127 was renamed, was a significant factor in the success of the remarkable Falklands campaign of 1982. And today the news is that an 'advanced'

Harrier is being produced for the American Marines, with a number being built for the RAF in a joint Anglo-American programme. Rumour also has it that following on the Harrier's success in the Falklands, British Aerospace have resurrected the concept of a supersonic version. Whether this ever proves technically and economically realizable, in the sense of resulting in an aircraft which is operationally manageable, and which fills a military operational requirement, remains to be seen. Arnold Hall always felt that the idea was technically possible, given enough time and sufficient resources. He may be right. After all, it was largely the faith of a few MWDP American officials in the jump-jet idea, who were ready to risk US resources to add to those which the UK could afford, that led to the emergence of an aircraft that was to prove critical to victory in a precarious operation that took place twenty years later.

The enterprises in which the UK engaged on an international basis in the few years that followed my futile efforts to organize cooperative R&D projects make an unhappy story. The French had not been disinterested spectators as they watched the British aircraft industry driving itself into the ground with its burden of commitments. For reasons that I never learnt, we had distanced ourselves from the one big NATO cooperative project that had been a success – the Breguet Atlantique maritime reconnaissance aircraft, which the French had masterminded. While the French aeronautical companies had long been eager to cooperate with us, with some exceptions our industry went on treating them as, at best, second-rate partners. When Rolls-Royce spurned a request for help from the French nationalized aero-engine company, SNECMA, the latter then turned, successfully, to Pratt and Whitney, one of Rolls's two American competitors. Jim Pearson of Rolls was not, of course, the only leader of the British aviation industry who failed to appreciate how quickly and successfully the French aircraft industry was going to revive, and in particular how much Marcel Dassault, a designer and industrialist – to whom France owes its Mystère bomber and Mirage fighter-bomber, as well as a number of civil projects – was to achieve. Whenever cooperation was suggested, the response was that if we ever did cooperate with France, British requirements had to come first – and that we had to be the 'lead player'. We have paid dearly for our easily understood conceit.

I was introduced to the French aeronautical industry partly through

227

'official channels', but what was to prove more important, by Paul Willert (p.122). Through him I first met René Lucien, the head of a company that produced undercarriages for aircraft, and which was allied to the UK company, Dowty. René Lucien in turn introduced me to the legendary Marcel Dassault who, as Marcel Bloch, had emerged from a concentration camp after the war to win singlehanded a competition for an aircraft design. Both men were friends of de Gaulle, with Lucien more outspoken than Dassault. Occasionally I lunched alone with Lucien, and learnt to take it as a matter of course that, wherever we were, a folding bed would appear after our meal so that he could stretch out and rest his bad heart. He was an ardent Anglophile, and brought into my life René Bloch (no relation to Marcel Bloch/ Dassault), a young naval officer who was then serving as Director of International Affairs to Pierre Messmer, the French Minister of Defence. It was René Bloch who had directed the successful Breguet Atlantique programme and, as a staunch Anglophile as well as a Gaullist, he was determined to set an Anglo-French project in train.

I found the frail, quietly spoken Dassault a forbidding character, but my meetings with him were always memorable. He entertained in a large house on the Champs Elysées near the Rond Point, where a superb meal would be served, accompanied by claret in bottles bearing his own labels. I also once met him alone in Geneva – we were there for different reasons, but had arranged to take advantage of the occasion. The purpose of our meetings was to consider the possibilities of Anglo-French cooperation. Through René Lucien I also got to know General Henri Ziegler who, after retiring from the army, had become the Managing Director, first of the Breguet company, and then of the nationalized group, Sud Aviation. Years later I had a lot to do with Henri Ziegler over the Concorde, in whose production he was the project manager for the French Government. Dassault in turn introduced me to General Gallois, whom he had taken on to his staff after Gallois's retirement from NATO, where he had been an Air Deputy to Larry Norstad when the latter was Supreme Commander.

In the UK Roy Jenkins, when Minister responsible for the British aircraft industry, was foremost in wanting to organize cooperative projects with the French. The first that was arranged, with René Bloch as the effective agent for the French Government, was the Jaguar, a French design which at the start was regarded essentially as an advanced trainer, of which we took over the production of the rear half of the fuselage and tail. It seemed an odd industrial proposition to me, but it worked. The second joint project was far more ambitious. It was for an Anglo-French variable geometry aircraft (AFVG), in the design of which George Edwards insisted that the British Aircraft Corporation should take the lead. This project, initiated around the time of the cancellation of TSR2, was also successfully negotiated by Roy Jenkins, and work was duly started. However, before a year had passed, the French Government cancelled the agreement, the ostensible reason being lack of funds. George Edwards was once again in despair. So was René Bloch, who welcomed his release from the post which he then occupied in the French Ministry of Defence because he felt that Messmer's abrupt cancellation had affected his 'credibility' in Anglo-French circles. René was then posted to take charge of the big missile-testing centre which the French were building in Les Landes to the south of Bordeaux. Here he remained, in the rank of vice admiral (and the last serving senior Gaullist officer), until removed by President Mitterand, and placed *'en disponibilité'*. We have been close friends from the day we first met.

For his part, George Edwards, then some sixty years old, fought off his frustration and helped manoeuvre the UK into the discussion stage of a German–Italian project to build a fighter-bomber which George saw as taking the place of the cancelled TSR2 and AFVG. Gradually, and to me not surprisingly, the project took on more a British than a German or Italian complexion. It succeeded, and the Tornado is the outcome. George had retired from BAC before it entered squadron service in 1982.

PART V

Nuclear Independence and Reality

Skybolt

Duncan Sandys's 1957 White Paper was a forthright warning that the strain imposed by our armed forces on the Exchequer had to be reduced.[1] National service – a costly item – was to end. Our security was to be based on our alliances, and on the concept of nuclear deterrence, which from now on was to be the keystone of our central strategy. We would deter aggression by threatening nuclear retaliation – despite the fact that there was no way by which our own population could be protected. Supersonic manned bombers were no longer to be developed. The era of ballistic missiles had dawned. Our status as a nuclear power depended on Blue Streak, the liquid-fuelled ballistic missile, the development of which had started a year or two before.

Two years later, Harold Watkinson replaced Sandys, and soon after warned Parliament that the future of Blue Streak was being reviewed.[2] Less than two months later,[3] he announced that the project was being brought to an end.* Harold Macmillan writes that the decision to cancel was based mainly on the advice of the Chiefs of Staff about the inadvisability of the UK relying on missiles in fixed sites.[4] In retrospect, it seems odd that they did not think of this three years before. When Parliament was first informed about the project, there were many questions about the wisdom of deploying a stationary ballistic missile in so small an island as ours.

What I find interesting in the light of later developments is that in the Commons debate that followed the announcement of the cancellation, Harold Watkinson referred to British nuclear policy as the maintenance of an independent British *contribution* to the nuclear deterrent of the West, not as the British nuclear deterrent, *tout court*.[5] Lord Hailsham put the Government's view in equally clear terms when

*One stage of the rocket was kept in being for a time for possible use by the European Launcher Development Organization (ELDO).

winding up a debate on Blue Streak in the Lords.[6] An 'independent deterrent' was not a nuclear force powerful enough 'to engage one of the great powers in the world on our own with a hope of victory. . . .' The UK's independent contribution was 'a significant part of the Western deterrent under our own control, for the good reason that all its components, aircraft and bombs, were made in Britain and paid for by British money'. That, however, was said before Skybolt, and before Polaris.

My views about the cancellation of Blue Streak were never specifically sought, but it was known that my Air Ministry committee had been less than enthusiastic about the project. Brundrett, now retired, felt himself free to declare publicly that the decision to 'scrap' was thoroughly bad, as also did Aubrey Jones, who had been Minister of Supply between 1957 and October 1959.[7] For obvious reasons, Duncan himself could not say publicly how much he regretted the decision, but he often reproached me later for not having used what influence I had to preserve a weapon system that he had called the mainstay of the UK's defence policy. My reply was always the same – Blue Streak had ceased to make sense from the moment that the Government had decided that it should be buried in concrete silos. He, Duncan, had declared that the country could not be protected against a nuclear assault. It was equally certain that we could not protect a handful of buried Blue Streaks in order that they might serve as retaliatory weapons in what Harold Macmillan once called an act of 'posthumous revenge'. A small number of Blue Streak missiles might have had some strategic significance in a 'first strike' role. If words meant what they said, the logic demanded, I went on, that one Blue Streak should have been mounted in Parliament Square, one in the forecourt of Buckingham Palace, and one on Horseguards Parade, on to which the garden of Number 10 Downing Street opens. They would be there as a threat of possible use if the Government decided our national interests were at stake. But either way, I argued, it made no difference to the future of the United Kingdom – were our missiles ever fired, we would be destroyed.

My Air Ministry committee had been aware that in the customary American inter-Service battle for funds, the US Navy had committed itself to the submarine-launched Polaris missile, and the Air Force (USAF) to Minuteman, a fixed and buried ground-launched rocket.

With Soviet air-defences improving fast, the Air Force also wanted a supersonic bomber – a nuclear-powered Polaris of the skies – and an air-launched ballistic missile system called Skybolt. The latter would help keep manned bombers flying. Other ideas for 'strategic systems' were also being bandied around at the time, including space satellites from which missiles would be fired onto enemy territory. The triad of strategic nuclear forces which the United States now deploys came about not because of some rationally conceived plan. It represents the residuum of a host of ideas for new weapon systems that were being advanced in the fifties.

From the moment that the idea of Skybolt was conceived, the American Air Staff sought the support of the RAF which, from early 1959, had started to send officers and Ministry of Aviation officials to the States to keep in touch with what was afoot. John Rubel, who later was made responsible for monitoring the programme for the American Secretary of Defense, has told me that this was happening before the Defense Secretary's office had even started to consider the project. It suited both Air Forces to keep in touch, since any UK interest was useful ammunition in the arguments in which the American Air Chiefs would have to engage with the Defense Secretary about the need for such a weapon system. Both Air Forces were fighting for the survival of manned bombers. Both also already had an air-launched cruise missile. The American version was called Hound Dog. Blue Steel Mark I was ours, and when I became CSA it was already being argued that an improved version of Blue Steel that was under development would have to be cancelled since it would be 'too late into service' – although by what criterion of 'lateness' was never made clear. The reality was that Blue Steel did not seem as up-to-date as Skybolt, which was a ballistic missile with a much greater range, and which the RAF therefore urged was the only way the life of the V-bombers could be prolonged beyond the sixties.

Air Commodore Hughes, the officer who reported jointly to me and to the Air Staff, lost no time in telling me about Skybolt. At his instigation I therefore spoke to Herb York, and he agreed to provide a full account of what Skybolt was and what its development entailed. Herb's post as head of the Directorate of Defense Research and Engineering had been established by Act of Congress in 1958 in order to help the Defense Secretary control the ever-burgeoning R&D

235

demands of the three Services. Skybolt was the first strategic weapon system with which Herb and, in particular, John Rubel, his deputy for 'strategic systems', had to deal. When in Washington early in March, only some two months after becoming CSA, I was accordingly given a briefing by the two of them. At the time, Tom Gates, the American Defense Secretary, barely knew about the project.

John was introduced to Skybolt by the US Air Force in a way which he has told me seemed 'almost insulting in its superficiality and gross incompleteness'. He had the experience to judge, since during his distinguished career in industrial R&D, he had often briefed the US military. This was the first time that they had briefed him. But under the 1958 Defense Reorganization Act, it was his responsibility to 'approve' the project before the Air Force could commit funds to a programme of development. At the time there was no proper procedure for considering all 'strategic nuclear weapon systems' as belonging to a class that should be examined as a whole – more than a year was to pass before Robert McNamara introduced 'Program Budgeting'. In the meantime it was business as usual in the Pentagon, except that the Air Force and the other services now had to contend with the new office of the DDR&E.

After a number of meetings with Air Force officers and officials, as well as with the main contractor, the Douglas Company, John demanded that specific proposals should be spelt out about the way certain technological problems were going to be solved if the Skybolt dream was ever to be realized. He was then asked to see General LeMay, at the time the US Air Force's Deputy Chief of Staff. In the course of what must have been a fascinating meeting, with LeMay in his characteristically aggressive mood, John asked him if he knew how much had already been spent on Skybolt. The answer was no, he didn't. John told him, about $10 million, and then added, 'Do you know what you have got for that?' The answer was again no. John pointed to some papers on LeMay's desk. 'You have reports about as thick as that thin pile of papers. Do you know what they are worth?' He answered the question himself. 'About as much as the paper they are printed on.'

When John gave me my first briefing, the project was not much further ahead than it had been when he saw LeMay. Nor was it two weeks later when Harold Macmillan was in Washington to confer with

President Eisenhower about a moratorium on all nuclear tests. As Macmillan records in his memoirs, he also used the occasion to get the President to agree 'in principle' that now that the UK was about to cancel Blue Streak, we could purchase either Skybolt or Polaris.[8] As Macmillan understood the situation, both were in full development; his preference for Skybolt would help justify the enormous investment that had already been made in the V-bomber force. What was more, the Royal Navy did not then want Polaris – its share of the UK defence budget was barely sufficient to assure the more urgent needs of a surface fleet. Demands that NATO had made for medium-range ballistic missiles (MRBM) also came up in the discussions between the President and Prime Minister, for the United States was then being pressed by Larry Norstad, the Supreme Commander, to establish a Polaris force as a component of NATO's MRBM system. Macmillan disliked the idea that in exchange for a promise of Skybolt, the UK should allow the United States to establish a Polaris base in Scotland – although, as it was to turn out, the Americans started to treat such a base as part of a Skybolt 'bargain'. In their eyes it was the least we could do for them, since they were not asking us to contribute to the development costs of a missile that we wanted. Some two weeks after his return to London, and during the course of the Commons debate in which the cancellation of Blue Streak was announced, the Prime Minister referred to his Camp David talks, but without mentioning Skybolt.

The stage was now set for the next step, that of formalizing an agreement to 'buy' Skybolt. Accordingly, about a month later,* and immediately after a visit by John Rubel to London, Harold Watkinson, Richard Chilver and I flew to Ottawa, and then on to Washington where, after we had seen Tom Gates, John Rubel gave us a detailed briefing about Skybolt. He made it as clear as he had when he had first briefed me, that the project was a very speculative one. He explained his doubts about finding solutions to a number of technical problems, and his worries about the slow progress that was being made by the Douglas Company. It would therefore be some time before the United States could decide whether Skybolt was a reality, and in consequence it was far too early for a government-to-government 'contract to

*27 May 1960.

purchase'. He also warned that, if the US decided to cancel, it was highly unlikely that the project could be kept going for the sake of the UK alone. John was clear-cut and impressive. The upshot was that Tom Gates and Harold Watkinson signed a short 'memorandum of understanding', in which the United States undertook to make every reasonable effort to complete the R&D, and the UK to buy 100 missiles if the project succeeded. A detailed financial and technical agreement was then hammered out between the USAF and our Ministry of Aviation. This took some three more months – in retrospect not surprising, since the officials of the two sides were negotiating about something that did not exist.

John and I had established friendly relations by the time of this meeting, and he urged me to post a personal representative in the Pentagon, through whom he would keep me informed about the progress of the project. He also recommended that we should strengthen the Skybolt technical team that we already had in the United States to determine what modifications would be needed in the Vulcan bomber to make it compatible with the missile. As it turned out, John's suggestion led to considerable confusion. The Air Ministry and the Ministry of Aviation insisted that my representative should also represent them, and in due course a Group Captain, whom I had not met before, was sent to Washington. Since the American Air Staff has its HQ in the Pentagon, it was to the former, not to John Rubel, that the Group Captain mostly turned for information.

In consequence, his reports, like those of the UK team at the Wright Development Center, were always optimistic, in contrast to the far more sober information with which I was being provided directly, and which I immediately passed to Harold Watkinson. My information came not only from John Rubel and Herb York, but also from the President's Science Adviser, George Kistiakowsky, and from members of the President's Science Advisory Committee (PSAC), none of whom ever expressed high hopes for the project.* Rabi and Bob Robertson, as well as some other members of PSAC, in particular Jerry Wiesner, were unreservedly sceptical. They had no axes to grind when commenting on the technical aspects of the many weapons systems

*George B. Kistiakowsky, in his diary entry for 23 December 1959, noted that the White House scientists were opposed to the Skybolt programme, 'partly on the grounds of its unfeasibility, but also on operational grounds'.[9]

which they studied. They were nobody's servants, unlike the scientific staff that served the USAF chiefs who, while technically 'under' the Defense Secretary, were really a power unto themselves – except when it came to money.

Before we left Washington, Tom Gates impressed on us the strength of the US concern to provide NATO with a force of medium-range ballistic missiles, and the American wish to establish a Polaris base in the UK. Watkinson was cautious, almost discouraging, on both issues. But it took the Americans less than two years to get their base – at Holy Loch. It was twenty before NATO became possessed of its own medium-range missile force (apart from a few Polaris submarines which were notionally assigned to SACEUR). When the MRBM force eventually materialized, it consisted of cruise missiles and Pershing IIs, whose deployment on European soil in the early eighties caused so much political trouble.

I find it interesting that while the name of the German Chancellor, Helmut Schmidt, is usually associated with the plan to deploy MRBMs, the seeds of the enterprise were planted during Eisenhower's administration, at a time when it was assumed that the existence and deployment of nuclear missiles would, like all NATO's armament, help deter Soviet aggression. As it was to turn out, when the time came to deploy the MRBM force, few believed that it had any military, as opposed to political, significance. By then even that most stridently anti-Communist of American Presidents, Ronald Reagan, was declaring that a nuclear war could never be won, and that it should never be fought. It is also an indication of how long it takes to develop a new weapon system that Pershing II, about which the public never heard until the end of the seventies, was being thought of at the same time as was Skybolt.

Our business in Washington completed, we flew to Los Angeles where we were given detailed technical briefings by the staff of the Douglas Company. Mr Douglas himself chaired some of the meetings, and was obviously very anxious to persuade us that all was well with the project.

Immediately after our return, Harold Macmillan summoned us to a meeting at his country home, Birch Grove, to hear a blow-by-blow account of what had happened during the visit, a written report of which had been put together by Watkinson on our way back. As

Macmillan notes in his memoirs, Watkinson had successfully disassociated the British Government from the notion that a submarine base in Scotland should be a *quid pro quo* for Skybolt.[10] I used the occasion to speak forcibly about the American concept of a NATO medium-range ballistic missile force, arguing that were the latter to materialize, we would be providing a 'strategic' weapon to an organization which, while it existed to fulfil a strategic purpose, deployed forces that were there to deal with tactical situations as they arose.

This, I think, was the first opportunity I had had of expressing my heterodox views about nuclear war to Harold Macmillan. A senior Foreign Office official, Sir Patrick Dean, who was at the meeting, and I were then charged to prepare the draft of an agreement which might be needed if a Polaris base were to be set up in the UK. I left the job to him. A couple of days later the PM called us together again for a further discussion about those matters which had come up during our visit that he felt had to go to the Cabinet.

About four months later, at a NATO meeting in Paris, I learnt that all was not well with Skybolt, which by then was beginning to be implanted in the public mind as the symbol of the UK's status as an independent nuclear power. Watkinson accordingly suggested that I should deliver a personal letter from him to Tom Gates in Washington, asking him to discuss the situation with me 'with the utmost frankness'. This Gates did over several days and many hours of meetings, in which the Deputy Secretary of Defense, Jim Douglas, as well as John Rubel, participated. I was also shown a confidential and highly critical and objective report that Professor Frank Long, a member of PSAC, had prepared on the subject for George Kistiakowsky, whom I also saw. To all of them I stressed the mounting political importance of Skybolt to the UK.

Each day I sent back a message reporting what I had learnt, and before leaving I wrote a detailed report, which was already in Watkinson's hands by the time I returned. My message was simple. It boiled down to the fact that, while the American Administration fully recognized that the project had assumed enormous political importance in the UK, to President Eisenhower and the Joint Chiefs of Staff Skybolt was no more than a very costly R&D programme in which they had little faith. The pressure for Skybolt came from the American Air Force, which was anyhow hedging its bets by according land-based

Minutemen a higher priority. The USAF had also succeeded in getting Gates to reinstate the B70, a highly controversial supersonic bomber project that had been cancelled, at the same time as it was beginning to press for the F111 swing-wing fighter-bomber. The signs were that the allocation for Skybolt in the next year's defence budget was going to be severely reduced.

As soon as he received my first telegram, Watkinson let the Prime Minister know what I had learnt, and, as the latter records in his memoirs, he immediately asked President Eisenhower to explain what was happening. Back came a reply which the Prime Minister regarded as reassuring. This happened while I was still in Washington. I was shown a copy of the draft which the Pentagon had sent to the White House as a possible answer to the Prime Minister's enquiry, but which I was told had then been 'torn up'. In substance, however, its message was the same as the one that the President sent, the gist being that all was continuing in accordance with the agreement the President had made with the PM at Camp David, and also with the Gates–Watkinson memorandum of understanding. The President's reply had deleted from the Pentagon draft any reference to difficulties.

Before I left Washington, Gates asked me to warn Watkinson not to 'overplay the hand'. Watkinson tried hard not to. He fully appreciated that Skybolt was an R&D project, and while it had grown in importance politically since our June visit, he also realized that if it failed to materialize we would look foolish if we went on saying that all was well when the American Defense Secretary was saying the opposite.

Gates had agreed to a suggestion that I put to him to visit London in early December – which would have been after the Presidential election – when he was due to attend his final NATO meeting as Defense Secretary. Unfortunately, the Douglas Company let the press know before he arrived that the allocation of funds for Skybolt was to be significantly reduced. The cut was a consequence of a general reduction in the size of the outgoing Administration's defence budget which it proposed leaving for its successor, whether Republican or Democratic. Eisenhower's views about the power wielded by the military–industrial complex, which he spelt out in his valedictory address, were already well known. All Tom Gates could do when he turned up was to express his sympathy with the UK's position. The reduced budget was not to be regarded as a cancellation. It would be up to his successor to decide what happened to Skybolt.

If what Tom Gates told Watkinson accorded with all that I had reported, it was completely at odds with the glowing reports which the RAF officer in the Pentagon and the RAF teams at Wright Field continued to send back. To them, the wish continued to be father to the thought, and Tom Pike, the CAS, as well as his colleagues, regarded my reports as being designed to weaken not only Watkinson's interest in the project, but also that of the American Defense Secretary. The RAF had ridiculously exaggerated views about the extent of my influence.

Skybolt had rapidly become less of a military than a highly charged

U.S. TO
SCRAP
SKYBOLT

For Solly
from Osbert L

'Ah well, I suppose we can't expect even the Americans to go on footing the bill for rockets and for Elizabeth Taylor.'

Osbert Lancaster
11/12/62

political issue. The Government had publicly indicated that the UK's status as a nuclear power depended on it. To impress this fact on the Americans, inspired pieces about the success of the development programme were published in the British press, regardless of contrary rumours that were appearing in the well-informed and influential American journal, *Aviation Week*. What was worse, all the emphasis that was being placed on Skybolt implied that without it we were defenceless. The divergence between what was being said publicly on the two sides of the Atlantic worried me considerably, and towards the end of 1960 I protested formally to Watkinson about the impression of 'bland innocence and supreme confidence' that was being spread about by the Ministry of Defence's Chief Public Relations Officer.

After the Presidential election on 8 November, there was the usual lull while the new Administration took over. It was now up to Robert McNamara, the new Defense Secretary, to decide whether Skybolt was going to be funded more liberally than the $50 million provided in Tom Gates's final budget. Herb York had recommended nothing.

In those first few weeks, John F. Kennedy, the new President, had to review the whole field of his responsibilities. It was little more than nine months since Eisenhower and Macmillan had met at Camp David, and arrangements for a submarine base in Scotland were already being negotiated. The question was whether we should now put pressure on the Americans to regard Skybolt as the other side of a bargain about the base. I was due to be in Washington during the first week of February, and it was agreed that I should try to find out exactly what was happening. Jerry Wiesner, a brilliant MIT professor of electrical engineering, had become Science Adviser to the new President, while Herb York and John Rubel were still in charge of R&D in the Pentagon.

It turned out that as part of an overall review on which he had embarked, Bob McNamara had charged Herb with the task of examining contentious R&D items that added up to some $500 million in the budget that Gates had left, a job in which Herb was working with Jerry Wiesner and members of PSAC. Included in the figure of $500 million was the item of $50 million allocated to Skybolt, and one of $70 million for SACEUR's MRBM force. It had already become clear to the President and his Defense Secretary that the presumed missile gap, about which he had castigated his predecessor during the election campaign, was a myth. The Soviet Union had not outstripped the

United States in the development of missiles. During the course of my first visit to Jerry in his capacity as the President's Science Adviser, he introduced me to President Kennedy. Kennedy began by asking me about some mutual friends, and told me that he had helped Hugh Fraser win his first election as an MP by ministering to his needs when he came in from electioneering. He described Hugh as lying exhausted on a sofa while he, Jack Kennedy, dropped grapes into his mouth. The President then asked, 'What do you think of my missile gap?' I could only answer, 'What missile gap, Mr President?' at which he laughed as though the whole thing had been a vast joke. 'I hope you and Jerry will work closely together,' he said as we left. 'Come in and see me whenever you're here,' which I did on the occasions when the President was free.

During that week in Washington, I saw Jerry, Herb and John Rubel constantly, and also had several talks with Paul Nitze, who had been appointed by McNamara as Assistant Secretary in charge of International Security Affairs. All were concerned to explain the reasons for their doubts about the technical feasibility of Skybolt, in the same way as I was concerned to emphasize the trouble that was bound to occur in Anglo-American relations if the project was not funded above the level proposed by Tom Gates. The President was fully aware of the considerable political significance of Skybolt to the UK. Equally, he did not think highly of the project. When a Senator, he had commissioned a report about Skybolt that had been very discouraging.

By common consent, Skybolt was the most daunting technological project that had yet been attempted by the United States. If the missile was to be controllable, the precise point in the skies at which it was launched had to be fed into its computers, which meant that the navigational system of the aircraft not only had to be near-perfect, but also able to transfer the information in its computer system into that of the missile at the moment of release. Information also had to be fed into the bomber's navigational system from a star-tracking telescope which the missile carried, and which had to 'lock on' to a particular star or constellation. The missile then had to right itself before starting on its ballistic course. I did my best to understand the technical details and options, but, while appreciating the difficulties, I always had to return to the political dilemma facing the British Government. Whatever problems there were in the R&D programme, I hoped that it would not be stopped.

When I left Washington I was confident that both Herb's office in the Pentagon and Jerry's in the White House would take the political factor into account when tendering their advice – knowing that while they were highly dubious about Skybolt's prospects, they were even less enthusiastic about some other items in McNamara's $500 million list, including the idea that NATO should deploy MRBMs. There our views were identical. I have no doubt at all that after my visit, Herb, John Rubel and Jerry used their influence in persuading McNamara to increase the allocation for Skybolt above the level proposed by Gates. As a result, a new figure of some $500 million to cover the entire development programme was agreed with the American Air Force. The British Government could breathe again.

That was at the beginning of 1961. It was not until the following January that the boat was rocked again. The President was entertaining Julian Amery, the Minister of Aviation, to lunch, and told him that there were increasing doubts about Skybolt, and that the UK should not bank too heavily on it. Amery exploded, saying Skybolt had to be made to work, and that if it failed, the future for Anglo-American relations would be very bleak. The President could only reply that all that could be done was being done.

But costs continued to soar, and it became clear that Skybolt could never materialize in the time that had been promised – if at all. As before, the information that I was being given by those in final charge of the project, and which I sent on to Watkinson in minute after minute, continued to conflict with the picture the RAF was painting, which was even rosier than that which the USAF could see.

Sometime in May, I therefore decided to pay another visit to Douglas and Nortronics, the main electronics subcontractor, to hear what they had to say, another reason for going being the fact that McNamara, who had recently been in London, had sounded a new warning about the technical obstacles that still had to be surmounted. Both contractors were perfectly honest with me about the further steps that had to be taken before a prototype Skybolt could be tested in the fully-guided launch which was programmed to take place in October, five months away.

I returned from the West Coast to Washington greatly impressed by what I had seen. Some, although not all, of my enthusiasm was immediately knocked out of me by Harold Brown, now the Director of Defense Research and Engineering, and by John Rubel. They had their own people, all specialists, working in the plants, and their news was that there was no chance whatever of a full test taking place in October. Only when one had been carried out would they know whether or not the guidance systems in the missile were able to interact properly with those of the aircraft. The delay, they told me, would cost at least $50 million, and it looked as though the total sum that would be needed for the R&D was likely to exceed the limit of $500 million that had been set by McNamara. Despite this setback, John did not think that the Defense Secretary would cancel Skybolt. In his view the project had proceeded beyond the 'point of no return'. I went over to the White House to hear what Jerry Wiesner had to say. He and his expert panel had also recently visited Douglas's and their information was in general the same as that of Harold Brown. Back in London I gave a detailed report of all that I had learnt.

Bob McNamara certainly had bigger financial problems on his hands than the cost of Skybolt. The Joint Chiefs had requested a budget a quarter more than what Gates had proposed, and were making inordinate demands for more and increasingly costly nuclear weaponry. One of the first of McNamara's many decisions was to cut SAC's demand for some 10,000 Minuteman intercontinental missiles to 1000. He and his advisers believed that a smaller number would be adequate for the Minuteman component of the USA's nuclear arsenal, but he also knew that he would be running into endless argument with Congressional supporters of the Air Force had he insisted on going below the thousand.*

On 13 July 1962, when Jerry Wiesner and some of his colleagues were in London for discussions with me on a variety of matters, a note was passed to me asking if I could slip away for a moment to see the

*Walter McDougall[11] records the amazing range of figures which the three Services were bandying around to whip up enthusiasm for the missile programmes for which they were each seeking Presidential and Congressional support. The USAF declared that the USSR had deployed at least 300 ICBMs by 1960. The Navy's corresponding figure was 10. The Army and CIA's estimate was 125 to 150, but after the reconnaissance satellite Samoz 2 had orbited the earth in January 1961, the figure was reduced to 60. A few months later, after further space reconnaissance, the figure had become 'at most fourteen'.

Minister – whose office was only two doors from mine. As we were near the end of our session, I scribbled a reply saying I would be with him as soon as possible. Harold Watkinson wanted me to know, before the news broke publicly, that he and the Prime Minister had agreed that he would leave the Government in order to return to private life. I was more than a little taken aback. We had established a trusting relationship over the two and a half years we had worked together, and he had been skilful in steering a course on the Skybolt issue which did not allow the political clouds to obscure the technical obstacles. After arranging that we would meet on the Monday morning, I returned to my room for a sandwich lunch with the rest of the party. Harold did not know who was going to be his successor.

The following day, Saturday, was degree day in the Birmingham University Calendar, and I had arranged for Jerry and Rabi, who were to spend the weekend with me, to be invited to the Friday night dinner for Honorary Graduands. When we arrived at the University, we were shown into the anteroom where the party that was due to sit at or near the high table were drinking sherry. I introduced my two American friends to Lord Avon, the Chancellor, who suggested that I should congratulate another of the guests, Enoch Powell who, he told me, had just been promoted by Harold Macmillan. I moved across to Enoch Powell, and, as I offered my congratulations, I asked whether he was Watkinson's successor. The reply was no, he was remaining Minister of Health, but with a seat in the Cabinet. He didn't know who had been appointed to succeed Harold Watkinson. Indeed, he had not known that Watkinson was going. As was reported in the press the following day, seven of Harold Macmillan's cabinet colleagues had been 'retired', after an operation that some papers called 'the night of the long knives', and which Macmillan later admitted might have been carried out less dramatically than it had been.

After the speeches, the Avons returned with us to Carpenter Road, where we went on talking till near midnight, with Rabi elaborating a favourite theme of his – that for Britain's own good, we had to turn to Europe and break the assumed special relationship we enjoyed with the United States. Because of Suez, Rabi declared, Eden was the only Englishman who might be able to influence the French to let us in. The closer and longer we clung to the United States, the worse for us. It was an odd conversation. It was widely believed that Anthony Eden had been responsible for seeing to it that we did not join the Community when it was launched. Anyhow, it was a pleasant end to a tumultuous day, and I went to bed not knowing the name of my new Minister.

The next morning the papers carried the news that Peter Thorneycroft had been appointed Minister of Defence. Peter turned out to be an amiable man to work with, firm in decision, as transpired when, with practically no consultation, he cancelled the Army's pet project, Blue Water (p. 210). He also quickly absorbed what he had not already learnt about Skybolt when he was Minister of Aviation. In September I accompanied him to the United States where, in discussions with McNamara, he too made no secret of the political storms that would be generated were the project to be cancelled. There was also a meeting in the State Department where, with a team that included Walt Rostow, then the head of the State Department's Policy Planning Council, and Robert Bowie, he argued against the idea of establishing a multilateral NATO Polaris force (MLF). I had a feeling that the Americans did not quite appreciate Peter's style of debate as he dismissed the whole idea.

The high point of the visit was an unexpected invitation to join a Presidential team on a three-day tour of a number of NASA's space centres. 'You'll enjoy it,' said the President, when he saw I was to be one of the party. 'You'll never again see so many billions of dollars being spent in so short a space of time.' Peter Thorneycroft and Bob McNamara were in the party for its first leg, but then flew back to Washington in a separate plane. I was in the 'back-up' plane which carried Vice President Johnson and a group of scientists, among them Jerry Wiesner and Harold Brown. What I best remember about the first part of our journey was the bare-torsoed Vice President coming back to talk to us, leaning with his elbows on the backs of two seats on either side of the centre aisle. He had a glass in his hand, and wanted to know whether all was well with us and whether we would like a drink. It was during the course of that trip that the President, oblivious of the presence of reporters, triggered an exchange between von Braun and Jerry Wiesner about the best way to land a man on the moon.*

---

*The Presidential party stopped in Houston to witness a test firing of the first stage of the Saturn rocket which was destined to take men to the moon. Jerry Weisner, Harold Brown and I were standing a couple of yards away from Wernher von Braun as he introduced the President to a line of his senior colleagues, most of them ex-German

During the rest of September the President was fully occupied with the Cuban Missile Crisis. But early in October I got news from Will Hawthorne – my man in the Pentagon – that the future of Skybolt was again looking very bleak. A few weeks later John Rubel came to London, and in good faith told Peter Thorneycroft, who had him to lunch, that at the time he left Washington no decision had been taken to cancel the project. What John did not know was that during the few days that he had been away, McNamara had decided, with the consent of the President and of Dean Rusk, the Secretary of State, that the time had come to discuss the matter of cancellation with David Ormsby Gore, our Ambassador. The two met on 8 November and, during the course of their talk, McNamara made it plain that, while no final decision had been taken, cancellation was all but certain. The Ambassador could only say that were that to happen there would be an explosion in London. On the following day, McNamara telephoned Peter Thorneycroft to repeat what he had told David Ormsby Gore, and to arrange for a further discussion when McNamara stopped in London on 11 December, that is to say about a month later, on his way to a NATO meeting in Paris.

During the intervening weeks, reports about the failure of the flight tests of Skybolt got into the news and, despite every effort on both sides to suppress them, there were leaks that the project was to be cancelled. With the writing on the wall becoming clearer every day, we sat down to consider what options were open to us, and how best the projected McNamara–Thorneycroft meeting should be steered. In accordance with the signed memorandum of understanding, McNamara's only legal obligation was to consult with us if Skybolt was going to be cancelled. If that were to happen, our concern was to get the Americans to agree to sell us Polaris 'without strings'. Polaris had to be independent in the same sovereign sense as Skybolt would have been, and not subject to American control.

I returned to Washington in early December, and saw McNamara in company with Paul Nitze and John Rubel. They were clearly very worried. McNamara broached the possibility of the UK taking the

---

rocketeers. Without lowering his voice, Harold said, 'They haven't had so grand a day since they were introduced to Hitler at Peenemunde.' I had a feeling that the President heard him, but not von Braun, who was far too busy making his introductions.

project over on the understanding that we would not have to reimburse the United States for the considerable sum which the project had cost so far. Another option was that we should buy some Minutemen – an idea which I said was unlikely to be entertained since we had cancelled Blue Streak because it was a fixed target. A third idea was that we should make do with Hound Dog, the American superior equivalent of our Blue Steel. When I suggested that Polaris was the obvious answer, I was told that this would prove difficult for the United States.

Several accounts of the meeting that took place between McNamara and Thorneycroft on 11 December, the day after my return from Washington, have been published, and all are correct in describing it as tense and dramatic. Press reports about cancellation had multiplied in the preceding week. There were also stories that the United States intended to deprive Britain of her nuclear status. Despite the advice which George Ball, the American Under-Secretary of State had given him, McNamara spoke to the press when he and his party landed at Gatwick. He told them that all five of the flight-tests of Skybolt that had been carried out had been failures, making it plain that the project was therefore being cancelled. George Ball describes the meeting as having been 'a foregone disaster'.[12]

When the Defense Secretary and his party arrived at the Ministry of Defence (among them were Paul Nitze and John Rubel, as well as David Bruce, the American Ambassador), and after the customary preliminaries, McNamara proceeded to read from a document that detailed the history of Skybolt, and which explained why the project was both a technical and financial disaster. He ended by saying that the United States realized the problem that the cancellation would create for the UK, and that in order to help, they were ready to give us free, gratis and for nothing the results of the work that had already been done, leaving it open to us to carry on with the project on our own if we so wished. Alternatively, we could buy their Hound Dog, or we could participate in a NATO multilateral Polaris force, an offer which, according to the account published later by Neustadt, McNamara was not even authorized to make.[13]

In reply, Peter Thorneycroft focused on the effects which a decision to cancel would have on Anglo-American relations, his speech ending with the question – did the United States want to deprive the UK of its independent nuclear status? One account of the meeting describes

Thorneycroft's performance as a brilliant forensic display.[14] John Rubel noted that 'a major refrain' of Thorneycroft's speech was that the UK had 'depended absolutely' on the United States. 'He said it in a way which evoked images of the most dire betrayal, and I remember reflecting at the time on his skill in evoking a sense of guilt, of obligation, on the part of the Americans who had, in fact, done nothing more than cancel a development that should never have been started, to which the British had contributed nothing, for which the Americans had no real military need, and which the British had identified as *their* "independent deterrent".'[15]

Thorneycroft's reaction was clearly the last thing that Bob McNamara had expected. Harold Watkinson had publicly acknowledged that Skybolt was an R&D programme, not a certainty.[16] And here was Thorneycroft behaving as though the whole notion of cancellation was a total surprise. What was worse, when he had spoken to Peter Thorneycroft over the telephone in early November, McNamara had been led to expect that the UK would consider its options, not from a political but from a technical point of view. He therefore tried to turn the discussion back to the question of technical alternatives. When he repeated his offer of turning the project over to us if we thought we could make a better job of it than they had, I urged Thorneycroft to ask what seemed to me to be the only relevant question – did McNamara believe that Skybolt could ever be made to work? The answer was no. Thorneycroft rejected Hound Dog out of hand, and as for our participation in a NATO MLF, what about the UK's sovereign rights over its own defences? Unless McNamara could guarantee this in a Polaris deal, the matter would have to be referred to the Prime Minister.

McNamara had no answer to any of this. He had come to explain to his opposite number the technical and financial reasons why Skybolt was going to be dropped, and to suggest ways by which the UK might be helped. Instead he had been subjected to a reply which implied that the United States had a more far-reaching obligation to the UK than had ever been spelt out in any memorandum of understanding or agreement.

The concentration on the political repercussions of the cancellation was so intense, and the atmosphere so charged, that I have completely forgotten exactly how the meeting ended, or what we did when we got up from the table. I can remember the beginning of the meeting, and the order in which we sat, with Peter Thorneycroft at the head of the table and McNamara and his party on the left side. But I have no vision of how it ended. Tempers were certainly kept under control, but nothing was settled. Did we shake hands? Did the two leaders say they were going to continue to talk in Paris at the NATO meeting which both were attending? I do not know.

Henry Brandon, the Washington correspondent of the *Sunday Times*, pieced together the strands of the story in a lengthy and notable piece that was published a year later.[17] He says that at the end of the meeting I accompanied John Rubel back to the airport, and that we discussed a sheet of paper which dealt with Polaris. John's story is that 'at the very last minute', when he got into a taxi to go to the airport, I jumped into his cab and 'closing the window that isolates the driver from the rear compartment, we held a frantic meeting all the way to the airport laying out the basis for an early meeting between UK and US representatives charged with preparing a program for introducing Polaris to the UK'.

Even that I do not remember. Obviously the two of us must have discussed Polaris several times, for he shared my view that the idea of a 'third nuclear force' under the NATO flag was dangerous. To my mind, a bi-polar nuclear world, with the UK integral to the Western side, was a far safer bet than any third force. I suppose that the sheet of paper to which Brandon referred must have been a series of technical questions that I had had prepared. At that moment John and I were not concerned with politics.

Soon after the Skybolt affair was laid to rest, President Kennedy charged Richard Neustadt, a member of the White House staff, to make a detailed enquiry into the steps that had led to so serious a crisis of confidence between two governments that were supposed to be bound by a 'special relationship'. While regarding it as a crisis that was 'superficially as sharp as that of Suez', Neustadt judged the Skybolt saga to have been a chapter of spoken and unspoken misunderstandings between the leaders of the two sides.[18] From where I stood, it seemed somewhat different.

The Americans with whom I dealt fully understood the political importance of Skybolt to the UK. On our side, however, few were ready to give proper weight to the financial and inter-Service problems with which McNamara was wrestling, nor did we have 'experts' to match John Rubel or Jerry Wiesner in assessing the technical feasibility of the Skybolt concept as a whole. As some Americans put it bluntly: who was the crazy guy who had first thought that an air-launched 'farting' ballistic missile could have its starting point fixed in space by means of stellar navigation accurately enough to hit a given target in the USSR? If it hadn't been for the fact that 'anything went' in the weapons field in the latter days of Eisenhower's Presidency, the idea would never have got off the drawing-board. In retrospect, John Rubel regrets that he did not resist much harder than he did when the Air Force demanded his approval to go ahead with the project. By the end of 1961, the R&D programme had already cost $400 million dollars, equivalent to $1,300 million today, and it had been estimated that if it were assumed that Skybolt could ever be made to work, it would have been necessary to set aside some six times as much for further R&D.

While Thorneycroft was not technically minded, I believe that as Minister of Aviation he had had enough experience of over-ambitious R&D programmes to appreciate the problems posed by Skybolt. But his main concern was political. The quasi-official leaks about cancellation in the American press had been a considerable embarrassment to the Cabinet. Some American accounts have it that when the news of the unsuccessful tests appeared, Macmillan protested, 'This is too much. The lady has been violated in public.'[19] Britain had been exposed in its nuclear nakedness. Nonetheless, I doubt very much whether Watkinson, or Thorneycroft, or Macmillan, or even Hugh Fraser, then Minister for Air, ever believed the RAF reports that Skybolt was certain to materialize. But those reports, encouraged by the USAF, helped Peter Thorneycroft make the USA feel that they had a moral obligation to do something to help.

Even when Polaris took the place of Skybolt, there were protests in the press – and in Parliament – that the UK had been misled, and that there had been nothing wrong with Skybolt, that indeed it had been a major technical achievement. Whether by coincidence or intent, at about the same time as the decision to cancel was made, the Douglas Aircraft Company announced that a sixth test had been successful. What this meant technically or operationally was never stated. But Dermot Boyle, who had been Chief of the Air Staff at the start of Skybolt, wrote a forceful letter to *The Times*, in which he hinted that its cancellation was all part of a plot. An equally angry letter from Marshal of the RAF Sir John Slessor, who had been the Chief of the Air Staff in the early fifties, scathingly condemned the decision to replace Skybolt with Polaris. 'It is a really appalling thought', he wrote, 'that a couple of Ministers and a zoologist can slip off to the Bahamas and, without a single member of the Chiefs of Staff Committee present, commit us to a military monstrosity [i.e. Polaris] on the purely political issue of nuclear independence – which anyway is a myth.'

I liked that 'and a zoologist'. The words echoed that occasion early in 1944 when I first attended one of Winston Churchill's Defence Committee meetings – 'midnight follies' as they were called – and heard him read from his brief that a plan to disrupt the communication network of northwest Europe before the Overlord landings, a plan which he opposed, was 'the brainchild of a biologist who happened to be passing through the Mediterranean'.

When the political dust had settled, I asked John Rubel whether a British team could examine the Skybolt hardware to see if there was anything to salvage. 'As soon as I have finished doing just that, you can have a go,' replied John. Some time later came the message, 'We've found nothing. You can send your team.' It too found nothing.

But one thing was not lost. The Vulcans which had been adapted for Skybolt remained in service much longer than the RAF had supposed they would – the first date that used to be bandied around when I was CSA was the mid-sixties, later extended to the end of the decade. As I have said, a few Vulcans were still in operational service at the time of the Falklands War in 1982. One day I read that a Vulcan had bombed the airstrip at Port Stanley. I thought this a pretty costly and useless operation, however brilliant from the point of view of arranging in-flight refuelling for an 8000-mile flight. There were reports of other Vulcan operations. After the surrender of the Argentinian forces, I asked a senior RAF officer why it had been thought worthwhile to bomb an airfield when the defenders had all the time in the world to fill in such craters as were made. The answer was that there had been only one Vulcan attack on the airfield, and that all the others were against the enemy radar. We used, he told me, anti-radar missiles purchased from the Americans. And would you believe it, he said, the fittings and electrical components we had made for Skybolt were just the things we needed for the missiles that were used.

23

Polaris

George Ball has described the meeting that took place between President Kennedy and Harold Macmillan immediately after the cancellation of Skybolt as 'probably one of the worst prepared summit meetings in modern times'.[1] In fact, it had been arranged many months before, for what was then assumed would be a friendly exchange of views about the state of the world. The cancellation changed all that. McNamara had told Ball that he proposed to be at Nassau with the President. Since Dean Rusk, the Secretary of State, was pinned down by another engagement, Ball knew that as Under-Secretary he would have to be there. He accordingly warned McNamara that since he, Bob, intended to be at the meeting, Peter Thorneycroft was bound to turn up. Skybolt and the UK's nuclear status had obviously become the focus of the meeting.

It began on Tuesday 18 December, and ended on Friday 21st. Ball tells us that, during the nine days that intervened between the Thorneycroft–McNamara London discussions and Nassau, he took what he calls a 'careful look' at the State Department's concept of a Multilateral Nuclear Force, since the likelihood that the UK was going to ask for the Polaris missile could prove an obstacle to any agreement about 'nuclear sharing' within NATO as a whole. That possibility also worried both McNamara and William Tyler, the Assistant Secretary of State for European Affairs. They anticipated that were the US to agree to sell the UK the Polaris missile, it would be playing into de Gaulle's hands, and so set back the concept of European integration – the State Department's 'Grand Design' – and, in particular, the UK's chances of being admitted to the European Community.

Harold Macmillan had spent the weekend before Nassau with President de Gaulle at Rambouillet, the main purpose of the visit being to discuss that very thing. But he also took the opportunity to tell the

General about the crisis that had developed over Skybolt, and about the UK's 'determination *coute que coute* to maintain an independent nuclear force'.[2] The fact that the UK's determination was to depend on the Americans was not lost on the General, and the Prime Minister returned to London on the Sunday with, as he says, 'a heavy heart'. On the same day Peter Thorneycroft had held a somewhat lengthy meeting to discuss Skybolt and Polaris. He had had a further opportunity to talk to Bob McNamara at the NATO Council in Paris a few days after their London encounter, and had become convinced that further discussion with him would get nowhere. Whatever else, the attitude of the two at Nassau in the following week did not suggest that they had become friends!

The PM flew to the Bahamas with Philip de Zulueta, one of his private staff, and with Lord Home, the Foreign Secretary. Peter Thorneycroft, Sir Robert ('Rob') Scott, who had succeeded Eddie Playfair as Permanent Secretary, and I, followed in a second aircraft. Dickie Mountbatten was indignant that he was to be left behind. The President rightly regarded the Nassau discussions as strictly political – as did Macmillan. Had Dickie been there, the American party would have had necessarily to include the Chairman of the US Joint Chiefs of Staff, which the President did not want. Dickie, however, found time to arrange for me to have the run of a luxurious villa, Shangri La, which belonged to a friend of his. Alas, I had time to visit it only once, and even that visit was somewhat spoilt by Randolph Churchill, who was one of the horde of journalists who had come to cover the occasion. Randolph latched on to me when he discovered where I was going to bathe that afternoon, but he knew me well enough not to persist when he saw that he was not going to get any more information from me than was being disclosed in the official bulletins.

The President and the Prime Minister had their separate villas, while the main British and American parties were comfortably housed in the Lyford Cay Club. George Ball describes the mood of the British team as subdued and grim. I do not, however, recall that I allowed the occasion to prevent me from fraternizing with the American party, which included David Bruce, whom I knew well, and John Rubel. I was also on friendly terms with George Ball, whom I had first met towards the end of the war, when we had cooperated in the study of the effects of bombing. If anyone was grim, I would say that it was Bob

McNamara. The meetings were held in Bali-Hai, Harold Macmillan's villa, the garden of which had been turned into a kind of outdoor office, where those like myself who were not at the negotiating table, spent the first day mainly chatting, and the rest of the time, certainly in my case, enjoying the delightful weather, and inventing something to do.

Lengthy accounts of what happened on the opening day have been provided by Macmillan himself, and by several of the Americans who were concerned. By every account, Harold Macmillan's performance was a *tour de force*. He pulled no punches in letting the President know what would happen to Anglo-American relations if Skybolt were not replaced by Polaris – and replaced in a way that did not imply that Britain's status as an independent nuclear power was being demeaned.

No new arguments were deployed by either side on that or the following day, and despite his powerful belief in the State Department's Grand Design, the President in the end gave way. The upshot was an agreement which specified that, in exchange for the right to purchase the missile, the British Polaris force would be assigned to NATO, but with the proviso that it could be withdrawn when HMG 'may decide that supreme national interests are at stake'. What these could ever be, or whether, when it came to the crunch, we would be allowed by the Americans to fire a Polaris missile without them agreeing, was never discussed.

Before he yielded to the Prime Minister's arguments, the President repeated the offer that had been made by Bob McNamara about the UK taking over the Skybolt project, with the United States making a gift of what had already been achieved with the money that had been spent. The President even suggested that, were we to accept the offer, the United States might share half the cost of the further R&D that needed to be done, but without any commitment that the missile, if it ever materialized, would be bought by the United States. The Prime Minister would have none of this. During one of the breaks, however, he once again sought my opinion before finally saying no. It could only have been as a matter of form that he put the question to me, for I am sure that the idea of accepting had never crossed his mind. My answer was no different from what it had been in London. If the best advice the President could get was that the Skybolt system could never be made to work effectively, what chance had we to do better than had the Americans, with the added handicap that we would have to manage from London a major and highly speculative project on the West Coast of America?

Strictly speaking, the United States had not been bound to provide the UK with a substitute were Skybolt to be cancelled, nor was there any formal linkage between Skybolt and the UK granting the US facilities for their submarines in Holy Loch. The whole affair had become a network of gentlemanly understandings. But the Americans, and particularly those at Nassau, were increasingly amazed by the extent to which the UK Government seemed to have been strung along by the RAF and by the USAF's propaganda machine, and so had allowed Skybolt to become *the* symbol of British independence.

Late in the afternoon of the second day John Rubel was asked by Bob McNamara to obtain answers to certain questions about the contractual arrangements that had been made with the UK when Tom Gates had been Defense Secretary. In order to check whether there were any verbal commitments that had not been recorded, John had to get in touch with Gates, which he did from his room while he and I were enjoying a drink. I was amazed by the ease with which it was all done. He simply picked up the telephone, got himself connected to the White House exchange that is always set up wherever the President happens to be, and having been put through to the Pentagon, instructed his secretary to find Gates wherever he might be. Within minutes there was Tom Gates on the line! He had been tracked to a restaurant in New York. John told him that he was in Nassau, asked a few questions and, having been answered, said, 'Say hello to Solly who is with me.' Tom Gates and I exchanged greetings, and I acknowledged that he had been right about the likely fate of Skybolt.

During the course of that day, a joint drafting team was in more or less continuous session trying to contrive a mutually acceptable text of an agreement entitling the UK to purchase the Polaris missile. Successive drafts were flashed to London as they were turned out since, not surprisingly, the Prime Minister was anxious that the Cabinet should be in full agreement with what was being set out on paper. The outcome was a document in which, as Arthur Schlesinger puts it, the drafters 'outdid themselves in masterly ambiguity',[3] and which George Ball describes as 'a monument of contrived ambiguity'.[4] It referred to a joint commitment by the UK and the USA to establish a NATO multinational or mixed-manned nuclear force, and also to a multilateral force. It also declared that the nuclear defence of the Western World was indivisible, a proposition which at first sight seemed to be at odds with the proviso that Britain's nuclear forces might in dire emergency operate on their own!

My only contribution to the final text was the addition of the words 'on a continuing basis' after the statement that the United States was prepared to sell us Polaris missiles. At the time of the meeting, two types were available, the A1 and A2, but I knew from John Rubel that the US Navy was already developing a longer-range version, styled the A3, and that there were even further plans. There was also the question of spares. The UK having just been burnt in the fires of Skybolt, it was essential that we did not land ourselves in trouble over another missile which, despite the good reports about the progress being made in its development, might in the end also fail to materialize. As it has turned out, that seemingly simple contribution of four words was more significant than I realized at the time. They made it legally straight-forward for the US to sell us, nearly twenty-five years later, the Trident missile, since it could be regarded as part of 'the continuing basis'. The same words are repeated in the formal and published exchanges of letters regarding the sale of Trident.

The Prime Minister had gone to Nassau not only disturbed by de Gaulle's attitude at Rambouillet during the preceding weekend, but smarting from a remark that had just been made by Dean Acheson, a previous Secretary of State, when he had observed in the course of a speech that 'Great Britain has lost an Empire and has not yet found a role' – a remark that no doubt had been drawn to de Gaulle's attention before he greeted Macmillan at Rambouillet. But whatever de Gaulle may have thought about Britain's lost role, he was indignant about a speech that McNamara had given at Ann Arbor earlier that year, when he had said that the nature of nuclear war made a unified deterrent imperative, and that weak national nuclear forces were 'perilous in peace' and 'disastrous in war'. As he put it, 'Limited nuclear capabili-ties, operating independently, are dangerous, expensive, prone to obsolescence, and lacking in credibility as a deterrent.'[3] Macmillan, too, called it a foolish speech.

Time has shown, however, that it certainly was not. Nor do I believe that Macmillan would have dismissed it as he did had it not been for de Gaulle's strong reaction, and for the fact that Britain's status as an independent nuclear power had then become a critical domestic political issue. He did not share de Gaulle's belief that nuclear weapons are essential instruments of war, and therefore of defence, although he might have admired the General when he declared that France was not going to be told by anyone what it could or could not do in the interests of its own security. The fact is that Macmillan was passionately concerned about the dangers of the nuclear arms race. He had declared several times that enough nuclear weapons were already deployed to destroy the Western World more than once, and he had also spoken about the futility of the belief that they could be used in battle – of which the First World War had left him with the most gruesome memories. On the other hand, it was not surprising that he also took pride in the fact that British scientists had played a significant part in the development of nuclear weaponry. It was difficult not to want to 'keep up with the Joneses'.

I doubt if either McNamara or Ball felt at ease with the Prime Minister. Both admired the dramatic way in which he had put the UK's case, but they knew that it was an act designed to sway the President. And they felt sure that the Prime Minister and Peter Thorneycroft were 'pretending' when they expressed surprise at the failure of Skybolt, and when they implied that the UK had been deliberately let down. Both must also have smarted inwardly when the Prime Minister contemptuously dismissed the idea of a ship-of-war manned by 'multinationals' – the State Department's MLF – with the remark, 'You don't expect our chaps to share their grog with Turks, do you?' George Ball's riposte, he records, was, 'Wasn't that exactly what they did on Nelson's flag-ship?'

I also knew that Bob McNamara did not like the imprecise way in which the UK, knowing that Skybolt was a highly speculative project, had dealt with its own fall-back position. The UK had been told that the USA did not intend to make Polaris available to the UK except as part of a multilateral NATO force. And, as I have said, McNamara was at the time wrestling with many proposals for new systems that added senselessly to the nuclear 'overkill' that already existed.

Before the final session of the 'summit' on the Friday morning, Rob

Scott and I were becoming increasingly worried by the implications of the course on which we were being impelled. The task of drafting the agreement had been entrusted to Philip de Zulueta on our side, and McGeorge Bundy on the American, and as successive versions appeared, we started searching for possible hidden meanings that could be read into the ambiguities that had been 'so cunningly contrived'. The earlier memorandum of understanding about Skybolt had no political overtones. The Polaris agreement did. Before the principals sat down to their final session, Rob and I therefore composed a joint minute in which we set out the matters that we found disquieting. Rob typed it out with two fingers on his own portable machine and, since Peter Thorneycroft was our departmental Minister, addressed

'Jahwohl, Herr Kapitan!'
'Aye, Aye, Sir!'
'Merde!'

Osbert Lancaster
21/5/63

the minute to him. We would have been defying normal civil service practice had we sent our note directly to the Prime Minister. Whether the PM ever saw it we therefore never knew. Nor, so far as I know, was it ever acknowledged by Thorneycroft. In it we said a way had been found whereby Skybolt could be replaced by Polaris in the maintenance of the British deterrent, but that the claim that it was 'independent' could be made only with difficulty – particularly as a cardinal feature of the President's policy was to deny his allies independent nuclear forces. As it was, we would therefore be providing vast sums of money as a contribution to a multilateral force, the object of which was political rather than military. We then went on to say that by committing ourselves to Polaris we would be losing some of our freedom of action in deciding how best to support NATO militarily, both in nuclear and non-nuclear fields, and that we would be under constraints in discussing the military policy of the Alliance and the shape and size of its forces. In so far as we were put in a straitjacket within the NATO alliance, we would correspondingly lose some liberty of choice and action elsewhere.

What also worried me was that I knew how hard the Prime Minister was working to achieve a comprehensive ban on all nuclear tests, and how much his views on this subject had already had to give way to American pressure. It was there that I felt that our independence was most threatened.

Having delivered our warning note, Rob and I hung around until the agreement had been signed at the final session of the 'principals', when we were due to sit down to a luncheon that Harold Macmillan had insisted should mark the end of the meeting. Bob McNamara had excused himself, and as he walked to his car from the compound – for that is what the garden of Bali-Hai had become, with all the guards and security men around – he called to me to walk the few yards with him. He was grim-faced and, in so far as Bob ever shows frustration or anger, he did so then, even more so than did the State Department representatives, George Ball, Tommy Thompson and William Tyler, all of whom saw better than we did what the European reaction would be to the deal. As Bob said goodbye to me, he remarked, 'If the tubes on your Polaris boats ever have to open, I hope that the first missile that is shot out is that public relations officer of your defence department.' Bob knew full well that the newspaper campaign that had painted the

Americans as villains who were determined to cheat us out of our rightful possession of Skybolt had been encouraged – or certainly not discouraged – by Brigadier Hobbs, a nice man who, together with his deputy, Colonel Sammy Lohan, were much liked by British defence correspondents. The two knew how to do their job.

We lunched on the terrace of Harold Macmillan's villa, with the Prime Minister presiding over one of the four tables round which members of the two delegations were distributed. President Kennedy was on his right, and Mr Diefenbaker, the Prime Minister of Canada, whom Macmillan had invited to hear at first hand how the Anglo-American crisis of confidence had been resolved, on his left. I was placed diametrically opposite the Prime Minister, and was much pleased to find on my right Derick Heathcoat-Amory, who had retired from the post of Chancellor of the Exchequer to become our High Commissioner in Canada.* We had first met when he had been posted in 1944 as the Army's liaison officer to the HQ of the Allied Expeditionary Air Forces – Leigh-Mallory's HQ – a posting from which he had taken French leave to join the paratroopers in the Arnhem operation, in which he had been badly wounded and taken prisoner. 'Derry' Amory had accompanied Diefenbaker that morning from the snows of Canada, for which his heavy suit was more appropriate than for the Nassau sun.

Suddenly – it must have been when we were more than halfway through the meal – President Kennedy called across to me, 'Solly, have you been up to see my nuclear rocket?' 'No, Mr President,' I replied, 'I thought you had given up all that jazz.' I was in fact right. 'What's it for?' asked Macmillan. 'To get a man to the moon,' said the President. 'But how?' was the next question. 'You tell him, Solly,' answered the President. So, with the whole table now listening, and improvising as I went along, I built on what I had learnt during the three-day Presidential tour of space centres, speaking about a non-nuclear rocket with sufficient thrust to carry its final stage, to which a 'lunar module' was attached, into the moon's gravitational field. 'Then what?' asked Macmillan. 'Oh, the lunar module would be automatically detached from the mother-ship, and with the help of its retrorockets would carry the crew gently down to the surface of the moon. They would be talking

*Later Viscount Amory.

263

all the time to ground-control at NASA's headquarters.' 'And then what?' By now I was allowing my imagination full rein. 'I suppose they'd look at each other, wait a while before opening the hatch, and then lower their landing steps. The leader would stick his head out and step down onto the moon's surface, still talking to HQ.' 'Saying what?' asked Macmillan. There was a laugh as I said, 'Oh, I suppose his first words would be, "Momma, we're here".' My words were a far cry from astronaut Armstrong's 'giant leap for mankind'.

'That sounds very easy,' said the President, 'but I don't understand how one of those small pocket-radios works. Tell us, Solly.' I was all but stumped, and looked around to see if John Rubel was at one of the other tables. But he was already on his way to Washington. I started to talk about different frequency-bands of electro-magnetic waves to which a radio could be tuned. 'I still don't understand,' said the teasing President, to which I could only reply that it was nonetheless the sort of thing a schoolboy understood. 'But *I* don't understand,' said the President. 'That's not surprising,' I said. 'You're not a schoolboy.' Some time later I told the story to Jerry Wiesner, who referred to it in a short and moving obituary he wrote after the President's assassination.

The President, as Macmillan tells us in his Memoirs, was persuaded only 'under great pressure' to stay to the lunch. When we got up from the table, Mr Diefenbaker drew me aside to congratulate me on the light-hearted way I had handled my exchanges with the President and Macmillan. I do not think that he realized as much as I did that President Kennedy might possibly not have enjoyed the meeting, and that at the time he wanted to put out of his mind what he had agreed. Macmillan had got what he had come for and, contrary to what he must have thought best, Kennedy had given it to him. His attempt to repair part of the damage by sending de Gaulle a message from Nassau offering him what he had agreed to give the UK, was rejected out of hand, even though it was backed up by a personal letter of explanation and encouragement from Macmillan. De Gaulle was not going to tie France to the American chariot.

Nearly ten years later, when Edward Heath became Prime Minister, I had to arrange his first full 'nuclear briefing', in the course of which he was given an account of the arrangements under which our four Polaris boats operated, and about our continuing exchanges with the Americans. As we walked back to Number 10 from the Ministry of Defence, the PM asked, 'How is it that the French do all this on their own?' I reminded him that it was a political decision that the UK would continue as a nuclear power but with American help, adding that 'Given the resources, we might have continued on our own.' The decision was the Cabinet's, of which Heath had been a member, but he was then devoting himself to the goal of getting the UK accepted as a member of the European Community. Nassau had certainly not helped him.

Today I wonder whether we could have 'gone it alone'. As the Americans suspected, we had no technical fall-back position when we went to Nassau. Having abandoned Blue Streak, itself based on an American model, we were unlikely to embark on another 'stationary' ballistic missile. Nor were we skilled in the technology of casting the large blocks of solid fuel that now power long-range ballistic missiles; Minuteman, for example, and some Soviet rockets. We would have been forced to fall back on V-bombers and free-falling bombs, and perhaps would have reinstated the longer-range Blue Steel II which had been cancelled when the vision of Skybolt appeared on the horizon.

Some Ministers were waiting at Heathrow to congratulate the Prime Minister on his return, and two or three were still there when Peter Thorneycroft's aircraft landed. Julian Amery was amongst them. So far as I can recall, that was the only time I ever again heard about the minute that Rob Scott and I had addressed the day before to Peter Thorneycroft. 'One day', Julian Amery said to me, 'you will be proud of that Minute; not that it has made any difference.' Even before we returned from Nassau, naval staff and officials had started to arrange for a follow-up team to fly to Washington to put flesh on the bare bones of the agreement that the President and Prime Minister had signed. There were any number of things we had to know in detail – the design of the submarines to accommodate the rockets, the control mechanisms for firing, the contractual arrangements with the firms that were building the missile, the way the nuclear warhead, which was our responsibility, would need to be designed, and so on.

It is a curious fact that so determined was Macmillan to get Polaris that he never bothered to consider what the cost would be. It really was a case of *coute que coute*. The belief in RAF circles that the Royal Navy, particularly in the person of Dickie Mountbatten, had been intent on stealing the nuclear deterrent role from Bomber Command was, to the best of my knowledge, groundless. Until the December 1962 meeting between Peter Thorneycroft and Bob McNamara, I do not recall any costings, even 'back of an envelope' figuring, for Polaris submarines and missiles. On the other hand we had costings galore for Skybolt, starting at a figure of under $1 million per missile for a buy of a hundred, and ending with something like $3 million each for a purchase of 150. Moreover, I cannot remember that the Navy protested when Macmillan returned from his meeting with Eisenhower in March of 1960 with the news that the President was ready to make a deal over Skybolt. Dickie Mountbatten had never referred to the replacement of Skybolt by Polaris until he read the depressing reports that I had sent from Washington in November 1960. On that occasion, he sent me an urgent personal letter by the overnight diplomatic bag, asking me to enquire discreetly whether, given that Skybolt was cancelled, the United States would sell the UK two Polaris submarines, including their full complement of missiles, for £100 million! As the figure implies, no serious thought had ever been given to the possibility that the Royal Navy might one day have to assume the burden of maintaining Britain's position as a nuclear power. Dickie had not even been on the scene when, in 1955, well before he became First Sea Lord, steps were taken to develop a naval nuclear reactor. According to some of his contemporaries, he never threw as much weight behind that particular development as he did to promote aircraft carriers. Dickie did, however, help influence Admiral Rickover, without whose help it looked as though we would make little progress with our own nuclear submarines. Rickover was one of those who, in 1958, spoke up in favour of amending the McMahon Act, and he gave us critical support in the purchase of a complete American nuclear propulsion plant.

After Nassau I was immediately involved in the preparations for the follow-up visit to the States, and little more than a fortnight later, after a much-needed Christmas break, I was back in Washington leading a large team of naval and nuclear 'experts'. The Pentagon official who had been put in charge of the American follow-up was John McNaughton, a friendly and shrewd man whom I had already got to know. The American Chief of Naval Operations and I had to make ritual speeches about friendly cooperation.

Needless to say, during the days that our Polaris team was conferring with the American Polaris experts, I had several meetings with Bob McNamara, Harold Brown and John Rubel, as well as with Jerry Wiesner. I was staying at the Embassy, and so was able to give the Ambassador, David Ormsby Gore, a daily report about what was happening (he was, of course, also getting reports from his naval staff). One piece of news was disquieting. Bob McNamara proposed that the UK should contribute towards the R&D for the follow-on to the A2 Polaris missile by an amount which he said would need to be negotiated, but which he thought should be a proportion that corresponded to the number of missiles we bought relative to the total cost of the whole production run. The proposal did not sound unreasonable to me, but when I returned to London and gave Peter Thorneycroft a verbal account of the results of the mission, he treated what I told him about our share of the cost of the R&D as though it was the only thing that mattered. 'They will tear me limb from limb in the House if this ever comes out,' he said.

Ormsby Gore, who was officially told by McNamara what he proposed about R&D costs, immediately sent a message to Harold Macmillan who, in his Memoirs, writes that he 'was much concerned' by the news.[6] Whether Peter Thorneycroft had already passed on to him what I had been told informally, I do not know. At Nassau the Prime Minister had assumed that Polaris would be made available on the same basis as Skybolt, on an 'actual end cost'. As soon as he received the message, he instructed the Ambassador to see the President and offer 'to add five per cent to the retail cost', an offer that was eventually accepted. Ormsby Gore later told me what happened. 'I went to the White House and in some embarrassment passed on Harold's message to the President. He looked at me, whistled, and then said, "I wonder what Bob will think about this?" ' He was straight-away connected by telephone with McNamara and repeated to him the message that he had just received. The Defense Secretary was indignant, but in the end agreed. 'Not a bad bargain,' Macmillan notes in his Memoirs.

As I have suggested, the Prime Minister did not seem to understand Bob McNamara, whom I had got to know well, and who, more than twenty years after Nassau, I still meet regularly. Macmillan writes that 'the American Defense Minister has been very grasping.' What the PM failed to realize was that while his performance *qua* performance had been greatly admired at the Nassau meeting, the outcome was not. George Ball wrote that he 'found Macmillan both shrewd and impressive:[7] shrewd in the way he played on the President's sympathy, and impressive when he suddenly spoke about the need for a United Europe' – a concept which, as the Americans saw it, was going to be badly compromised by the Polaris deal, as indeed it was.

During the time I was in Washington negotiating the Polaris purchase agreement, I was surprised to get a message from London asking me to see whether the Americans would increase the size of their financial stake in the P1127 vertical take-off aircraft project. It did not seem to me the right moment to raise the matter, but McNamara agreed in principle, at the same time as he expressed his concern that nothing of consequence had resulted from the memorandum of understanding on complementarity that Harold Brown and I had encouraged him and Harold Watkinson to sign a year before (p. 202). Officials in London had held back because of their inability to find a form of words which automatically allowed the Americans, in the interests of national security, the full use, without payment, of any developments that might be made in the UK under the agreement.

Lawrence Levy, who was using all his energies to get the American Marine Corps to 'buy' the P1127 (p. 226), was also becoming frustrated by the lack of action. So, too, were my representatives in the Pentagon, Will Hawthorne and J.R. Christie. I was therefore not surprised when, soon after my return to London, John Rubel sent me a personal letter in which he said that he had asked McNamara what precise steps the USA should take so as to expedite the P1127 project. The answer was none, not until Thorneycroft submitted a real plan. McNamara's complaint was that the Pentagon had never received a document explaining how the P1127 project was being managed, nor a schedule of operations that provided information about such matters as the service life or overhaul rate of the engine. What McNamara wanted was the kind of detailed plan that he was now demanding for all big R&D projects proposed by the US Services. He was not going to release funds for the P1127 until he had it.

John went on to warn me that there was a feeling in the Pentagon that the UK was concerned to obtain political and financial understandings at a high level, without really bothering about the substance of complementarity. Clearly there were more people in the Pentagon than just McNamara who were smarting because of the Nassau agreement and Macmillan's refusal to contribute to the R&D, adding instead 5 per cent to the retail cost. Peter Thorneycroft found McNamara's message gloomy.

Despite what had been publicly announced in the Nassau agreement, we were also dragging our feet about the MLF. Harold Macmillan had revealed how much he disliked the idea. Peter Thorneycroft had also been scathing, and the British press was in general hostile. My own view was also highly critical. By the early 1960s the USSR had become as effective as the USA in its ability to threaten nuclear retaliation as a response to military action, and particularly action in which nuclear weapons had been used either against its forces or its territory. My own view was that a third force under NATO command would complicate matters every bit as much as the idea of independent national nuclear forces in the Western alliance had disturbed McNamara. If it ever came to ordering the use of nuclear weapons, who was in command? The Supreme Commander was himself subject to the American President. To whom would a multilateral Polaris force be subject? That was one of my main reasons for believing that a bi-polar nuclear world was a safer bet for the future than a world of separate nuclear forces.

The meetings which were held in Washington to formalize the Polaris arrangements were followed by another in London, when we were visited by Paul Nitze and Walt Rostow. It was all very low-key in comparison to Nassau and Washington, but it was clear that both of them, and Rostow in particular, were deeply concerned about the British attitude to the concept of an MLF, and about the problem of assuring the cohesion of NATO after the French reaction to the Nassau agreement. They had reason to be. Not long after their visit, de Gaulle took France out of the alliance.

24

Mountbatten and the Bomb

Nuclear weapons had been stockpiled in Europe from the early 1950s, and by the end of the decade, the NATO armoury must have included thousands of warheads, with yields ranging from a few kilotons to several megatons – some, it is now known, as many as twenty! I have read that the American Chiefs of Staff had considered a plan for the possible use of atomic bombs in a 'first strike' against the USSR as far back as September 1945; that is to say, before there were any bombs to implement such a plan, and well before the Western alliance was formed. In the summer of the following year, General Spaatz, the head of the American Air Forces, had made what amounted to a private deal with Lord Tedder, then the Chief of the British Air Staff, to adapt a few RAF stations for the reception of B49 bombers and for the storage and handling of atom bombs.* Hundreds of American aircraft were still deployed on British airfields, but it was the new arrangement that helped turn Britain into what some call America's 'unsinkable aircraft carrier'. The presumption was that, were war to break out, the homeland of the USSR would come under 'strategic' nuclear attack, while the Soviet armies would face nuclear as well as conventional fire. As Field Marshal Montgomery, the Deputy Supreme Commander of NATO, had put it very simply, 'I want to make it absolutely clear that we at SHAPE are basing all our operational planning on using atomic and thermonuclear weapons in our defence. With us it is no longer: "They may possibly be used". It is very definitely: "They will be used, if we are attacked." '[1]

The military had welcomed the emergence of nuclear weapons in the belief that they could easily be fitted into the conventional scenario

---

*This information comes from the Spaatz papers in Washington. There is no reference to this arrangement in those Chiefs of Staff or Cabinet papers of the period that are available in the Public Record Office.

of land warfare. Moreover, the development of small atomic, including radiation or 'neutron' battlefield weapons had been favoured by Robert Oppenheimer, Chairman of the General Advisory Committee of the Atomic Energy Commission, not only as an idea good in itself, but also as a way of deflecting attention from Edward Teller's crusade to have the weapons laboratory at Los Alamos focus its efforts on the design of the hydrogen bomb, the need for which Oppenheimer, like many other prominent American physicists, seriously doubted, and which, as Winston Churchill later put it, was to carry mankind 'outside the scope of human control', and into 'a situation both measureless and laden with doom'.[2] But Oppenheimer knew as little about field war as the military who welcomed his ideas about designing atom weapons for battle use appreciated that there was a critical difference between a chemical and a nuclear explosion. When, years later, I read the tragic story of how Oppenheimer, who during the war years had so brilliantly directed the scientific and engineering effort to develop 'the bomb', had in 1954 been declared a security risk, largely on the basis of Teller's intervention, and how Teller then emerged as the guru of destruction, I found myself asking whether so intelligent a man as Oppenheimer would have promoted the small-nuclear-weapon programme in the way that he did, had it not been for the blinkered influence of Teller who, no sooner had he won the fight for the superbomb, began to promote small nuclear weapons as well.*

In the late fifties, the American Government had said yes to Norstad's request for medium-range nuclear missiles, and in 1957 had asked their partners in NATO to do the same. As Supreme Commander, Norstad already had at his disposal aircraft that could strike targets a thousand miles behind any possible zone of battle, and every one of which, if it were ever hit with a megaton bomb, would have disappeared in a flash. Given a war, and with the Russians now able to reply in kind, I could see Brussels, Liège, Bonn, disappearing from the map just as instantaneously as would the deep targets that NATO would strike. If the NATO high command were to consider that

*I happened to be lunching at the Athenaeum Club with John Cockcroft, then the Director of the Harwell nuclear establishment, the day the news of Oppenheimer's 'disgrace' was flashed to the world. We read it on the ticker-tape. John was silent and grey-faced as we drove off in his car to a meeting. All he said was, 'It will take America decades to get over this.'

MRBMs with a range of some 1000 miles were part of its effective armoury, the planning of land battles would become totally befuddled by the Douhet–Trenchard doctrine of strategic air power.

When I joined the then small Ministry of Defence, I suppose I had at least as much experience as anyone else in the office of the problems involved in the planning of heavy-bomber operations, either in direct support of a land battle, or in so-called interdiction attacks. In 1943 I had planned the air component of a combined operation for the capture of the island of Pantelleria, as a prelude to the invasion of Sicily. Later I had been deeply involved in the planning of direct-support and inderdiction-bombing operations in Sicily and Southern Italy and, more important, in the Normandy campaign. Field units which I had directed had made detailed analyses of the results of most of these operations.

It was therefore only to be expected that I should try to fit what I knew of the enormous and devastating effects of nuclear weapons into the context of an assumed European battlefield. My background was very practical, consisting as it did of the work on conventional explosives for which I had been responsible during the Second World War, including the field studies that I had carried out into air-raid and battle casualties, and also the experimental studies into the anti-personnel effects of small nuclear warheads in which I had been engaged in the fifties.

The Army's Operational Research Group (AORG) had already carried out some theoretical studies of tactical nuclear warfare, particularly of the numbers of battlefield weapons that would have to be used 'to force a pause' were the Russians to attack the section of the central front that was held by British troops. AORG's results had been taken into account in devising a tactical doctrine that assumed that nuclear weapons had a practical use. But when I read the available reports, I got the feeling that no-one had thought the matter through. No account had been taken of distant interdiction strikes or of the battles that would be raging on the flanks of the central part of the front that was held by British troops. It was also assumed that the Russians would not have enough nuclear weapons to reply at a rate of more than one to every two or three we used – an assumption which I could not imagine was still valid by the beginning of the 1960s. And I was also worried that the AORG studies had not considered the possibility that the morale of our own troops, as well as that of the Russians, might be shattered in the environment of a nuclear battlefield.

These thoughts were well in my mind when early in 1960 I paid my first visit to the United States as the Ministry of Defence's new Chief Scientific Adviser. One of the responsibilities of my office was the oversight of the technical exchanges that had been made possible by the 1958 and 1959 amendments of the McMahon Act of 1946 (p. 182n). I flew with Bob Press to visit first, Los Alamos in New Mexico, and then Livermore in northern California. Bob, my aide on nuclear matters, had made all the arrangements for the trip, and for almost the first time in my life I enjoyed the luxury of travelling without having to bother either about hotels or appointments.

We first stopped in Albuquerque, where I made myself known to the officials of the Sandia base, the pre-production establishment that was concerned with the design of nuclear weapons. By good fortune it turned out that the general manager of Sandia was General Kenner Hertford, whom I had first met when he was a military attaché in the US Embassy in London in the rank of major. During the first two years of the war, Kenner had been a frequent guest of my dining club, the Tots and Quots, and he also knew a fair bit about my subsequent career. He and his colleagues could not have been more patient with someone who until that moment was all but ignorant about the technicalities of nuclear warheads. As a memento of the visit I was presented with a large synthetic-quartz crystal.

We were also warmly welcomed by Randy Lovelace and Sam White at their nearby establishment, and were told about the progress that they had made in the research programme of 'nuclear-effects' that I had laid out for them nearly ten years before. Los Alamos, which came next, was then directed by Robert Oppenheimer's successor, Norris Bradbury. Norris, whom I always enjoyed meeting when in later years our paths crossed, never minded my heterodox views about the military utility of nuclear weapons, sometimes, I think, because secretly he agreed with them. The purpose of that first visit was to make me known to his warhead designers. But no-one in Los Alamos tried to persuade me about the merits of some exotic new weapon that was still on the drawing board, or to urge on me the need to break the moratorium on nuclear testing which was then in being.

That was not the case at Livermore, essentially Edward Teller's creation. Its Director at the time was Harold Brown who, little more than a year later, was to take Herb York's place in the Pentagon. I have a vague recollection of Teller looking in during the course of one of the meetings that had been arranged for me, and a more vivid one of Harold Brown's young lieutenants explaining the merits of the weapons they were designing.

The first nuclear devices that had been developed for presumed use on the battlefield exercised their effects through a combination of heat, blast, and radiation – the first two being responsible for the immediate devastation that the explosion caused. In 1955 the use of nuclear weapons had been simulated in a NATO field exercise, from which it had become clear that if real weapons had been used, millions of civilians in the battle zone would have been wiped out. Not surprisingly, the upshot was considerable disquiet in West Germany.

The Livermore scientists reacted by setting to work to devise a warhead whose effects would be essentially due to radiation – the so-called neutron bomb – regardless of the fact that they knew little or nothing about the way troops were deployed and behaved in battle. Another of Livermore's creations was the Davy Crockett, in effect a small nuclear bazooka that could be carried by an infantryman. Having listened to 'presentations' on nuclear tactics by the Livermore enthusiasts, I returned to the UK even more worried about the concept of tactical nuclear warfare than I had been when I set out. The weaponeers seemed to have no idea at all about the way battles are fought, or about what would happen on a European battlefield if scores, and possibly hundreds, of nuclear weapons were to explode in a short space of time. I could only marvel at their naive belief that any commander would welcome the responsibility of coordinating the use of thousands of nuclear bazookas that fired warheads with an explosive power of about 100 tons.

The belief that nuclear weapons could compensate for any weakness in the conventional strength of NATO's armies had surfaced in the early 1950s, when it had become clear that the members of the alliance were not going to increase their forces to the levels that the military hierarchy had then estimated would be needed to match those of the Warsaw Pact. Were the new dogma questioned, the problem of finding the resources to increase the conventional strength of the West would rear its ugly head. Another drawback was that hardly anyone seemed to want to let his imagination dwell on the reality behind the oft-repeated proposition that a nuclear war could mean the end of Western civilization.

I enquired into the restricted nature of the 'war games' that had been carried out by AORG. The answer lay partly in the terms of reference which the army scientists had been given by the military staff. They had not been asked to consider what might be happening outside the confines of the battle zone on which they had been told to focus. What was equally important was that they worked independently of the corresponding unit of the RAF which, for all I knew or could find out, had never analysed a scenario in which both sides were using nuclear weapons to destroy airfields or railway centres or munition dumps a thousand miles from the area of contact of the opposing armies. I therefore prepared a fairly comprehensive note about the further studies that I felt would have to be carried out in order to derive a more realistic picture. Of one thing I was sure. If it were assumed that the Russian forces could call on as much nuclear fire as could NATO, the outcome would be millions of civilian and military casualties and the total devastation of vast areas. NATO doctrine for the actual use of nuclear weapons seemed to me to be pure wishful thinking. On the other hand, it was equally absurd to suppose that we could afford to forget about nuclear weaponry when we faced an enemy that was similarly armed.

At a meeting of the NATO Science Committee in Paris in the spring of 1960 I told Rabi about the disturbing conclusions to which my enquiries were leading, and he suggested that I should invite George Kistiakowsky and a few members of PSAC to come to London to discuss the problem. This I duly did, on the strict understanding that the talks would be unofficial and off the record, and that we would not discuss State secrets or actual military plans. That was the start of a series of biannual meetings that I had with the President's Science Adviser and PSAC on matters of mutual concern, to which I would invite a small number of UK scientists who I hoped could contribute to the discussion. Kistiakowsky was followed by Jerry Wiesner, President Kennedy's adviser, and he by Don Hornig when President Johnson succeeded to the White House. Then came DuBridge, the President of Caltech, and finally Edward David. President Nixon abolished the post of Science Adviser as well as PSAC after one of its members had spoken out publicly against a project which the President favoured.

In so far as its members were 'cleared' to deal with any subject, whatever the level of secrecy, PSAC differed from the Advisory Council on Scientific Policy and, for that matter, from any other British advisory committee one could think of – including the DRPC. It was also much less formal in the conduct of its meetings. From then on, if PSAC happened to be in session when I was in Washington, I would often be invited to sit in when matters not too sensitive for my ears were being debated. My exchanges with a succession of Presidential science advisers and PSAC continued for some six years, and as a result my circle of friends among the American top scientists kept widening.

Our first meeting spanned four days of July 1960. To focus the discussion, I prepared a paper in which I enunciated a few general propositions, followed by sixteen precise questions. My central proposition was that neither NATO nor the Warsaw Pact would deliberately embark upon hostile action in Europe if doing so carried the risk of an all-out nuclear exchange. This proposition, or assumption, I wrote, needed to be seen 'as the fact it is', and 'not merely as the cliché it has become'. Thirty years later it has become even more of a fact than it was then. Most of my questions related to one central issue. Could the use of nuclear and conventional weapons be so integrated and controlled that, given a war, all-out escalation did not occur?

Rabi and Jerry Wiesner were in the team that Kistiakowsky brought with him. I had Bill Cook and Nyman Levin, both of whom knew about nuclear bombs, and John Kendrew, Victor Rothschild and Derman Christopherson,* all of whom, I hoped, had enough general experience to contribute to the discussions.

The meeting was a success, and I summed up the proceedings in a fairly lengthy document which, while it had no official status, was bound to be read by others in the Ministry of Defence – and no doubt in the Service departments as well. The general consensus, as I put it, 'was that once nuclear weapons became used in an engagement in Europe, both the speed of operation and the inadequacy of any

*Sir Derman Christopherson FRS, as he now is, was Professor of Applied Science at Imperial College, and then Vice Chancellor of Durham, before becoming Master of Magdalene College, Cambridge.

technical system for surveillance and control would be likely to result in escalation to (a) weapons of longer range, (b) weapons of higher yield and (c) targets of a non-specific kind'. Such an outcome, I continued, 'appears to be far more likely than that a pause would occur after the first nuclear exchange had taken place'. It followed, therefore, 'that the deployment of nuclear weapons in the field was of little, if any, value to either NATO or Russian forces except in an abstract military sense'. Were they ever used, the outcome would be defeat for both sides. Moreover, given an incipient stalemate on the battlefield, 'strategic air and missile forces' would most likely 'have been called into action in an all-out attack on the homelands of the main contestants'. Equally important, therefore, was the implication that the equipment of ground forces with nuclear weapons meant the abdication by the political authority of its power to intervene once hostilities had started, and before the process of escalation was well on its way.

As I have said, the record I made was a personal one, and I did not attempt to agree it either with members of my own party or with Kistiakowsky who, I was sure, would prepare a record of his own. That he clearly did, because in his diary, published in 1976 under the title *A Scientist at the White House*, is a lengthy entry in which he records his immediate impression of our meetings.[3] It begins with the note: 'A worthwhile trip to London', and it goes on to say that 'only Harold Brown, out of a dozen present, maintained that small nuclear weapons could be used in a land campaign without escalation'. But, as George continued, 'One of the useful results of the meeting seems to be that Harold had begun to doubt his own viewpoint.' Nearly twenty years later, in his final report as Defense Secretary before Ronald Reagan was elected President, Harold made a ritual, almost obligatory, obeisance to the hoary doctrine of the value of battlefield nuclear weapons. But he did so in words that indicated his total disbelief in their military, as opposed to political utility. As he put it:

> Our targeting plan allows sufficient flexibility to selectively employ nuclear weapons as the situation dictates. Such a capability, and this degree of flexibility, we have believed for some years, would enable us to:
> – prevent an enemy from achieving any meaningful advantage;
> – inflict higher costs on him than the value he might expect

to gain from partial or full-scale attacks on the United States and its allies; and

– leave open the possibility of ending an exchange before the worst escalation and damage had occurred, *even if avoiding escalation to mutual destruction is not likely*. [the italics are mine][4]

At the end of his published note of the meeting, Kistiakowsky wrote: 'I understand now why the meeting was set up by Solly: there is a struggle in England as to where to put their defense money – into small nuclear weapons or conventional forces. The minutes of the meeting will be used heavily, I suspect. When our JCS [Joint Chiefs of Staff] see it, they will hit the roof, because we definitely poached on their territory, and I understand that the British chiefs of staff made a determined effort to kill the meeting.'[5]

If Dickie Mountbatten ever told the Chiefs of Staff that I was convening a meeting to discuss military tactics, he never told me that he had. And if he had, the Chiefs did not have the authority to veto what I proposed doing. All I needed was an assurance of the necessary funds with which to entertain my guests in London (their fares and hotel bills were presumably looked after by Geoge Kistiakowsky). The fact is that before I started my enquiries into the military utility of nuclear weapons, Dickie had not given much thought to the problems that their deployment and potential use would raise. Both he and Harold Watkinson soon became interested in the questions that I had started to ask.

George was also wrong in believing what he did about my reasons for organizing the meeting. My concern was far more basic than the simple question whether British 'defence money' should be spent on nuclear or conventional munitions. What worried me was that NATO military policy was wholly based on the highly dubious assumption that nuclear weapons had some specific military utility.

George's reference to the American Chiefs was, however, interesting. They clearly did not like the idea of 'independent' civilians discussing an issue about which their ignorance could have been said to have been no less profound than that of 'the man in the street'. In an entry in his diary for 30 August the same year, George notes that he had to seek the approval of General Goodpaster, the defence liaison officer on President Eisenhower's staff, and later the Supreme Commander of

NATO, as well as that of Chris Herter, the Secretary of State, and of Tom Gates, the Defense Secretary, before he could invite me to Washington for a 'return match'!* This took place in October, both of us fielding somewhat different teams. Our main topics were the vulnerability of naval carrier task forces and the problems of reconnaissance and communications in the context of nuclear war. Harold Watkinson and Dickie Mountbatten were as interested in the record I made of this meeting as they had been in that of the first.

Soon I was becoming overwhelmed not only by my enquiries into the tenets of nuclear policy, but also by the increasing number of matters that were referred daily to my office, not least our worries about TSR2 and Skybolt. Terry Price, Cliff Cornford and Bob Press had more than enough on their hands. There were, however, four scientific civil servants in the Ministry, notionally members of the Chiefs of Staff machine, whom I then took over as *de facto* members of my staff. They were known as JIGSAW, an acronym for the Joint Inter-Service Group for the Study of All-Out Warfare.

As soon as the summer holidays of 1960 were over, I got the JIGSAW team to undertake more realistic studies of what the use of nuclear weapons would imply than had been carried out before. It was already recognized, but in a purely abstract sense, that a megaton bomb could destroy a city, and that a 15-kiloton bomb, that is to say one with the yield of the weapon that had devastated Hiroshima, would be more than enough to 'take out' an airfield or a railway centre. But railway centres were treated in NATO doctrine as though they were set in a wilderness, and not where most of them are, in the middle of heavily populated cities or towns. Munition dumps and tank-parks also seemed to be located in deserts, not, as they normally are, close to railway centres. The political message that came out of NATO's simulated nuclear field exercise of 1955, that towns in Western Germany are a megaton's distance apart, and villages a kiloton, had been noted, but it had had no impact on so-called military tactics. The

---

*I was much amused when I was formally asked to call on Mr John Hay Whitney, the American Ambassador to London, to tell him what George and I proposed to discuss. Jock, as he was known to his friends, and Betsey, his wife, the daughter of the pioneer brain surgeon, Harvey Cushing,[6] were already close friends of mine. After their return to the States in 1961, and whenever time allowed on my visits to Washington, I stayed with them at Greentree, their country house on Long Island.

world of the nuclear strategist and tactician was uninhabited except by Russians. Someone once said that after a nuclear exchange the living would envy the dead. But which 'living', and which 'dead', he did not say.

In an effort to impart a modicum of reality to the picture, I designed two studies for JIGSAW, the first to show what would happen to Birmingham were it struck by a single one-megaton bomb, and the second to provide a picture of the small town of Carlisle, after it had been hit by a 20-kiloton warhead. I selected Carlisle because it was an important railway junction, of a kind that corresponded to hundreds of others that might be struck as an 'interdiction' target in a European war. And I chose Birmingham, first because I knew the city well – the layout of its business and industrial areas, of its hospitals and of its different residential districts; second, because my University colleague, Philip Sargant Florence, had published an important study of the economic and communication links that held together the conurbation of which Birmingham was the centre; and third, because Birmingham had been the subject of a major enquiry into the overall effects of German bombing early in 1942. This was the study of which I had been the co-director, and which had been used by Lord Cherwell, Churchill's personal adviser, to help justify the area-bombing strategy of RAF Bomber Command. That he had misused its findings did not matter to my new enquiry.[7]

The technique followed in both studies was the detailed one that had been devised for the analysis of the actual results of conventional bombardments. The results were later summarized in the Lees Knowles lectures that I delivered in Cambridge in 1965. I did not know at the time whether anyone else had made similarly detailed studies, and indeed, for lack of any other, mine had to be used in a United Nations report entitled *Effects of the Possible Use of Nuclear Weapons*.[8] This was prepared in 1968 for the Secretary General by a group of international 'experts', of which I was the UK member. Neither the American nor the Russian representative knew of any similar studies in their own countries. Nor did Jerry Wiesner in the White House or Paul Nitze in the Defense Department, both of whom requested and were sent copies of the detailed reports.

What emerged was that Birmingham would have been utterly devastated had it been struck by a single one-megaton bomb. A third of its million inhabitants, a figure that excluded those who lived in the built-up areas contiguous with the city, would have been instantaneously killed as a result of blast and fire, or would have died from a lethal dose of radiation. Streets would have disappeared and fires would have been raging and spreading everywhere. Most of the immediate fatalities would have been due to blast. Within a radius of a couple of miles from the point of burst there would have been total destruction and few survivors. About another hundred thousand who lived close to the zone of total destruction would have been serious casualties, trapped in the debris of their houses, unable to look after themselves. Further away the incidence of casualties would have fallen. But hardly a house anywhere would not have been damaged and, depending on the direction of the prevailing wind, the whole built-up area to one or other side of the point of burst would have been affected by radioactive fall-out.

The analysis also showed that essential services would have ceased to exist in the main area of destruction. Those parts of the city that might not have been affected by the direct effects of the blast, or even by radioactive fall-out, would have been without water or drainage, power or food supplies. People who had been trapped in the wreckage of buildings, and those who were still able to fend for themselves, would have known that if they themselves could not crawl or make their way to safety, the chances were that there would be no-one to help them. Able survivors would have been either fleeing or searching for help, for food, for relatives, or for some place of shelter better than the one in which they happened to be when the bomb went off. The general conclusion of the study was that the explosion of a single megaton weapon over any one of Britain's large cities would inevitably lead to its elimination.

The corresponding analysis that we did of Carlisle, a town that then had a population of 70,000, showed that the scale of destruction from a 20-kt strike would have been *pro rata* the same as for the megaton weapon which destroyed Birmingham.

In recent years similarly detailed analyses have been carried out both in the USA and USSR (and no doubt in other countries as well). In one where the 'target' was assumed to be Detroit, it was estimated that, even if they could have been mobilized, all the medical services of the United States would have proved insufficient to deal with the aftermath of the explosion of a single bomb on the city. Today one often reads that a one-megaton attack on a big city can be equated to a million deaths – a figure which presumably is meant to include delayed deaths from fall-out beyond the city limits. No matter whether this is an exaggeration; there are no words that could impart reality to the idea of millions and millions of deaths occurring were not just one, but dozens of cities in Europe, the USA and the USSR, to be struck simultaneously.

Soon after the formation of NATO in 1949, it became customary for the Supreme Commander to convene an annual summer get-together of NATO military commanders, together with the Chiefs of Staff of all the member countries. Officials from the NATO HQ and from the defence ministries of the member states also attended. The meetings came to be called SHAPEX, and I attended my first in 1960 when Larry Norstad was the Supreme Commander. In his pep-talk to the assembled might of the Western alliance, he had stated that were the Russians ever to attack, he would have to strike back with any or all the weapons he chose. In the parlance of the day, SACEUR's conventional forces were described as being NATO's shield. If the shield proved inadequate to hold back a Soviet attack, SACEUR would strike with his nuclear sword, the understanding being that he might find himself compelled to do so with practically no delay.

Soon after the 1960 SHAPEX, Larry came to London to try to persuade Harold Watkinson that his request for NATO MRBMs should be supported by the UK. But as Supreme Commander he was also then pressing, as Harold Macmillan notes in his Memoirs, not only for an intermediate-range missile force, but also for what Macmillan calls 'small tactical atomic weapons'.[9] Presumably these were the Davy Crocketts, which were already in production. The Prime Minister was opposed to both ideas, and indeed had already ruled that British troops should not be armed with nuclear weapons except at such times as they were under the direct command of NATO's Supreme Commander. Britain had to maintain her nuclear independence. He was also passionately concerned, as I have already said, to bring the nuclear arms race to an end, in the first instance by securing agreement with the USA and the USSR to a comprehensive ban on all nuclear tests. The dilemma the Prime Minister then faced was not only how to reconcile these two goals, but how to muster arguments against the idea that NATO should have what was in effect a strategic armoury, at the same time as he defended the proposition that Britain, a member of the alliance, should continue to have one of its own.

I do not know whether Larry saw the Prime Minister the day he flew in from Paris, but I have vivid memories of his luncheon with Harold Watkinson in that ornate government hospitality centre, Lancaster House. There were three or four others, including Dickie Mountbatten and Frank Mottershead, a quiet civil servant who chaired a committee in the Ministry of Defence that had been set up to consider Larry's demands. We discussed the matter of NATO's nuclear strategy for hours, but Larry seemed to be deaf to what we had to say.

Having lived and worked with him in North Africa in 1943, I felt that I knew him well enough to realize that he meant what he said when he declared that he would not hesitate to initiate a nuclear attack. I accordingly once again drafted a lengthy minute to Harold Watkinson in which I spelt out my fears about a NATO MRBM force, a subject on which I had touched at our meeting with the Prime Minister at Birch Grove when we returned from our first talks about Skybolt (p. 240). Despite its length, Harold immediately sent it to a Cabinet committee that was then dealing with NATO policy.

The Supreme Commander already had at his disposal short-range nuclear artillery, as well as aircraft which could strike deep into Soviet territory. If he were now provided with intermediate range ballistic missiles, against which there was no defence, and which he might launch at the onset of hostilities, it was inevitable that the outcome would be an all-out nuclear exchange. The result would be a devastated Europe covered in radioactive rubble and dust, not a Europe that had been saved.

Harold Watkinson called a meeting of the Chiefs of Staff to discuss the whole issue, making clear that in general he agreed with my views, and that the entire question of NATO strategy needed to be reconsidered. Dickie and Eddie Playfair also agreed with my analysis. So, as I knew from many a talk, did Admiral of the Fleet, Sir Caspar John.* The CIGS, Field Marshal Sir Francis ('Frankie') Festing, was away, but I always felt confident that Frankie approved of my critical attitude to NATO nuclear policy. He had been a distinguished commander in

---

*Caspar occasionally stayed with us in Norfolk in the village where Nelson was born. It is to him that we owe some of the Nelson memorabilia that are displayed in the village hall.

Southeast Asia during the Second World War, and often contrived to convey a false impression that he took his responsibilities lightly. During the course of the 1960 SHAPEX meeting, Dickie, as Chief of the Defence Staff, asked me to join a small meeting of the Chiefs that he had called at our Paris Embassy. One of the items on the agenda was the future of the army anti-aircraft weapon Thunderbird. The question was whether there would be enough money to buy it as well as the corresponding RAF weapon, the Bloodhound. 'Yes,' said Frankie, 'there'll be just enough money to allow me one squadron of Thunderbirds. I can see how it will be. I'll deploy them along the west bank of the Irawaddy, and with their help you can just see me holding back the tide of Communism as it sweeps in from the East.' We all laughed. On another occasion, when Frankie and I happened to walk into a meeting of the Chiefs at the same time, he had an enormous pile of paper under his arm. 'Think,' he said, 'of all those poor fellows beavering away producing all these briefs for me, and they don't realize that it doesn't matter a damn whether or not I read them.'

After Harold Watkinson's meeting, I wrote a personal letter to Eddie Playfair saying that I could not imagine that the idea of NATO having its own strategic force of MRBMs would stop the French going ahead with the development of a 'national' nuclear arsenal that would be entirely under their control. There was therefore another spectre looming on the horizon, the possibility that if the UK agreed to the American MRBM proposals, the UK would find itself with no power of decision independent of the Americans. That freedom, I wrote, had already been sufficiently eroded without any reciprocal gains, and whatever influence we could still bring to bear on American policy was decreasing steadily. The past twenty-five years have more than justified my assessment.

But if I was worried by these general considerations, the Army was becoming concerned that I was meddling in what they, no doubt rightly, regarded as their problem. It was not long before members of the General Staff – not Frankie Festing himself – tried to apply a brake on my nuclear enquiries.

In addition to the studies that I had launched in order to impart a sense of reality to the term 'nuclear destruction', I had convened a small group, again including a few 'independents', to consider what kind of surveillance and communications network would in theory be called for if a nuclear battle were to be controlled – given that it ever could be. I had done this with the full approval of Harold Watkinson and the Defence Council, a body to which I refer later. Towards the end of my first year as CSA, it was therefore suggested that I arrange for a 'presentation' to the Council of my ideas of the problems implicit in the concept of tactical nuclear warfare.

General Sir Charles Richardson, at the time Director of Combat Development in the War Office, then wrote that the subject was, in effect, none of my business, even if I saw it as my duty to look ahead in order to sense what 'requirements' the Services might be calling for were battlefield nuclear weapons ever deployed for actual use.* Dickie, to whom I protested, immediately overruled Richardson, and also reminded me that it had been agreed by the Defence Council that the Chiefs of Staff themselves should attend my presentation. I forget whether they did, but the more I delved, and as more results of war-games carried out by JIGSAW and by AORG became available, the more convinced I became that the whole concept of tactical nuclear warfare was a delusion.

Equally, the more I enquired, the more bewildered I became at what I could only regard as blindness on the part of the military. As I saw it, the basic cause of my differences with the 'planners', all of the rank of one-star general, was that they were not prepared to step out of line. Battlefield nuclear weapons had been deployed and, however irrational the outcome, everything else had to conform. The doctrine that nuclear weapons could compensate for conventional inferiority might have made sense when only the Americans had large numbers of these weapons. But even though this was no longer the case, paper after paper continued to be written as if nothing had changed. The idea that escalation could be avoided was a matter of faith, and I only irritated when I asked how we could be confident that the Russians would not 'escalate' once we started to use nuclear weapons? Why, I asked, was it assumed that we would gain an advantage if the threat of nuclear fire prevented the Russians from concentrating their forces for a break-through? Our numerical inferiority would still leave us at a disadvantage in other sections of the enormous front across which we faced each other. As I put it in one of the many private notes I sent to Dickie, 'the

*I wrote about Richardson in *From Apes to Warlords.*

military have no more experience of the use of nuclear weapons than I or the man at the door.'

When Dickie in the course of our mutual learning process asked what I thought would happen if we failed to counter a Russian attack with conventional forces, I replied that we would then have to assume that the Russians, knowing that in desperation we might use nuclear weapons, had accepted the risk of all-out nuclear warfare. On the other hand, since I did not find it credible that the Russians would risk all-out nuclear war, I was not prepared to believe that they would ever launch a conventional attack on such a scale that it could not be held by conventional means.

I went on to ask him to provide answers to three questions: first, why was it assumed that we could not hold a conventional Russian attack? Second, did the military really believe that there was anything to be gained by multiplying the numbers and types of nuclear weapons in Western Europe, as opposed to merely reinforcing the strategic deterrent? And third, why did he suppose the multiplication was taking place?

Dickie got his staff to help him prepare answers, which he sent me, again in a personal minute. He was ready to agree that there was no point in multiplying nuclear weapons merely for the sake of so doing; it was just happening without adequate thought. On the other hand, he and his planners did not believe that we could stem a Russian attack with conventional forces alone, and consequently he felt that nuclear weapons would have to be used, in the hope that escalation would not occur. In his view, if the Russians attacked, they would withdraw if things became too difficult, and before the battle showed signs of escalating into a strategic nuclear exchange.

I knew that Harold Macmillan was interested, so, with Dickie's agreement, I sent copies of our exchanges to the Prime Minister. I had already sent the PM a 'personal' copy of the earlier and lengthy minute on MRBMs that I had prepared for Harold Watkinson, knowing that he shared my scepticism about their military utility.

I realized from the start that my nuclear dialogue with Dickie was easier for me than for him. Although the exchange was a personal one, what I sent him was seen not only by his own staff, but also by the Joint Planners, who served the Chiefs of Staff Committee.* The result was

*The Joint Planners were replaced by the Defence Planning Staff in 1968.

that Dickie's 'personal' replies often tended to be coloured by the hallowed dictum that NATO could use nuclear weapons in field war, regardless of the build-up of Soviet nuclear strength and of the fact, which both sides recognized by the dawn of the sixties, that it was within our power to destroy each other, regardless of who struck first.

Philip Ziegler was not exaggerating when he wrote that Dickie was deeply mistrusted by the Chiefs of Staff and, indeed, in many other corners of Whitehall.[10] Even if in theory they served the Chiefs of Staff, the Joint Planners were his invention, and Dickie could not bluntly reject their advice because he favoured mine. As long as nuclear weapons were believed to have some real value in battle as distinct from their political and psychological significance, the planners had to try to show how existing military tactics could be adapted to take the new weaponry into account. When his staff declared that escalation was not likely to occur, the furthest Dickie could go in writing was to say that he could not give a guarantee that it would not. That was fair enough for me. I had no need to say that escalation was inevitable; it was enough for me to make the point that the chances were that it would occur. But to insist, as the Army Staff occasionally did, that there was a 'principle of non-inevitability', and that in consequence nuclear weapons could be safely used in the field, was to me ridiculous.

One thing that kept worrying Dickie was the thought that if it were assumed that nuclear weapons were going to be used, military considerations might dictate that it would be better to use them straight away. If that were the case, I told him, all we needed in the way of conventional forces was a 'thin red line' of soldiers, and a policy of immediate and massive nuclear retaliation which, as I then reminded him, no political leader any longer regarded as credible. We are, I said, clearly faced by a classical dilemma, and one that could not be resolved 'merely by pursuing the same argument in the same words in ever decreasing circles. We have got to break the circle, either by re-examining the postulates of the argument, or by introducing into the circle some new considerations.'

It was not long before I was able to put my views to a wider audience. Early in 1961, Bob Robertson told me that Larry Norstad had asked him to organize a symposium for the 1961 summer SHAPEX to the general theme of 'Science and Warfare in the 1970s'. Bob thought that it was about time that the subject of the use of battlefield nuclear weapons was ventilated publicly, and that I should prepare a paper. I told Dickie, who also thought it was a good idea. Prepare a real 'shock piece', he said.

I was able to write it in the quiet of the country, for in the latter part of April my voice had given way, and I had to leave London and its endless meetings. But first I had to fulfil a promise that I had made to Lord Tedder to give the prizes at Dauntsey's School, of which he was a Governor. Just in case my voice failed utterly, Joan drove down with me from Birmingham to the school in Wiltshire, having undertaken, if necessary, to read a short speech that I had hastily scribbled. I managed to read it myself, but when I came to my final sentence, my voice simply disappeared, and all I could do was smile at the prizewinners as I silently handed them their awards. The Headmaster thanked me in a nice little speech, and then a boy came up to the dais and gave me my own prize – a pot of honey to soothe my vocal cords. Someone had slipped out and got hold of it during the course of the proceedings.

By the time of the SHAPEX meeting at the end of May my voice was completely restored. Dickie and Bob Robertson served as joint organizers, and the meeting was chaired by the Supreme Commander himself; that is to say, by Larry, who was flanked on the platform by General Earle ('Buz') Wheeler, the C-in-C of the American forces in NATO, and General Adolf Heusinger, the senior German in NATO.

I gave my paper the title 'Judgment and Control in Modern Warfare', and it embodied most of the conclusions that I had reached in the course of what had been a year's enquiry into NATO policy. I began by enunciating three general propositions. The first was that the military input into complex weapon systems was declining as fast as the technical input of the non-military weaponeer was increasing. The second was that neither battles nor wars are uniquely determined by matching units of destructive power. My third generalization was that the more extensive and scattered an organization, the more difficult did it become to coordinate its heterogeneous parts.

I then painted a realistic picture of the devastation that would result from a nuclear strike, using as illustration my Birmingham and Carlisle studies. Finally I turned to the results of war-games that simulated nuclear battles in central Europe. Here I referred not only to AORG's work, but also to field exercises that had since been carried out by

NATO commanders. I rubbed in the fact that, according to NATO plans, nuclear strikes would be made far behind the battle line – and by both sides, at the same time as short-range nuclear weapons were used in the battle zone itself. I reminded the audience of the enormous shortcomings of the command and control apparatus with which the Supreme Commander would have to try to direct a battle in which nuclear weapons were used – I knew of no nuclear war-game that had ended in victory for the defenders, only in devastation and disaster. Nuclear weapons, I insisted, could not be categorized as tactical or strategic. Whatever they were deemed to be depended on the target they struck. A few Soviet 'tactical' nuclear strikes could remove from the map some of the smaller member states of NATO. That could hardly be regarded as tactical warfare. After referring to the limitations of abstract operations analysis that left human beings out of account, I summed up by saying that when we spoke about the potential use of nuclear weapons, we had to avoid the conceptual framework that derived from the military terminology of pre-nuclear warfare. One could deter with nuclear weapons but, I asked, could one defend?

There was silence when I sat down. General Heusinger, shaken by the picture of destruction that I had painted, rose to express his disquiet about NATO nuclear policy. A few others in the audience commented in what I thought was an aimless way, and at the end of the meeting General Wheeler invited me to his room for a drink. He spoke as though my picture of what a nuclear battle would be like was the first he had ever heard. 'We have painted ourselves into a corner,' he said. 'How do we get out of it?' I had never heard that expression before, and it stuck in my mind. But I had no answer. He then suggested that my paper should be published, and after some rewriting and some excisions for reasons of so-called security, it appeared about six months later in the American quarterly, *Foreign Affairs*.[11] A footnote indicated that it was published with the authority of General Norstad, the Supreme Commander, and of Admiral of the Fleet, Lord Mountbatten. Publication had, of course, also needed Harold Watkinson's permission, and by implication, that of Harold Macmillan.*

---

*In December 1961, that is to say seven months after the SHAPEX meeting, I delivered the guest lecture in Ottawa at the annual meeting of the Canadian Defence Science Board to the title 'Field Warfare in a Nuclear Age'. My paper, which was intended for publication, gave a far more detailed picture of the results of our studies. I

I often wondered why Larry had not objected to the publication of my article, since the views it embodied were so contrary to the NATO doctrine that he, as Supreme Commander, was propounding. Did he really believe the doctrine, I wondered, or was it simply the accepted wisdom of the Pentagon? I remembered that in 1943, shortly after General Spaatz had moved his headquarters from Algiers to Constantine in Algeria, Larry, as Operations Officer, had had to lay on a small bombing attack on the town of Marsala on the west coast of Sicily. The raid did little damage, but Larry hated being teased by one of the other older members of Spaatz's small mess as 'Larry, the killer'. Larry must also have often thought hard about Hiroshima and Nagasaki, whose destruction he had helped to plan.

The publication of my SHAPEX paper attracted immediate attention. Several British and American papers declared that I was challenging accepted doctrine, and questions were asked in the House of Commons. The Labour front bench, led by Hugh Gaitskell and George Brown, pressed Harold Macmillan to agree that, since I was a full-time official, the publication of my heterodox views represented a change in government policy. No change in policy was implied, said the Prime Minister. The publication of my piece had the authority of the Government because it was felt that the issue was so important that it should be fully discussed and given the widest possible publicity.

Despite whatever remaining reservations Dickie may still have had about my views, he started to worry his military colleagues about NATO's policies. He was therefore disconcerted when, only a few days after our return from the SHAPEX meeting, he discovered a passage in a speech that Harold Watkinson had just delivered to the Western European Union which read 'we should give a firm backing of atomic fire power to all our field forces. By this, I mean nuclear weapons of an Army support nature, highly mobile, but of limited range and yield.'* Dickie had seen a draft of the speech, which presumably had been prepared for the Minister's consideration by one of Mottershead's staff (p. 283). Certain sentences that Dickie had thought 'would be dangerous' had been deleted, but he had not noticed the one about

---

made the point that nuclear weapons had no military utility even more forcibly than I had at the SHAPEX meeting.

*The WEU still exists side by side with NATO and the EEC.

'atomic fire power'. He sought my views about what he should do, and then drafted a letter pointing out to Watkinson that the ministerial statement conflicted with the line he was taking with his American colleagues, and would enable the War Office to return to the charge that, contrary to the Prime Minister's ruling, British forces should have nuclear arms even when they were not under SACEUR's command.

There was a lot more in the letter, a copy of which he sent me on the following day under cover of a 'personal and private' note, in which he said that perhaps he would not send the letter to Watkinson, but instead would use it as a brief from which to speak to the Minister 'more in sorrow than in anger'. Dickie then wrote saying that there was one small critical issue to which he wanted my answer: did I accept that the existence of a small number of short-range, small-yield tactical nuclear weapons under full political control in NATO can act as a deterrent to limited aggression in an era of nuclear sufficiency?

I replied somewhat lengthily in a letter that began: 'The answer to your question is not a simple "Yes" or "No". In fact, the question is better put: "How much more credible does the threat posed by the West's nuclear weapons become if a proportion of them are deployed by NATO forces?" A brief statement of opinion, or an affirmation of faith on this question, does not, by itself, help anybody.'

I went on to say that we agreed that nuclear weapons deterred, and that field battles could not be fought with nuclear weapons. 'If a few more nuclear weapons were to help to deter more,' I continued, 'then well and good. But since the very existence of *any* nuclear weapons constitutes a deterrent, I cannot see anything but the most expensive waste in multiplying NATO's nuclear stockpile. I am sure that this is already too big for whatever purpose NATO weapons could achieve in deterrence. The reason why I accept the *status quo* is *faute de mieux*. For no other reason. Putting more nuclear weapons into NATO would only help aggravate the situation and obscure the main problems.'

From that moment the argument was settled for him. Of course the army planners continued to write papers about an assumed reality of nuclear battles, and as CDS, Dickie had to keep the peace with the Chiefs, particularly when General Sir Richard Hull succeeded Frankie Festing as CIGS. Dick Hull was not ready to accept the view that nuclear weapons could not be fitted into the armoury of usable weaponry.

Mountbatten and Twenty Nuclear Propositions

Unlike the Permanent Secretary and the Chief of the Defence Staff, the Chief Scientific Adviser had no executive responsibilities. On paper, however, my status was equal to theirs in relation to the Minister of Defence. Other than my everyday duties as Chairman of the DRPC, I acted as a one-man 'think tank'. At weekends, when not on some official visit overseas, I could turn from a piece of laboratory research, or from the draft of a scientific paper to one on nuclear policy.* In London I would have been unable to write lengthy minutes – some more like essays – such as the one on NATO MRBMs that I sent Harold Watkinson in July of 1960, and which he had sent unedited to a Cabinet committee (p. 283). When arguing with myself about the *a priori* assumptions that always seemed to characterize NATO's plans, I needed the same kind of quiet that was called for in reaching a judgment about some challenging new scientific observation or piece of analysis.

When he took over from Watkinson as Minister of Defence, Peter Thorneycroft was already aware of some of my views about nuclear matters, and I was therefore not surprised when he asked me to prepare for him a statement of my 'personal views on the basic issues covering nuclear and conventional warfare and the use of tactical nuclear weapons'.

I answered in an essay that I entitled 'Twenty Propositions'. The views that it embodied were those that I had ventilated at the NATO SHAPEX a year before, plus some that related to the significance and reality of nuclear deterrence. I sent copies of my first draft to him as well as to Rob Scott, who suggested some minor amendments, which I

*My secretary at the University was 'cleared' to deal with all confidential matters, and as a visible sign of security, a vast safe stood in my office in the Department of Anatomy.

incorporated in a second draft.* In his Mountbatten biography, Philip Ziegler writes that sometime in 1962 I 'tabled a paper arguing against the multiplicity of tactical nuclear weapons and inferring that Europe should rely on the American strategic deterrent and itself concentrate on building up conventional forces'.[1] Dickie insisted that the paper 'should be considered by the Chiefs of Staff and its author given a chance to defend his view, "for, as matters stood, he was in agreement with Sir Solly Zuckerman's paper"'. The response from the Chiefs was friendly when the matter was raised at one of Dickie's COSIs, but the follow-up in writing was predictably less so, except for Caspar John who, speaking for the Navy, hoped that I would extend my analysis to warfare at sea.

To my surprise, what Tom Pike did not like was the fact that I had pursued my analysis having in mind a background of actual – that is to say, of potential – operations. He was also worried lest something that I had written could be taken as implying that Skybolt, which had not yet been cancelled, was not as sound a nuclear strategic system as a sea-based system might prove. In acknowledging his comments in a personal letter I told him that I was neither for nor against any weapon system. 'What I have tried to do,' I wrote, 'is set out the arguments in a dispassionate way and to draw the most reasonable conclusions one can from them. If my arguments are wrong, my conclusions – which I called "propositions" – would necessarily be wrong. Even if my arguments are right, I may have drawn the wrong conclusions.'

Dick Hull, the CIGS, was the only one who did not like any part of my paper, which he declared was written from 'an emotional and humanitarian point of view rather than from that of pure scientific advice on defence'. He rejected the view that the chances were that field operations in which nuclear weapons were used would become uncontrollable, and argued that, because escalation might not occur,

---

*Peter Thorneycroft received my first version early in September 1962. I did not bother to send him the final one which I had had typed in July 1963. My memory is that it was seen only by Dickie, Rob Scott and my own staff. I had changed the order of some of the propositions, made reservations here and there, and overall had been left with a document which was less coherent than the original – but without any real change of substance. But what I can now see is that, at least on paper, I managed to get a much greater measure of agreement from my service colleagues over twenty years ago than I believe would be possible today, despite the enormous growth of nuclear arsenals since then.

one could rely on it not to occur. Dick Hull had got it wrong. I was not arguing from 'an emotional and humanitarian point of view'. I may have humanitarian instincts, but my concern was that the army planners were living in wonderland. They did not seem to realize what a mess nuclear explosions would make of a battlefield; that all communications would be disrupted, so making command and control impossible, and that the scale of destruction would be so great that it would be impossible for such survivors as there might be to move in an organized way. It was not arrogance that made me think that I could see further than my critics. It was the fact that my life-long experience as a scientist had made me suspicious of conventional wisdom, and that I knew as much, if not more, than most of them did about the realities of destruction.

Dickie's staff agreed with all but two of my propositions. As professional military men, they thought I was wrong in not regarding the predictable annihilation of our own side as an acceptable military option. Dickie dissented. He accepted my view that 'fighting to the last man' had no meaning in a conflict in which nuclear weapons were used. The Joint Planners submitted their contributions, as did the separate planning staffs in each department.

My own staff helped in dealing with the mass of paper that I had inspired. In submitting some textual amendments, Terry Price wrote 'you may feel at times that I am no longer on the side of the angels. There is a simple explanation. I have suggested toning down some of what you have to say because of my feeling that this is such an important document that it would be a great pity if the forces of darkness could point to even one statement which if quoted out of context would appear unfair or exaggerated.'

It had never been my intention that a personal minute in which I had set out my own thoughts for Peter Thorneycroft would be subjected to such wide and critical scrutiny. That was Dickie's idea. But it helped refine my own views which, during the years that have followed, I have further sharpened in several published papers. Had Dickie not said that he was 'in agreement' with my first draft as it stood, I doubt if the staffs of the service departments would have bothered much about a paper written by a civilian who had dared to cast doubts on tactical doctrine.

Towards the end of 1961, well before I drafted my 'propositions paper', Harold Watkinson had thought it would be a good idea if I were to organize a 'presentation' for his ministerial colleagues, as well as for senior service officers and officials, to indicate the realities of nuclear war. It took place in the old Admiralty Building in a small room that had been adapted for the showing of films. As a background we borrowed from the Home Office a three-dimensional model that showed what a few acres of London would look like at the periphery of a nuclear explosion. For all I know, the model may still exist. Terry Price and the members of JIGSAW gave brief accounts of a series of our studies, including those that concerned the use of nuclear weapons in field warfare. For good measure I included in the agenda an account of the results of a detailed analysis of the disruption that would beset the industries of the USSR were Leningrad and other cities in the northwest of Russia to be struck by a few of the Blue Steel missiles that we had developed, but which were going to be withdrawn from service – despite Harold Watkinson's view, which I strongly shared, that they were a useful deterrent weapon. Obviously we could not expect busy Ministers and officials to sit through the whole programme, but at the end of the day I remember feeling that people just did not want to know what the term 'nuclear war' implied.

I was also not surprised that the War Office did not like the presentation. More AORG war-games had by now been completed, one of them somewhat more realistic than the usual kind, in so far as two divisional commanders had been summoned from the British Army of the Rhine to pit themselves against each other in a simulated nuclear battle. They and their respective staffs were separated from each other in different huts, each furnished with a vast relief model of the actual terrain where their forces were deployed, the defending British general commanding the Blue, and the attacking general, the Red. Both huts were connected by telephone to the umpires' hall, where a relief model displayed the disposition of both forces by means of little coloured flags which were moved in accordance with messages sent to the umpires by the Blue and Red commanders. When, as anticipated, the Red forces started breaking through, the Blue commander was allowed to call for the use of nuclear weapons. In due course Red replied in kind. The result was a shambles, with each 'game' grinding to a disastrous halt. I watched in the umpires' hall, saying nothing.

Wishing to teach me the error of my ways, Dick Hull arranged a contrary presentation for me at the War Office, which purported to show how a tactical nuclear battle could be controlled. All that happened was that my doubts were even further sharpened. There were the usual maps showing the disposition on the central front of our own and the 'enemy's' forces, with Intelligence and Operations officers indicating how our troops would react in the face of attack, and exactly how, when and where nuclear fire would be exchanged. I realized that the officers concerned did not have much idea about the amount of destruction that would result from nuclear explosions, or about the terror that would afflict not only the civilian population in the battle zone, but also our own and the enemy's troops. But there it all was, on the maps and on the board, scores and scores of nuclear explosions, and then victory for our side.

When it was all over, Dick Hull asked me whether I was now convinced that nuclear weapons could be used on the battlefield. 'Well,' I said, 'I don't see our fellows stopping in the middle of all that for a brew-up,' adding for good measure, 'nor do I see anyone being decorated for valour on the field.' Since Dick's staff were present, this was not the most tactful thing I could have said. But I could not help it. The scenario made absolutely no sense to me.

A month or two later, Dick Hull gave a still bigger presentation to a larger audience, which included Peter Thorneycroft. I read the script, and sent Peter a detailed commentary, which concluded that it was nonsense to talk of 'military success' after two hundred or more nuclear weapons with an average yield of 15-kt, had burst in an area equivalent to a narrow band that reached from Whitehall to Reading, some thirty-five miles away. 'A highly dangerous aspect of the presentation,' I pointed out, 'was the assumption of asymmetry in the use of nuclear weapons, by which I mean that the Russians would not use them at all, or would use fewer than we would. Or that one of their nuclear strikes would damage us less than one of ours would damage them.'

I do not, however, believe that it needed any comment of mine to make Peter Thorneycroft sceptical about the concept of nuclear field-war. After all, within days of becoming Minister of Defence, he had cancelled the Army's pet nuclear project, Blue Water.

Dickie's arguments with the Chiefs about nuclear policy did not stop, and all I could do was encourage him not to give way on the specific issue of the military utility of atomic weapons. The UK, I urged him, should not pay lip-service to the doctrine that nuclear war (as opposed to the concept of deterrence) was militarily feasible simply in order to give the impression that NATO had a united view on the subject.

He himself had made his own views clear at the 1962 SHAPEX meeting. Edward Teller had been invited to address the meeting, and had spoken mysteriously about the development of wonderful weapons which the Russians could never face. What he was hinting at, as though it were a dense secret that could not be revealed at so open a meeting, was the neutron bomb. He claimed that he was speaking to the military commanders of NATO on behalf of 'the scientific world' – which he made sound like a sorcerer's kitchen.

As soon as he had sat down, I rose and said that Teller was presuming when he said that he was speaking for the world of science. He was speaking, I said, only for himself and his small band of acolytes, in opposition to the majority of the defence scientists with whom I myself conferred. Neutron bombs were nuclear weapons, and could not be used on a European battlefield without accepting at the outset that their use could well be countered not only by similar weapons but by other kinds of nuclear armament.

I had told Dickie that I expected that Teller was going to talk about the wonders of tactical nuclear weapons, and that if I was right, I proposed to challenge him as I would have done at any scientific meeting. As soon as I sat down, Dickie got up and, in the course of some five minutes of criticism, said that Teller had been proclaiming dangerous military nonsense. I do not know whether it was this 1962 SHAPEX speech of Dickie's to which Ziegler refers as having given Dickie satisfaction, but it certainly gave me satisfaction to hear Teller's military fantasies being swept away so effectively by a man whose military credentials no-one could question.[2]

During a break in the proceedings, I was chatting in the sunshine with some uniformed friends, when Teller came up to me and, in his strange accent, said, 'I will never forgive you for that,' to which I replied that it would make not the slightest difference to me if he didn't. I knew that nothing could stop him. To this day he continues to expound what to me is dangerous military and political nonsense. Every now and then his name crops up in the European press, mainly in reports of speeches in which he extols the technical miracles that are, or will be, associated with President Reagan's dream of a space defensive system that is going to make nuclear weapons 'obsolete and impotent'. Not so long ago I read a paragraph which reported that he had 'reassured' an Italian audience that, given a nuclear war, they need not fear that all of them would be killed. There would be some survivors! And anyhow he wanted them to know that it would be relatively easy to construct a defence against nuclear weapons for Europe. Relatively easy, a cynic commented, when the opposing forces face each other from opposite sides of a street!

The debate about NATO nuclear policy that I had triggered in London, and which I had opened up in my exchanges with Kistiakowsky in the summer of 1960, was soon overshadowed by a wider one that Bob McNamara initiated in response to mounting disquiet among America's European allies about the Dulles doctrine of massive nuclear retaliation. In his Ann Arbor speech of June 1962, which both de Gaulle and Harold Macmillan had decried, McNamara had stated his conviction that the Western alliance could not tolerate divided nuclear command. McNamara fully appreciated the fears of a trigger-happy America that were entertained by some of her European allies. Therefore, in place of the Dulles doctrine, he proposed a policy of 'graduated response', which he first styled 'a full options policy', and which in due course became known as 'flexible response'. He writes in his *Blundering into Disaster*, that it took from 1962 to 1967 for the NATO Council to accept his proposal.[3] In theory it has remained NATO policy till today.

So far as I was concerned, the Pentagon's terminological changes did not alter the fundamental fact that, without adequate conventional strength to counter any attack by Warsaw Pact land forces, the threat of using nuclear weapons was tantamount to a declaration that the peoples of the northern hemisphere were ready to risk extermination because they could not settle their political differences with the USSR. I was convinced that it was a dangerous illusion to believe that NATO's difficulties could be disposed of by providing it with its own strategic deterrent – that is to say, its MRBM force. As I put it in my 'Twenty Propositions' paper, the idea was 'militarily worthless, and probably dangerous', and 'could not make sense unless real political unity were to develop both within Europe and between a coherent Europe and the

USA.' Since NATO's Supreme Commander had to dance to Washington's nuclear tune, Bob McNamara's changes of emphasis meant that SACEUR (Norstad had been replaced by General Lemnitzer in 1963) had to revise his so-called strike plan.

As CDS, Dickie was the UK's representative on the NATO Military Committee, and at times he all but despaired of getting his opposite numbers to recognize that any policy was better than one which implied that nuclear extermination was an acceptable option. I continued to send him personal minutes on the subject, one of which I entitled 'Consistencies and Inconsistencies in our NATO Strategy'. Rob Scott again wanted me to agree to it being put into 'the machine'. Having had so much time taken up when this had happened to my 'Twenty Propositions' paper, I declined, saying that in due course I would pull together all my writings into a comprehensive document. At the time I had more than enough on my hands, and anyhow, Dickie was there to drive the lessons home, if that was at all possible. As Philip Ziegler puts it:

> 'Mountbatten enjoyed playing the *enfant terrible* at NATO meetings, asking the questions that nobody else had dared articulate. . . . There was some relief mixed with the regret when Mountbatten made his final appearance in 1965. His valedictory address was a plea for sanity; for acceptance of the fact that, if nuclear warfare broke out, NATO would have failed and would have no serious part to play in the ensuing carnage; for an end to the accumulation of ever larger nuclear stockpiles and, instead, for the provision of mobile, well-equipped conventional forces capable of dealing with any sudden but limited incursion by a satellite country. His last words were 'a heartfelt tribute to this, the greatest peacetime alliance the world has ever seen. Its existence has ensured peace and stability. May it continue to do so.'[4]

But despite all the arguments of those days, the idea that nuclear weapons do possess a value as weapons for use in battle still holds sway in conventional military and political circles, and not least in the public mind. McNamara's concept of 'flexible response' was one step towards the goal of sanity. He has since taken another. There are no

299

circumstances, he now declares, in which nuclear weapons have military utility. Nuclear weapons can deter; they cannot defend.

Perhaps the whole argument would have gone differently, and with it the arms race, had we all been clearer about what would happen were a nuclear shell actually to explode over a battlefield. In 1960 it never occurred to me to ask whether anyone had ever witnessed the explosion of a nuclear weapon at the close quarters that would prevail in a zone of battle. My own views were derived by relating what I knew about the effects of nuclear explosions in general to situations with which I had become familiar during the Second World War. The fact that there was information about what would happen was unknown to me until 1983, when Bernard O'Keefe, a man with considerable experience of testing of nuclear warheads, published his account of what actually happened when a nuclear artillery-shell was fired.[5]

The test was apparently the only one of its kind that has ever been made in the West. The gun was fired by pulling a lanyard, and the twenty-five men who were at the 'exercise' then jumped into a five-foot-deep trench. Mr O'Keefe tells us that he snatched off his dark glasses and

> watched the fireball churning its way thousands of feet up into the sky, visible for fifty miles around, the familiar mushroom cloud identifying it to all the world as a nuclear explosion, then the shock wave, very powerful in the trench, rattling windows in Las Vegas, ninety miles away; I was aghast. . . . My dark glasses protected my eyes against the first flash. What of the soldiers on a battlefield? The first flash would sear the eyeballs of anyone looking in that direction, friend or foe, for miles around. Its intensity cannot be described; it must be experienced to be appreciated. The electromagnetic pulse would knock out all communication systems, the life blood of a battle plan. In addition to its effect on troops in the vicinity, everyone for fifty miles in any direction who lived through it would realize that it was a nuclear explosion. It would seem like the end of the world, and it probably would be, for any man who had a similar weapon under his control, who had a button to push or a lanyard to pull, would do so instinctively.

I sometimes wonder if the record of the test was deliberately buried at the time, even from those who had access to the most secret information, for fear that it would reveal the total irrationality of the concept of battles fought with nuclear weapons. Had the information been available, I cannot imagine that we would today still be listening to some of the extraordinary views of European politicians about the significance of nuclear weapons to the defence of their countries.

This particular issue was not the only part of my 'Twenty Propositions' that provoked controversy. I find it odd that twenty-five years ago I had to spell out the obvious point that the 'credibility' of our own strategic nuclear deterrent force depended not on what we believed about the technical effectiveness of our nuclear armoury, but on the views of the side which it threatened. As I put it then, one could not imagine that the leaders of a nuclear-weapons state would dare to engage in war with a similarly armed opponent, given the certainty that its own capital city and, say, ten of its other major cities, would be utterly destroyed. I could not see any British government ever believing that some political prize could justify the certain total destruction of London and of half a dozen of the other great cities in the United Kingdom. In my exchanges with the planners and intelligence authorities of the day, that was the criterion which I argued could be equated with the term 'minimal deterrence'. The contemporary American criterion of 'mutually assured destruction', or MAD, assumed the death of some fifty per cent of the population of the USSR, and the destruction of two-thirds of its industry. The concept of mutually assured destruction was truly mad.

In the real world, were a mad enemy to strike first, it would not matter how powerful one's own nuclear force had been. That means not thousands of retaliatory weapons, but scores, so deployed that they could not be destroyed. As I put it in another of my propositions:

> The state of mutual strategic deterrence, upheld by the threat of retaliation with nuclear weapons, will remain valid until (1) a meaningful defence is achieved against both ballistic missiles and low-flying aircraft . . . or (2) a weapons delivery system is perfected which, for all practical purposes, could successfully carry out a surprise attack which destroyed so large a proportion of the other side's delivery system before they could be launched, as to

301

make it impossible to make a retaliatory strike. [It was] . . . just technically possible, but immensely expensive in resources to devise an anti-ballistic missile capable of intercepting the simplest kind of incoming warhead. . . . But the balance is inevitably in favour of the attacker, and no Western scientist or technologist knows of any way of providing an anti-ballistic missile defence of the major targets in his country. If the Russians know of one, we have no idea of what it is.

Twenty-five years later that remains my view, SDI or no SDI. The state of mutual deterrence is likely to remain valid indefinitely.

What was then an even more controversial one of my 'Twenty Propositions' was that the solidarity of the Western alliance was dependent upon the acceptance of a single nuclear policy. This statement carried the implication that Britain's independent deterrent was a destabilizing factor within the alliance. I was implicitly supporting McNamara's Ann Arbor speech, of which I did not know at the time. This is how I spelt out that particular proposition:

In a game in which all players have the same objective, namely that of winning, the outcome becomes more incalculable as the number of players increases beyond two. The incalculability arising from there being two or more independent deterrent forces in the West could, therefore, increase the extent to which Russia is deterred by Western strategic nuclear forces. But there is no guarantee that if there were completely independent deterrent forces in the West, the political objectives of the states to which they belong would remain the same. In consequence the solidarity of the Western deterrent could be weakened by the multiplication of such forces.

For good measure, I added the thought that none of the small number of existing nuclear powers would welcome the emergence of others. The 1968 Non-Proliferation Treaty was still five years away.

NATO's nuclear doctrine was exposed in all its nakedness in October 1962 at the time of the Cuban Missile Crisis. There are many accounts of what passed between Washington and Moscow during the critical weeks, but little or nothing about what went on either at NATO headquarters or in the capitals of Europe. I told the story of what happened in London in an obituary of Dickie which I wrote immediately after his death.[6]

Because of the close personal ties between President Kennedy and David Ormsby Gore, our Ambassador in Washington, Harold Macmillan was almost certainly better informed about what was going on than were the leaders of the USA's other European allies. As the drama unfolded, Number 10 kept Peter Thorneycroft and his top advisers informed of the changing situation. This is what I wrote nearly ten years ago:

> The fateful Sunday, 28 October [1962], was approaching when, if the Russians did not give way, it was widely expected that 'the nuclear balloon' would burst. On the Saturday, word was sent to the Ministry of Defence's three top staff – the Chief of the Defence Staff, the Permanent Under-Secretary and the Chief Scientific Adviser – as well as to the Chiefs of Staff, to meet the Secretary of State the next morning. When I joined Peter Thorneycroft, the Minister, I learnt that the crisis was over, and that the Russians had accepted the Americans' terms without loss of face. We sat around the table just looking at each other. Dickie broke the silence. 'Well, what would we have done if the Russians had not pulled back? Do we know? We've got to work this out.' No-one knew, but he was the only one to put the question. To the best of my knowledge, neither he nor anyone else has yet provided an answer. Perhaps there is none.

Today I would delete the word 'perhaps'.

A day or so before Dickie Mountbatten set off for his last and tragic summer holiday at Classiebawn in Ireland, he wrote to me saying that he had sat next to the new Prime Minister, Margaret Thatcher, at a dinner, and that he had tried to explain to her some of the realities of nuclear weaponry. He had urged her to speak to me on the subject. Some three weeks later I was summoned to Number 10. Dickie and I had arranged to meet in the week that followed, when he was due to return from Ireland. So I wrote to say that I had seen the Prime Minister and that when we met I would tell him what had been said.

But Dickie never got my letter. It must have arrived at Classiebawn the very day he was assassinated.

He would have been less pleased to hear what I had to say about my meeting than he would have been to discover, as the months passed, that an ever-increasing number of military men of experience and distinction – and on both sides – had started to say openly, what they had probably always felt secretly, that the existence of nuclear weapons was a deterrent to war, but that their use could only spell disaster. That is what Dickie had come to believe.

PART VI

Arms Control

26

The Moratorium on Testing

Formal negotiations to bring an end to nuclear testing began in 1958. I became officially involved two years later, and thirty years on I still find the subject of absorbing interest. Public protests against testing had been growing steadily from the beginning of the fifties. At the same time, weapons experts were advising that a ban on tests would put the NATO alliance at the mercy of the Soviet Union. With all but limitless resources at their disposal, the American weapons laboratories were designing new varieties of nuclear weapons without waiting to ask how they were going to be used. Indeed, most of the people to whom that kind of question might have been addressed understood little about the significance of nuclear weapons, other than the single fact that they were enormously destructive. After the public humiliation of Robert Oppenheimer in 1954, the Atomic Energy Commission had become dominated by 'hard men'. Enthusiasts like Edward Teller pooh-poohed the idea that radioactive fallout was dangerous, and were even readier to promise that, even if it were, 'clean' neutron bombs were just around the corner.

Not surprisingly, scientists in the nuclear establishment at Aldermaston were sympathetic to the views of their opposite numbers in the American weapons laboratories, from whom there was much to learn now that Congress had passed the 1958 and 1959 amendments to the 1946 McMahon Act. Harold Macmillan, on the other hand, was committed to the view that a comprehensive test-ban treaty – a CTB – and an end to the nuclear arms race were crucial to the security of Britain and of the rest of the world. I recall one comment of his when it was suggested that domestic political considerations had led him to this view. No, he said, it was human decency and survival that demanded it, not political expediency. His undisputed authority as Prime Minister meant that, whatever contrary views they may have held, no British scientific civil servant nor any military figure could campaign openly against what had become both the Government's and the Opposition's declared policy.

Macmillan's problem, however, was the sharp hostility that prevailed between the USA and the USSR. If a treaty were to be negotiated, the climate of opinion in the United States made strict on-site verification a must. It was for that reason that in 1957 Selwyn Lloyd, then the British Foreign Secretary, proposed to the United Nations, on behalf of the United Kingdom and the United States, that scientific experts should get together in Geneva to consider how a test-ban treaty could be policed in order to make sure that neither side would try to gain an advantage by testing surreptitiously. The discussions, which opened in July 1958, were essentially tripartite – UK, US and USSR – with John Cockcroft and Bill Penney leading the British team. They had what amounted to instructions from the Prime Minister to work for an accord.

At the very start of the talks it became obvious that the views of the Soviet delegates differed from ours and the Americans' about the role that science had to play in the negotiations for a treaty. The Russians had come to Geneva to link the technical talks to a commitment that the three nuclear-power states would stop testing. Both sides were fairly certain that they not only had an accurate tally of all the tests that had so far been made, but also reliable estimates of the explosive yields that had been achieved. From analyses of the radioactive dust that had been carried by the winds they also had a pretty good idea of the nature of the fissile material that had been exploded at the test sites.

The difficulty was with underground tests, where the problem was the differentiation of the shock-waves generated by an underground explosion from those caused by earthquakes and other natural disturbances. Much, of course, was already known about earthquakes. Many countries had for long maintained stations equipped with seismometers that registered the shocks that are transmitted through the earth's crust from the epicentre of an underground disturbance. Given that an earthquake was sufficiently violent, seismometers were already sensitive enough to register disturbances from thousands of miles away, the intensity of the shock being calibrated in accordance with an internationally agreed scale that was known by the name of the American geophysicist, Professor Richter, by whom it had been introduced. By comparing the times and intensities at which widely separate seismological stations registered a shock, it was also possible to locate on a map the source of the disturbance. Better still, above a certain Richter level, it was possible to tell from the character of the waves whether what had occurred was an earthquake or an explosion. A severe earthquake would register, say, eight on the Richter scale; a minor earth-tremor, a million times less energetic, only two.

After some argument, the Russian team accepted the US and British view of what their business as experts was, and in about two months, the three parties tabled an agreed report to the effect that an earthquake could be differentiated from an underground explosion down to a level of a one- to five-kiloton device, that is to say, of a bomb less powerful than the one that had destroyed Hiroshima. To achieve this, it would however be necessary to establish a world-wide network of seismological stations by which quakes of whatever origin could be monitored and diagnosed. The three expert teams did not attempt to describe the form of the international control commission under whose charge the seismological system was to operate, and the threshold Richter level below which on-site inspection would be needed to tell an earthquake from an underground explosion. That was to be decided later.

Following this agreement, Aldermaston was allocated the necessary funds to launch a vigorous programme of research aimed at improving the available seismic techniques, with Dr H.I.S. ('Hal') Thirlaway in charge of a first-rate field experiments laboratory.

Before the start of the experts' meeting, the USSR had put forward a proposal that there should be a moratorium on all forms of testing until a treaty had been concluded. This was agreed when the political discussions on the draft of a comprehensive test-ban treaty were begun, again in Geneva. The leader of the British delegation was David Ormsby Gore, at the time Minister of State at the Foreign Office.* Again there were difficulties. The Soviet delegates had been instructed not to discuss verification procedures before the parties agreed that there would be a permanent end to nuclear tests. This approach was the reverse of that of the USA and the UK, and a month passed before the delegates started to consider the monitoring

---

*Later Lord Harlech and British Ambassador in Washington.

measures that would be necessary in order to satisfy their respective governments. But no sooner had the Russians yielded on this point than arguments about the size and control of the proposed international network of seismological stations became the order of the day.

Defence scientists, military people and politicians in the United States who were opposed to any ban on tests, had already started to pick holes in the 'position paper' that had been agreed in Geneva at the first technical talks. As Sir Michael Wright, the Deputy Leader of the British delegation at the Geneva disarmament talks, put it, 'a lesser order of technical people' had taken over. They dreamt up esoteric ways whereby the Russians could infringe a CTB, whatever its provisions. Ballistic missiles could be used to test warheads behind the moon or in outer space. They could be tested in vast underground cavities in which the nuclear charge, not being in contact with solid matter, would be 'decoupled', that is to say would generate seismological shock-waves of lesser intensity than if the explosion had been made at the bottom of a narrow shaft. Tests could be carried out in earthquake zones, and even to coincide with an earthquake. The records already showed that a large number of subterranean disturbances that might be due either to an earthquake or to an underground explosion, occurred every year in the Soviet Union. The higher the chosen Richter number – the magic figure that was first agreed was 4.75 – the greater the number of underground disturbances that could be regarded as suspicious events. Some disturbances that might be registered could not, of course, be treated as explosions because the worldwide network of seismic stations would show that their focal points were in the vicinity of Moscow or some other improbable test site. But even so, scores of suspicious events could be expected to occur every year in the USSR at a Richter level of 4.75.

In theory, this meant that given a CTB, the Soviet Union would have to accept as a necessary condition of a treaty the unlimited right of teams from the United States to move to the area of large numbers of suspected events to determine whether or not cheating had taken place. The Russians were adamantly opposed. They were totally unprepared to permit unrestricted entry to their territory. As Harold Macmillan relates in his memoirs, during the course of a visit to Moscow in 1959 he persuaded Khrushchev to agree to three on-site inspections a year, both leaders hoping that the Americans would also be satisfied with the same small number. But this independent move on the part of the United Kingdom proved highly unwelcome to the Americans, who were still demanding the right of unrestricted inspection. Well before the end of 1959, President Eisenhower was therefore suggesting that since the Russians were so opposed to 'intrusive visits', the goal of an agreement should be a treaty that did not preclude underground tests.

It was into these troubled waters that I was plunged when I moved to the Ministry of Defence. My interest in the proposed ban was stimulated, not only because of the general anxiety that existed about the deleterious effects of the radioactive fallout that followed atmospheric nuclear tests, but because of my conviction that the nuclear arms race had ceased to have any strategic meaning. A formal interdepartmental committee had been responsible for providing Ormsby Gore's Geneva delegation with briefs on the technical matters under discussion, but this had been wound up by the time I took over. Bob Press was, however, continuing to serve as a technical assistant to the delegation, and with his help I soon became familiar with all that had been going on. He was the right man for the job. Starting in 1948, before the United Kingdom had even tested its first bomb, he had held a succession of staff jobs in the British nuclear organization.

On my first visit to the American nuclear weapons establishments (p. 273), I had had to listen to a lot of 'hard-line' talk, particularly at Livermore, about the deleterious effect that a comprehensive test ban would have on the development of nuclear weapons. I was also told that a CTB would prevent the use of underground nuclear explosions in civil engineering projects. This still futile idea, which was then being strongly promoted by Edward Teller, went by the name of 'Plowshare'. Obviously, if underground nuclear explosions were going to be included among the 'peaceful uses of atomic energy', it would have been impossible to differentiate them from underground military tests without on-site investigation. The very idea of 'peaceful' explosions ruled out a comprehensive test ban.

Little that was new or even secret came up in the arguments against a test ban to which I found myself being subjected. The Chairman of the American Atomic Energy Commission, John McCone, was openly campaigning against the test moratorium that had begun in 1958, and I was certainly not the only British official whom he urged to bring pressure to bear on the UK Government to encourage the American President to authorize a resumption of testing. The formal American position was that the President had agreed to a suspension of testing only on an annual basis, and on the understanding that the moratorium would end if and when the Administration decided that there was no chance of an agreement to a comprehensive ban. On the other hand, the overt Soviet line was that the moratorium would continue until a treaty was agreed. Not surprisingly, Soviet suspicions became ever sharper as increasing numbers of prominent American officials raised their voices against the idea of a CTB.

I was exposed to more pressure from American officials who wanted to see an end to the moratorium than might have been expected. My new American colleagues knew that I had started out not by asking what could be learnt technically from testing, but by questioning the strategic or tactical advantage that could be expected to be derived from new nuclear weaponry. I also wanted to know whether, if there were any advantage, it was sufficient to offset the political disadvantages of resuming tests.

The situation worsened in May 1960 when Khrushchev abruptly walked out of a major summit conference in Paris. The Russians had not only just shot down a high-altitude American spy-plane, but had also captured Gary Powers, its pilot. At the meeting Khrushchev denounced the Americans for their duplicity and demanded an apology, which Eisenhower refused to give. That was the end of the summit. Two months later the Russians also left the Geneva talks on 'surprise attack', but not before the Americans had proposed that the goal of a comprehensive ban on tests should be abandoned, and agreement reached on a suspension of tests which did not preclude those carried out underground.

I had quickly become infected with Harold Macmillan's sense of frustration, and with his impatience about the way the Geneva negotiations were dragging on. No-one will ever know whether, when they proposed in 1958 that all tests should be suspended during the period of negotiations, the Soviet leaders had it in mind to break loose, and resume testing as soon as it suited them. Whatever their intentions, matters came to a head when, towards the end of December 1959, President Eisenhower announced that the USA would regard itself as free to resume tests during 1960 if the Geneva negotiations continued to drag on. History has it that Eisenhower took this step lest his successor – whoever he might be, whether Republican or Democrat – would have to bear the odium of being forced to make the same declaration when he assumed the Presidency. On the other hand, according to Glenn Seaborg, who succeeded John McCone as Chairman of the Atomic Energy Commission, the President was in fact already intending to resume tests. After Jack Kennedy's electoral victory in November of that year, Eisenhower advised the President-elect to start testing without delay.[1]

In July 1961, Jerry Wiesner, President Kennedy's Science Adviser, and I got together in Washington for the third round of the informal and unofficial 'mind-clearing' talks that I had started with Kistiakowsky, at which we had all agreed that the idea of using nuclear weapons in field warfare made no sense (p. 276). To focus the discussion with Jerry, I had prepared a short paper in which I outlined the same argument as the one that had been the basis of the address that I had delivered six weeks earlier at the annual SHAPEX meeting (p. 288). One of the many questions to which I proposed we should turn our attention was whether the renewal of tests by either side could change the prevailing nuclear stalemate. Specifically, I asked:

(1) If testing were resumed, what weapon could the West develop that might deter the Russians more than they would be deterred otherwise?

(2) If during the next five years the Russians can carry out clandestine tests and no Western country can, what specific advantage might the Russians gain sufficient:

(a) to make them believe that driving the West to initiating nuclear warfare or initiating it themselves might be a worth-while risk;

or

(b) to enable them to do serious damage to the morale and cohesion of the West by letting it be known that they had secured a lead in nuclear weapon technology?

My questions were precise and focused, and our discussions concluded with the general answer that nothing would be lost strategically if all testing were stopped. Jerry had no doubts about the futility of the further elaboration of nuclear weapons in order to enhance national security. I returned to London, reinforced in the thought that the UK stand about a CTB was fully justified.

Some two months later came the event which more than anything else focused my mind on the need for a treaty. We were aware of the strength of Soviet suspicions, and also weary of the way they were negotiating, but it came as a considerable shock when, on 30 August 1961, the Russians suddenly announced that they were going to resume tests. A day or two later, they began a series in which some fifty warheads were exploded, mostly above ground – one of them with an estimated yield of 58 megatons. I well remember Khrushchev's public boast that they had a 100 million ton bomb, but that they could not explode it because if they did 'we might break our own windows' in Moscow.[2] President Kennedy was constrained to announce that the Americans were going to follow suit, but that they would only test underground.

Now that the Russians had resumed atmospheric tests, the Geneva talks became meaningless, at any rate for the time being. To Harold Macmillan, the Soviet and American decisions were a considerable setback. The problem now was how to limit the damage that had been done to international relations, and to decide how negotiations for a CTB could be resumed. There were Russians, as well as Americans, who regarded the turn of events as disastrous.

This became clear barely two weeks later (11 September 1961), during the course of a five-day meeting of American, British, Soviet and French scientists, most of whom had been involved in the nuclear activities of their countries. The meeting had been organized by the Pugwash movement* well before the moratorium had been broken, and took place in Stowe, Vermont, under the auspices of the American National Academy of Sciences and the American Academy of Arts and Sciences. Professor Sir Nevill Mott, the Chairman of the British National Committee of the Pugwash movement, had warned me that a meeting was being arranged to consider ways of breaking the deadlock in the Geneva negotiations. Jerry Wiesner sent a message to say that he was going to be there, so, encouraged by the Foreign Office and with

---

*The Pugwash organization provides a forum for the discussion on an unofficial basis of major East–West problems. Its name derives from that of a small Canadian village in which the first meeting, sponsored by a wealthy Canadian, Cyrus Eaton, took place.

invitations to attend from Bertrand Russell, co-founder with Albert Einstein of the Pugwash movement, as well as from Mott, I flew over as 'observer' at a meeting where I met my first Soviet scientists/diplomats. The British party included John Cockcroft, Bill Penney, Patrick Blackett, Edward (Teddy) Bullard, Michael Howard and Philip Noel-Baker.*

I found the meeting remarkable in a number of ways. First, its general title was 'Conference on Science and World Affairs', and both President Kennedy and General Secretary Khrushchev had sent encouraging messages to speed the exchanges that were to take place. Second, several of the members of the delegations were officials, even though the discussions were by definition unofficial. As one of the Americans who attended put it to me, 'Before, we would have lost our security clearances if we had attended a Pugwash meeting; this time we've had to get special clearances to show that we can be trusted to be here!' Third, the general scientific calibre of the participants was very high, four of them being Nobel Laureates.

The Soviet team included Academician Topchiev, Vice President of the Soviet Academy of Sciences, and Academician Tamm, Sakharov's mentor. Some had been involved in the Geneva discussions. All took the line that the USSR was increasingly threatened by the West, and in particular by what they regarded as the nuclear rearmament of Western Germany – to wit, NATO. They were defensive about their own government's breach of the moratorium, offering the formal excuse that the American President had warned that the USA would resume testing, that the Russians had conducted far fewer tests than had the West, and that in any event the West had not given up testing since France had refused to be party to the moratorium and had not been condemned by the USA and the UK for its refusal to join. The Russians were sceptical when Francis Perrin, the head of the French

*Sir Edward Bullard was later Cambridge University's Professor of Geophysics. Teddy was a delightful extrovert, whom I had first met towards the end of the war, when he was working at the Admiralty with Patrick Blackett. Michael Howard was Professor of War Studies in King's College, London, and is now Regius Professor of Modern History in Oxford. He had served in the Coldstream Guards during the war. Philip Noel-Baker, later Lord Noel-Baker, had been in the League of Nations secretariat during the inter-war years, and became a Minister in Attlee's postwar Government. He was noted for his work for peace, for which he was awarded a Nobel prize. He died at the age of ninety, active to the last in his crusade against war.

Atomic Energy Commission, declared that France had not provided either the USA or the UK with any information derived from its nuclear tests. The Soviet line was that they were prepared to cooperate in the establishment of any controls, provided only that it was clearly agreed that the goal of the whole exercise was general disarmament.

But all this was by-play to the better part of the twenty-strong American delegation, which included Kistiakowsky, Rabi, Hans Bethe and Szilard, several of whom had played decisive parts in America's nuclear programme. There were also a few political scientists, among them Robert Bowie, Harvard's Professor of International Relations and a State Department consultant, and Henry Kissinger. The presence of so powerful a team was an indication that Washington wanted the door to be kept open. All the participants agreed about the desirability of a resumption of negotiations for a comprehensive test ban.

At the last moment Jerry Wiesner had been prevented from attending, so on the third day I left for Washington to find out from him the purpose of the nuclear tests which the Americans were preparing. Opinion in Whitehall had not been unfavourable to the American declaration that the US was going to resume underground tests, but there were hints that tests would also be carried out in the atmosphere.

Jerry was every bit as concerned as I was, even though he appreciated far better than I the political pressures to which President Kennedy was being subjected, and the attractiveness of the technical arguments for resuming tests – for example to improve the yield of warheads so as to allow reductions in their size and weight, and so increase the range of ballistic missiles. Tests of possible anti-ballistic-missile warheads were also in the programme.

More than anyone else, it had been Jerry who had instilled in me a total disbelief in the strategic value of anti-ballistic-missile systems, in the same way as I had converted him to my views about the lack of any military utility of so-called battlefield or tactical nuclear weapons. We shared the same fears that a renewal of the nuclear arms race would add nothing to the security of either side. But the political fact that we both had to accept was that President Kennedy had been forced to say that now that the Soviet Union had broken the moratorium, America would resume testing. We knew, too, that pressure would be exerted on the UK to help the Americans, even if only indirectly.

Throughout this period, Harold Macmillan was urging President Kennedy, as he had Eisenhower, not to yield to the demands of the Pentagon, the Atomic Energy Commission, and Congress. In his memoirs he writes that in 1959, when discussing ways of ending the arms race, he had said to Eisenhower that, 'We ought to take risks for so great a prize. We might be blessed by future ages as saviours of mankind, or we might be cursed like the man who made "*il gran rifiuto*".[3] In a message which Macmillan sent Kennedy soon after the Presidential election, he made it plain how much he deplored the Pentagon's wish to continue testing, and urged the President-elect to reach an early agreement on the test-ban talks.

Neither Macmillan nor Kennedy knew whether technical rather than political considerations had led the Russians to resume testing in the atmosphere. In condemning their action, the Prime Minister and the President announced that no atmospheric tests would be carried out merely as a matter of retaliation. Kennedy joined the Prime Minister – with de Gaulle abstaining – in a statement implying that testing that could result in fallout would be barred.

On 15 September 1961, two weeks after the Russians had started, the Americans began testing. But the 'hawks' were not satisfied. Claims continued to be made that American security was being undermined because of unspecified advances which the Russians were making as a result of their atmospheric tests.[4] All the President could at first do was call for greater urgency in testing underground. It was not long, however, before Seaborg had to tell him that the only way to make greater speed would be to resume atmospheric testing – which the President would then need to justify publicly. Like Wiesner and Kistiakowsky, Glenn Seaborg had his doubts, but as the official in charge, he had to comply with the President's wishes.

Harold Macmillan was dismayed by the new turn of events. In the record he made of his meeting with President Eisenhower in March 1960 he noted that while it was the argument of the Pentagon and the Atomic Energy Commission that no agreement could be reached with the Russians because 'a satisfactory system to distinguish the smaller *test* bangs from normal *earthquake* bangs' could not be devised, their real reason for opposing any treaty was that they were 'very keen to go on *indefinitely* with experiments (large and small) so as to keep refining upon and perfecting the art of nuclear weapons'.[5]

317

On 2 November, President Kennedy was impelled to announce that America would resume atmospheric testing in the Pacific, and he also let it be known that the United States had asked the UK to allow Christmas Island to be used as a test site. The island is part of the British Commonwealth (in fact an Australian territory), and agreeing the American request was highly sensitive politically. The Prime Minister therefore insisted on being told precisely what it was that the Americans thought they were going to gain from their proposed tests. Once again he also wanted to be assured that there was real evidence that what the Russians were learning in any way changed the strategic balance between East and West. An *ad hoc* committee of Whitehall officials was convened to consider the political implications of the President's request, while Penney and I were sent to Washington to enquire whether the Americans truly believed that the Russians had gained materially and strategically from the vigorous programme of testing which they had carried out. To provide answers, the President had also set up an *ad hoc* committee, of which both Glenn Seaborg and Jerry Wiesner were members. I also saw Bob McNamara, who was making no secret of his own view that the United States already felt deterred by the then smaller Russian nuclear arsenal, and that further nuclear tests could not change the strategic situation. The answer with which we returned to London, and with which the officials with whom we conferred agreed, was that nothing that the Russians might have learnt could have made any difference to the strategic balance between East and West.

That was not the only joint exercise that Penney and I, as his two main 'scientific' nuclear advisers, had to undertake for the Prime Minister. We did not always see eye to eye for, unlike Penney, I could find no merit in work on new nuclear warheads that was based on the premise that they necessarily had some military value. Penney, like Seaborg, viewed the problem differently. He had become the Deputy Chairman of the UK Atomic Energy Authority, but in effect was still the head of Aldermaston, where the view was that there is always something that.can be learnt from testing. This proposition, while manifestly sound, inevitably invited the question whether what was likely to be gained in technical knowledge had any military value or was worth its political price. When I argued that it did not matter militarily whether a small underground disturbance which seismic stations outside the USSR registered was due to an explosion or to an earthquake, the warhead experts were always ready with the reply, 'Who knows? Even the smallest explosion might have military signifi-cance.' There was also the political argument on which they could fall back. If the Government insisted on knowing whether a small under-ground disturbance in the USSR was due to natural earth movement or to a nuclear explosion, we would have to fall in with the Americans and insist on on-site inspection. If that were the case, I would then argue, there could never be a test ban, since the same reservations would apply to earth-disturbances down to any level, even to the explosion of a few sticks of dynamite in a quarry.

On one occasion when Bill and I were having an amiable discussion about our different points of view, I told him that Hans Bethe, the theoretical physicist and Nobel Laureate who had played a critical part in the development of 'the bomb', had just given a public lecture in which he expressed doubts about the scientific need for America to test in the atmosphere. Not long before, Penney had told the Prime Minister that the American scientific community was at one in believ-ing that atmospheric tests were necessary. Bill's response was a warning that Bethe had become 'unsound', and he also thought that 'young Harold Brown', a fire-eater when he was head of Livermore, had gone 'soft' after moving to Washington.

Years later, I read in George Kistiakowsky's record of his term as Chief Scientific Advisor to President Eisenhower, that in October 1959 – in the same month as the general election that provided Harold Macmillan with his final term of office as Prime Minister – Bill Penney had told George that now that Macmillan had been re-elected he would no longer be as insistent as he had previously been about the need for an agreement with the Russians. Kistiakowsky writes that next day he mentioned this to Spurgeon Keeny, who was well known to many of us in the UK.* Spurgeon told him that Penney had given him the same message.[6] In fact, Macmillan's resolve to secure a treaty had never wavered, and indeed in late October 1961, two months after the Russians had broken the moratorium on atmospheric tests, he had

---

*Spurgeon Keeny began his official career as a technical Intelligence Officer to the Air Force. He has held a succession of staff posts in the White House and State Department, and today is President and Executive Director of the privately funded Washington organization, The Arms Control Association.

proposed that the USA and the UK join together in announcing a six-month moratorium on *all* tests. Our American colleagues had presumably misunderstood what Penney had said.

There had been a long-standing arrangement that the two leaders would meet in Bermuda towards the end of December 1961, and it had become obvious that the use of Christmas Island would be the main item on the agenda. Harold Watkinson had advised the Prime Minister to be wary of the American request. So had I. One day I was asked to go over to Number 10 for a word with him. It was midday, and we were alone in the Cabinet room. 'You don't know why I've called you over, do you?' he began. 'I've been rereading all these minutes of yours about Christmas Island, and I want you to know that I agree completely with you. Yet there are reasons which make it impossible for me to say "no" to the President. But I also know that I shall live to regret what I have to do.' The other reasons were, of course, obvious – in many fields of politics we were more dependent on the Americans than they were on us. All I could add to what I had already said was that it seemed to me that the Russians had resumed atmospheric tests mainly for political reasons. Since they were clearly not worrying about world opinion, there was every reason to suppose that were the Americans to reply in kind, then as soon as the projected series of American atmospheric tests had been completed, the Russians would start another.

I was disheartened when I left him, but at the same time pleased that I had heard from his own lips, and in so graceful a way, that basically we were of the same mind. When one's advice has to be rejected, it's always nice to know why. To the end, Harold Macmillan always had style. There was another occasion that I recall, when he summoned me to Admiralty House when it was temporarily used as the Prime Minister's residence. He was in an armchair in a small sitting room on the first floor, reading what I assumed was one of Trollope's novels. He began by inviting me to fill a glass of sherry, and then before we started to talk about official matters, he asked me what I thought of his Canaletto. As I started to look round the room, he said, 'No, not here. Look out of the window' – from which one got a glimpse of the Embankment at the end of Whitehall Place. 'If I could only sweep Hungerford Bridge away, the view of the Thames would be just as he painted it.' We then got down to work.

Being as unsympathetic as I was to the American request, it was obvious that I would have been an embarrassment to the Prime Minister had he included me in his Bermuda party. Penney, however, was at the talks, as was Seaborg, who writes that he was there more as an observer who 'was able to take copious notes' than as a participant. Seaborg had met Penney in Washington a week earlier, when Penney had told him that the US experts had not as yet made as 'enthusiastic' a case for the use of Christmas Island as they would need to do if Macmillan were to be persuaded. The record Seaborg later published makes it plain that in Bermuda Penney was forthright about the dangers of nuclear weaponry. In reply to a question put to him by the Prime Minister, he warned the President that a single 100-megaton bomb (the Russian 58-Mt device would have had that yield had its fissile core been encased in uranium rather than lead) 'would burn up everyone in even the largest city'. He also said that it would take no more than eight warheads from the current stockpile 'to make a terrible mess of England'.[7] In later years, Macmillan used to tell the story as a wry joke. 'It was hot, and I could see that the President was becoming pretty bored by the technical presentation. I certainly was. So I asked Penney how many bombs would be needed to destroy England, and his answer was' – and then he would try to mimic what he thought was Bill's accent – ' "Well, let's say six bombs, or make it nine to be on the safe side. And now may I have a gin and tonic?" '

According to Seaborg, both the Prime Minister and Lord Home, the Foreign Secretary, tried to persuade the President that before he authorized testing in the atmosphere, a further major effort should be made to stop the nuclear arms race. But Kennedy was not deflected. When the two-day meeting was over, he returned to Washington, confident that he would get what he had come for – the use of Christmas Island.

Despite the fact that the USSR had been the first to break the moratorium, Harold Macmillan became more and more concerned lest a new round of American tests would make it all the more difficult to get the Russians to agree to a comprehensive test-ban treaty. Shortly after the public announcement that the Government had agreed to the American request, he therefore tried to secure even more specific information about the purpose of the proposed tests than what he had learnt at the Bermuda meeting. He also wanted to persuade the American authorities that the detection and diagnosis of underground explosions was not as difficult a job as they were making out. This meant still more work for Penney and me, and also a second joint visit to Washington, accompanied by a small team of seismological experts, including Thirlaway and Teddy Bullard. We carried with us a paper that Ministers had endorsed, and which stated that the UK was satisfied that recent advances in seismic science made it possible to monitor a comprehensive test ban without the need for unrestricted on-site inspection. I had arranged with Jerry Wiesner that our latest findings would be presented to a group of US specialists, and that we would argue with them the case for not insisting on more than a few on-site inspections. We failed to convince, although, as Harold Macmillan writes, we were received amiably.[8] The momentum of the drive for tests was far too strong for the US to be moved by the technical arguments of her closest ally.

The American tests began on 25 April 1962, and ended six months later on 4 November. The first Russian 'retaliatory' test, a 30-megaton shot, took place on 5 August. A further series of American tests was then planned to start early in 1963. It never took place. By then worldwide demands for a cessation to all testing in the atmosphere had become so overwhelming that negotiations for a partial test-ban treaty had to be opened. In the meantime, both sides continued with underground tests.

The overt obstacle to the conclusion of a comprehensive ban was the American insistence on a right to 'inspect' Russian territory. The secretive and suspicious Russians were determined to deny what they regarded as a free ticket for American spying. President Kennedy began the new phase of negotiations by demanding, as had Eisenhower, twenty inspections a year. Later he was compelled to reduce the figure partly, according to Seaborg, because of a misunderstanding that had arisen during a discussion between Jerry Wiesner and a senior Russian official. What had happened was that Jerry, in a conversation with the Russian, had suggested that the USSR should propose a low figure and then settle for one midway between it and the President's higher one, which by then had been reduced to twelve.

Matters came to a head in December 1962 when the President received a formal letter from Khrushchev in which the Russian leader said that, in order to bring about a ban on all testing, he would agree to an annual quota of three on-site inspections – the figure that he had already agreed with Macmillan, and which he had mistakenly assumed the President would be ready to endorse. Kennedy replied by saying that, while he welcomed the Russian readiness to accept the principle of on-site inspection, the lowest number of inspections to which he could agree was between eight and ten. Khrushchev reacted as though there had been a breach of faith, and declared that in the circumstances he would not allow a single one.

In retrospect, it is obvious that the argument about numbers was an empty and spurious exercise. As the President reduced the number for which he was prepared to give battle with a hostile Senate, so those who were opposed to any accommodation with the Russians started to demand that the geographical area that would have to be investigated in each inspection would need to be increased! I sent a note to the Prime Minister in which I bluntly said that the world would now be able to regard the inability of world leaders to narrow the gap between three and seven inspections – both of them arbitrary figures – as the reason why a test-ban treaty could not be concluded, and the nuclear arms race brought to an end. Dickie Mountbatten, to whom my office usually sent copies of my minutes, even though he was not directly involved in the test-ban discussions, wrote 'well-spoken' on his copy.

Glenn Seaborg writes that during the course of the Bermuda meeting he had had a conversation with the President and the Prime Minister, in which both had expressed their regrets that the USA had 'overemphasized what the Soviets could gain from cheating on underground testing'.[9] They had also agreed that the failure to secure a treaty when one was within sight had worsened the relative position of the West. In private the President seemed 'to be considerably more in favor of accepting risks and making compromises in order to achieve a test ban than either he or US negotiators ever allowed themselves to be in public'.[10] That may well have been the case, but I suspect that Kennedy was never quite as convinced as was Macmillan about the need for a fully comprehensive ban. One day Jerry telephoned to say that his man was 'getting cold', and would I get mine (i.e. Macmillan) to give him a shove. The code was somewhat obscure, but the message clear enough.

The Partial Test Ban

Whenever I visited Jerry he would take me round to pay my respects to the President, given that he had a few minutes to spare. Bill Walton, a writer and painter whom I had met years before, and with whom I often stayed when in Washington, was a close friend of the President. One evening Bill took me to a small party that Joe and Susan Mary Alsop had laid on for the President and his wife.* Joe was then one of the most influential newspaper columnists of the day, and a propagandist for a strong America. The President drew me aside to discuss Harold Macmillan's concerns about the use of Christmas Island. On that occasion I had to hedge. Soon after, when I was again in Washington, I had a much longer talk with him. Together with Bill Walton, I was invited by the President to dine with him at Glen Ora, his small retreat in Virginia, to which he occasionally went when he wanted to get away from the White House. Bill and I arrived before him, to find Jackie, 'the First Lady', in the small sitting room, teaching her small daughter some dancing steps. Apart from Lee Radziwill, her sister, no one else was there. After the President arrived we chatted over drinks, before moving across the small hall into the dining room. As he sat down, the President said, 'I'm taking off my jacket.' Bill followed suit. 'Take yours off, Solly,' said the President. 'I can't,' I replied, 'I'm wearing braces.' 'Who cares about your suspenders?' remarked the President as I sheepishly did as he said. After dinner, he and I were left alone to talk 'nuclear matters'. He kept returning to one question – why do you think the Russians are now prepared to agree a partial test ban? – to which I could only reply, 'for the same reason that you should be, because they must be scared stiff about the possibilities of proliferation and the prospect of an unending nuclear arms race'. That evening,

*I had first met Susan Mary when she was married to Bill Patten, a member of the American Embassy in Paris in the immediate postwar years.

rightly or wrongly, my impression strengthened that at heart Kennedy was not as firm as was Macmillan in believing that it was in everyone's interest to secure a comprehensive test-ban treaty, regardless of the possibility of occasional cheating by the Russians.

The skies had been grey when we drove down on the Saturday afternoon, and it was snowing heavily when, near midnight, we got up to leave. Because of the worsening weather, the President suggested that we should spend the night, although where we were to sleep in so small a house was not clear to me. However, I insisted on leaving as I was booked to fly back to London on the Monday.

The next and last time that I saw Jack Kennedy was some three months later, at the end of June, when he spent a day and a night at Birch Grove with Harold Macmillan, shortly before the start of formal negotiations for a partial test-ban treaty.

I had not expected to be at that weekend meeting, of which accounts have been published from the British point of view by Macmillan,[1] and from the American by Seaborg.[2] On the Thursday and Friday, I was at a NATO meeting in Paris, and Joan was due to join me for our annual weekend in Bordeaux. Our visits there had become important events in our lives, with their high point the magnificent luncheon which my 'godfather in wine', Raymond Dupin, always arranged for us at Grand Puy Lacoste, his property in Pauillac. At the end of the NATO meeting on the Friday evening, I was, however, told by our Embassy that the Prime Minister wanted me to be at Birch Grove the next day, and that an RAF plane would take me back to the UK on the Saturday morning. It was too late for Dupin to rearrange his Sunday luncheon, so I telephoned Number 10 and was assured that I was wanted at Birch Grove only for the Saturday afternoon, and that I would then be flown straight back to Bordeaux.

The next morning I therefore waited at Le Bourget until Joan's plane arrived from London, and having explained matters to her, she went off to the Gare d'Austerlitz, taking my suitcase with her. I then boarded a small aircraft which flew me to Gatwick, from where I was driven the few miles to Pooks, the small house on the Birch Grove estate where Maurice Macmillan, the Prime Minister's son lived. Neither he nor his wife, Katy – David Ormsby Gore's sister – seemed to know exactly what was going on, nor did the others who trooped in and out of the house. As the afternoon wore on, I became more and more concerned, wondering when I was going to be called upon to do whatever it was that had required my presence and, what at the time was equally important, whether a plane had been laid on to get me back to Bordeaux. Not until the evening was I told to go over to the 'big house' and to wait until the Prime Minister summoned me.

I managed to get a message to Joan, telling her that our arrangements had been totally disrupted, and that she would have to grace next day's luncheon without me. At one moment Lady Dorothy, Harold Macmillan's wife, came to tell me that I would have to spend the night at Birch Grove, and that she would lend me a pair of Harold's pyjamas. As it turned out, it was nearly midnight before the Prime Minister emerged from the drawing room where he and the President had been conferring on their own. He beckoned me to follow him into his study, saying that he wanted me to help him find a book. Puzzled, I moved with him to the corner furthest from the door, where he started to fiddle with books on a high shelf. 'Stand closer,' he said, 'closer still. I'm slipping into your pocket a paper that the President has given me, and which he should not have done since it sums up the objections of the American Joint Chiefs of Staff. I want you to stay up,' he said, 'and have ready for me by the morning your answer to their arguments.' He then returned to the drawing room. As I waited in the hall for a car to take me back to Maurice's house, the President came out of the drawing room and, as he walked to the staircase, called out, 'Hello Solly. I'm off to bed.' He looked very tired – or bored.

When I got back to Pooks, I told Maurice that I had some work to do before settling down to sleep on the sitting-room sofa which, as he and Katy had had to put up other unexpected guests, was all that was now available as a bed. I then started to read the memorandum. It contained not a single new argument, just the old warnings that the Russians would cheat, and that there was always something to be learnt from new tests. The PM had already read several minutes in which I had dealt with the same arguments, and so, after struggling for an hour or so trying to write something new, I decided to get some sleep in the hope that at six or so in the morning I would find myself in a mood to write something more original and inspiring.

Glenn Seaborg writes that Bill Penney was also at Birch Grove.[3] If he was, he must have left by the time I arrived. What happened was that early on Sunday morning, while I was sitting on the sofa where I had slept, scratching my head as I wondered what I could write that was new, in came Frank Long, who in addition to being a member of PSAC, was the Assistant Director of the State Department's Arms Control and Disarmament Agency (ACDA), together with John McNaughton, to tell me that they knew that the President had given the PM the Joint Chiefs paper, but that what was really wanted for the President and the Prime Minister was an agreed statement about a few specific issues, which Frank and I could sign jointly. They had already prepared a draft which, after some amendment, I duly signed. I felt that it was a real step forward for someone of Frank's standing in the Washington establishment to put his name to a document which said that if the Russians were to test secretly even down to a level as low as 3 Kt, there was a significant chance that the disturbance could be picked up by seismometers outside Russia, and that the risk of detection increased greatly were they ever to carry out a series of low-level clandestine tests. A single test would make no difference.

The Prime Minister now had two documents to read: a hasty critique of the Joint Chiefs Paper, which said nothing new, and the joint one signed by Frank Long and me.

Harold Macmillan writes that while it was not really necessary, a meeting was arranged on the Sunday morning in order to give the members of his and the President's staff 'a show' – all the serious matters having already been settled tête-à-tête between him and the President.[4] The meeting was indeed little more than a show. I can remember Jack Kennedy in a rocking chair, a few questions thrown at Frank Long and me, and then some desultory talk that did not appear to relate to anything in particular.

I managed to get to Bordeaux that evening, and my mouth watered when Joan told me what I had missed by not turning up for the luncheon earlier in the day. But Dupin had arranged an impromptu lunch for the Monday in a small inn frequented by foresters in the woods that run down to the coast of the Medoc. The party consisted of Dupin, the Pautrizels, the Mayers, Joan and me. We lunched out of doors, and I can still remember every course that was served, and also some recently bottled 1961 vintages which Dupin, as the doyen of the Medoc, had commanded a few of his co-propriétaires to send by messenger to Grand Puy Lacoste before we set off for the woods. I doubt if any other of those who had been at Birch Grove enjoyed as pleasurable a sequel.

Barely a fortnight later, on 15 July, I was in Moscow as a member of the British team that was to negotiate with the Russians and Americans for a treaty to ban all nuclear tests in the atmosphere, in the seas or in space. By then the Russians had formally withdrawn their offer of an annual quota of a handful of inspections, and the idea of a comprehensive ban to prohibit underground tests had been abandoned. Lord Hailsham, or Quintin Hogg as he was soon to become on renouncing his peerage, was then in the Cabinet as Lord President of the Council and Minister for Science and Technology.* Quintin had been chosen by the Prime Minister to lead the British team; Averell Harriman led the American; Andrei Gromyko, the Russian.

Lord Hailsham had not been involved in the negotiations that led up to the talks, and Duncan Wilson,† a senior Foreign Office official, who had long been involved in the test-ban debate, and I had been deputed to brief him. We clearly did not do a good job. When Harriman arrived in London the British and American parties greeted each other formally on opposite sides of a long table in Richmond Terrace (where Quintin then had his office). It was soon clear that Quintin had not appreciated that the 'position paper' which we were taking to Moscow, although first drafted in Washington, was a document that the UK had already agreed at official level. To Harriman's surprise Quintin, saying that he was speaking as a lawyer, started to criticize the text. After a few minutes, John McNaughton pushed a note to me that read: 'Solly, what's going on?' I scribbled a quick and joking reply saying, 'If you think you've heard anything yet, wait.' Harriman remarked that if that was the way Quintin felt about the paper, the American party might as well pack their bags and return to Washington. I then whispered to Quintin that the document had been agreed at the official level. He quickly changed the tone of the discussion, and all ended happily. But Harriman never did seem to get to like Quintin. According to Seaborg's account,[5] Quintin had been told by Harold Macmillan to play second fiddle to Averell, a role which he did not like. Although I

---

*Though Quintin renounced his hereditary title, he is today again Lord Hailsham as a life peer.
†He was later our Ambassador, first in Yugoslavia and then in Moscow. After retirement he became Master of Corpus Christi, Cambridge.

became very friendly in later years with Averell, I never once heard him refer to Quintin – which is more than I can say for some other members of the American team.

Penney was also a member of the British party, and Frank Press, a geophysicist, was attached to the American team. The two disappeared after our first day in Moscow, when the Russians reaffirmed that they were not prepared to discuss underground testing. Quintin stayed at the Embassy with Sir Humphrey and Lady Trevelyan, while the rest of the British team were quartered in an ornate but shabby pre-First World War hotel, from which the Trevelyans soon moved me to their second guest room.

Quintin's first duty was to pay a courtesy call on Mr Khrushchev in the Kremlin. The Ambassador, Duncan and I accompanied him, but all I remember of the meeting is Khrushchev teasing Quintin because of the way the British Government had fallen in with the Americans in refusing to sell to the USSR wide-bore pipes for a gas-line they were then laying. 'We now make our own,' said Khrushchev, 'and next time we'll sell you some.' The first meeting to discuss a ban on testing also took place in the Kremlin, with Khrushchev in bantering mood. The meeting was brief, both sides expressing the hope for a successful and speedy end to the negotiations.

These took place in a vast room in the Spiridonovka Palace. The principals with their immediate advisers sat at a round table. Gromyko was flanked by Zorin and Tsarapkin. With Averell Harriman were Frank Long, Foy Kohler, the American Ambassador, 'Butch' Fisher of ACDA and Carl Kaysen, McGeorge Bundy's deputy on the National Security Council. Quintin had Duncan Wilson, Humphrey Trevelyan and myself – with Bob Press sitting behind taking notes. The Russians had prepared a draft of a treaty that was very much shorter and less detailed than the one that the USA and the UK had agreed, and which, after it had been translated into Russian, became the definitive text on which the discussions of the next fortnight focused. There we sat, day after day, examining the draft, sentence by sentence, agreeing or amending. The interpreter for the Russian delegation, a man whose face I was later to recognize in many a photograph of high-level or 'summit' meetings, was most impressive. He had been educated at the English public school Radley, and it was difficult to believe he was not an Englishman.

There is little that I can add to the detailed reports that Seaborg and others have published of what went on during the days that the meetings lasted. Towards the end, Quintin felt that Harriman was making unnecessary difficulties, and sent a message to the Prime Minister asking him to intervene with the President. Macmillan duly telephoned the White House and was speaking to Kennedy at the very moment that Carl Kaysen had got through on another line to McGeorge Bundy, seeking the President's approval for a final trivial textual change which the Russians wanted in the clause that dealt with the accession to the Treaty of 'further parties'. Bundy happened to be in the room when the President was talking to Macmillan, and passed him a note saying that all was settled. The President immediately assured the Prime Minister that there were no difficulties, and that the draft treaty was ready for initialling. I shall always remember Carl Kaysen's call. It was made to the White House on an open telephone line from the Spiridonovka Palace. It seemed like a real sign of trust.

It took about two hours to prepare bound copies of the English and Russian versions of the agreed document, and with the three teams now waiting, I suggested to Quintin that it might be opportune to propose a quick informal meeting to see whether the Russians and Americans would agree to a resumption of technical talks about underground tests. A few of us got together, with Tsarapkin in the chair, but it was immediately apparent that my initiative was unwelcome both to the Americans and the Russians. There were no hard feelings, but I was determined to bring the matter up again as soon as possible.

After our brief abortive meeting, we all moved back to the main conference room, where we waited for bound copies of the agreed text which the three principals had to initial. With the cameras of a horde of photographers flashing away, each page was initialled separately. I blotted Quintin's copy as he applied his customary 'H', and decided to keep the blotting paper as a memento. Carl Kaysen saw what I was doing, and after the initialling ceremony had been completed, he passed me the blotting paper that had been used for Harriman's initials. So did the member of the Russian team who had been blotting Gromyko's. I still have them all, bound together as a souvenir. Seaborg writes that *Life* magazine reported that 'Harriman signed WAH, and

Gromyko wrote, in Russian letters, AG.', but, as was 'fitting for an English lord', Quintin signed only with the single letter H, and that Harriman remarked that 'it was very beautiful!'[6]

On the following evening Khrushchev gave a party for the three teams in the Catherine the Great Palace in the Kremlin. I do not remember much of what happened except that it was a very jolly affair, with toast following toast.

During what turned out to be a stay of nearly three weeks, we had had very little time for anything but the business that had brought us to Moscow. As a rule the American and British teams got together after the formal meetings, alternately at each other's Embassy. But I do not remember that we fraternized much otherwise. Quintin and I paid a formal visit to Moscow University and to the Academy of Sciences. We also called on Academician V.A. Kirillin, a Deputy Prime Minister of the USSR and Chairman of the State Committee for Science and Technology. The weather was fine and our hosts in the Embassy generous to a fault – although Humphrey Trevelyan grumbled that the whole affair could have been settled more effectively at ambassadorial level than by Ministers. I managed to spend a few hours in the Tretyakov Gallery, where I was amazed to discover the wealth and sweep of nineteenth-century Russian painting. I had been under the mistaken impression that the only paintings worth looking at in Russia were those of the French impressionist and post-impressionist schools which a few Russians with money had had the wit to collect – the bulk of these are now in the Hermitage in Leningrad.

A niggling worry that was at the back of Quintin's mind did not seem to dampen his interest in all that was going on. Rumour already had it that Harold Macmillan was likely to retire from the Prime Minister-ship, and that Quintin's name was one of those mentioned as a possible successor. To be in the running, however, he would have to renounce his hereditary peerage, a matter about which he spoke freely to Humphrey and me in our leisure moments. Some time after our return to London, when Alec Home, having renounced his ancient peerage, had become Prime Minister, I was amused to read in a newspaper that I had told Quintin that in fairness to the electorate he simply had to get off the fence and declare one way or another whether he was a 'runner'.

It was all of three years before I was able to make what, at the time, seemed like a meaningful move to reopen discussions about the technical aspects of a comprehensive test-ban treaty. By then Harold Wilson had become Prime Minister. Negotiations for a non-proliferation treaty (NPT), talk of which had started when Harold Macmillan was still at Number 10, were in full swing, with strenuous efforts being made by the nuclear-weapon states to persuade other countries that there was no merit in having nuclear weapons. I was sent to Bonn and Delhi to try to help put this message across. The Germans suspected that the nuclear powers enjoyed technological and economic advantages that would be permanently denied any non-nuclear state that committed itself to a treaty that barred it from developing nuclear weapons – a fear that history has shown to have been groundless. The Indian view was that there was an element of humbug in the whole idea, since while an NPT would disallow what they called 'horizontal proliferation', it would not put a stop to 'vertical proliferation', by which they meant that the existing nuclear-weapon states would continue to elaborate their nuclear arsenals. Other important nuclear negotiations were also in progress – such as the one that resulted in the 1967 treaty that banned the emplacement of nuclear weapons in space. But I continued to believe that if the nuclear arms race between East and West were to be brought to an end, the primary consideration had to be an agreement that banned all nuclear tests.

The chance to reopen the question of a CTB came in June 1966 at a meeting that had been convened in Toronto by a number of organizations, including the London Institute for Strategic Studies (ISS). Alastair Buchan, the founder of the ISS and one of the convenors of the meeting, had persuaded me to prepare a paper on what he called the 'technological aspects of proliferation'.

A small Russian delegation at the Toronto meeting included Professor Emelyanov and Dr Pavlichenko. Emelyanov was a much respected figure, a scientist–engineer, who had played a significant part in helping the USSR to become a nuclear power. Pavlichenko was the link between the Academy of Sciences and the Foreign Ministry and, so it was rumoured, with the KGB. He has always been a familiar figure at talks on disarmament.

In my paper,[7] which I did not have time to finish until I got to Toronto, I emphasized the importance of a CTB, and towards the end of the meeting, Emelyanov and Pavlichenko approached me to ask whether I would be ready to accept an official invitation to visit

Moscow, together with a British seismological expert, to see whether the CTB ball could be set rolling once again.

It was on Hal Thirlaway's advice that Penney and I primarily depended for information about the detection and diagnosis of underground disturbances. Both of us also relied heavily on the views of Teddy Bullard, the UK's senior geophysicist, who kept a close eye on the work of Thirlaway's team. It was on the basis of the evidence which the two of them had given us that I had advised Harold Macmillan in 1961 and 1962 to be less demanding than the Americans about the scientific need for on-site inspections. An official report under the title *The Detection and Recognition of Underground Explosions* had been published at the end of 1965 by the Atomic Energy Authority.[8] The story which it told about the improvements that had been made in seismic techniques since the 1958 Geneva technical talks was based, in the main, on Thirlaway's work. I imagine the Russians knew about it before extending their invitation.

As soon as I was back from Toronto, I asked the Prime Minister for permission to agree to Emelyanov's suggestion. Diplomatic considerations prevented him from giving an immediate answer, and I began to wonder whether the Russians would not regard my silence as implying a lack of interest by the UK in matters of arms control. But as soon as it was agreed that my going would be a useful step, the Russians wasted no time in responding. Academician Millionchikov, then First Vice President of the Academy, sent what was literally an immediate reply proposing dates, but asking at the same time that there should be no publicity. We were unaccustomed to such swift action from Moscow, and the inference we drew was that they regarded the matter of a CTB very seriously.

Only Thirlaway and Bob Press accompanied me, and our departure at the end of September turned out to be so bizarre a business that we wondered whether we were the unwitting subjects of an MI5 or CIA exercise. First there was a delay of two days because Moscow had not told their Embassy in London to issue us with visas. It was then arranged that we would fly directly to Moscow by Aeroflot. When we got to Heathrow, however, we were told that the aircraft on which we had expected to leave had been delayed, and that we would have to wait while the matter of our travel was sorted out. Some two hours later we were led out to an aircraft, and then told that we were flying to Warsaw.

When we arrived, the British Ambassador, Thomas Brimelow,* met us at the gate of the terminal building, and shepherded us past the immigration and customs officials to his car. We had no visas for Poland. His instructions from London were to meet us, to put us up for the night, and to see that we boarded an Aeroflot flight the next morning. He behaved as though he had no idea why we were in Warsaw, or why we were going to Moscow, and we did not tell him. When we reached Moscow the next day, the scientific attaché at our Embassy whisked us to a hotel where we deposited our bags, and where we were met by an anxious emissary from the Soviet Academy of Science, who had made a fruitless trip to the airport the day before to meet the flight on which the Academy had assumed we would be travelling. Everything having been explained, our attaché then drove us to the British Embassy where I put the Minister in charge – the Ambassador was away – in the picture. On the following morning we were driven to the central office of the Soviet Academy, a somewhat heavy eighteenth-century mansion.

Our discussions spread over three days, with Millionchikov in the chair most of the time. The Russian team included Emelyanov, Academician Artsimovich, then the leading fusion physicist of the USSR, Professor M.A. Sadovsky, an Academician who was Director of the Academy's Institute of Earth Physics, and Professor Keilis Borok, who was, in effect, Thirlaway's opposite number. As always, there was Pavlichenko, as well as two interpreters, ours having been provided by the Embassy. But despite the fact that we were in Moscow at their invitation, the Russians were at the start suspicious. Whether it was because of the delay in responding to their invitation, I do not know, but they seemed to think that our purposes were political rather than scientific. I also gained the impression that they were wondering whether I had not already discussed the possibility of new tripartite talks with the Americans, so much so that I found it necessary to assure them that it would have been pointless to do so before knowing whether the Russian authorities were serious about reopening talks on the monitoring of underground tests.

When we got down to the hard talking, Thirlaway explained the seismological advances that he felt had been made since 1963, and

*Now Lord Brimelow.

which, as he later told an American audience, he had used to convince me that the time was ripe to reopen the debate.[9] He and Keilis Borok saw eye to eye. There was endless discussion about the details of the problem, and I had constantly to remind Millionchikov that our task was scientific, not political. What had to be done in the first place was to see whether we could agree that there was a reading on the Richter scale above which seismological stations outside Russian or American territory would be able to differentiate explosions from earthquakes, and a level below which we would be dealing with such minor disturbances that they were not worth attention. Our problem was to narrow the range within which doubts could arise. Thirlaway and his colleagues in the Atomic Weapons Research Establishment were satisfied that in normal circumstances we could now detect and diagnose explosions with a force of only a few kilotons. It was for the military, I insisted, to speculate whether underground disturbances of much lower intensities could have any strategic significance, and for politicians to argue whether international trust demanded on-site inspections. These were not scientific matters; our job – and that included the American seismologists – was to strive to narrow the band of uncertainty.

It was not until the morning of the third day that Millionchikov agreed that I could now try to find out whether the Americans would also be willing to reopen the tripartite technical discussions that had been broken off in 1962. To mark our agreement, the Russians invited us to a sumptuous luncheon, at which Millionchikov made it plain that he doubted my ability to dissipate US fears about possible Russian cheating. In one of his toasts in which he referred to the American obsession with verification, he told a story about an old Russian who, after years of wooing, had managed to persuade a young woman to marry him. But no sooner had he succeeded, than he started to be tormented by the thought that she had a young lover. He poured out his fears to an old friend, asking how he could be sure that, even while the two of them were talking, his wife was not entertaining a lover in his apartment. 'How should I know?' was the answer. 'Spin a coin, and if it comes down heads she has a lover; if tails, she hasn't.' 'But,' continued the worried old man, 'if tomorrow she says she's going to see her dressmaker [the story, which I now know has many variants, obviously came down from pre-revolutionary days], how can I be sure that she

335

hasn't gone to her lover's apartment?' The answer was the same. 'But you don't understand,' moaned the old man. 'Supposing she is faithful to me?' 'Ah,' was the response, 'in that case the coin will remain suspended in the air.' We all laughed. What Millionchikov was getting at was that the Americans would always suspect that the Russians would cheat.

When I proposed a toast in return, all I could do was to say that the CTB was so important a prize that we had to take risks, emphasizing the point by recalling that during the war, when operational research was born, a cynical French scientist, whom I had recruited to work with my team when Paris was liberated, had said that all that the new so-called discipline implied could be illustrated by a simple proposition: since most traffic accidents in towns occur at street crossings, intersections are obviously the most dangerous points in a traffic system. *Ergo*, you spend as little time as possible at crossings. Consequently, when driving, put your foot down as hard as you can when approaching one. Obviously new technical talks were going to reveal new suspicions, I said, but we simply had to try.

In his final toast, Millionchikov spoke seriously. Remember what has happened in the past, he said. 'When you and the Americans agreed, we have disagreed. When the Americans are about to agree with us, you disagree [a remark that I remembered twenty years later when the question of the UK's Polaris missiles being counted in the inventory of 'theatre' or of strategic weapons became a matter of dispute]. Now that you and we agree, the Americans will disagree.'

On one of our nights in Moscow, we were taken to a magnificent performance at the Bolshoi Theatre of Benjamin Britten's *Midsummer Night's Dream*. We also managed to visit the Moscow Zoo to see how Chi-Chi, London Zoo's female giant panda, was getting on with the Russian male An-An, the two having been brought together in the hope that they would mate. We discovered that the animals were being kept in separate, miserable cages. 'That's no way to get them to mate,' I told the heavily built female curator who was taking us around. 'Get them together and if they fight a little, so what? Isn't that what men and women often do, even in Russia?' Thirlaway added that that was precisely what we were trying to get the Russians to agree to do with the Americans.

Although we had been 'smuggled' out of London – I assumed in an effort to mislead newshounds – someone had let a reporter know that we were in Moscow. The British press almost immediately started speculating about 'secret talks'. As soon as Bob Press had completed his report for the Prime Minister, I therefore wrote to Don Hornig, President Johnson's Chief Science Adviser, telling him that I had been to Moscow and that I would shortly be in Washington, when I would give him a full account of what had transpired. Barely a day passed, however, before I received a call from Gerry Tape of the American Atomic Energy Commission, wanting to know what I had been up to. I had to tell him that both Harold Wilson and George Brown, the Foreign Secretary, had decreed that the matter was so important and delicate that I was not to make any report to my American friends until Brown had spoken to Dean Rusk, the Secretary of State, whom he was due to visit before very long. I was to go with him. Shortly after his telephone call, Tape came to see me in London, but all I could do was repeat what I had said over the telephone. Pointing from my window to the garden of Number 10, I assured him that I was only too anxious to give him a full account of my talks, but that it would be up to him to get the necessary authority for me to do so from the Prime Minister himself. Otherwise we had to wait until Brown had spoken to Rusk. Harold Agnew, who had succeeded Norris Bradbury as Director of Los Alamos, also called to see me to find out what was afoot.

I was sure that the embargo was a mistake. It was Gerry Tape's responsibility to satisfy the Congressional Joint Committee on Atomic Energy that nothing incorrect was happening in the field of Anglo-American nuclear exchanges. There had already been enough leaks in the papers to make him suspect that we, the junior partner, had discussed with the Russians a resumption of scientific exchanges which could be preliminary to political negotiations for a comprehensive test ban. He made it plain that if there were going to be any such talks, the initiative would be taken by the United States. All I could therefore do was assure him that all would be disclosed when George Brown had seen Rusk. I passed the same message to Harold Brown in the Pentagon, and to Don Hornig in the White House, both of whom were, of course, aware of Tape's and Agnew's visits.

My initiative ended in failure. Some three weeks after my return from Moscow, George Brown set out on his trip. It had been assumed that I would travel with him, but when I learnt that he was first going to

337

Ottawa, I arranged to fly directly to Washington, and to arrive the evening before he was due to see Rusk. When I arrived at the Ambassador's residence, the footman who let me in told me that a dinner party which Sir Patrick Dean, the Ambassador, had given for the Foreign Secretary had broken up. I was delighted to hear this, because all I wanted was to get into a bath and then bed. I was half undressed when a very gloomy Pat Dean came into my room. There were no secrets between Pat and me; we had got to know each other well from the moment that I had joined the Ministry of Defence. The dinner party, to which Pat had invited the senior members of the Embassy staff and their wives, had turned out to be one of those occasions when George had drunk too much. He had done his best to upset the ladies, as he hurled insults at their husbands for their presumed shortcomings. Pat then told me that there was to be a briefing meeting with the Foreign Secretary at 9.30 the next morning, and that he hoped that I would be there. I had already arranged to see Don Hornig at eight, and Philip Handler, the President of the National Academy, at 8.30, to give them an idea of what had happened in Moscow, but said that I would be back in time.

The briefing turned out to be a meeting that never was. Since the Foreign Secretary had not appeared some ten minutes after the appointed hour, and since time was short, I asked Pat whether he would like me to try to stir George. In matters of this kind I never regarded myself as a civil servant. I went up to his room, and went in to find him still in the process of dressing. 'George,' I said, 'I gather you behaved like a shit last night, and now you're keeping a pack of your officials waiting for what should be a serious meeting.' 'I know,' he said contritely, 'should I go down and apologize?' I said, 'No, but you shouldn't keep them hanging around any longer.' And with that we went down for as desultory a briefing as I can ever remember.

I did not accompany him and Pat on their visit to Rusk. Despite the American desire not to disturb the status quo, George succeeded in getting the Secretary of State to agree that I should try to arrange matters with Hornig. Later that day, I gave him and his staff a full account of my Moscow talks, and despite some doubts, Hornig agreed that I should try to convene a tripartite meeting in London, but on the understanding that we had strict terms of reference agreed by the State Department and the Pentagon.

338

A week after our return to London, I was visited by Academicians Kirillin and Artsimovich, and although they had called to discuss other matters, the question of the press reports that had followed my Moscow visit came up. I assured them that I had never spoken to any reporter, that I did not know who had, and that the slant of two pieces which implied that I had been disappointed by the results of my exchanges in Moscow was totally false. Since they had obviously taken the reports seriously, I straightaway sent a corresponding message to Millionchikov, reaffirming the British Government's wish to see the tripartite technical talks reopened.

In late November, two months after my meeting with Millionchikov, George Brown visited Moscow for talks with Andrei Gromyko. Shortly before this, the Russian Academy had been told that the Americans had not only agreed formally to new talks, but had also agreed terms of reference. Gromyko was uninterested. The USSR no longer wanted its scientists to engage in new tripartite talks. The matter was entirely political. The Russian authorities were confident that seismological records alone were all that were wanted to detect and diagnose underground explosions. When I was told this on George Brown's return, I immediately let Hornig know. My impression was that the American scientists who were involved, and some of whom I knew had also been urging the need to reopen technical talks, were just as disappointed as I was.

Early in the new year, that is to say in February 1967, Kosygin, the Soviet Prime Minister, was in London on a formal visit. I was among those who were invited to dine at Number 10, and before we went in to dinner, George Brown beckoned me to join him and the Russian leader. George was expressing his regrets that the Russian political authorities had frustrated the arrangements for technical talks. Kosygin, through his interpreter, simply repeated what Gromyko had said – that there was no need for talks. Russian scientists were able to register American underground tests, as no doubt the Americans monitored the Russian. Over and above this consideration, the Russians had not yet ruled out the possibility of using nuclear explosions for major civil engineering projects! I had thought it was only Edward Teller who enjoyed this dream.

When Carter became President in 1977, tripartite negotiations for a CTB were once again resumed in Geneva. Paul Warnke was appointed

US Ambassador and leader of the American team, his opposite number for the UK being Percy Cradock, who at the time also served as British Ambassador to East Germany. A year later Warnke was replaced by Herb York, and Cradock by John Edmonds, a Foreign Office official. Herb stayed with me twice on his way to and from Geneva, and I arranged for him to see some senior British officials whom he would not otherwise have met. But before President Reagan abandoned the talks in 1981, they had all but lost their purpose. Under pressure from the Pentagon, what had begun as a proposal to agree a CTB of unlimited duration became a seven- or five-year and finally a three-year moratorium, with the UK reluctantly having to follow the US line. To my way of thinking, a three-year moratorium had little or no significance – it took almost that time to prepare a series of new tests. What was worse, the Americans had hinted that the USA would very likely resume testing once the three-year period ended, whereas the Russians assumed that the ban would continue unless political circumstances had changed completely. There was a great deal of frustration in Whitehall.

But the talks did result in some real gains. The Russians agreed to the principle of on-site inspection, and to the emplacement of monitoring stations on their territory. This was a major advance. As a *quid pro quo*, however, they insisted that the UK, as a presumed co-equal in the talks, should be responsible for the same number of seismic stations as the USA and the USSR had undertaken to install, an unwelcome proposal about which we were still arguing when the negotiations came to an end. Some Americans were then saying that if the UK was so poor that it could not find the money to pay for its quota of stations, private American foundations would be ready to help.

In the years since Reagan suspended the negotiations, the whole purpose of a test ban – to help to stop the nuclear arms race and to reinforce the 1968 Non-Proliferation Treaty – has been turned on its head. The Americans have declared that they have no intention of abandoning tests, and that testing must go on so long as they produce and deploy nuclear warheads. When Gorbachev, the new Russian leader, called in 1985 for a CTB, and declared that the USSR would unilaterally forego testing, the response from Washington was negative. When the Russian leader declared that he was ready to permit on-site inspections of events which the USA deemed to be suspicious,

President Reagan invited the Russians to visit the USA's main test site in Nevada, to see how expertly the Americans tested. The Russians have since formally invited the Americans to use test sites in the USSR. For me the supreme irony came when in 1985 the British Government tabled a paper in Geneva on seismic monitoring which, from the scientific point of view, implied that our seismological techniques were less advanced now than they had been when I had visited Moscow twenty years before. Dr David Owen, who had been Foreign Secretary during the period of the negotiations that President Carter had initiated, publicly protested about this paper.[10] As he put it, 'Seismological advances and satellite technology have transformed the possibilities for verification, and it is sad to see scientific evidence bent to buttress the job prospects of nuclear scientists in Aldermaston, Los Alamos and Livermore, or to fit the political judgements of leaders who are not prepared to state openly their true wish, namely to continue to test.' Harold Macmillan had said it all before. As he wrote in the note he made during his March 1960 visit to Eisenhower. 'The real reason' why we were getting nowhere with a CTB was 'that they [the Americans] are very keen' to go on testing endlessly.[11] The difference today is that the UK has for the moment become part of the 'they'.

Glenn Seaborg described the failure to achieve a comprehensive test ban in 1963 as 'a world tragedy of the first magnitude'.[12] This is what I also believe, as do – or did – so many of those of my American friends who had played a part in trying to achieve a CTB, among them Averell Harriman, Jerry Wiesner, George Kistiakowsky, Herb York, and Herbert Scoville.*

Of course, the American scientific advisers had a more difficult job than mine, as also did, I suppose, the scientific advisers to the top political and military authorities of the USSR, caught up as they so constantly were in a web of suspicion. I was working to a leader who did not have to face any political opposition when he declared his belief in a CTB. Eisenhower, Kennedy, Johnson and, I imagine, the Russian leaders of the day, did. It is sad that a Macmillan and a Gorbachev have not yet been in office at the same time as a President who thought like them – or a like-minded Prime Minister and President with a like-minded General Secretary.

*When I first met him, Scoville was chief scientist of the CIA, a job which he left for a corresponding position with ACDA.

I sometimes ask myself whether the outcome of the 1963 negotiations might not have been different if the American scientists with whom I had been conferring for so long, and who favoured a CTB, had been able to join as a coherent body in public debate against men such as Teller, by whom it was opposed. They always had to work in separate cells of secrecy, while those in favour of the continuation of the arms race could shout from the rooftops that to stop testing would imperil American security, as they now claim do the SALT and ABM Treaties of the seventies. The message of the hawks not only reinforces their vested interests, it also distorts public understanding. Many years ago Jerry Wiesner said that we were running a race between catastrophe and understanding. Understanding has not yet taken the lead.

Arms Control at the United Nations

I have already referred (p.280) to my participation in an enquiry about nuclear weapons that was launched by U Thant in response to a resolution of the United Nations' General Assembly. I was also the UK member of the two other 'expert' groups that he set up. The report of the first, which dealt with 'the effects of the use of nuclear weapons and their security and economic implications', appeared in 1968. As I have said, the analyses of the probable effects of attacks on centres of population were based on the results of the studies of Birmingham and Carlisle that I had directed in 1960, while the technical sections of the report drew on information that had already been published. The only part of the report that caused trouble was the one that dealt with 'security implications'. To resolve the difficulty the American representative on the expert group, John Palfrey, who had been a member of the US Atomic Energy Commission, proposed that Vasily Emelyanov, the Russian member, should prepare one text in Moscow, and I another in London, the idea being that the two drafts would then be pulled together at a meeting of the full team. Wilhelm Billig, the Polish member, then arranged for a preliminary meeting in Warsaw in order to help Emelyanov and me iron out whatever differences there might be in our two texts. Billig was then Minister for Posts, having previously been head of the Polish Atomic Energy Authority. Bob Press came with me to Warsaw, but at the time we had done no more than jot down headings for the kind of chapter that we thought was needed. Both Emelyanov and Billig spoke English, so we had no need of interpreters.

It turned out that Billig had also prepared a draft, which he had had translated into English. Emelyanov's Russian text had not yet been translated. No sooner had we sat down than Emelyanov said that his draft was in all essentials identical with Billig's one (they had no doubt collaborated in its preparation). Bob and I therefore spent half an hour or so looking through the translated Polish text, and decided that there would be no difficulty in reconciling the lines it took with what we would write. When I explained this, Emelyanov and Billig happily agreed to leave the final drafting to me. Our Warsaw meeting, for which two days had been set aside, had thus taken no more than about an hour.

With time to spare, we were asked what we would like to do. So on the following day we were driven miles across the flat Polish countryside to the Bialowieza Forest on the Russian–Polish border, where the Russians, in an effort to preserve the then almost extinct European bison, had gathered together after the war the nucleus of a breeding herd, whose descendants were now running wild. On a day that proved enjoyable in spite of the mosquitos, the only bison we saw were confined in paddocks. Before we left Poland I also paid courtesy calls, at Billig's suggestion, on the Polish Deputy Prime Minister and on the Minister for Industry and Technology.

The only serious difficulty that I then had to resolve was with Vikram Sarabhai, the Indian member, who was clearly under orders, and who refused to accept the view that nuclear weapons were significant only in a deterrent role. In that case, he kept asking, why did the nuclear powers continue to elaborate their nuclear arsenals? His arguments, in fact, were a preview of the considerations which later led the Indian Government to refrain from signing the Non-Proliferation Treaty.

That was the first of the technical United Nations reports with which I was concerned. It was child's play in comparison with the second, which dealt with Bacteriological and Chemical Weapons (B&CW), and which was published a year later.[1] I was made responsible for the 'general' editing of the report (in which I was helped by two British experts and by Bob Press). In addition, William Epstein, a senior member of the section of the UN Secretariat that dealt with disarmament, suggested that I should draft the chapter on the economic and security implications of B&CW. The Russian delegates, who were led by Academician O.A. Reutov, whom I had never met before, disagreed. They were going to be responsible for this critical chapter. I readily assented.

Our first meeting took place in New York, and went tolerably well.

The second, in Geneva, was all but a disaster. The Russians arrived without the text that they had promised, but said that there would be one before the end of the week's meetings. It was obvious that they held me in great suspicion, probably because the UK had already tabled a formal resolution about the banning of biological agents, a resolution to which the Russians were at the time opposed.*

Reutov, who spoke fairly good English, seemed to be under instructions to oppose any views that I might express, and by the end of the week it also became obvious that there was no Russian text. After consulting with Epstein, I accordingly sat down, and with the help of Bob Press and my two experts, drafted a version of what I thought a chapter on 'security implications' should look like. On the Monday of the second week we had a draft ready to present to the group. When Reutov again failed to table a Russian text, Epstein told the meeting that I had prepared a draft for discussion. The Russians were indignant, but Reutov was made to accept a copy of what I had written.

On the following day, Russian annoyance at what I had done became even more pronounced. After discussing the matter with Ivor Porter, the UK Ambassador to the Disarmament Committee, I decided to make a protest to his Russian opposite number, so as to indicate my disquiet at the way the meetings were going. Porter first suggested that I should go on my own, but then decided that the protest should be more formal. He and I therefore visited Ambassador Roshchin together. I explained the situation, without making it appear that I was putting in a formal complaint about Reutov. Roshchin said that he had no authority over Reutov who, in any event, ranked higher than he did, being a full Academician who was receiving his instructions direct from the Foreign Ministry in Moscow.

---

*I worked closely with Fred Mulley when he became Harold Wilson's Minister for Disarmament in 1967 and when he set about the task of securing international agreement to a ban on the use of 'biological agents' – to wit, bacteria and viruses – in warfare. The BW Convention did not come into force until 1972, by when the Labour Party was no longer in power. Securing agreement was a remarkable achievement. In a world clouded by suspicion and by hostile intent, it was not only the nuclear test-ban negotiations that had broken down after years of talk because we demanded monitoring and verification procedures that the Russians regarded as excessive. Since it is impossible to 'verify' that all parties to the BW Convention would desist from producing some viral or bacterial agent in a secret laboratory, it made the initiative associated with Fred Mulley's name all the more impressive.

The next morning, Wednesday, there was still no Russian text. I therefore told the group that I would be unable to remain in Geneva after Friday. At this Reutov said that he hoped to be able to have his text ready by then. In the meantime the text I had tabled continued to be discussed.

That evening the Americans gave a cocktail party, in the course of which Reutov drew me to a balcony where he protested at my having been to see Roshchin. I replied lightly by saying that my visit to Roshchin could not have made any possible difference to him, since he, Reutov, was senior in rank to the Ambassador, from whom he did not take his instructions. Reutov agreed that this was so, but nonetheless clearly remained disturbed. We continued talking for about a quarter of an hour, after which Reutov said that we ought to go in since anybody looking through the windows could see that we were arguing.

On the following day, Thursday, there was still no Russian draft. The entire group was by then getting restive. On Friday, Reutov swore that the Russian text was nearly ready, but that it could not be available until Saturday morning. I repeated that I had to be back in the UK on Friday evening, but said that if there was an absolute assurance that a draft would be available on Saturday morning I would try to arrange transport so that I could be back in London by midday. To make my gesture all the more impressive, I explained that there was no commercial flight available at the time, and that I would have to make special arrangements. I then left the meeting and telephoned a friend who for a brief period in those days possessed a small jet, an HS125. Without any explanation, I asked whether, as a matter of extreme urgency, he could send it to Geneva to stand by and fly me back to the UK at a moment's notice.

The next morning the group of experts assembled at the Palais just before nine o'clock. The Russians were about ten minutes late, saying that they now had a translated text, but that they had not yet had time to have it copied. It then turned out that the UN secretarial organization did not work on Saturdays, and consequently it was necessary to do some 'breaking-in' in order to get at a copying machine. I suggested that while we waited, we might as well go to the cafeteria. But this, too, was closed. Reutov, who by now was beaming, said, 'If we can't get coffee, let's have brandy.' We all agreed that this was an excellent idea, but the question was, where could we get brandy if we could not get

346

coffee? 'Here,' Reutov said, and pulled a couple of bottles and some small glasses from his attaché case. We each had a glass or two – this at 9.30 in the morning – until the English version of the Russian text was brought in and passed around.

That turned out to be a bigger surprise than Reutov's brandy. His text was a photocopy of the one I had tabled, the one that he had all but refused to accept when it was passed round on the Monday, five days before. The Russian delegation had not even bothered to have it retyped. It still carried the few handwritten textual changes that I had made before it was first photocopied. Some additional but minor textual changes had been made, presumably under instructions from Moscow. Indeed, we all had a feeling that that was where Reutov had sent my draft and where the alterations had been made. The changes were so trivial that they altered nothing of substance, and so were accepted by the rest of the group. I congratulated the Russians and immediately left for England. There was no further trouble.

The third report in which I was involved, on the 'Economic and Social Consequences of the Arms Race', proved to be an even more arduous and tricky exercise.[2] M.E. Chacko, the Indian Deputy to the Under-Secretary-General for Political and Security Council Affairs, was made chairman of the group of 'experts', which again first met at the UN headquarters in New York. At the end of our opening session Chacko suggested that I should be made responsible for the preparation of a skeleton of the report that we were charged to present to the Secretary General. The outline that I produced was redrafted three or four times during the remainder of the week's meetings, at the end of which Chacko allocated the writing of the separate sections to different members of the group. Acting on the Secretary General's instructions, Chacko proposed that I should then be made responsible for editing the whole report. He did not consult me about the way he partitioned the work. I was also made responsible for writing two of the chapters.

The second session, during the course of a very hot fortnight, also took place in New York. It was immediately apparent that the drafts that the members of the group had produced could not be fitted together into a coherent document. Everyone was at cross-purposes with everyone else. In particular, a young Rumanian, Gheorghi Dolgu, insisted on bringing in matters that seemed totally irrelevant to the

Western group – in particular to William Duisenberg of Holland and Henry Wallich of the United States, both of them distinguished economists. The discussions became so heated that I took advantage of an attack of asthma to absent myself from two of the meetings.

Towards the end of the week, it was clear that the group was getting nowhere, and Chacko then consulted separately with some members of the group, in particular, as he told me later, with the Canadian representative, Douglas Le Pan, Jacques Mayer, the French, Mullath Vellodi, the Indian, as well as with Duisenberg and Wallich. The upshot was a suggestion that I should be asked to try to pull together such material as had been agreed into a draft report for further discussion at our next series of meetings. At a luncheon at which he entertained the group, U Thant formally announced that this was to be done.

I did not welcome the suggestion. When Chacko put the proposal at the next – and equally disagreeable – meeting of the group, I said that I would be prepared to undertake the task, but only on three conditions: first, that I would base my text only on the written contributions that had already been discussed and amended; second, that I would be free to consult such members of the group as I chose, as well as other authorities if I thought that necessary; and third, that our next discussions should focus on the text that I would submit, and not on any that other members of the group might table. Whatever I produced could be amended, as necessary, at our next meeting. I still remember the frozen look on some faces as I left the room, saying that the Secretariat could inform me if the group accepted my conditions.

I did not feel it appropriate to attend the final meeting of the series on the following morning. Later in the day I was told that the group had reluctantly agreed my conditions, and that they had done so because Chacko had warned them that, were they not accepted, it was unlikely that there would be a text available for the next series of meetings, which were due to take place in Geneva.

I was given two months in which to prepare a draft. It was not a difficult job, and everything was going fairly well until Chacko decided to call on me in London, ostensibly to see how I was getting on. The real reason for his visit was to tell me that there had been complaints that I had not consulted any members of the group. The reason why I had not done so was that I judged that the result would be even more confusion than we had already experienced.

A few days later I gave him a text – it had been a simple matter to write – which he sent without delay to the other members of the group, with instructions to inform him whether they were content with the text as it stood, or whether it would be acceptable, subject to amendment. Emelyanov, the Russian member, insisted on seeing me, and came from Moscow with two Foreign Ministry officials. After two meetings at the Russian Embassy in London, their difficulties were apparently settled, and Emelyanov assured me that he would now support my draft, which I had already amended in three or four places to take account of other comments.

But when the group reconvened in Geneva, my draft, far from gaining the acceptance it had been promised, and despite considerable support given me by Henry Wallich, was all but torn to pieces. After consulting with our Ambassador, I told Chacko that if he could not secure agreement, I would like him to withdraw my text, and to leave the group to produce whatever alternative draft it wanted, and on which I would comment. I then decided to take a few days off, leaving the group to sort matters out. I had in any event warned Chacko that I wanted to participate in a conference in Basle on the Future of Medical Science. The Basle meeting proved much more friendly and stimulating intellectually than the one I had left, although I found the American anthropologist and publicist Margaret Mead, who was one of the participants, almost as irritating as were some members of the Geneva group. At one session, and before a large audience, I chided her for speaking only in headlines – a remark which she justifiably resented.

The experts were still at sixes and sevens when I got back to Geneva, but nonetheless, with some vigorous redrafting here and there, and largely because of the support given me by Wallich, Duisenberg, Mayer, and Akira Matsui, the Japanese delegate, I managed to produce a text that was endorsed by the whole group. As so often happens, it turned out to be much the same as the one that I had prepared in London.

Not long after the report had been presented to U Thant, I received a telephone call asking whether I would be ready to serve as the UK member for a fourth enquiry which the Secretary General wanted to launch, this time on the general subject of disarmament. I had no hesitation in saying no. I had had enough of formal arms-control discussions. U Thant then sent me as a memento inscribed copies of the three reports in whose production I had been made to play so central a part. Despite their wide circulation, I never did learn whether any one of them had much effect on world opinion. The way the arms race has proceeded over the past two decades, I would think not.

PART VII

Changes in Organization and Government

Defence Reorganization

When I joined the Ministry, the preparation of the 1960 Defence White Paper had all but been completed. While it contained nothing new or startling about defence policy, it gave me my first sense of the vast scale of our military commitments. In not a single one of the fifteen years since the end of the Second World War had we not been engaged in military operations. The break-up of Empire, starting in 1947 with the partition of India, had left us with an enormous legacy of military as well as political problems. We were burdened with defence commitments in the Middle and Far East, in Africa, in the Caribbean, and in the Pacific. We had become an 'independent nuclear power', and we were now members of the North Atlantic Treaty Organization, in the establishment of which, as Nicholas Henderson relates in his book *The Birth of NATO*,[1] we had played a star role.

The 1960 White Paper conveyed a comforting impression that everything was on course in accordance with the Duncan Sandys plan of 1957. Even Harold Watkinson's announcement that Blue Streak was being cancelled, and that in order to remain a nuclear power we were considering the purchase of Skybolt, seemed to me little more than a statement of the continuation by other means of a policy that was both clearly set and realizable.

The announcement did, however, cause a parliamentary stir, and it was then that I became acutely aware of the fact that despite the Sandys cutbacks, we simply did not have the resources to match our military commitments. This was not something that Dickie Mountbatten seemed prepared to accept at the time, or if he did, he succeeded admirably in disguising his true feelings. When in Washington soon after the debate on the White Paper, I accompanied him to a meeting with the American Chiefs of Staff. They always liked to have him call on them, and I was amused when, without any hint of doubt, he gave them the impression that we could dispose of far greater military power than we obviously possessed. Dickie put words into their mouths as he got them to agree that it was essential to world peace that we should continue to deploy strong naval forces in the Far East – a message that he duly transmitted on our return to a quizzical Watkinson.

Later, in May 1965, Dickie and I arranged that a visit I had to make to India coincided with one that he was paying, but in which his official business was to discuss the level of immigration of Commonwealth citizens to the UK (p. 382). It was not a happy visit. The Chinese had moved in from Tibet and occupied Indian territory high in the Himalayas. Indian and Pakistani forces were in arms against each other over the Kutch–Sind border. The Indian Chiefs could not have been more polite to him than they were at a meeting that we had with them, but they told us nothing about their concerns, and asked no questions. An interview that we had with Lal Shastri who, when Pandit Nehru died, had become Prime Minister, was even less revealing. Our time with him dragged on through a forced and disconnected conversation punctuated by moments of silence. When we left I asked Dickie why he had not cut the meeting short. 'An hour had been set aside for it,' said Dickie somewhat bitterly, 'and I was not going to let him off for a minute.' It was all very different from the relations he had enjoyed with Pandit Nehru.*

The following night was the occasion of a grand dinner in the Rashtrapati Bhavan palace that Shastri gave in Dickie's honour. Dickie had taken great trouble with his speech, and was disappointed when only one newspaper bothered to notice it next day. He also felt that not Shastri but the President, a delightful man who had been Professor of Eastern Religions and Ethics in Oxford from 1936–52, should have been the host at the dinner, and not simply at the luncheon which he had given us on the preceding day.

---

*He had arranged for us to stay in a wing of Lutyens' enormous Viceroy's House, which was now, under its new name of the Rashtrapati Bhavan Palace, the home of the President of India. Our return from the meeting with the Indian Chiefs of Staff coincided with President Radhakrishnan's return from an afternoon ride. He was in an open carriage, preceded and followed by detachments of the marvellously garbed Indian Household Cavalry. We looked on from a corner as the President was helped down from his carriage and mounted the steps into his palace. At that moment Dickie said, 'There were twice as many cavalry when I was Viceroy.' I reminded him that one half might have gone to Pakistan.

Dickie and I parted company the day after the dinner, he to leave India, and I to stay on for a few days to continue my talks with Dr Bhagavantam, the director of defence research in Delhi, and with Homi Bhabha, the head of India's Atomic Energy Programme. General Chaudhuri, the Indian CDS, had also invited me to visit the area in the Himalayas where Indian troops were facing the Chinese.

Very early in the morning after Dickie's departure, Bhagavantam and I flew up to Srinagar in Kashmir where, after breakfasting in an officers' mess in excellent company, we were taken, first in cars and then in jeeps, up to about 8000 feet, which was as far as they could go. We then climbed gently for about a mile and a half across rough ground covered with snow to the Mountain Warfare School. The scenery was magnificent, but it was bitterly cold. The unit that ran the school had been cut off for some months, and were delighted to receive visitors and to tell us about their work. The senior officer, Lieutenant Colonel H.C. Chadha, was the only one who was old enough to have served in the Indian Army when it was under British command. But all his officers were immensely 'British' and, as I was to discover, they also constituted a nursery of Everest climbers. When I left, the commanding officer presented me with a set of their regimental brass buttons. Later he wrote to give me news of the successful climbs his men were making.

In the mid-afternoon we scrambled down to our jeeps, where a small column waited to lead us back to Srinagar – two armoured cars in front and two behind. 'What's all this about?' I asked, but all my guides knew was that there had been trouble in Srinagar. I was deposited in a splendid hotel on the outskirts of the town and later taken to dine in the same officers' mess where I had breakfasted that morning. Again, everything was very British. At dawn the next morning I was driven to the airport, the plan being that Bhagavantam and I were to be flown to Leh, the highest base – 17,000 feet – where troops were deployed. But the weather was worsening fast, and the pilot, who would have had to fly over snow-covered peaks to Leh 'by the seat of his pants', decided that the trip was not on. We therefore decided to return straightaway to Delhi. On our arrival, I learnt that on the previous day the Kutch–Sind fighting had hotted up considerably. I congratulated my hosts on their security. No wonder they had not told Dickie anything. He would have wanted to run their war.

The President had invited me to stay on in Rashtrapati Bhavan on my return from Kashmir, but I declined as it was more convenient to spend my remaining three days in Delhi with John Freeman, our High Commissioner. General Chaudhuri wanted to see me again, mainly to discuss the further talks I was to have with Homi Bhabha, which were mostly concerned with India's negative attitude to a non-proliferation treaty. Chaudhuri, a handsome Sandhurst-trained officer who had achieved the rank of brigadier under the British Raj, was against India participating. 'Why do you want to deny us the Bomb?' he asked with a smile. 'We are a nation of phallus-worshippers, and we need to set up this phallus and worship it.' I laughed and replied that it was indeed a phallic symbol, a symbol of power, but for a soldier it was an impotent one. We were dining in his scented garden, he, his beautiful wife and I. She smiled, and I went on to ask how India could conceivably strike at Peking (China had exploded its first bomb in October 1964, little more than a year before): 'You are not, I hope, intending to threaten Karachi with a bomb?'

I paid a courtesy call on the President before flying on to Bombay to see Homi Bhabha. Homi and I had first met soon after the war, when he invited me to spend some time in India as a strategic and scientific defence planner. Homi was a wealthy bachelor, an amateur painter and, in a small way, a patron of struggling young artists. After obtaining a first-class honours degree in engineering at Cambridge, he had become one of Rutherford's disciples, remaining in Cambridge until 1939. His election as a Fellow of the Royal Society at the early age of thirty-two was a recognition of his brilliance as a theoretical physicist.

Homi took me to the nuclear establishment that he directed, and which I had visited once before (on the only occasion when I ever handled a piece of plutonium). Nehru and Homi had been intimate friends, and it was Nehru who had seen to it that Homi was given the resources with which to establish his vast and elite scientific institute. But, like Chaudhuri, Homi wanted India to have 'the bomb'. He was totally uninterested in the idea of a non-proliferation treaty.

That was the last time we ever met. I had told him about the house I was rebuilding in Burnham Thorpe, and he suggested that his young artist friends could produce some tiles with which to brighten the walls of my bathrooms. I accepted the gift, as I had always accepted the occasional basket of mangoes which he sent from Bombay. Homi said

356

that he proposed to take the opportunity of seeing the tiles in place after a meeting that he had to attend in Vienna early the following year. He never came. As his plane was coming in to land at Geneva Airport, it crashed into a snow-covered peak. Whenever I am in Geneva, I find myself nodding towards Mont Blanc in salute to his body, still lying in an inaccessible spot high up in the snows. I have been to India two or three times since Homi's death, but although always a fascinating place, it has never been as exciting to me as it was when he was alive.

A few months after that trip to India I accompanied Dickie on his 1965 and final world tour as CDS. After a night in Aden and another on the small island of Gan, we flew to Singapore and then Borneo, where he inspected the British forces that were facing the Indonesians on a 1000-mile front. We were flown by helicopter to small clearings in the evergreen forest, each manned by a small company of men, usually including a few Ghurkhas. The young commanding officers received him as though they were being reviewed by Caesar. I could not help asking myself how many of them realized that the days of our military presence in the far East were fast coming to an end.

This was not something that could have been read even between the lines of the annual Defence White Papers of the early 1960s. There was no hint there of the speed with which all but the last vestiges of Britain's imperial power were about to be swept away. Dean Acheson's quip about our having lost an Empire and not found a role was not something that our political leaders were ready to admit, however clear the writing on the wall, nor were our armed forces ready to adjust themselves to an impecunious future. The Ministry of Defence was then a small island to itself, geographically isolated from the quasi-independent and separate empires of the three Services.

In 1958 a Defence Board had been set up in order to bring the four departments closer together. It met fairly regularly, but during my time I do not recall it engaging in any significant discussion of strategic policy. We were a shadow of the concept of a unified Ministry of Defence, a concept that had first started to take shape in 1902, when the Committee of Imperial Defence was formed. Maurice Hankey, the Marine major who was its Secretary from 1912 until 1938, invited me to lunch shortly after I had joined the Ministry, and explained to me how difficult it was to achieve inter-Service cooperation. By then he was Lord Hankey, and Chairman of Porton's Bacteriological Research Advisory Board, about whose problems he also wanted me to be aware.

Winston Churchill's assumption of the post of Minister of Defence during the Second World War had in effect been little more than a public declaration that he had assumed the powers that Lloyd George had wielded in the First World War. He was Chairman of the Cabinet's Defence Committee, the country's generalissimo and, as such, the coordinator of the plans for all our armed forces. When the Government changed on 25 July 1945, Attlee, in an effort to maintain the authority of a defence ministry, deprived the three Service Ministers of their separate seats in the Cabinet. It was a step that achieved very little. The three Services settled down and resumed their independent ways.

The idea that a single Minister should have the final executive say over the whole field of defence was formally redefined in 1957, when Harold Macmillan publicly announced that, unlike his predecessors, Duncan Sandys would have the authority, as Minister of Defence, to decide on all matters that affected both the shape and size of the Services and their deployment. It was to be the end of 'defence by committee'. In the following year, Sandys published a White Paper, entitled *Central Organization for Defence*.[2] Unfortunately, the small Ministry over which he presided simply did not have the staff to wield the authority it had been accorded. As Harold Macmillan noted in his Memoirs, what he had achieved still meant that 'the system was to remain basically one of coordination' and the Chief of Defence Staff (CDS) 'was to have no control of his own'.[3]

Ziegler has written that Dickie told Alan Campbell-Johnson, a close friend who had been his press attaché in his Viceregal days in India, that Harold Macmillan offered him the job of Minister of Defence.[4]Macmillan makes no mention of this in his Memoirs, and I wonder if Dickie's story was not simply a manifestation of what Philip Ziegler describes as his inability in the last few years of his professional life 'to distinguish between what had happened and what he would have liked to have happened'. Harold Macmillan must have known that despite Dickie's powers of leadership, his drive, his ambition and determination, he was mistrusted by his military peers, and would have been a political liability in any effort to effect a reform that he, the Prime Minister, had already failed to achieve.

Anyhow, whoever reopened the issue, the fact is that almost as soon as Dickie became CDS, he and Harold Watkinson arranged that there should be overall Commanders in the Near and Far East, as opposed to three separate Cs-in-C reporting back to their Service Chiefs in Whitehall. The next step was to make a reality of what had begun under Sandys in 1957 – that of ensuring that a Secretary of State could exercise full authority over the Services, with adequate powers being accorded to the office of Chief of the Defence Staff. Dickie received little encouragement from Eddie Playfair. 'If you hear the sound of feet scraping outside your door,' Eddie told him, 'they'll be mine, dragging my heels if you go on with this silly scheme.' I smiled when Eddie told me this. Dickie had once got down on his knees to teach both of us how to use his own variety of double knot when tying our shoelaces. I still do it his way.

If Eddie, the Permanent Secretary, was lukewarm about the proposed reforms, I, the Scientific Adviser, was the reverse. The committee on the control of Government R&D that I had chaired had been dealing with one aspect of the whole problem, and I had found it amazing that in the Ministry as it then was there was no-one who, for example, could give a ruling about the way troops fighting on the ground should be provided with close air-support, whether by a vertical or short take-off subsonic aircraft or by supersonic fighters and fighter-bombers (there were no helicopter 'gun-ships' in those days). Nor could I see why each Service should run its own senior training college, or quasi-university when, by combining the three, a single powerful university could be formed that would also be able to cater, as necessary, for the specialized interests of the Navy, the Army and the Air Force.

Eddie Playfair had resigned from the Civil Service in 1961. His successor, Rob Scott, was much more sympathetic to Dickie's ideas. Rob's experience as Commissioner General in Southeast Asia, had fitted him admirably for a task that was going to flout service tradition.* Peter Thorneycroft was as ready to support the move as Watkinson had been. He realized that some form of executive unification was essential. Draft after draft of a paper on integration was prepared by Dickie's office in consultation with other sections of the Ministry, with the

---

*Rob had been the prize prisoner of the Japanese after the fall of Singapore, and a central figure in the postwar War Crimes trials.

Chiefs providing their own commentaries and recommendations as the deliberations proceeded.

Thorneycroft then arranged that Dickie's staff paper should be discussed with the Prime Minister, who invited him together with Dickie, Rob Scott and myself, to a meeting on the evening of Sunday 9 December 1962, at Admiralty House – which had become the PM's temporary home and office while Number 10 Downing Street was being treated for dry rot. It was a foggy evening, and we arrived well before the Prime Minister, who had been held up on his way back from an engagement that he had had to keep outside London. Every now and then Tim Bligh, the head of the Private Office, came into the hall to tell us how much longer we would have to wait. When at last the PM came in, followed by Philip de Zulueta, he was deep in thought and walked past us without acknowledging our presence. Philip just smiled and went on, no doubt to prepare a note about what had transpired at the engagement from which they had just returned.

After about ten minutes, Tim Bligh beckoned us into the temporary Cabinet room. The PM was seated in his usual chair at the centre of the long Cabinet table, his hands over his eyes, and his thoughts obviously still far away – we were in the middle of the Skybolt upheaval. We took our places opposite him and, after about a minute or two's silence, the PM, having peeped at us between his fingers, opened the discussion by saying, 'Ah, yes, I know why you're here.' A somewhat uninspiring hour was spent discussing the integration of the Services, with the PM, who for years had been committed to the idea, occasionally making a remark that echoed something that had obviously cropped up in the talks he had had that afternoon. He then suggested that we should go into an adjoining room for a drink, where he cheered up remarkably. Dickie was teased because of his single-minded concentration on the powers that a CDS should have, the PM telling him that there was more to the matter than the bickerings of Chiefs of Staff. 'Why,' he said, 'speaking as an old grenadier, the good soldier doesn't bother about you people at the top. You'd be lucky if he knew the name of any officer above that of his company commander.' Dickie was not amused. The PM was his usual self by the time we moved to the dining room and a splendid cold supper. The party ended only when Philip de Zulueta came in to suggest that it was time for the Prime Minister to go to bed.

I have no memories, nor do I know of a record of any more such meetings, although I do remember that one had been arranged for the following Sunday. Dickie, however, often said that the five of us, the PM included, got together on successive Sundays to plan what should be done.[5] What did happen was that Lord Ismay and General Sir Ian Jacob were asked to prepare a report on the organization of defence, taking into account the views of all concerned. I was asked to prepare a memorandum on the work of my division of the department, and to say what I thought was wrong with the way things were going.

The first part of the paper that I prepared was easy. It was merely a factual account of the way the DRPC functioned and of the role of my office in the nuclear and disarmament fields. Providing a personal view of what was wrong was not so simple. Trying to implement the recommendations of my committee on governmental R&D had revealed that what we had advised related more to the symptoms than to the underlying causes of the problem that worried the Government. The central issue was not how a project was managed, but the fact that the cost of the R&D for a new piece of defence equipment and, if carried to completion, of the finished product, were as a rule several times what had been the estimated starting price when the project was authorized. We were over-ambitious. I had indicated some of the difficulties in the argument that had led me to what I had called 'the inexorable law of R&D' (p. 206). But inordinate and often uncoordinated demands on a limited R&D budget were still being made separately by the Services. I repeated my view that the R&D programme did not reflect a coherent defence policy – given, of course, that there was such a thing, which I doubted.

Another cause of concern was that the scientists who worked for the defence departments were 'men who could contribute materially in the taking of major decisions' but they tended 'to be regarded as "technicians"'. They took no direct part in the discussions where the decisions were taken. In this way, so I wrote, 'narrowness and exclusion become perpetuated', and scientists become isolated in departments within their specialities. This, I pointed out, also conduces to isolation from the very thriving world of science in the universities. The particular kind of isolation that we practised means that 'our scientists, as often as not, are in a less favourable position to give of the best of which they are potentially capable . . . than their opposite numbers in

361

other countries who in most cases are not only concerned with the business of bringing science and technology to bear on defence, but also in the administration of R&D, and in the determination of policy'. There was 'a far bigger gap in the United Kingdom world of defence between the "decision-maker" on the one hand, and the scientists and technologists on the other, than one now finds in industries which are correspondingly technologically based'.

The consequence, I argued, was the erosion of the nation's scientific capital. Despite the fact that we had been first in the field with most of the major innovations that had helped win the Second World War, we were no longer adding in a comparable way to the fund of scientific and technological knowledge from which we now drew for defence. We had been in at the birth of many new postwar developments, for example, variable geometry aircraft, computers, and semi-conductors, but had been overtaken by other countries to whom we were also fast losing men. We had become far more dependent on the Americans for advances in defence technology than they were on us, in spite of the fact that we still remained pre-eminent in fields of science where sheer intellect counted.

My memorandum made it clear that I did not believe that an ideal system for defence R&D could ever be devised – there were too many unknowns and constraints for that. But if the system was to be improved at all, I felt that an effective ministry of defence should not only be responsible for formulating all operational requirements for new equipment, but should be provided with the means of monitoring the progress of every R&D project that was authorized. To help promote a coherent defence policy, the separate operational research groups of the three Services also had to be brought together into one integrated inter-Service organization.

Ian Jacob discussed my memorandum with me before he and Ismay submitted their report at the end of February 1963. A few days later Thorneycroft informed Parliament about the principles of reorganization that were in the wind. As Harold Macmillan records, there followed a long period of discussion during which he kept urging Thorneycroft 'to see that we do not fall into this trap [that of doing nothing] again as we did in 1958'[6] – a reference to the abortive effort made by Duncan Sandys to bring about the executive integration of the Services. Elsewhere the PM writes that he told Thorneycroft that he 'would rather drop the whole idea than say that we have been defeated by the Service Departments. Pray take no notice at all of any obstruction. You should approach this the way Lloyd George used to approach problems with dashing, slashing methods. Anyone who raises any objection can go, including Ministers. . . . I beg you to take an axe to all this forest of prejudice and interests.'[7]

A fair amount of compromise did, however, prove necessary before Thorneycroft, in July 1963, was able to lay before Parliament his White Paper on the *Central Organization for Defence*.[8] Rereading it after a gap of twenty years, I can see that even if Dickie had had to yield a point or two to his colleagues, he had succeeded overall in achieving something that was very dear to his heart. One point that he failed to win was the removal of the Chiefs' right to tender their own advice to the Secretary of State and Prime Minister when their views clashed with those of the CDS.

He also enjoyed some victories of a somewhat symbolic nature. The title of the military head of the War Office was changed from Chief of the Imperial General Staff, as it had been traditionally styled, to Chief of the General Staff. After all, the Empire was vanishing fast. The Chief of the Air Staff remained the Chief of the Air Staff, but Dickie saw to it that the Chief of the Naval Staff retained as an additional title that of First Sea Lord. He also persuaded Peter Thorneycroft that the 600-year-old title of Lord High Admiral, which traditionally had been vested in the First Lord of the Admiralty* and 'the Lords Commissioners of the Navy', should be preserved and passed to the Queen.

My own proposals, which were consequential to the main idea of full authority being vested in a Secretary of State for Defence, were accepted. A single Defence Operational Requirements organization was established, Operational Research was coordinated, and a Defence Research Committee, as well as a Weapons Development Committee, set up. It was also agreed that the chief scientists of the three Services were to be full members of their respective boards.

I took part in an inspection of the splendid new committee room that the Chiefs were to use in the new Ministry of Defence. The room and its furniture were magnificent, and none of the Chiefs had anything to say when Dickie asked for our comments. When my turn came I

---

*Now within the area of responsibility of the Minister of State for the Armed Forces.

remarked, almost as a joke, 'Why isn't there a blackboard? If we're going to discuss strategy and policy, it might come in handy' – recalling, what we had all noticed in the Pentagon, that practically every room one visited had a board on which a speaker making a point could write. 'Not a bad idea,' said Dickie, and next time I was in the room, there was a board. I don't recall ever seeing it used, nor do I know if it is still there.

In the obituary I published immediately after Dickie's murder in 1979, I wrote:

> I can think of no Service Chief other than Dickie who would have been prepared to upturn centuries of tradition and to take the decisive step of depriving the separate Services of their independence. That was Dickie's strength. He was ready to defy tradition in big things, in the same way as he upheld it in small matters.[9]

Obviously, without the authority and political strength of Harold Macmillan, the process of reform could never have been started. Richard Hough reports Macmillan as telling him that he did not mind that 'Dickie always claimed the credit' for the reforms.[10] In theory Macmillan could have brought about the reorganization without Dickie's help. In practice, it was a major advantage to have had at his side a Service Chief who was prepared to dispose of the objections of his military equals. But change did not end with the 1963 reforms. The arrangements made then have gone on being changed – and an ideal system of defence organization has not yet been achieved.

The growing volume of work that kept coming my way had already led to some small increases in the size of my office. Indeed, on the occasion when I lost my voice and had had to retire from London (p. 288), the fear that I was overworking had taken the matter of additional staff out of my hands, with the Minister and CDS's office themselves treating with the Treasury on the subject. The formation of the new Ministry called for further reinforcements. In 1964 Bill Cook (p. 187) joined me as Deputy for Projects. His previous experience made him admirably suited for the job. A second deputy post, for 'Studies', was established and filled by Professor Alan Cottrell FRS,*

*Later Sir Alan Cottrell.

who resigned his chair in metallurgy in Cambridge to join me. The designation 'studies', which up to then had been Terry Price's, was a very loose one, and implied any enquiry other than those that dealt with R&D for new weapons systems. Unlike Bill Cook, Alan Cottrell was relatively innocent about the ways of Whitehall. Terry Price accepted the responsibility of combining the three separate operational research teams of the Services into a single organization.

The reformed Ministry of Defence, headed by a Secretary of State, formally began to operate on 1 April 1964. The responsibility for the enormous administrative task of transforming the new super-department into a reality, fell to Sir Henry Hardman, who had succeeded Rob Scott as Permanent Secretary. Unified procedures for preparing the Defence Estimates, organizing new measures for financial and accountancy control, and a host of other administrative matters had to be sorted out. It was all done smoothly. Indeed, I can remember only one moment of friction. Henry had not worked before in a military environment, and as was normal practice in big departments, he tried to arrange that, whatever advice was to be tendered to the Secretary of State, whether it came from the Chiefs of Staff organization, or the scientific, or the financial side of the department, should be coordinated by him, and sent on from his office. Dickie reacted politely, saying that he could not see the Chiefs agreeing that their advice to the Secretary of State should be filtered. Nor did I like the idea. Having discussed it with Terry Price, I wrote to Henry saying that while I was sympathetic to what he had in mind, and while I was sure that normally there would be no difficulties, I nonetheless feared that the bureaucratic procedure he was suggesting could slow down action, particularly when minutes from my side of the Ministry were pored over by people who could not understand their scientific and technological significance. More important, I warned of the danger that too much coordination could 'frustrate the creative and critical kind of study which affect the major issues of policy'. Nor was I ready to surrender my right to say what I wanted, regardless of the views of the rest of the Ministry, and even those of my staff. This manifesto in favour of free speech was in the end to bring about my departure from the department.

30

A Change of Government

Neither in 1963 nor in 1964 was there time to embark either on a new review or an updating of defence policy. There was too much going on. British forces had had to be called in to quell disturbances that broke out when old colonial territories had become republics within the Commonwealth. In April 1963 Indonesian forces started to 'confront' the Malayan Federation, beginning with an attack on Sarawak, and following a year or so later with armed landings in the Malay Peninsula. Our own, as well as Commonwealth forces had become involved. In June, France declared that those of her naval forces as were still assigned to NATO might be withdrawn in the event of war.* In August there was the Partial Test-Ban Treaty. In October Harold Macmillan resigned and Sir Alec Douglas-Home, having renounced his heredi-tary title, took his place.† In November President Kennedy was assassinated, to be succeeded by Vice President L.B. Johnson. Finally, there was a General Election. On Friday 16 October 1964, Harold Wilson became Prime Minister.

On the following day, a Saturday morning, Henry Hardman telephoned me in Birmingham to say that Denis Healey had been appointed Secretary of State for Defence. Healey himself telephoned about midday to ask whether I could call on him on the Sunday morning. He also asked me to let Dickie Mountbatten know. I telephoned Glyn Owen and Terry Price, asking them to collect together such papers as I might wish to discuss with the new Secretary of State, and said that I would join them that evening. I then telephoned Dickie and told him what was afoot. I had met Healey on one or two social occasions, but could hardly claim to know him. Dickie said that

*This step had been expected as a reaction to the US–UK Polaris agreement.
†He returned to the House of Lords in 1974 as a life peer in the style of Lord Home of the Hirsel.

he too only just knew him, and suggested that I find out on Sunday morning whether Healey would be free that evening, when the three of us could meet at my house.

Before I left Birmingham for London, the telephone rang again. An unfamiliar voice said that it was Frank Cousins speaking, and that he was calling at the Prime Minister's request. He had been appointed Minister of Technology, and Harold Wilson wanted him to see me straight away to get my help in formulating broad terms of reference for the post. Harold Wilson knew that although publicly I was Chief Scientific Adviser to the Ministry of Defence, I had also served in the same capacity to Harold Macmillan. Cousins wanted to see me next morning. When I asked where, assuming that as a trade union leader he had an office in London, or had been assigned one in Whitehall, it turned out that he had neither. He therefore asked if he could call on me. I suggested 11.30 the next morning at my house, guessing that my appointment with Healey would be over well before then. I then went off to the train, and joined my two colleagues in the Ministry, leaving Terry to bring round to Hasker Street the papers on which they were still working. He arrived near midnight.

While waiting, I telephoned Roy Jenkins to congratulate him on having been appointed Minister of Aviation. He told me that Patrick Gordon-Walker had been given the Foreign Office, and that George Brown, whom he was at that moment going to see, had been appointed Secretary of State for Economic Affairs. I asked Roy to congratulate George on my behalf, but Roy suggested that I should do so myself. I telephoned and was surprised when George proposed that we should lunch together the following day. Sunday was becoming increasingly odd. Healey at nine, Cousins at eleven-thirty, and George Brown at one.

The next morning I sat with Healey in his garden in Highgate in North London, and went over the matters that were my particular concern in the Ministry, and some of the problems with which he would have to grapple straight away in an already overloaded defence budget. He seemed well-informed, and I was much encouraged by the strength of his commitment to NATO. We discussed the nuclear problem in the context of the Labour Party's election commitments, but I was careful not to pursue the subject except to tell him that all the studies which I had done, and all the intimate talks I had had with

American colleagues, had led firmly to the conclusion that the idea of fighting a field-war with tactical nuclear weapons was military non-sense. Nuclear weapons were for deterrence. He liked the idea of my introducing Mountbatten to him that evening.

Frank Cousins, whom I recognized from newspaper pictures, was waiting on my doorstep when I got back. I found him easy to talk to in spite of my not knowing anything about the way the new Government proposed to put science to work to help industry. A committee that Dick Crossman had chaired, and of which Patrick Blackett had been a member, had been considering the problem in the months leading up to the election, but I had declined an invitation to appear before it, and had also said that I would not encourage my then part-time deputy, John Kendrew, to do so. Harold Wilson had himself more than once made speeches about the need for a Ministry of Technology, and Cousins explained what little he had been told. At the end of about an hour, I drafted a few paragraphs which indicated what we sensed should be the objectives of his new Ministry, including the suggestion that the administrative position of those governmental research institutions whose activities related to the specific responsibilities of executive departments of state should be examined.

On Monday, Maurice Dean who, until the election, had been Joint Permanent Under-Secretary in Lord Hailsham's small Department of Science and Technology, was appointed the first Permanent Secretary of Cousins' Ministry of Technology. I had told Cousins to ask for him since Maurice was the very man for the job. A new government department is not created by the stroke of a pen, and it needed someone of Maurice's experience to confer with Sir Laurence Helsby, the head of the Home Civil Service, and with the heads of all the other departments that would be affected by the creation of a new one. Maurice and I had known each other since the last days of the war, when he was in the Air Ministry. During the first week of the new Government he came to see me several times so that we could both be satisfied that the terms of reference he was putting into shape would satisfy our new masters.

But back to that Sunday. I had booked a table in the restaurant of the London Zoo for my lunch with George Brown. He turned up punctually with Sophie, his wife, and before going to the restaurant we drank a glass of sherry in my room. I can still see George, swinging his legs as he sat on a table in my small room, in a seventh heaven of delight as he told me how he was going to put the country's economy to rights. He was even more in that heaven after lunch when I went back to my house to arrange a cold meal for the two guests I was expecting that evening.

Then came the biggest surprise of the day. One of the Downing Street private-office staff whom Harold Wilson had inherited telephoned to say that the PM wanted to see me early that evening. I explained that I would have to be away by 7 p.m., and was told to be there as soon as I could. I did not have to wait more than a few minutes before the Prime Minister led me into the Cabinet Room, nodding to a sombre-faced C.P. Snow who was sitting at a small round table in the hall. The PM took his seat in the prime-ministerial chair, looking very confident. Beckoning me to sit next to him, and with barely a word of introduction, he said that he wanted me to join his Government and go to the Foreign Office as Minister of State to deal with disarmament negotiations. I was, he said, well known internationally, had many Washington friends, and was the man for the job. He was organizing a 'ministry of all talents' – at which point I turned to look at the door outside which Snow was sitting – whereupon he said, 'Oh, that's public relations, that's not serious. This is. You'll have to go to the Lords, of course, and I propose that you also become a member of the Cabinet's Defence Committee.' Without a moment's hesitation, I declined – using words less polite than a simple no. 'Either I serve this Government as I have its predecessor,' I went on, 'or I leave Whitehall,' adding that I was not a politician, and had no intention of becoming one, and that anyhow I was not a member of the Labour Party. 'I know better than you why I want you to do the job,' replied the PM. 'Think.' My refusal became firmer.

I got up to go, repeating what I had said about leaving Whitehall if I couldn't continue to serve as an official. 'Turn it over in your mind,' was his answer. 'I'll telephone you this evening. Speak to your wife.' I told him that Healey and Mountbatten were joining me for a cold meal, and asked for his permission to tell them what he had suggested, since there would be no point in my talking to them about defence policy if the consequence of what was in his mind was that I had to leave Whitehall and return to full-time academic life. 'By all means,' was the reply, and I left, thoroughly shaken.

The first time I had met Harold Wilson had been when he was a member of Attlee's Government. Our first and only social encounter was one evening in 1951 when, over a drink, Nye Bevan told me that he was leaving Attlee's Cabinet and that 'young Harold', who was lolling on a sofa in Nye's sitting room, beneath a gloomy picture by Michael Ayrton – it seemed to reflect the gloom on his face – was going with him. Our paths had rarely crossed after that evening, but 'young Harold' knew that Joan and I were friendly with Nye and his wife Jenny. He may have followed my career in Whitehall, but I had a feeling that what really counted in his eyes was that I had been a friend of Nye.

When Denis Healey and Dickie Mountbatten arrived at my house we started to chat over a glass of sherry about the UK's defence problems. After about ten minutes I blurted out that I might not be working with them. 'The chances are that I'll be returning to academic life.' I told them about the exchanges that I had just had, that my mind was absolutely shut to the PM's proposal, and that if he insisted, my only course would be to leave Whitehall. Dickie backed me up. Healey, although he knew me only by reputation, took the line that he wanted me as his Chief Scientific Adviser. Then the telephone rang. It was the PM. 'Well, have you given any more thought to my proposal? Have you changed your mind?' 'No.' 'Have you spoken to your wife?' 'No, there's no point. I've made up my mind.' 'Can I speak to Healey?' They conversed for about five minutes, with Dickie and me just looking at each other. 'He wants another word with you,' said Healey, handing me the telephone. 'Sleep on it, and come and see me tomorrow morning at nine,' said the PM.

The three of us then moved to my dining table and, over a cold meal, settled down to talk about the problems of the Ministry of Defence, with Dickie and me answering Healey's questions as well as we could. Needless to say, Labour's pledge about abandoning Britain's status as a nuclear power came up, but for tactical reasons was not pursued. I went to bed a troubled man, wondering whether it was the last time I would find myself discussing defence policy in an official capacity.

My meeting with the Prime Minister next morning lasted only a few minutes. Once again he said that he could see further than I could, and that I would be serving the country better as Minister of State in the Foreign Office than as Chief Scientific Adviser. I repeated that, if I could not carry on serving the new Government as I had the old, I would have to go. He then said that Patrick Gordon-Walker, the

Foreign Secretary, wanted a word with me straight away, and that when I had spoken to him I was to return to Number 10.

That morning the newspapers reported that I was to be Minister of State in the new Government. There had been a leak from Number 10. When I got to the Foreign Office, I ran into Harold Caccia, who was now the permanent head of the Office, and Nicko Henderson, the head of the Foreign Secretary's private office, and had to suffer their badinage as they said that the best suite of rooms in the building was being prepared for me. They had been told by the private office of Number 10 that I had said no. Patrick had also been told by the PM about my refusal, but he wanted to satisfy himself that my mind was really made up. He did not press me. I then returned to the PM who, in the thirty minutes or so that had elapsed since I had left the Foreign Office, had obviously been told by Patrick that I had not budged. This time the PM accepted my answer as final, but said that in the circumstances, from now on I was to be styled Chief Scientific Adviser not only to Defence but to the Government as a whole, with responsibility to the Foreign Secretary for matters relating to disarmament – which, of course, was what I had been *de facto*, although not publicly, ever since 1960. For good measure I was also to be known as Head of the Scientific Civil Service, an empty title and one that had not been accorded to anyone before – or indeed since. That decision provoked some argument with Sir Laurence Helsby, who as Head of the whole Civil Service, an office that had been in existence for many years, saw in it a derogation of some of his authority. But the PM insisted.

My refusal to accept the PM's invitation was not the end of the matter. When he realized that my 'no' was final, he asked me to suggest another scientist who was both internationally known and *persona grata* with the Americans, someone whom he could invite to be Minister of Disarmament. I offered the name of John Cockcroft. He was one of our nuclear pioneers, and the Americans knew him well. Would I get in touch with him and bring him along? asked the Prime Minister. I did so, and on the following day the PM put the same proposition to John, with me at his side, as he had to me. John explained that he was a member of the Liberal Party. That, said the PM, was no hindrance, since he was forming a 'Ministry of all talents' – the same words he had used with me. John undertook to consider the proposal, which he then discussed with me. He also saw Patrick Gordon-Walker. Some years

371

later John's brother told me that John had thought hard before he, too, declined the offer.

With all the leaks there had been about the appointment, Harold Wilson was in a jam, and called for help from George Wigg, his defence crony, whom he had already appointed Paymaster General. Rumour had it that the source of some of Wigg's views about defence was Alun Gwynne Jones, a professional soldier who had resigned his commission to become military correspondent of *The Times*, but who still had close connections with the War Office. Wigg put his name forward, and Alun became Minister of State for Disarmament, joining the Labour Party and taking the title of Lord Chalfont. He held the post for three years.

As I reflected in later years on how little I managed to achieve in debates on nuclear disarmament, I sometimes wondered whether Harold Wilson had not seen further ahead than I had, and that I might have done better than I did if I had enjoyed the authority of a government minister rather than that of an official. But I doubt it. Britain's fading power was already barely adequate to tip the scales one way or the other between the USA and the USSR. Anyhow my saying no did save me from being the butt of Barbara Castle's crack at Alun's appointment – 'a dangerous gimmick'.[1]

The only time I ever heard Harold Wilson refer to my refusal was some years later when he entertained President Nixon to dinner at Number 10. The party round the dinner table had been fairly small, but a number of Ministers and senior officials had been invited to meet the President when the dinner was over. We were lined up in a semicircle to be introduced, and when it came to my turn, the PM introduced me by saying, 'He made the mistake of preferring to remain an official rather than accept my invitation to become a Minister.' I doubt if Nixon understood what the difference was.

31

Defence Under Labour

Harold Wilson had frequently chided the Conservative Government about the claim that the UK was both an independent nuclear power and 'interdependent' with the United States. On an occasion when I had met him in the months before the election, he had asked me – fully aware of what the answer had to be – whether he was justified in saying that it was a 'pretence' that Britain had an entirely independent nuclear weapon. The Chiefs certainly expected that the new Government would honour its electoral pledge and change the UK's nuclear policy. A lot of shadow-boxing did take place, but in the end the policies remained essentially what they had been before. In retrospect I doubt if the changes in Britain's military establishment that have occurred since the early sixties would have been much different from what they have been whatever government had been in power.

The Labour Government was, of course, fully aware that the defence budget was woefully small in relation to the commitments it was trying to underwrite. To Harold Wilson, it must have seemed like 1951 all over again, when he and Aneurin Bevan, together with John Freeman, had resigned from Attlee's Government in protest against Hugh Gaitskell's final budget, in which the resources allocated to defence had squeezed out other items of expenditure, particularly in the National Health Serice. No doubt he also remembered that a few months after Winston Churchill's return to office, he had reduced the defence vote. What was different in 1963 was the nuclear element.

Wilson immediately learnt that the construction of the hulls of four Polaris submarines had already gone beyond what was claimed to be the 'point of no return' (a point which in the defence world varies arbitrarily case by case). I do not, however, believe that he was made aware of the fact that some of the Navy Chiefs had cautiously assumed that the new Government would scrap Polaris. As a fall-back position, they had in mind to do what Denis Healey had suggested when in Opposition, and eliminate the centre section of the hulls – the section consisting of the 'tubes' for the missiles – in order to transform the boats into what they irreverently called the Wilson class of nuclear-powered hunter-killer submarines.[1]

What happened was that the new Cabinet immediately endorsed a recommendation of its Defence Committee that the four boats, when completed, should be deployed, 'as a fully committed part of the NATO defence forces. There was to be no nuclear pretence or suggestion of a go-it-alone British nuclear war against the Soviet Union.'[2]

The Prime Minister then convened a conference at Chequers over the weekend of 21 November 1964. It was attended by all the Service Chiefs and their new Ministers, as well as by the new Foreign Secretary, the Chancellor of the Exchequer, the Minister of Aviation, and the new Secretary of State for Economic Affairs. Its purpose was to consider how defence expenditure could be cut in the light of the Party's electoral pledges and of the country's critical economic condition. As the Defence White Paper that was issued two months later stated, our forces were 'seriously over-stretched and in some respects dangerously under-equipped'. There had 'been no real attempt to match political commitments to military resources, still less to relate the resources made available for defence to the economic circumstances of the nation'.[3]

At the time of the Chequers meeting the Defence Chiefs were still feeling their way with their new political masters as they defended the interests of their own Services. What stands out in my memory was the way the Prime Minister steered the discussion towards the American proposal to establish a NATO 'mixed-manned multilateral nuclear force', an idea for which only Western Germany had expressed any enthusiasm. Harold Wilson was as much opposed to the idea as Macmillan had been, but since he was soon due to confer with President Johnson, who was even keener on the MLF than President Kennedy had been, he devised the alternative plan of 'internationalizing' the British nuclear deterrent through the creation of a NATO Atlantic Nuclear Force, the so-called ANF, to which our Polaris boats, and 'at least an equal number of American Polaris submarines', would be irrevocably committed during the lifetime of NATO. 'The United

States, the United Kingdom, and any other participating country which so wished, would have a veto over the release of the weapons of the Force.'[4] If the ANF seemed to be a gimmick designed to get rid of the MLF, it certainly succeeded in its purpose.

I was in the party that the Prime Minister took with him to Washington at the beginning of December. He seemed to get on well with President Johnson, but I do not believe that anything very significant happened except that the Americans agreed to examine the concept of the ANF in relation to that of the MLF – an examination which, after a year or two of discussion, came to nothing. I attended the meetings in the White House, and the usual formal dinner, and also spent some time with my friends in the Pentagon, and with Don Hornig in the Executive Office.

Soon after the Prime Minister's return, there was a Commons debate on defence and foreign affairs, with the opposition highly critical about the PM's ANF proposal, and equally so about Labour's declared policy 'to remove the clause in the Nassau agreement which was based on a fictitious assertion of independent nuclear action by Britain'.[5] In the late afternoon of the second day of the debate I was summoned to the Prime Minister's room in the House of Commons, where he was about to dictate the outline of the speech with which he proposed to wind up the debate. He asked me to confirm that, quite apart from the Polaris missile, we were then dependent on the Americans for one of the components that goes into the making of a nuclear warhead. I did so. He then asked me to stay with him while he dictated his speech, a few pages at a time, to two secretaries, each of whom returned with what they had typed for me to scan in order to make sure that his text did not contain any serious technical error.

I was amazed by the speed with which he worked and, not having followed the long debate that he was due to close, impressed by the force of what he intended to say. Say it he did, as I learned next morning from the newspapers and from *Hansard*. His main point was that we were not only dependent on the Americans for the weaponry on which our nuclear independence was based, but that it was inconceivable that a British Prime Minister would ever embark alone on a nuclear war with the Soviet Union. Bob Press told me that the director of Aldermaston, as well as Aldermaston's main representative in MOD – who technically was on my staff – were indignant that the PM had

375

taken it upon himself to deliver a speech on nuclear policy without having cleared it through the usual channels which, at the end of the day, would have meant themselves. Bob knew that I had been with the PM when he was preparing the speech. When I pressed him he said that the main complaint was that the PM had referred to the nuclear component which we were then getting from the Americans as a fissile material, when he should have said a nuclear material. I told him not to worry. The PM had made his point. It was years before the issue of our strict independence was again raised publicly, and when it did come up, it did so in totally different circumstances.

During the decade before he became Secretary of State for Defence, Denis Healey is said to have proposed the creation of a 'non-nuclear club', and to have espoused a policy that would have disengaged the UK from Europe.[6] None of this was apparent during his first year in Defence, which he spent reviewing our commitments and future policies, with particular emphasis on 'cost-effectiveness'. I soon learnt that Denis was neither one to accept ready-made recommendations, my own included, nor necessarily committed to views that he may have forcibly propounded before. Barely six months after he had taken office, he invited me to comment on the draft of a speech, parts of which flew in the face both of views that he himself had expressed in public and of conclusions that had been endorsed by his two ministerial predecessors. I never knew what part officials may have played in the preparation of the paper, nor do I remember whether the speech was ever delivered or, if delivered, whether it was first amended to take account of comments which he received. One of the points in the draft was that the deterrent posture of NATO's forces should be made to depend on the acceptance of the idea of nuclear escalation from the outset of hostilities. SACEUR should therefore continue to deploy battlefield nuclear weapons and also be given control of strategic nuclear forces. Bob McNamara was still at the start of the lengthy process of changing this policy to that of 'flexible response', a goal which Denis soon endorsed, and which he worked hard to encourage the West German Government to accept.

It was clear to everyone in the Ministry that when Denis began his first defence review it was going to be stamped by his own strong personality. Economies had to be made, and commitments adjusted to accord with a force structure that a £2000 million budget (at 1964 prices) would allow. This was the target that the Cabinet had set, and which was supposed to be reached by the year 1969–70. All three Services had to suffer, the Army less than the other two. The RAF would lose the TSR2, the P1154, and the short-take-off transport aircraft, the HS681, while the Navy had to renounce its dream of building a vast aircraft carrier. Needless to say, there had to be something to compensate for the cancellations, and that is where my views started to diverge from those of Denis, and from what became dominant departmental policy. Dickie Mountbatten had left office by the time serious drafting began, and whether or not he would have agreed with my own general conclusions, I was well and truly isolated so far as Healey was concerned.

My own view was that in deciding on our overseas commitments we had to bear in mind at the start the demographic changes due to differential population growth that would have transformed the world by the year 1980. As I wrote in a lengthy minute, experience showed that while precise estimates of future population growth could never be relied upon, the broad trends could not be ignored; if they, as well as the speed of education and economic growth, were taken into account

> it is impossible not to envisage vast changes occurring in our own strength relative to that of our present allies and enemies, and vast political alterations in the world as a whole. Every sane man hopes that we achieve the goals of our 1970 economic plan. But when we have done so, we shall still have to face the fact that, in the light of population changes in the world, our status and influence as a military power cannot but be lower ten, twenty years hence than it is today. If the forces we can now afford to deploy overseas already seem dangerously close to the threshold of military effectiveness, even less will they reach that threshold in 1980. The decision about what we do now depends more on general and political considerations than on a technical and military assessment. We are used to saying that we are no longer in the military first league. Short of a miracle, I do not see us, as an independent power, in the third league twenty years hence. Our future as a military power depends mainly on our alliances, on the outcome of disarmament negotiations, and on the prospects for the UN. Nonetheless, for the time being, it remains a fact that we

are stuck with the military commitments history has imposed on us, and with forces whose value is basically political.

Like many others, I failed to see how our forces could underwrite our existing 'East of Suez' strategic commitments once 'confrontation' with Indonesia had ended. The previous Tory administration had decreed that South Arabia would become independent by 1968, when we were due to withdraw from Aden. Healey, on the other hand, no doubt for political reasons, declared that we would continue 'to maintain a military presence in the Far East as long as the governments of Malaysia and Singapore agree that we should do so on acceptable conditions'.[7]

As soon as a date had been set for the cancellation of the TSR2, Healey announced that the American F111 would be bought to help 'bridge the gap' until an Anglo–French variable geometry machine (p. 229) was in production. It was not difficult to appreciate why the RAF had to be placated, but it did not make sense to me to buy an American aircraft to replace the TSR2, when one of the publicly stated reasons for its cancellation was that it did not serve any relevant strategic purpose. The decision also seemed odd against the background of the views that were emerging from a 'scenario committee' on which sat senior representatives of the Services, and of which one of my two deputies, Alan Cottrell, was chairman. I made no secret of my scepticism about the UK's need for the F111. One day Henry Hardman came into my room with a copy of a minute that I had just sent Healey, and indignantly asked how I could disavow policies in whose formulation my own staff was playing a part. The minute dealt with the differences in performance between the specifications of the F111 and those of the Navy's advanced Buccaneer project, which to me meant little in relation to our operational commitments. My answer was that whatever scenario the studies seemed to be revealing, I had not joined the Ministry to subcontract my own judgement. It was one of the few occasions on which Henry and I clashed.

In the knowledge that the Navy had been denied the vast aircraft carrier that it wanted, the Air Staff started to promote a new doctrine – that the RAF could compensate for the Navy's weaknesses by what was called an 'island strategy'. Maps were drawn which presumed to show that, if they were not there already, bases could be built on small islands within range of each other, so that a force of F111s could patrol the globe. (I never made my own checks, but it was being rumoured that the position of islands on the RAF map were being shifted 100 miles one way or the other so that their distances apart would be compatible with the range of operation for which the F111 was being designed.) The Navy spokesmen were no match for those of the RAF at the various committees where the presumed new strategy was debated. So 'island strategy' became the departmental doctrine.

From the start the idea seemed unreal. It was being seriously proposed that our ground forces, wherever they happened to be, could be protected by fewer than a hundred strike aircraft, which could be deployed worldwide in an offensive–defensive role. I failed to see how aircraft alone could support forces which it was presumed might be engaged in land operations East of Suez. I remember asking at one meeting whether it was seriously proposed that an 'opposed landing', such as that in Anzio in Italy in 1943 (in which Healey had taken part), could be covered by aircraft based in the UK. If that were the case, I added, count me as the first deserter. It was not the sort of remark that added to my then waning popularity with the Air Staff.

My own argument was simple. If we were ever to be on our own in an operation overseas, we would need both transport and supply ships. Clearly these could not rely on being protected just by a handful of aircraft operating from widely dispersed island bases. In short, if our commitments East of Suez were going to continue, we could no more dispense with naval forces than we could with air forces or men on the ground. I regarded the statement in the Defence Review White Paper that, 'in the future, aircraft operating from land bases should take over the strike-reconnaissance and air defences functions of the carrier', as a groundless claim.[8]

In my capacity as Chief Scientific Adviser to the Government as a whole, and not just to the Minister of Defence, it was accepted that I could discuss the Defence Review with members of the Government other than Denis Healey, whether in answer to questions that were put to me or on my own initiative. I can now see that this made life more than difficult for Denis, whose affairs should have been my primary concern. From his point of view my behaviour was intolerable. The end came when one day he called me to his office, and after his private secretary had left the room, said that he understood that I was briefing his Cabinet colleagues not only against his views, but against policies that had been elaborated with the help of my own staff. How was it, he wanted to know, that I was opposed to the purchase of the F111 when I had not been opposed to the cancellation of the TSR2? I replied that the concept of the TSR2 as a nuclear-strike aircraft for a European battlefield had become, as he himself had admitted, strategically untenable. The same argument applied to the F111. What was more, the F111 would prove financially disastrous to us and, at that stage of its development, it was also technologically 'dicey'. The answer to his question about my briefing his colleagues was yes, and for good measure I added that as soon as our talk was over, I was seeing George Brown, at the latter's request. Denis's question about my staff got the same reply that I had given Hardman.

The Review ended my days in the Ministry of Defence. It also ended even more stormily than its progress had threatened. The Navy Minister, Christopher Mayhew,* resigned from the Government, and the First Sea Lord, Admiral of the Fleet Sir David Luce, from the Service, while Vice-Admiral Sir Frank Hopkins, the Fifth Sea Lord, was transferred from his central post to that of C-in-C Portsmouth. Then my name came up publicly. Christopher Mayhew explained the reasons for his resignation at a meeting of the Parliamentary Labour Party, and in the course of doing so referred to me by name. Denis Healey was present and the inevitable followed. A Parliamentary question was tabled in which the Government was asked about my disagreement with the Defence White Paper. The customary reply – that it was regrettable that the names of civil servants were bandied about in such circumstances – was given. But with banner headlines in some newspapers, it was also said that I had been involved in a major quarrel not only with Healey, but also with Dick Hull who had now succeeded Dickie as CDS. The story in the papers was that Dick Hull and I had 'rowed' both about the Air Force island strategy and about the potential value of nuclear weapons on the battlefield.

I never did discover why the papers had suggested that there had been a quarrel between Dick Hull and me. Perhaps it was because there was no love lost between Dickie Mountbatten and Dick Hull. For some time Field Marshal Montgomery had also been cultivating my acquaintance, the first occasion being when he wanted me to read the

*Now Lord Mayhew and a member of the Liberal Party.

draft of a speech that he was proposing to deliver in the House of Lords. I had never met him during the war, and the fact that the great man occasionally called on me must have been known throughout the Ministry. Monty was also no friend of Dick Hull and, worse than that, he had been intriguing to block Dick's succession as CDS. He had both spoken and written to me on the subject, urging me to help him persuade the Government to agree that Mountbatten's appointment should be extended rather than that Dick Hull should succeed. Obviously I did nothing. Philip Ziegler has written that whether Monty was 'more anxious to keep Hull out or Mountbatten in is a finely balanced question'.[9]

In fact, in one of our conversations Monty had dropped a hint that he himself should be called out of retirement to succeed rather than let Dick Hull in!

I do not believe that Dick seriously supported the RAF's mythical concept of an island strategy. The only issue on which he and I were known publicly to differ was about the utility of nuclear arms in field warfare. But even so, I doubt whether Dick believed in the concept of a nuclear battlefield. He always reacted with undeserved restraint to the forthright way I stated my views, and I am happy to say that on the few occasions that we have met in retirement, we have greeted each other like old friends.

It would, of course, have been surprising if the Service Chiefs had got on happily with one another in the course of a Defence Review. Every year they had to fight each other for a share of constantly declining defence resources. In 1966 the RAF appeared to have won with its island strategy. In the end it fared no better than did the Navy. For the F111 'option', around which the new strategy had been devised, was also in due course cancelled. Struggle as Denis did with his Cabinet colleagues, the money simply was not there to allow of the purchase. Indeed, in the end the RAF suffered almost more than had the other two Services. Healey cancelled the TSR2 in his first year. The F111 followed three years later. The Anglo-French variable-geometry aircraft foundered in 1967. By that time, of course, no more was being heard of the island strategy. It was not until 1982, by which time the strength of the Air Force had been greatly reduced, that the Tornado, the lineal successor of the TSR2, the F111 and the AFVG, came into service.

I never knew how Denis got on with the Service Chiefs, but I suspect that once Dickie was out of the way, it was easier for him to show that he was master. Denis did not protest when, at the Prime Minister's request, Dickie spent most of the three months preceding his retirement visiting Commonwealth countries to urge a slow-down in the flow of immigrants to the UK. Indeed, Denis had encouraged him to undertake the mission, and Dickie was therefore out of the country during the critical stage of the Review. Denis's biographers have said that Dickie wished to continue as CDS.[10] This I do not believe, even if he may have been flattered that there were a few who thought that his term of office should be extended more than it had already been. I also feel that Healey's biographers oversimplify in their account of the quarrels which ended with the resignation of Christopher Mayhew and Admiral Luce. On the basis of information which they say was provided by Henry Hardman, they make it appear that the argument boiled down to the single issue of whether or not the Navy should have had a carrier fleet, and in particular the vast ship known as CVA-01, which Denis is said to have cancelled contrary to the advice given him by Dickie Mountbatten and myself. The facts are otherwise. CVA-01 had already been ruled out of court by Peter Thorneycroft, Denis's predecessor, and I do not believe that Dickie ever thought that the money would be available for so vast a project. So far as I was concerned, the CVA-01 had never been more than a naval architect's dream.

What I specifically advised Denis was, first, that the procurement programme that would flow from the decisions he was taking should not be based on the premise that we would be engaged in military operations East of Suez after 1980. Second, we should forget about the RAF's island strategy. If pursued, it would only end in cancellations and waste. Third, he should confirm that there was no future in the idea that the UK could build giant carriers such as CVA-01, and that no more money should be spent on modernizing the *Hermes* (one of the carriers that was still in service). Instead, we should take up an offer, which the Americans had made, to buy two of their mothballed carriers. Lastly, we should abandon the F111, and as an interim measure equip the RAF with an advanced version of the Buccaneer until such time as our project with the French to build a variable-geometry aircraft had borne fruit.

Apart from troops, our goal should therefore be a coherent mobile naval task force that could be moved around, as required, when the moment came for us to abandon our bases in the Far East and the Gulf. In my mind's eye I even saw a mobile force – which had been a central feature of the policies that Harold Watkinson favoured – helping to evacuate British citizens from the east coast of Africa! Nothing like the Falklands operation then entered my mind, nor did I ever hear anyone suggesting such a possibility.

A cynic might be excused were he to judge today that the concept of an island strategy was only a smoke screen behind which the RAF, deprived of the TSR2, could campaign for an aircraft other than the Navy's Buccaneer. There are some who still believe, however, that the decision to cancel the TSR2 was misguided, that the P1154 could have been developed, and that the decision to stop work on both destroyed the British aircraft industry. I have heard others, including, as I have said, senior RAF officers, argue that the RAF should have accepted the Buccaneer. My own view is that the industry would have suffered even more than it has if the decision to cancel had not been taken. The P1154 was both a technological and an economic impossibility in the early 1960s – as it may still be – while had it entered service, the TSR2 would have been outmoded within a year or two by the French Mirage, the Soviet MiG-23, and the American variable-geometry F111. The real trouble was that without the TSR2 or the F111, there was a gap in the armoury of a modern air force.

It is, of course, true that at the time of the 1966 Defence Review, the UK could not have withdrawn summarily from East of Suez. We were still engaged in operations in Borneo and in South Yemen, and were also under considerable pressure from Australia, New Zealand and Singapore not to abandon the positions we still maintained in the Far East. But I have always regretted what was said in the 1966 White Paper about island bases.* Not only did it foreclose the option of starting the development of a coherent combined Services task force, it also misled us about our future, as well as doing us little good at the

---

*We already had a base at Gan, a desolate spot and the southernmost of the Maldive Islands, south of Ceylon. We were also casting eyes on Diego Garcia, some 300 miles south in the Chagas Archipelago which, despite the public protests of the Indian Government, has since been developed as an American base. The only possible new one that was then being spoken about was the island of Aldabra. This proposal caused

time. Had the Navy and Air Force not been at each other's throats, the foundations could then have been laid for a task force that could have been modernized and built on as the years passed. And had that been done, there would have been no need for the improvisation, brilliant though it was, that made the Falklands operation possible. That war was won by the kind of coherent task force which Frank Hopkins and I had in mind when, in September 1965, several months before the publication of his White Paper, I sent Denis what I called a Review of Reviews.

As it turned out, it was barely two years after the publication of the 1966 White Paper before the Government had to declare that our defence effort would from then on be focused mainly on Europe and the North Atlantic, and that we would be withdrawing from East of Suez during the ensuing five years. This conclusion, as Patrick Gordon-Walker later wrote, may have been unwelcome, but we were 'pushed and coerced into it by unforeseen events'.[11] The economy was simply not strong enough even to allow for the financial target for defence expenditure that had been set in the 1966 Review.*

In November 1967, Roy Jenkins took over as Chancellor, and set to work on the preparation of a package of major cuts. Harold Wilson tells us that steering the expenditure review through the Cabinet, and particularly its defence component, was 'the most formidable task' that he had attempted in over three years of government.[13] The account of what happened, as detailed in the diaries of his two Cabinet colleagues, Barbara Castle and Dick Crossman, make it plain he was not exaggerating.

The Prime Minister anticipated that the proposal to bring forward to 1971 the already announced date for our withdrawal from East of

---

an uproar. Aldabra lies off the East African coast, north of Madagascar, and is the home of some creatures so rare that they are not found anywhere else in the world (among them a giant tortoise, a bird called a pink-footed booby, and another, the flightless rail, a kind of extant Dodo). Representations against the proposal were made both by our own Royal Society and by other national scientific bodies, including those of India and the United States. Questions were asked in Parliament, and in the end the Ministry of Defence was persuaded to seek an alternative staging-post. The whole idea was subsequently dropped, to the relief, I suspect, of the Government and of Denis Healey who, according to Crossman, was from the start only half-hearted about the idea.[12]

*£2000 million at 1964 prices.

Suez, and to cancel the order for the F111, would cause particular difficulty. I was a member of the committee of officials that serviced the Cabinet's Defence and Overseas Policy Committee (DOPC), and had kept him advised about the technical difficulties that were afflicting the development of the F111, and delaying the date of its possible deployment in the UK by 1969.* Even more important was the fact that the eventual cost of the aircraft was likely to be the same as that of the ill-fated TSR2, and not the much lower one that had been announced to Parliament, a likelihood which would have been highly embarrassing politically – as embarrassing as Peter Thorneycroft had three years before thought a charge for Polaris R&D would be. Denis worked hard to avoid the cancellation and, as I have already said (p. 224), was at first prepared to sacrifice the P1127 to save the F111. According to Dick Crossman, the PM's success in steering the package of cuts through the Cabinet was largely due to Roy's skill. Denis, he says, 'was no match for Roy', who throughout remained the 'dominating force in the Cabinet'. Despite some mutterings about resignation, this time there were none.†

It is a mark of the robustness of Denis Healey's character that he was able to survive the personal setback that he suffered from the cancellation of the F111. When Roy was in charge of the Ministry of Aviation, he often urged me to be 'nicer' to Denis than he believed I was. He was no longer doing that when he had become Chancellor.

By then I had left the Ministry of Defence. The stormy meeting I had had with Denis about the F111, had obviously made it impossible for me to continue as his Chief Scientific Adviser. As soon as the necessary arrangements could be made, I therefore transferred myself and my immediate staff to the Cabinet Office to start operating as CSA to the Government 'as a whole'. When I left Defence, Denis sent me a letter which, in the light of the difficulties that I had made for him, I did not deserve. It was as warm a letter of appreciation for my critical approach to defence policy as could ever have been written.

*The first F111s went into service in the United States in 1967.
†Healey's biographers[14] have commented that it was surprising that Dickie Mountbatten did not oppose Denis during the period of the Defence Review. The reason was simple. Dickie was out of the country at the critical time. He was, however, anxious to display his indignation at the time of the Mayhew resignation, and proposed doing so in a speech in the House of Lords. I cautioned him against doing so. So did David Luce, and the speech was never delivered.

Chevaline

Claude Pelly (p. 145) had attained the rank of Air Chief Marshal, and had become the Atomic Energy Authority's member for Weapons by the time I joined the Ministry of Defence. It was the period of the moratorium on nuclear tests, and Claude knew that Harold Macmillan was committed to securing, if at all possible, a comprehensive test ban. On my first visit to Aldermaston, he confessed to me his hope that Macmillan's dream would be realized, in which case, as he saw it, Aldermaston's activities would be much curtailed. Since the position he held in the AEA was the last in his long and distinguished service career, the prospect of Aldermaston closing down did not imply any conflict of interest for him. But he appreciated, as I did, that it was a worrisome time for the Aldermaston scientists and engineers. A comprehensive ban was an implicit threat to their livelihoods as much as to their careers. Their future depended on having Ministers and civil servants believe that their work was essential to the national interest. This, of course, was not difficult, since the Aldermaston scientists worked in strict secrecy on mysteries which the ordinary civil servant or politician could not begin to understand.

Designing a warhead for Skybolt and then, after Nassau, for Polaris, had breathed new life into the Establishment. But by that time the American weaponeers and those in the USSR had begun to conceive of ways whereby offensive warheads could be destroyed either in space or after they had re-entered the atmosphere. One American anti-ballistic-missile (ABM) system that governmental and industrial defence scientists had devised, and for which they had campaigned hard, had been vetoed by President Eisenhower as early as 1959. It was known, however, that the Russians were still trying to devise an ABM system to defend Moscow. Our own weaponeers therefore had to show, as their opposite numbers in the United States had already done, that an enemy's defensive system could be defeated by incorporating decoys in the nuclear warheads. We had intended doing this for Blue Streak's warhead. There was open discussion at the time of other forms of 'penetration aid', and of the possibility that a single ballistic missile could carry several independently manoeuvrable warheads (MIRVs) in order to overwhelm any defence.

I discussed the ABM problem endlessly with John Rubel, Jerry Wiesner and others in the United States, and also with Robert Cockburn,* then the Scientific Adviser to the Ministry of Aviation. Bob was one of the pioneers of radar, and admirably level-headed. His view was that whatever technological developments might be made in one or more of the many components of an ABM system, it would prove impossible to devise a defence that could not be defeated or, at the least, rendered strategically impotent. It was because I was so persuaded by the facts and by the argument that I formulated the particular 'proposition' that I have quoted on page 301.

Unfortunately, the fact that there was little or no faith at the top in ABM systems did not mean that the weaponeers of the two sides stopped furnishing the warheads they were designing with costly penetration aids. One of our reasons for wanting Polaris was the political one of 'keeping up with the Joneses'. The Royal Navy and Aldermaston felt the same about the A3 Polaris and the newer Poseidon missile on which the Americans were embarking. They wanted to keep up with the Americans. Admiral Sir Varyl Begg, David Luce's successor as Chief of the Naval Staff, called on me soon after I had moved to the Cabinet Office, to tell me that the production of the A2 Polaris missile would be coming to an end, and that even the future of the A3 was now threatened by more ambitious projects. Varyl wanted me to use what influence I had to see that the Royal Navy was kept in line with the US Navy. But he said nothing about penetration aids or ABM systems, and he left with a smile on his face when I asked what difference it made what our Polaris tubes contained, provided that the Russians believed that they were nuclear missiles that could hit Moscow or Leningrad. What we believed was irrelevant.

By the mid-sixties the debate about the possibility of defending American cities and missile-batteries against attack had become

*Now Sir Robert Cockburn.

public. When writing about the MLF, Harold Wilson describes Walt Rostow, the head of the State Department's planning division, as being 'a persuasive salesman – to both sides'. He had to persuade his colleagues in the State Department that Germany and Italy wanted the MLF, at the same time as he was trying to persuade Germany and Italy that NATO needed the MLF. Whether this remark about Walt Rostow was justified is neither here nor there. But it was certainly the case that some of the Aldermaston staff were persuasive salesmen to both sides. Their friends in the Pentagon and in the American Atomic Energy Commission had to be encouraged to warn that unless Aldermaston was provided with the resources necessary to pursue a vigorous programme of warhead development, it would not be provided with information that it might one day want. Buying from the Americans, that is to say, keeping in with them, meant selling the idea that we should do so to the UK Government.

I had arranged that one of the visits I had to make to the West Coast of America coincided with one that Rabi was making. He thought that it would be a good idea if I were to meet Herman Kahn, who was then at RAND, the US Air Force 'think-tank'. Kahn was the nuclear enthusiast who had invented the phrase, 'thinking the unthinkable', and who became the model for the film character, Dr Strangelove. We were brought together at a small luncheon, which Kahn turned into a debate. One of his points was that the United Kingdom was rich enough to build a force of nuclear missiles that could deliver so effective a first-strike that the USSR would not be able to retaliate. All you need to do, said Kahn, is take an economic decision. Your economy is growing now, or could grow, at something like three per cent a year. What you must do is keep your standard of living at its present level, and divert your annual increments of wealth to your nuclear weapons programme for, say, five years. It was all straightforward to Kahn. I had to explain that the United Kingdom was a democracy, whose electorate was unlikely to tolerate a clampdown on its standard of living. No party would ever be elected were it to go to the polls declaring the policy that he was advocating. Rabi added some salvos of his own. He appreciated that Kahn had a lively mind, but he regarded him as a nuclear madman.

It was in 1965 that Johnny Foster, fresh from Livermore, succeeded Harold Brown as Director of Defense Research and Engineering in the Pentagon. Johnny liked the link with Aldermaston – not that the American authorities ever told us anything except on a 'need-to-know' basis. We knew only about those parts of their weapons development programmes that related to our own requirements. I had got to know Johnny well. He was no Herman Kahn, and he amused me with his naive political and military views about the significance of nuclear weapons, and by his implicit assumption that the UK could and should pursue the nuclear path that the USA was blazing.

He had been egged on by his Aldermaston friends to urge on me the message that, without an assurance that Aldermaston was going to be provided with the resources to proceed beyond Polaris, the US could not go on giving us technical help. It was a kind of blackmail. I did not know anyone in Whitehall who opposed the idea that the UK should maintain a nuclear 'deterrent' force, or who wanted to disrupt our special, even if ephemeral, relationship with the United States. But there were always the underlying questions – how much independence were we having to sacrifice because of the 'relationship', how much had it already cost us, and how much more were we prepared to pay? The minute that Rob Scott and I had written at Nassau (p. 261) was often in my mind.

The way Aldermaston succeeded in its aim has been recounted in a lengthy television programme in which a number of retired Ministry of Defence officials described the course of events in the later 1960s and early 1970s which led, first, to the Chevaline–Polaris programme, and then on to Trident.[1] One of those who took part was Victor Macklen, a nuclear specialist who had taken Bob Press's post in Defence when Bob joined me in the Cabinet Office. Macklen explained that the Americans had warned us that the production of the A3 Polaris missile, the system that we had bought, was going to be discontinued, and that in its place they were prepared to offer us either 'the technology' for 'hardening' our warheads and incorporating the penetration aids that they had designed, or the right to buy the newer Poseidon missile. The first part of his story I can confirm, but the second I find strange.

Long before the initial letters SDI – Strategic Defense Initiative – were made familiar by President Reagan, it had become known that one feature of an anti-ballistic-missile system could be the explosion of a nuclear bomb in the path of an attacking missile whose warhead would be irrevocably damaged by the X-rays that the explosion generated. The antidote for the attacker was to encase his warheads in a material that was immune to X-rays – the technique called hardening. Penetration aids – 'penaids' – were 'decoys' of various kinds that could be incorporated in the nose cone of the attacking missile, and which would be released in order to confuse the 'acquisition radars' of the defensive ABM system, these being the 'sensors' which first spotted the offensive missile as it flew through space towards its target.

Regardless of any strategic considerations, and egged on by the weaponeers in the States, Aldermaston wanted both to harden and to incorporate penaids in our Polaris warheads. In the television programme Macklen also stated that 'we were offered Poseidon as an option in 1967 by the American technical people' but this 'never really reached the level of final offer and decision at a political level because we had to ask for what we wanted from the things that they described to us were possible.'

That was the way things were done. Matey exchanges would take place between quite low-level British and American technical experts, ideas would be tossed around, the Americans would suggest that we did this or that, with an indication that, if asked, they might be able to help. Our 'experts' would then inform and persuade their civil service and military colleagues – not a difficult task – and the idea would then find its way upwards until as often as not it reached Ministers.

But if Poseidon was 'offered' at the technical level, it was never requested at the political. In his memoirs, Harold Wilson tells of a visit he paid General de Gaulle in June 1967, in the course of which the Prime Minister told the President that he had just decided 'not to ask for the Poseidon missile in place of Polaris'.[2] That, I am sure, was the way it was. Poseidon may have been mentioned at Johnny Foster's level in the Pentagon, and was no doubt discussed between the American and British naval staffs. But knowing how McNamara had felt at Nassau, and of his conviction that the Western alliance could neither afford nor tolerate divided nuclear forces, I cannot imagine him 'offering' Poseidon to Denis Healey nor, and I have asked him, does he recall ever having done so. At the time he was also highly sceptical about the arguments that were being advanced in technical and industrial quarters about ABM systems, and it would have been odd if he had encouraged us to embark on a programme of 'hardening'

Polaris warheads – which, again, he has no recollection of ever having done. Poseidon would have cost us much more than just the missile. Expensive changes would have had to be made in the submarines that we had already completed or were still building.

With Bob Press and myself no longer members of the Ministry of Defence, the departmental officials who, together with Macklen, were now responsible for nuclear policy at the technical level were men who instinctively shared Aldermaston's aspirations. Johnny Foster had warned that the A3 missile that we had contracted to buy no longer existed in its original form. It would therefore cost more than we had bargained for, plus the 5 per cent of the costs of the R&D that it had taken to transform the A2 into the 'improved' A3. Since the US Navy had decided to continue deploying some of their new A3s as well as Poseidon, we could therefore buy the new version of A3 and, if we so wanted, the American penetration aids. Alternatively we could see whether the US Government would sell us Poseidon. That was Johnny Foster's message to me, and that was what Denis Healey must have been told by his people, and passed on to Harold Wilson. The Ministry's nuclear experts would also have told him that the Russians were deploying an ABM system to defend Moscow, which our Polaris warheads would be unable to penetrate if they were not hardened and redesigned. Unless we changed the warhead, our nuclear deterrent would, they said, therefore lose its 'credibility'. What the Russians might have thought about the 'credibility' of our nuclear force was another matter.

Although there was nothing new in any of the arguments, Healey then became an advocate of the Aldermaston case within the small court of Ministers which dealt with nuclear matters. He was dealing with a small but powerful band of civil servants and military men who had a blind faith in anything that was nuclear. In the field of nuclear weaponry, anything which enhanced technological sophistication or multiplied variety and numbers was assumed to bestow some strategic advantage. There was also the implicit assumption that the nuclear arms race was never going to stop. The Twenty Propositions I had formulated five years before had stimulated a lively debate in the Ministry. But there was no longer any debate. I had to start all over again trying to answer, in minutes addressed to the Prime Minister and the Foreign Secretary, the case which Denis had started advocating in late 1966 and which he continued to argue until the change of government in 1970.

If there was little new in the way that Denis promoted his case, there was equally little that was new in my counter-arguments. My first point always was that the public debate that was going on in the United States indicated that there never could be an effective ABM system, however much the Americans and Russians might spend in a futile nuclear and ABM arms race. At the very least a proportion of the nuclear warheads carried by ballistic missiles would always get through. Why, therefore, should we spend money and effort that could be ill-afforded in elaborating the UK Polaris warhead? Second, our nuclear force, which was assigned to NATO, was there to deter, not to fight nuclear wars. We were never likely to engage the USSR in a nuclear exchange on our own. Warheads, I also argued, do not carry national flags. Were the Americans ever to fire their own weapons, either in a first or in a retaliatory strike, the ABM system round Moscow would be overwhelmed by the onslaught of American missiles before ours needed to be launched – if indeed they ever were. What difference would hardening and penaids then make? As a further argument, I suggested that the deployment of ABM systems would put an end to ideas of 'graduated' or 'flexible' response. Supposing one or other side believed that it had deployed an effective defensive system, or even if both shared the same belief, neither would ever know how many of its warheads in a nuclear exchange would have been put out of action by the other side's ABM nuclear explosions in space – hardening and decoys could never be expected to be one hundred per cent effective. Logically, therefore, a nuclear attack against targets protected by presumed ABM systems would call for the launching of all one's armoury of strategic weapons. Years later the same argument was deployed by Henry Kissinger in his support for President Reagan's SDI – as he saw it, 'uncertainty enhanced deterrence'. If you did not know how effective your opponent's defence system was, you had to 'drench' it in the hope that a proportion of your warheads would reach their targets.

But credibility, I kept insisting, was what we believed about the potential destructive power that the enemy could bring to bear against us. The extent of our fear of annihilation at Russian hands would not be reduced if we thought that a proportion of their weapons were 'duds'. Finally, I kept pointing out that since we knew that the two superpowers were already engaged in negotiations to stop the development of ABM systems, would it not be advisable for us to wait until we knew what the outcome would be?

My arguments were of no avail against Aldermaston's insistence that it had to be technologically equal to the American and Russian Joneses. Denying them the chance to show that they were, would be damaging to our national prestige and would impair our 'special relationship'.

Sometimes I went too far. At one meeting, when called upon to comment on the view that hardening was necessary to maintain the 'credibility' of Britain's nuclear deterrent, I began by saying that if credibility was an issue, one had also to guard against gullibility, against being 'blinded by science'. Denis was not amused. I forget whether it was at that meeting or an earlier one that I took exception to him saying that the advice I was giving the Government was not the same as that which I had given him during the year and a half in which I had been his scientific adviser. At the Prime Minister's suggestion, I sent Denis a personal letter, in which I reminded him that he had blessed the texts of the Lees Knowles lectures which I had delivered in Cambridge at the end of 1965, when I had advanced the same arguments as those to which he now took exception.

Denis must surely have realized that we were being subjected to American arm-twisting when we were told that we would find ourselves in trouble were we to insist on buying the A3 missile that we had ordered rather than its more expensive replacement. McNamara was being impelled along the path of 'modernization' by domestic technological and industrial interests, not by fear of what the Russians might be doing. Rumour had it that he had authorized the Poseidon missile because it was one of the only ways open to him to counter the campaign to deploy what he knew would be yet another ineffective ABM system. He had to convince the American public that their missiles could always get through. He had to do something, even though the debate about the political and strategic futility of ABM systems had crystallized in the United States before the end of 1965 by a call for a moratorium on all work on ABM systems.

My views about hardening and 'penaids' were opposed to those of Bill Cook and Bill Penney. But my objections were based on strategic, and not on technical considerations. Not only did I fail to see any strategic advantage for the UK in a programme of hardening, I saw us having to pay a considerable political price if we followed the path of the American weapons laboratories. In June 1967 Harold Wilson had told de Gaulle that he proposed to 'turn Nassau on its head', that he wanted to reduce our nuclear dependence on America, and that he also wanted to cooperate with France on nuclear matters. What Aldermaston wanted made nonsense of this political objective, and also of the Government's arms-control policies – we were still working hard for a CTB. Harold Brown also regarded the issue as far more political than technical. If the ABM talks between the Russians and the Americans were to end in an agreement that both sides would desist from going ahead with defences against rocket attacks, there was no point, he told me, in our 'improving' Polaris. It would be a 'credible' deterrent even in its pristine form.

Bill Cook and I visited Washington in order to obtain information about the technicalities of modernization. Our joint report changed nothing, nor was there any likelihood that it would have done, since there was no argument between us about the technicalities or probable costs. But our report reinforced Denis Healey's concern about the future of Aldermaston, even though he did not carry his Cabinet colleagues with him. As Harold Wilson informed the House of Commons at the end of 1967, the Government was 'not embarking on a new generation of nuclear weapons or warheads in relation to our Polaris programme', adding for good measure that the Government's intention remained the same as it was when it took office, 'not only to renegotiate the Nassau agreement, but to internationalize our deterrent'.[3]

Harold Wilson was not the first Prime Minister who had thought that cooperation with France in the nuclear field would be a good thing in itself, as well as a means of helping to reduce our dependence on the Americans. Before his visit to de Gaulle he had agreed that when I was next in Paris I should have a word with Bertrand Goldschmidt, a friend who was then a prominent figure in the French weapons programme. This I did in May 1967, during the course of a meeting of the NATO Science Committee. It had been arranged that I should first see Hervé Alphand, the Secretary General at the Quai d'Orsay. Alphand's main concern was the extent to which we were tied to the Americans, and to discover what real possibilities there were of cooperation in the nuclear field. All I could do was repeat what Harold Wilson had declared to be his policy. In turn Alphand urged me to impress on the Prime Minister that 'the only key' which would get the UK into Europe, a matter which the Prime Minister had discussed with de Gaulle in January 1967, was a 'nuclear key'. I left him – late – to go to Bertrand's apartment, where he had gathered to meet me his three colleagues who were then respectively in charge of the weapons, reactors and computers divisions of the French nuclear authority. We had a pleasant lunch and spoke in generalities. They were all ready to cooperate, if cooperation became the order of the political day. I suddenly remembered that it was my birthday.

Two days later I was a member of the party that the Prime Minister took with him on a curtailed visit to President Johnson. I had been under the impression that nuclear matters and Nassau would be among the items on our agenda. As it turned out, and as Harold Wilson relates, the crisis in the Middle East, which was about to erupt in the Six Day War between Israel and her neighbours, overshadowed everything else.

We spent the morning of our arrival in the White House, with the Prime Minister and the President closeted together most of the time, leaving Burke Trend, the Secretary of the Cabinet, and me to face, on the opposite side of the Cabinet table, an array of the President's senior colleagues, including the Secretary of State and the Defense Secretary. Harold Wilson had decided not to have any of his Ministers with him. Only during lunch, when the President placed me at his table on his left, with Harold Wilson on his right, did the latter raise the issue of renegotiating Nassau, and then in a somewhat unconvincing way. When, to change the subject, he brought the topic of the 'environment' into the conversation, the President called out, 'Where's Hornig?' The President's Science Adviser was duly summoned and arrived in time for coffee. Don Hornig – who promptly spilt the cup he was given – had not even known that we were in Washington!

After lunch a number of us returned to the cabinet room. The PM then took his party to the British Embassy for a debriefing, after which I was driven to the Pentagon to see Harold Brown, with whom I had yet another lengthy and intimate talk about the ABM problem and about hardening. I then returned to the White House Executive Building for a further talk with Don Hornig.

That evening the President laid on a grand dinner, and finding myself next to Bob McNamara, we discussed, as we had so often before, various aspects of the nuclear dilemma. It was a strange prelude to an open-air concert of nostalgic American music. I was placed next to Mrs Johnson. When some of George Gershwin's *Porgy and Bess* was played, I proudly told her that I had attended rehearsals of the opera in the thirties.

Two weeks after our return from Washington, Harold Wilson visited de Gaulle for the second time that year. His talks with the President, as his published account of the visit shows, ranged widely over the political spectrum, with the Prime Minister again telling the President that he wanted to reverse Nassau, and to cooperate with France in the nuclear field. The Prime Minister's record reads as though the President was not convinced that Harold Wilson was ready to weaken the UK's special relationship with America in order to build one with Europe, and especially with France. The fact is that, whatever the reasons, nothing of substance resulted from the visit.

Geoffroy de Courcel was the French Ambassador in London at the time, and Gerard André his Minister. I was on friendly terms with both – with Gerard in particular – and both wanted to see Harold Wilson's proposals on Anglo–French nuclear cooperation turned into a reality. For weeks afterwards Gerard kept asking me what we proposed to do since, after the talks with de Gaulle, the nuclear ball was now at our feet. I dutifully passed the messages on, but to no effect.

One reason for the lack of any follow-up was the fact that only days after the talks between the Prime Minister and de Gaulle, Pierre Messmer, then the Minister of Defence, cancelled the Anglo–French project to build the swing-wing fighter-bomber on which the RAF was counting. Harold Wilson had in fact let the General know that rumours of cancellation were in the air. An era of potential nuclear cooperation could not have been heralded in a worse way. The news of the cancellation had been passed to me in Geneva where I was attending a meeting, and General Henri Thoulouze, the French air attaché in London, had taken the trouble to find out the time of my return flight, and was waiting at Heathrow when I returned to tell me how much he regretted the cancellation. Henri had flown with the RAF during the war, and was an ardent Anglophile. Like René Bloch, he had worked hard to get the variable-geometry project launched.

The reaction of the press to the cancellation was inevitably hostile, and Denis Healey found himself attacked for ever having embarked on a programme to deploy either the F111 or the Anglo–French VG aircraft in a European role for which, so the papers claimed, they were unsuited, in order to fulfil a presumed worldwide role that we could not afford. The 1966 Defence Review had left us with a disaffected Navy, and now he had to deal with a disappointed RAF. Aldermaston was pressing all the time, and in the circumstances it was not surprising that Denis continued to urge his Cabinet colleagues to agree to the 'modernization' of Polaris. He succeeded to the extent that the establishment was provided with additional resources with which to carry out 'studies' to define clearly what it intended to have done – which no doubt was enough to indicate to Aldermaston's opposite numbers in the States that all was not lost.

Aldermaston had friends not only in the MOD and the Foreign Office, they also had them in the press. About two weeks after Edward Heath became Prime Minister in June 1970, the *Daily Express* carried a signed piece by Chapman Pincher in which he urged the new Government to start straightaway on the proposed programme of 'updating' our Polaris warheads without awaiting the outcome of the talks about limiting strategic nuclear systems and ABM defences that were then in progress betweeen the USA and the USSR. On the same day, *The Times* devoted its entire editorial column to the same theme, with the added and inconsistent frill that we should join with France to form a third nuclear force. The two pieces had clearly been concerted. I lost no time in telling the new Prime Minister that the unique Anglo–American nuclear relationship to which the *Times* editorial had referred, would make it extremely difficult for the UK to start negotiating with the French. We would first have to clear our decks with the United States.

But Ted Heath did not need this reminder. The exchanges that he had had with Harold Wilson and Denis Healey in the last Parliament must have made him fully aware of the difficulties. The 1958 and 1959 amendments to the McMahon Act, which allowed American information to be passed to the UK, expressly prohibited us from passing what we were told to a third party. We had run into trouble on this score when we set up the tripartite scheme with the Dutch and the West Germans to enrich uranium for civil nuclear reactors (p. 443).

Moreover, as I also reminded him, the two superpowers were close to agreeing that the development of ABM systems should be stopped, since not only would they make no strategic or political difference to the existing situation, a consideration which the protagonists of hardening invariably played down, but because the ABM race merely exacerbated the nuclear arms race. It had been highly unfortunate that the British press had paid little if any attention to the vigorous public debate about ABMs that was then in progress in the United States, with reams of informed governmental and non-governmental evaluations of the pros and cons of developing and deploying an ABM system appearing almost daily. The treaty that banned their development was signed in 1972.

My life as an official had ended before that happened. From what I have heard and read since, the pressure to do more about Aldermaston's programme increased after I had left, with the result that sometime in 1973, formal, although only hesitant, approval was given to the hardening programme, which became known by the codename Chevaline. According to retired senior officials who participated in the television discussion on Chevaline, including Sir Frank Cooper, the Ministry's Permanent Secretary from 1976 to 1982, the programme proceeded in six-monthly review periods, and what had been estimated at the start would cost only a few tens of millions of pounds, ended up by costing a billion, and did so well after a treaty had been agreed between the USA and the USSR which made penaids unnecessary. In a recent television programme, I heard an Aldermaston man who had helped direct the Chevaline programme say that it is to Chevaline that we now owe our independent nuclear deterrent status. It would be difficult to imagine an observation that better illustrates the irrational consequences of a technological obsession.

David Owen tells us that when the Labour Party returned to power in 1974, it had a chance to cancel the programme which, in his view, is what should have been done.[4] He himself did not learn about Chevaline until he became Foreign Secretary in mid-1977, by which time the project was nearing completion, with little left to cancel. Denis Healey has also told me that one of the things he regrets most about the period when he was Chancellor of the Exchequer is that however far the programme had gone, he did not cancel it.

'Kill them when they are no bigger than sprats,' Harold Macmillan had advised me. Defence R&D projects become almost impossible to get rid of when they reach the size of a herring. The rationale behind Chevaline was as irrelevant at the start as it was when the project was completed, some ten years after the 1972 ABM Treaty had been signed. As the Government's committee on the control of R&D had pointed out more than a decade before, however much money had already been spent, it is wiser to cut one's losses than to continue spending on projects that have ceased to have any significant purpose.

Work on Chevaline might have given Aldermaston a new lease on life, but it has not given the United Kingdom anything in the way of additional security. My view has not changed. Our A3 Polaris force was enough to deter the Russians from ever attacking us. Why, I continue to ask, should Moscow be the only target for retribution? If our Polaris force were ever used, we would never even know whether our missiles had struck. There would be no newspapers to tell us, no television to show what had happened, and maybe no 'us', just the crews of those of our Polaris boats that had been at sea.

Dickie Mountbatten had retired from official public life when hardening first surfaced as an issue. I once asked him whether he thought the project might have been blocked had he still been in service. He thought not, and I think he was right. Our weaponeers would just have waited until he had gone. But what would Ernie Bevin have made of it all? He wanted us to become an independent nuclear power so that we would not be leaned upon by the USA. What would he think of interdependence and dependence now? What would Churchill have thought? Are the defence scientists determining the direction of foreign policy as Dean Acheson once suggested?

PART VIII

The Government's Scientific Adviser

33

Crises and the Environment

My move from the Ministry of Defence on one side of Whitehall to the Cabinet Office on the other could not have proved smoother than it did. Burke Trend immediately allocated to me the suite of offices that I was to occupy for the next five years. They were in the central part of the Office, architecturally one of the more interesting of Whitehall's monuments to the past. My own quarters, which overlooked Horse Guards Parade and the garden of Number 10, were as they had been left in the eighteenth century, except for the absence of chandeliers, and for the addition of layer upon layer of white paint on what I presume had started out as plain pine panels. I was told that William Kent had been the architect.

The announcement of my transfer, and the fact that the duties that had been mine in the Ministry of Defence were from then on to be shared between Bill Cook and Alan Cottrell, did not stimulate the slightest interest. Even the resignation of the Navy Minister, Christopher Mayhew, and the departure from the Ministry of two of the country's distinguished admirals, David Luce and Frank Hopkins (p. 380), proved to be only a seven-day wonder, and in the context of the country's economic problems, little more than a storm in a teacup. To mark the occasion of our joint departure from the Ministry of Defence – they had all discussed with me their intention to leave – I was presented, not long after, with a magnificent model of Nelson's flagship, *Victory*, made, I was told, from the ship's own copper nails.

Glyn Owen came with me, and I left it to him and to Dr Fergus Allen, a new member of my staff who had been posted to the Cabinet Office, to make all the other necessary arrangements. Fergus had been recruited to represent me in the Office after the announcement in 1964 that I was to be 'Chief Scientific Adviser to the Government as a whole'. He had been Director of DSIR's Hydraulics Research Station, from which he was about to be moved to a corresponding position in the much bigger Road Research Laboratory. In accepting the post in the Cabinet Office, he had sacrificed a rise in salary, but helping to create something new, and possibly important, was, he felt, adequate compensation. Before I moved from Defence, he had made sure that I read such papers as came his way about which he felt I should be aware; for example, minutes about space technology, coastal erosion and the 'brain drain'. He also alerted me to any item of governmental policy that he judged could be affected by scientific considerations. It was his responsibility, too, to scrutinize the reports that were published by bodies such as the Research Councils, and to see that I paid adequate attention to matters that Frank Cousins, the new Minister of Technology, or his Permanent Secretary, or Patrick Blackett, the Department's part-time Chief Scientific Adviser, wanted me to know about. Fergus was not, however, concerned with nuclear or arms-control matters. Until my move to the Cabinet Office, I continued to deal with these from the Ministry of Defence and, since they were high on the list of my responsibilities, I arranged for Bob Press to join me soon after I had settled into my new office.

As the Government's Chief Scientific Adviser, the other matters that were of greatest concern to me were the promotion and use of the country's technological resources, and the protection of the environment, together with the associated problems of the growth of population and the exploitation of our own natural resources. It was not long before the volume of work that came my way became so great that a Deputy Scientific Adviser post had to be established. So it was that early in 1968 Alan Cottrell joined me, with few regrets at leaving his post in the Ministry of Defence.

In the account that she has left of life in Number 10, Marcia Williams, Harold Wilson's personal and political secretary, writes that, 'Whenever there was a crisis where scientific advice was required, the first name to be heard was the name of Solly Zuckerman. It always sounded something like a court of law. You felt any minute some flunky would throw open the cabinet room door and shout down the long corridor of Downing Street, "Call for Solly Zuckerman." Yet at the end of the incident, whatever it might be, and whether it was successful or not, very curiously Solly Zuckerman seemed not to have been involved.'[1]

It reads as though there was a cloak-and-dagger quality to my life as the Government's CSA. There never was, and I can only suppose that if that is how it seemed to the Prime Minister's personal staff he succeeded in keeping them in the dark about matters with which I dealt, particularly in the nuclear field. My designation as Head of the Scientific Civil Service did not involve me in any administrative duties, while the term 'chief scientific adviser' meant precisely what the words implied. I was an adviser, as all the members of the Cabinet Office staff always are. During the seven years that I was the Government's CSA (including the two before I moved to the Cabinet Office), I reported directly to the Prime Minister. If a Cabinet Office brief had to be prepared for the PM on an issue about which I had a view, Burke Trend would add either a sentence that indicated that I concurred in what he sent, or a note that I would be submitting a separate brief. In the latter case, my usual purpose would be to bring to the PM's attention a particular consideration that had not been fully dealt with, or that had not been touched on in the departmental brief. The occasions when I advanced a view that opposed what Burke, as Cabinet Secretary, had advised, were few and far between.

There were times when I had to deal with what I assume Marcia Williams meant when she spoke of crises – what might be called 'one-off jobs'. For example, in late 1967 there was a serious outbreak of foot-and-mouth disease, and the Prime Minister wanted to be kept informed about the adequacy of the measures that were being taken to prevent its spread. That simply meant that the veterinary official in the Ministry of Agriculture, whose responsibility it was to see that the outbreak was kept in check, provided me with a daily account of what was happening. The same procedure applied to the discovery of gas and oil in the North Sea, when I coordinated for the Prime Minister information about the exploratory drilling that was going on – and about which my initial prognostications could not have been more off the mark. Sometimes I was able to shuffle on to someone else's shoulders a job that would otherwise have been mine. This happened, for example, when Dickie Mountbatten was asked by Roy Jenkins, then Home Secretary, to conduct an enquiry into prison security. At the outset Dickie, then retired, made it a condition of his acceptance that I should be a member of his small team. I was far too busy at the time with other matters, and I soon got Dickie and Roy to appoint in my place a member of the Royal Aircraft Establishment, a man who was much better qualified for the task than I was.

The only spectacular 'crisis' in which I had to play a somewhat central role was the wreck of the *Torrey Canyon*, not because it was assumed that I knew about the construction of giant oil tankers or about what would happen when thousands of tons of oil were spilt near our coastline, but because I was in a position to find out who did know about these things. As Harold Wilson records, I 'was put in charge of the scientists of all the departments concerned' to improvise a plan to deal with the wreck.[2]

The 120,000-ton *Torrey Canyon* disaster was the first one of its kind. On the morning of Saturday 18 March 1967, the fully loaded ship ran onto the Seven Stones Reef some sixteen miles west of Land's End. Until the following Tuesday, I knew no more about the event than what I had read in the papers. I had gone to the ballet that evening, and when I returned home I found a message asking me to telephone the Duty Officer at Number 10. The Prime Minister wanted me to attend a meeting which the Navy Minister, Mr Maurice Foley, was holding the following morning. It was then that I learnt for the first time about the scale of the disaster, and that a Dutch salvage team had boarded the ship in the hope of floating it off the rocks. The Royal Navy's chief salvage officer thought very little of their chances, and my job was to suggest a way of getting rid of the 90,000 tons of oil that remained in the compartments that had not been breached, and to find the best way to deal with the oil that had already washed onto the beaches. Having heard what was known about the way the ship had driven on to the rocks, I boldly said that nothing would ever pull her off. I was even more pessimistic than the salvage officer.

In those days I was subject to slipped-disc trouble, and a painful bout of sciatica had started when I was on my way to Covent Garden the night before. I was therefore not at my best, but I managed to convene a meeting that afternoon of a number of scientist and engineering colleagues from various departments and research stations. A blueprint of the vessel was provided by Lloyds' Shipping Register, and before long we had agreed a basic plan, having first rejected the idea of pumping the remaining oil from the ship to tankers standing by. The sea was too rough for that, and since the *Torrey Canyon* was a vast floating petrol bomb, the whole idea too dangerous. Knowing the thickness of the plate over the intact oil compartments, we decided instead to lay 'line charges' of the precise and safe amount of explosive necessary to open the compartments, with incendiary bombs being detonated simultaneously to fire the oil they contained. Given good weather, it seemed that this was the best thing to do. We also had to try to find a way of getting rid of the oil slicks that were already polluting the Cornish beaches. I sub-divided the operation into separate areas, delegating each, with full responsibility, to the different members of the group. But then came the snag. With the Dutch salvage team aboard – the team's chief salvage officer had been killed and other members injured in an explosion three days after they first boarded the vessel – and, if I remember correctly, the master of the vessel as well, we would be committing an act of piracy were we to board the vessel and lay explosive charges. Nonetheless, everything was got ready in the hope that the salvors would leave the ship in time.

My bout of sciatica had become steadily worse, and on Thursday I decided to leave London for the country. As Home Secretary, Roy Jenkins was in charge of the Government's Emergencies Committee and, in that capacity, the ministerial responsibility for dealing with the disaster was his. He tried to dissuade me, but I asked the Prime Minister to overrule him, and left for Burnham Thorpe. A telephone at my bedside kept me in touch, and all seemed to be going well, except that none of the inducements offered by the Government proved adequate to persuade the salvage team to abandon their potential prize.

There was nothing that my scratch scientific team could do except wait. Then on Saturday both Roy and Fergus Allen telephoned to say that the Prime Minister wanted me to attend a meeting on the following day at Culdrose Air Station in Cornwall. I told Roy that I was in no fit state to go, but he kept urging me to make the effort. Early on Sunday morning the Station Commander of a local RAF airfield telephoned to say that an aircraft had been laid on to fly me to Cornwall. I again telephoned Roy, who said that the Prime Minister wanted me to be at the meeting. I therefore telephoned Number 10 and was connected through their exchange with the Prime Minister, who was spending the weekend at his holiday home in the Scillies – it happened to be the Easter weekend. I told him about my physical state, but he nonetheless said that he would like me to attend if I could make it; if not, I had to see to it that Fergus Allen was there. Joan then telephoned Roy to say that I would not be going.

About an hour later the local Station Commander again telephoned, this time to say that my plane would be landing in about forty-five minutes. Could I join him within the hour? Further protest seemed useless. I got out from under the physiotherapist's lamp, and within the appointed time had boarded an ancient Pembroke of the kind I had known more than twenty years before. What made it somewhat nostalgic was that the crew consisted of two ex-wartime RAF officers – the pilot a squadron leader, and his navigator a flight lieutenant. I sat back and made the best of things, chatting about old times.

The Culdrose meeting, of which a detailed account has been given by Harold Wilson, was already in session when I limped in.[3] The PM asked me to explain the plan we had drawn up to deal with the ship, and the preparations that had been made to counter any further oil spills. But the only thing that mattered to me was whether Sir Elwyn Jones,* the Attorney-General, was going to succeed in buying off the owners and the manager of the salvage team, with whom he was bargaining in another room. As long as their people were on board, we could do nothing. Moreover, were the ship to break up, the precise measures that we had prepared could not be implemented. The only option then would be to bomb the wreck and to try to ignite her remaining cargo by means of incendiary bombs.

Nothing seemed to have been decided by the end of the meeting. A helicopter then took the PM back to the Scillies, the Whitehall party left in their 'executive jet', and I boarded my ancient Pembroke to return to Norfolk. When we were airborne, I asked the pilot to fly out to sea to try to find the wrecked tanker, which we reached at the critical moment when her back was breaking. We circled very low over her, watching an enormous gush of oil pouring out to sea. The stern of the vessel was attached by tie-lines to a tug, and we could see that a man was still on board. We then turned east for Norfolk, and I reached home in time to change for dinner. We had guests that night, and they were greatly impressed by my account of the day's adventures. The next day I was amused to learn that the Whitehall party had also flown

*Now Lord Elwyn-Jones.

out to see the wreck, but that their fast-flying jet had failed to find it. Slow aircraft have their uses.

All, however, was not over. After the ship had broken its back, and the owners and salvage operators had become reconciled to the fact that it could never be pulled off the rocks, the question was whether bombing could be relied upon to fire the oil that remained in the tanks. I had again taken to my bed, but every now and then there was a call from London telling me about the state of play. An attempt to fire a large oil slick on the surface of the sea had failed, and a big question now hung over the whole operation as more and more oil was washed onto the rocks and beaches of Cornwall. If it was all going to end with a bombing exercise, my concern was that the right mix of incendiaries and HE was used, and the right fusing. Joan came into my room at about midday on Monday to say that Roy, to whom I had already spoken that morning, was on the other line, now wanting to know whether he should give the order to bomb. I said yes. The rest of the story is in the books. When I returned to London the following day, the joke was whether the Navy and RAF fliers who had done the bombing were going to be decorated for valour. The fuses of many of the bombs had failed to work.

The *Torrey Canyon*,[4] which for a week or two filled the papers, may well have been the most spectacular of the 'one-off' jobs that came my way, but it was certainly not as important as some others; for example, the UK's space programme, to which, despite the interest of several departments, the Government had accorded a very low priority. My efforts to improve the situation were a failure, and Britain's space programme remains minuscule to this day. I had set up a committee in 1964 to consider how the exploitation of space affected Britain's security, and had approached Hermann Bondi, then Professor of Mathematics at King's College, London, to see whether he would take on the chairmanship. He had already served on one or two of my other committees of 'independents', and I gave him twenty-four hours in which to let me know whether he would do the job. The answer was yes. In 1967, when the European Space Research Organization – ESRO – was formed, I was told that the UK could put in a nomination for the post of Director-General. One or two scientific civil servants were suggested as candidates, but were not eminent enough in the international world of science. Hermann was the obvious choice, given that he was prepared to disrupt his academic career, which fortunately he was. The responsibility for putting his name forward became that of the Minister of Education and Science, and he was duly accepted. Hermann did an excellent job in transforming the embryo organization into the institution it is today. Later, when Alan Cottrell moved to the Cabinet Office, I suggested Hermann's name to Denis Healey as a possible successor, but nothing came of that move. Then, three years later, Bill Cook retired from his post as CSA to Defence. In June of the same year the Government changed, and Lord Carrington succeeded Healey as Secretary of State for Defence. Again I suggested Bondi's name as a successor, and took him to see Carrington. He was appointed, and remained CSA to Defence until 1977. He then moved to the Department of Energy, where he served until 1980.

Some time before his appointment to the Ministry of Defence, Bondi had also chaired a small committee that was set up to consider the dangers to which Londoners would be exposed were the Thames to overflow its banks. This was another 'one-off job' in which I became involved.

It had long been known that a minute but measurable increase occurred in the height of the tides that flowed up the Thames each year, due, I was told, to the fact that the southeast corner of England was being gradually tilted downwards by movements of the earth's crust. In 1953 there had been a freak North Sea tidal surge that had broken through the sea defences along the east coast of England and the northern coast of the Netherlands. Many people were drowned in the subsequent flooding. At the back of people's minds was the fear that the coincidence of a very high tide with a tidal surge like that of 1953 would make the Thames overflow its banks and drown thousands of Londoners. However remote the danger, it had been made all the greater because of the strengthening of the sea defences after the 1953 floods. A committee under Lord Waverley* had recommended that the banks on either side of the mouth of the Thames should be raised.[5] Given another surge, this meant that water which would otherwise have flooded the parts of Essex and Kent that form the estuary, would possibly have overflowed the banks as far upriver as Westminster, if not even further. It was possible to calculate the height to which the

*Sir John Anderson, as he was in Churchill's Cabinets.

river could rise and the extent of the ensuing flood using estimates of the likelihood of a surge occurring, and such basic data as the measurement of the heights of tides as they had been recorded over the years at Tower Bridge. Some of the conclusions about the numbers of people who could be exposed to the risk of sudden drowning were pretty horrifying. As the ex-director of the Hydraulics Research Station the problem was right up Fergus Allen's street, and he kept me informed about the studies that were being made. I was a ready listener.

Our home in the village of Burnham Thorpe, which lies within the Holkham estate that belongs to the Earls of Leicester, is no more than two miles from the north Norfolk coast, parts of which had suffered severely during the 1953 floods. A few people had been drowned, and a lot of livestock lost. I had been particularly impressed by the sight of some thousands of acres of coastal land that had been covered with water when a sea wall on which I often used to walk had failed to hold back the high seas. In my mind's eye I can still see bales of straw that had been washed into the branches of trees a mile or so from the normal high-water mark.

The Lord Leicester at the time of the flood – Tommy, to his friends – was a slightly eccentric character who was then engaged in an argument with the Council of nearby Wells-next-the-Sea. They wanted to erect a line of lampposts along a second sea wall that had been breached, and along which a road led to the Wells bathing beach. Tommy was opposed. Repairing the breach and draining more than ten feet of flood water had been a considerable engineering feat, and Tommy, who owned the land that had been flooded, wanted me to join in his argument with the Wells authorities. I still smile as I remember him saying that if the lampposts were ever erected, 'the next time the sea comes in, I won't let it out'. His eighteenth-century ancestor who had reclaimed the land from the sea would have thought differently – but then he would not have had to argue about lampposts.

The day came when the Government had to decide whether to provide the money to build a protective barrage at the mouth of the Thames. It fell to me to explain to a small meeting of Ministers, chaired by the Prime Minister, the scope of the problem to which the barrage had been proposed as an answer – or at least as part of an answer. The calculations had indicated that the probability of thousands of

Londoners being drowned was remote in the extreme – in any one decade, a matter of one chance in tens of millions. 'Why bother?' was the natural reaction, to which my reply was that, while the chances were utterly remote, no-one could guarantee that the disaster would not happen in a month's time. This gave Harold Wilson, as a professional economist and statistician – he later became President of the Royal Statistical Society – the opportunity of giving his colleagues a short tutorial on the concept of probability. The money was duly voted, and nearly twenty years later – that is to say, some thirty years after the risks had become apparent – the Queen pressed a button to activate what is one of the most outstanding engineering constructions of our times.

The Labour Party's 1964 election manifesto had indicated a strong interest in environmental matters, and included a pledge to create a Land Commission. To this end, Harold Wilson had established a Department of Land and Natural Resources,* with Mr Fred Willey as Minister. Not surprisingly, I assumed that the new department would breathe life into the Natural Resources (Technical) Committee, to which the Whitehall establishment had paid little attention during the preceding four or five years. The committee had, however, remained in being, and when the new Government came in, was busy on a detailed study of the economic and social problems of marginal land.

I had never met Mr Willey, but I knew the two civil servants who were charged to make a reality of the PM's initiative – Freddie Bishop, who had been a member of Harold Macmillan's private office in my first two years as CSA to Defence, and Richard Chilver, my chief tutor in the ways of Whitehall. Both agreed that their new department should assume the sponsorship of the Natural Resources Committee, of which I was still nominally the chairman.

But the Prime Minister had not reckoned with the opposition into which his new Ministry was going to run, and which, to his regret, led to it being wound up after only three years.[6] Difficulties immediately arose about its responsibilities for planning decisions in relation to those of the long-established Ministry of Housing and Local Government, of which Dick Crossman had been appointed Minister. Dick took pleasure in frustrating Harold Wilson's initiative. 'I must confess,'

*In his memoirs he refers to it as Land and Planning.

he confided to his diary, that 'I couldn't help smugly reflecting on the contrast between what we were doing in the Ministry of Housing and the miserable performance going on at the Ministry of Land and Natural Resources.'[7] Dick was determined to kill the new department. But he was not as far-seeing as he supposed. He had failed to see looming on the horizon the beginnings of the environmental movement. The Natural Resources Committee came to an end at about the same time as did the new department, but the problems with which it wrestled are still with us – the reconciliation of the social and economic with the amenity and conservation aspects of land use.

My long-standing interest in environmental protection had, not surprisingly, been sharpened by the experience of the 1953 floods and by the *Torrey Canyon* disaster. I had followed up the latter by enquiring into the responsibilities of different governmental departments for environmental matters, with the result that the Prime Minister asked me to form a 'central unit' of scientists to help in the task of coordinating inter-departmental work on the environment. In effect this meant little more than naming me as the official in the Cabinet Office into whose field of responsibility the subject of 'environment' fell. What Harold Wilson shortly afterwards referred to in Parliament as the 'central unit' which I directed to deal with environmental matters, consisted of no more than a single scientific civil servant, Martin Holdgate, who had been seconded from the Natural Environment Research Council.* Securing the interest of Roy Jenkins in environmental matters was almost more important than obtaining the support of the Prime Minister. Well before the emergence of 'green' parties in different countries, I remember the two of us speculating about the likelihood that the issue of environmental pollution would become a powerful political force throughout the world.

In the summer of 1969, I brought the matter of environmental protection and conservation to the attention of the Central Council for

---

*I first met Holdgate when accompanying Harold Wilson and Tony Crosland on a visit to the Nature Conservancy's Monks Wood Experimental Station, of which Holdgate was the Deputy Director. I was struck by the uninhibited way in which he described to us the work of the station, and accordingly recommended him for the post in the Cabinet Office and then for his transfer to the new department that was about to be created. Harold Wilson, in his memoirs, describes the visits we made that cold January day to a number of stations concerned with environmental protection and conservation.[8] Holdgate became a deputy secretary in the Ministry of the Environment.

Science and Technology – I discuss the Council in the next chapter. After surveying the problem, the Council recommended that a standing commission on environmental pollution should be established. A few months later, this idea was made an issue at the Labour Party Conference in Brighton, the Prime Minister declaring that we not only had to make good the devastation of the past, but that we also had to see to it that new industry did not bequeath 'a similar legacy to future generations'.[9] Soon after, Parliament was informed that the Government proposed to set up a commission, and that Tony Crosland was to be appointed Secretary of State for Local Government and Regional Planning, with responsibility for both Transport and Local Government, and with special personal responsibility for the protection of the environment.*

Crosland was then President of the Board of Trade and on an official visit to Japan. He was hurriedly summoned back, and asked by the Prime Minister to prepare 'an urgent report on steps which should be taken immediately'. He would have, the Prime Minister added, 'the advantage of a considerable amount of preparatory work' that I, as the Government's Chief Scientific Adviser, had carried out.[10]

A few days later, Crossland asked me to call on him in the temporary office that he had been given – it was the same office that Harold Watkinson and Peter Thorneycroft had occupied in the old Ministry of Defence – and having signalled his new private secretary to leave the room, Tony moved from behind his desk and asked, 'What is Harold up to? Am I being sold down the river?' All I could do was assure him as best I could that he had a major and responsible job on his hands. When I left he did not seem the least bit happy. The next time that he called me to his room, there was a new painting over the mantelpiece. It was of a complex of factories with tall chimneys from which smoke

*Wilson's plan to merge the departments that were concerned was put into effect after the election of June 1970 by Edward Heath, who created what is now the Department of the Environment, with Peter Walker as its first Secretary of State. Once set up, I kept well out of the new department's way and, indeed, my next serious contact with it was not until twelve years later, when I discussed the future of the Regent's Park Zoo with the Secretary of State, then Michael Heseltine. The Ministry's first Permanent Secretary telephoned me a year or so after my 'central unit' had been transferred to his department to ask why scientists were concerned about environmental matters, and what the official concerned was supposed to be doing. He was half serious, half joking. It was indeed difficult to see where scientific matters fitted into the evolving administrative framework of a major government department.

poured in horizontal plumes. Pointing to the canvas he said, with a smile, 'That was once a sign of Britain's prosperity; now I've got to stop it all.'

He then asked whom I thought should be appointed chairman of the Royal Commission on Environmental Pollution.* I had not given the matter any thought, but the name of Eric Ashby immediately sprang to mind. He was Master of Clare College in Cambridge, and a botanist by profession. I arranged for Crosland to meet him over lunch at the Athenaeum the following day – Ashby was about to leave on a visit to the United States, and everything had to be done in a hurry. The two got on well and Ashby agreed. In the following week, Tony Crosland made a major speech on the environment in the Commons, described by Harold Wilson as 'one of the most important and factual statements on the subject ever made'. But he went on to say that, as far as he and Crosland could judge, 'not a word of it appeared the next day in a single national morning paper'.[11]

I was one of the Royal Commission's original members, and during my four years as a commissioner was involved in the discussions that led to the first three of the many reports that the Commission has now produced. The third dealt with the pollution of estuaries and coastal waters, and so far as I am aware, is the only one so far produced by the Commission that was not unanimous. Wilfred Beckerman, the economist, and I joined forces in signing a minority report that proclaimed the virtues of the principle 'the polluter pays'. Our fellow commissioners thought that the 'principle' would be difficult to apply, and that anyhow it was going too far.

Now that the environment has become a dominant political cause in so many different countries, it is not surprising that less is heard today of the deliberations and reports of the Royal Commission than was the case at the start. But my own interest in the subject never waned, particularly as public interest in the complex of issues that were concerned increased. Soon we were hearing battle cries such as 'population explosion' and 'limits to growth' ringing out in the United States and, to a lesser extent, in Europe. I found myself reacting against extremist warnings that the human species would prove incapable of

---

*It had been the PM's idea to secure the Queen's permission for the body to be a Royal Commission, which meant that it would be a continuing institution that could not be dissolved without the agreement of the monarch, to whom it formally reported.

adapting to the environmental changes for which it was in large part responsible, and which, it was pessimistically said, it could no longer control. I expressed my concern at the over-reaction at the UN Conference on the Human Environment that was held in Stockholm in 1972,* where I delivered one of the six lectures that had been specially arranged to complement the inter-governmental discussions. My central theme was that the prevailing concern about the deleterious environmental consequences of the industrial exploitation of science and technology was leading us to forget the benefits – the improvements that had occurred in social conditions, in education and in medicine. I admitted that new environmental dangers, such as 'acid rain' and the disposal of nuclear waste, were looming on the horizon, but gave as my view that they were far more manageable than were 'the social and political problems that exist in a world in which we have so far not discovered how to eliminate war, in a world in which nuclear weapons could finally devastate not only ourselves but our physical environment as well, and in a world in which the disparity between rich and poor is an endless source of tension'. We had, I urged, to face our environmental and population problems 'in a hopeful and scientific spirit and not in one of hysterical computerized gloom'.[12]

A year later I chaired a conference on 'Population and the Quality of Life in Britain'.† In my opening remarks I reminded the audience of what John Stuart Mill, that distinguished economist of the mid-nineteenth century, had written when he spelt out what he saw as the advantages of a 'stationary state' that he expected would follow 'the progressive growth of the economy' as a result of improvements in 'the productive arts'. 'The density of population,' he wrote, 'necessary to enable mankind to obtain, in the greatest degree, all the advantages both of cooperation and of social intercourse, has, in all the most populous countries, been attained.' What Mill feared was that if population went on growing we would end up with a world in which nothing was 'left to the spontaneous activity of nature; with every rood of land brought into cultivation, which is capable of growing food for human beings; every flowery waste or natural pasture ploughed up, all quadrupeds or birds which are not domesticated for man's use exterminated as his rivals for food, every hedgerow or superfluous tree

*The United Nations had launched its Environment Programme in 1971.
†Organized by the Royal Society of Arts.

rooted out, and scarcely a place left where a wild shrub or flower could grow without being eradicated as a weed in the name of improved agriculture.'

When Mill wrote this, the population of Great Britain was less than half of what it is today. I quoted his words to remind my audience that judgments about environmental matters are often purely subjective, and that one cannot therefore separate the problems associated with environmental protection and conservation from the political and economic consequences of population growth and rising demand.[13]

I suppose that it was because my middle-of-the-road views about population and the environment were beginning to sound like those of a cautious elder statesman, that I was asked to deliver the 'keynote' address on the environmental responsibilities of industry at the 1970 Vienna meeting of the International Chamber of Commerce[14] and, even more daunting, to follow President Ford and Sheikh Yamani, then the spokesman for the OPEC countries, at the opening plenary meeting in Detroit of the Ninth World Energy Conference in 1974. As I noted on page 125, I also chaired a small commission that was sponsored by a group of international mining companies to outline the principles by which to reconcile mining and environmental interests.

Population having been one of my academic professional interests, it was not long before it, like the environment, was added to my responsibilities in the Cabinet Office. It was in that capacity that I had to appear early in 1970 before a parliamentary Select Committee that was dealing with population growth in the United Kingdom. During the course of a lengthy cross-examination, I was pressed to say what I thought would be the optimum size of population for the UK. I replied that I was sceptical about the concept of optimum population when regarded in terms of economics, but not 'when considered through a politician's eyes'.[15] Despite fears about over-population that had been voiced by economists in the early part of the nineteenth century, Britain had always been able to adapt. I then added, almost as a joke, that if people were willing to do so, and provided that the necessary resources, including food supplies, were available, we could live like battery hens. In that case the country would be able to accommodate twice the number of people it was then estimated would have to be catered for by the year 2000. That light-hearted remark got me into the papers! 'Scientist advocates that we live like battery hens.'

34

The Central Advisory Council

A month before the Labour Government came to power, the Advisory Council on Scientific Policy was abolished and replaced by a body called the Council for Scientific Policy, which was answerable, not to the Lord President of the Council, but to the Minister for Education and Science. These steps had been recommended by a committee that had been chaired by Burke Trend.[1] The establishment by the new Government of a Ministry of Technology, with its own Advisory Council, now threatened to create what some called an 'institutional split' between science and technology.

The Trend Committee's recommendations also meant that even the limited influence which the ACSP had been able to exert at the centre had now disappeared. From where I had been sitting in the Ministry of Defence, the changes did not seem to be the best way to correct the weaknesses of the old Council. I had become convinced that what was needed was a central committee for science and technology that was answerable to the Prime Minister himself. Despite the fact that action had already been taken on the advice tendered by his committee, Burke raised no objections when Harold Wilson agreed a proposal I put to him that a Central Advisory Council for Science and Technology should also be set up, reporting directly to him, and with the authority to delve into the scientific activities of departments as well as into the work of the Research Councils.* After I had consulted extensively with Ministers and Permanent Secretaries, the new Council started work under my chairmanship in January 1967.

In his *Diaries*, Dick Crossman refers somewhat scathingly to the Council.[2] He writes in similar vein about a ministerial committee on Science and Technology which, like all Cabinet committees, was

---

*Its terms of reference were 'to advise the Government on the most effective national strategy for the use and development of our scientific and technological resources'.

serviced by a committee of officials drawn from the relevant departments, and which it was also my responsibility to chair. Dick, who was then Leader of the Commons, describes the ministerial committee as having been 'pretty awful', and the Central Council as 'a pretty good waste of time'. As the father of the system of parliamentary Select Committees, Dick's money was on a Select Committee for Science and Technology, whose enquiries he almost certainly imagined would be hampered by the existence of the other two bodies.

He also writes that when I heard that it was proposed that the Select Committee should begin its work with an enquiry into the Agricultural Research Council, I 'came barging in' to his office and said, ' "Your Select Committee on Science and Technology can't do an investigation of the Agricultural Research Council; I've already started one." ' Dick goes on to say that my attitude revealed what 'Whitehall warriors' thought about his parliamentary reforms. All this is supposed to have taken place at a small meeting at which Wedgwood Benn, who had taken over from Cousins as the Minister of Technology, and Tony Crosland, then the Secretary of State for Education, were present.

Well, I may be forthright, but I doubt if the occasion could have been quite as Dick describes. I would certainly have told him that the Central Council had already embarked on an enquiry to see how the Agricultural Research Council's relations with the Ministry of Agriculture could be improved, but the idea that I also tried to forbid three Cabinet Ministers, with only one of whom I was on personal terms, from proceeding with what had been agreed by leaders of the Opposition, is nonsense. So, too, was Dick's judgment about the value of the Central Council, about whose affairs he probably knew little or nothing. Had he taken the trouble to find out, he would have realized that the Council was in a position to help, indeed to complement, the Select Committee on which he had set his heart. Dick was always too impulsive and egotistical.

The membership of the Central Advisory Council reflected the Prime Minister's aim that it should help avoid an 'institutional split' between 'pure' science and practical technology. Frank Cousins, who before his resignation from the Government had chaired the Advisory Council of his own department, was one of its members. So was Sir Harrie Massey, an astrophysicist who chaired the recently formed Council for Scientific Policy that reported to Tony Crosland, the

Secretary of State for Education and Science. They and the other nine who constituted the Council served in a strictly personal capacity, and not as representatives of government departments or as spokesmen for academic or industrial interests. Advising on 'the most effective national strategy' for developing and deploying the country's scientific and technological resources implied that the Council would be informed about the way these resources were being deployed at any given moment. This requirement was fairly easily met, partly by the Government's Central Statistical Office, and partly by the personal knowledge and judgment of the Council's own members.

The formulation of a 'best strategy' did not, however, mean that it would be possible to devise a list of scientific priorities in order of national importance. This often mooted idea has always been, and continues to be more than a little naive. Scientists are not interchangeable. For example, the vast majority of the men and women who are employed on defence R&D are not qualified for work outside their narrow specialities. Sudden shifts of scientific manpower are consequently impractical, and frequently impossible. Furthermore, the average British scientist (and most scientists are 'average') is pretty immobile geographically, compared say, to his opposite number in the United States. He dislikes being moved from one job to another if that means moving house and home. Moreover, the way the government at any given moment deploys the scientific resources which it commands is embedded in past political decisions, and is strenuously defended by the spending departments. So it is that at least half of the resources that are made available by the Exchequer for R&D is always committed to defence, with the bulk of it going to aerospace. In the few years that the Central Council existed, about a quarter of the money allocated to civil science went to the nuclear reactor programme – a field in which, as in aerospace, we did not shine in export markets. But, however allocated, there is always criticism that R&D resources are being wasted – for example, on abandoned projects such as Blue Streak, or TSR2, or on reactor designs that fail to meet the challenge of competition. Today the latest casualty in the billion pound R&D league is Nimrod, the early-warning aircraft which the Government rejected in favour of the American AWACS. It is hardly surprising that to the layman the way our R&D resources are distributed never seems to reflect a rational appreciation of what might or might not be best in the national interest.

The truth is that national needs in R&D can never be judged *post hoc* in terms of money allocations. It is pointless to moan about the benefits that might have been derived from work in some field of enquiry that was starved of resources had it been allowed, say, a year's allocation of the money that was going to the development of a new aircraft that was then cancelled. Different objectives have different price tags. Above all, as Otto Clarke kept reminding me, while Permanent Secretaries might well agree that there should be a rational set of priorities of scientific needs, when economies are called for they will fight to prevent any reduction in the volume of R&D that is already allowed for in their departmental estimates. It was against this background of reality that the Central Council worked.

The ministerial committee to which Dick Crossman referred dealt essentially with new items of R&D that called for relatively large increases in government expenditure – for example, a new radar installation to complement the famous one at Jodrell Bank. To help guide the committee, Otto Clarke helped me draft a set of general criteria which it was hoped Ministers would bear in mind when considering the merits of new projects. Here his experience as a Treasury watchdog on public expenditure and his knowledge of the ways of departmental officials made him an invaluable colleague. The ministerial committee never attempted to review the general pattern of governmental expenditure on R&D, even though it had been publicly stated that it was governmental policy to shift R&D resources from the defence to the civil sector of the economy.

Judged by any standard, Roy Jenkins was a sucessful Chancellor. During the years that he held that office, there had been requests from several departments for additional funds for R&D, and because great restraint was being exercised in public expenditure, I was encouraged to see whether the Chief Scientific Advisers of the 'richer' departments could be persuaded to reduce their R&D budgets in order to help their poorer cousins. In my time it was usual for the directors of research establishments to 'pad' their estimates above the level that was actually needed. They did this because there was always the likelihood that their figures would be trimmed, whatever the level they proposed. Even so, and since it was 'unwise' for establishments to have unspent balances, it was sometimes the case that enough would be available towards the end of a financial year to cause a flurry of spending, mainly on equipment. I once made a rough analysis, and discovered that the annual cost, exclusive of salary, of a scientist or engineer in a governmental defence or nuclear-energy laboratory was higher than it was in corresponding laboratories in industry. Not surprisingly, departments with 'clout', such as Defence, were thus inadvertently able to help distort the total pattern of govenmental R&D.

The outcome of my meetings with the departmental CSAs was that the richer R&D departments – and in particular Defence – offered to release something like £25 million. One of the departments in need was Transport, which was begging that year for money that it needed to develop a high-speed train. At the time it was spending thousands of millions on roads and railways, with a budget of less than £5 million for R&D.

During the course of the exercise rumours reached me that the Treasury was likely to claw back any money that I managed to persuade the CSAs to surrender. I therefore called on Roy Jenkins, and warned him that were he not to instruct his officials that whatever R&D money was going to be 'released' should be redistributed, I could guarantee that it was in the highest degree unlikely that the kind of voluntary share-out that was now in progress would ever again be undertaken. No-one, I told him, would believe that it was an honest exercise; government scientists were not going to reduce their allocations for R&D just to please the Treasury. Roy assured me that he would do what was necessary. He did, and Transport got the money it wanted to develop a high-speed train – not that the train ever proved the success that had been promised.

The Central Council was kept informed but was not directly involved in this particular exercise. It was, however, expected to comment on the merits of all the Government's outlays on R&D as part of the process of devising a pattern of R&D in 'the best national interest'. This proved to be extremely difficult, and by the time the Government changed in 1970, our studies were far from complete. I doubt if they have been completed yet, for it certainly looks as if the governmental R&D scene, both civil and defence, is in far greater disarray now than it was in the sixties. In July 1986, the Comptroller and Auditor General presented a report to Parliament which implied that, despite all the watchdogs and committees that have enquired into the shortcomings of Defence R&D, the position is much the same as it was when I wrestled with the problem at the end of the fifties and in the early sixties.[3] One vast R&D project after another still ends on the scrap heap. Today, with the total government outlay on R&D (corrected for the effects of inflation) less than it was in the days of the Central Council, the Government is still chasing that will-o'-the-wisp – an immediate return for the resources spent on science and technology.

Paradoxically, part of the difficulty that the Central Council faced in discharging the responsibilities defined by its terms of reference was due to Otto Clarke's move in 1966 to succeed Maurice Dean as the Permanent Secretary of the Ministry of Technology, which by then had incorporated not only the old Ministry of Aviation, of which Otto had been Permanent Secretary for a year, but also major parts of the Research Council that was still known as the DSIR. 'MinTech' was also busy with the reorganization of the civil side of the Atomic Energy Authority, whose military responsibilities had been passed to the Ministry of Defence.

Wedgwood Benn was immensely enthusiastic about all the reorganization that was being planned for his new empire. So, too, was Otto. In a long and distinguished career as a civil servant, it was his first appointment outside the Treasury (apart from a year preparing for the incorporation of Aviation into MinTech), and his performance as a Permanent Secretary soon became every bit as outstanding as it had been when he was the Treasury official whose job it was to see that the Government's R&D programme was, so far as possible, kept in balance. He used to complain that the pattern of R&D in civil science and technology was distorted by the relatively enormous sums that went to aerospace and nuclear technology. Now it was his turn to defend what was being done in both. Earlier he had encouraged me in my usually futile efforts to bring the Research Councils administratively closer to Departments of State with an immediate interest in their work. Now, as Permanent Secretary, he wanted to keep even the old DSIR's Building Research Station in the Ministry of Technology rather than have it transferred to the Ministry of Public Building and Works. And while previously very much in favour, he became strongly opposed to the idea of an annual review of R&D expenditure.

Whose idea it was I do not know, whether Wedgwood Benn's or Otto's, but their Ministry soon started floating the idea of establishing a 'British Research and Development Organization', with 'British' soon replaced by the word 'Industrial'. Otto published a long article on the idea in a prominent national paper. A Green Paper that spelt it out was presented to Parliament early in 1970.[4]

Benn was delighted to appear before the Central Council to reveal his department's vision of a vast R&D contract organization. He came three times as we pushed him to justify his proposals. One of his arguments was that the proposed organization was needed to control the applied research establishments of the old DSIR. As he put it, what research needed to be done should be decided by 'the customer', whether the customer was a government department or private industry. The fees from 'contract science' would pay for the enormous agency which his department had dreamt up. That was the first time that I had heard the term 'customer–contractor principle' used in discussions of the organization of government science. It was not to be the last.

At a separate meeting, Otto provided the Council with an exposition of MinTech's grandiose proposal to establish a giant national organization that carried out any and every kind of non-biological R&D on a contractual basis. The Council's view was that it all sounded fine in theory, but that it would be bad for industry if it ceased to carry out its own R&D. Nor could we see industry, especially companies working in highly competitive fields, paying a government organization to carry out its research. So far as Government was concerned, what was being proposed also flew in the face of the alternative view, which was being encouraged by most members of the Council, including Patrick Blackett, that government research establishments should be linked to the Ministries most concerned with their work – that is to say, Road Research should be sponsored by the Ministry of Transport, Forest Products Research by the Ministry of Public Building and Works, and so on. MinTech's plans all but implied a government within a government. In the end, Wedgwood Benn's and Otto's dream, as set out in their Green Paper, died a natural death when Harold Wilson was defeated at the polls in 1970.

Shirley Williams, when Secretary of State for Education, also appeared before us, in her case to argue the conventional view that the Research Councils should be allowed to devise their own programmes of work, without worrying about the affairs of executive departments. By the time the Council ceased to exist, other than defence and the nuclear weapons establishment, we had considered the scientific activities of most of the government departments that employed

424

scientific civil servants. What we were trying to do was construct a basis of fact not only about the Government's use of science and scientists, but about the brain drain, and about the mobility – or rather immobility – of scientists.

The Council met at monthly intervals – sometimes twice a month. It also provided most of the membership of several panels that were needed to enquire into specific problems – including some in the nuclear field. I sent the Prime Minister many reports about our enquiries, and it was on our recommendation that the Royal Commission on Environmental Pollution was set up. During the three and a half years of the Council's existence, we published only one report – an account of Technological Innovation in Britain.[5]

Not surprisingly, some Ministers felt aggrieved, in my view justifiably, that despite the fact that we never discussed any aspect of a department's affairs without giving the department as much opportunity as it wanted to present its views, departments that were affected by our deliberations and recommendations were denied regular access to our formal minutes. As a body working within the Cabinet Office, the trouble was that we were bound by the convention that what goes on there is not broadcast. With, I believe, the single exception of the Overseas and Defence Policy Committee, whose existence has been officially admitted, there is still a pretence that Cabinet committees and the committees of officials that service them do not exist – regardless of the fact that it is common knowledge that they do, and that they are always referred to openly in the memoirs of ex-Cabinet Ministers. I used to say – and without exaggeration – that we were so secretive about the way the Government dealt with scientific matters that it was easier for someone to become informed about the affairs of the President's Science Advisory Committee in Washington than it was to obtain information about the Central Council in London. So little was known about our activities that, years later, when the House of Lords Select Committee on Science and Technology asked questions about the work of the Council, Alex Todd, who had been Chairman of the defunct ACSP, and who as Lord Todd was a member of the Select Committee, observed that so far as he knew the Central Council had met only once and had then been wound up.

In 1970 Ted Heath appointed Lord Jellicoe Lord Privy Seal and Chairman of the ministerial Committee on Science and Technology, of which Margaret Thatcher, as the new Secretary of State for Education and Science, was also a member. As the chairman of the committee of officials that served the ministerial committee, I always attended its meetings, and from the start had been expected to take an active part in its discussions. In his *A Balance of Power*, Jim Prior writes that Margaret Thatcher became a 'disruptive influence' in the committee, and that she complained to the Prime Minister that Victor Rothschild and I 'were only officials and had no right to speak. They in their turn had complained about her.'[6] If she did complain about Victor, it must have been on another occasion, since he was not a member of the committee of officials that I chaired. George Jellicoe, a friend from the days of the war, told me about Margaret Thatcher's complaint, and said that he would explain to her my unorthodox position, which she clearly had not understood.

What was more important than this incident was a letter in which she criticized the way the independent Central Council on Science and Technology operated. George discussed this with me, since it related to the secrecy which shrouded our affairs. Here I was fully in agreemnt with her main point. On the other hand, she had not been correctly informed about the way we enquired into departmental affairs. She seemed to believe that the Council learnt about what went on in departments, and in particular her own of Education and Science, only from myself and my immediate staff. This was the reverse of what in fact happened. As I told George Jellicoe in a personal letter:

> The main series of meetings engaged in by the Council were in the nature of seminars conducted by the Permanent Secretaries of the Civil Departments plus their advisers, who informed us about their policies, their difficulties in implementing them with sufficient R&D under-pinning, and their hopes for the future. The results of this series of meetings are not yet assembled in a form in which they can be presented to your [i.e. ministerial] Committee (this for lack of staff and time). It is my intention that what we have learnt from departments should be dealt with by your committee, of which Mrs Thatcher is a member. Let me repeat – at no time has the Council ever discussed departmental policies on the basis of information provided them by the Cabinet Office.

It was, of course, understandable that officials of major spending departments would be jealous of their independence, and that they would be hostile to any body of 'independents' that had no axe to grind when considering the ways that departments used their R&D resources. The Otto Clarke of the Ministry of Technology, for example, was no longer the Otto Clarke of the Treasury. At the same time, and because one department could well be ignorant of another's policies and plans, the sum total of departmental R&D plans did not necessarily imply 'the best national interest'. In order to discharge its responsibilities the Central Council had had to look across the whole board, and not at the activities of departments taken in isolation. And it had had to take account of government policy as a whole, since that was always the Prime Minister's main concern.

Since questions had been raised about the functions of the Central Council, and since it had caused ministerial friction, I was not surprised when Ted Heath, who at first was in favour of its continuation, started to ask questions about the value of keeping it in being. Perhaps – but I am guessing – that was one of the reasons why he allowed the Council to lapse towards the end of his first year as Prime Minister and shortly before my retirement. Another may have been the opposition of the Permanent Secretaries of the big spending R&D departments – Defence and Technology – to an external body that was digging into, and passing judgment on, their affairs. A third could have been the fact that he had appointed a Central Policy Review Staff – the now-defunct 'think-tank' – which was chaired by Victor Rothschild, also a scientist. I can think of other reasons, but equally I can think of reasons why, and how, a Central Council could work effectively within our bureaucratic system. But this is not the place to spell out the ideas I now have about the subject. I described one possible scheme a few years ago in an address that I delivered at the Royal Institution to the title 'Scientists, Bureaucrats, and Ministers'.[7]

Since the days about which I am writing, many changes have taken place in the governmental organization of science. The Council for Scientific Policy of the Department of Education and Science has become the Advisory Board for the Research Councils. With possibly the single exception of the Medical Research Council, the activities of the Research Councils have been significantly curtailed for lack of funds. To some extent they have also been dismembered. A so-called

427

customer–contractor principle for government-sponsored research was introduced as a result of proposals made by Victor Rothschild when he was head of Ted Heath's think-tank. It, too, now seems to be on its way out. An Advisory Council for Applied Research and Development was set up in the Cabinet Office which, judging from its published papers, is mainly concerned with the neglect of science by British industry, and with suggestions about the way the situation could be improved. What does not exist, and what I still believe should exist, is a body like the Central Advisory Council that died nearly twenty years ago. There is now talk that Margaret Thatcher, who undoubtedly played a part in bringing about that demise, is going to resurrect the idea in a new form. I hope that she succeeds.

35

Technological Revolutions and Cooperation

Harold Wilson had got to know several Russian leaders during the course of the many visits that he had paid to the USSR before he became Prime Minister. It was not at all surprising, therefore, that when in office he tried hard not only to improve Anglo–Soviet relations, but also to reduce the tensions that bedevilled those of the USA and the USSR. Burke Trend and I, together with Denis Greenhill, at the time the number two official in the Foreign Office, accompanied him on the visit that he made to Moscow in January 1966, the main item on our agenda being the situation in Vietnam, which we discussed mainly with Prime Minister Kosygin, but also, over a lengthy luncheon, with General Secretary Brezhnev. I remember the occasion less for what it achieved – which in the light of events was very little, if indeed anything at all – than because of a somewhat theatrical landing in the dark before a guard of honour that seemed to consist of equally matched seven-foot-tall soldiers in greatcoats and fur caps, standing impassively to attention, oblivious of the falling snow, and for a performance of *Carmen* that was given by the Bolshoi at the Kremlin's Palace of Congresses. We were in a box, but the pleasure of the occasion was marred because Harold Wilson and Kosygin talked through most of the performance. In Wilson's memoirs, he writes that at various points there were loud 'shushes' from the audience, but that they ceased when they saw who the people in the box were.[1] But as I remember it, they went on shushing until the two lowered their voices to a whisper. The audience did not seem to be in the least impressed by the company in the box. It was the opera they had come to see and hear.

Another reason why I remember the visit is that I was then trying to arrange a second trial mating of the Moscow and London giant pandas, An-An and Chi-Chi; Chi-Chi was the female that had been presented

429

by the Chinese Government to Ted Heath when he was Prime Minister. Our hope was that the better conditions of the London Zoo might prove more favourable for a fertile get-together than had Chi-Chi's visit to Moscow (p. 386). The press was much interested in the zoological negotiations, which were still in progress when the Prime Minister flew to the USSR. I never did know whether he was amused or displeased when the newspapers referred to the giant pandas in connection with his 'summit' meeting. Anyhow, An-An's subsequent trip to London proved just as sterile as Chi-Chi's had to Moscow.

Our industrial links with the USSR are probably little stronger today than they were at the time of that 1966 visit. I would judge, however, that our scientific and cultural links have improved. In theory, nothing

'Now what you must realize, Chi Chi, is that there is nothing shameful about sex and that properly used it can form the basis of a very, very beautiful relationship.'

Osbert Lancaster
10/3/66

can impede the flow of basic scientific knowledge across the 'iron curtain'. The national academies of the two sides have always kept in touch, and in recent years many intergovernmental agreements have been made to encourage specific cultural and scientific exchanges. Their effectiveness fluctuates, however, in accordance with the vagaries of the political climate, and at all times they have been subject to the COCOM agreement, which inhibits the transfer from the West of any materials or information which, in the opinion of the Pentagon, might strengthen the USSR's strategic position. This has occasionally led to clashes between the US Administration and American scientific societies about the publication of papers reporting advances in basic science. We ourselves have not had that kind of trouble.

In 1967 we negotiated a formal agreement to facilitate technological collaboration with the USSR. As Chief Scientific Adviser I was automatically involved, and therefore accompanied Wedgwood Benn to Moscow to confer with Academician Kirillin in his capacity as Chairman of the State Committee for Science and Technology. Nothing of value came from that trip, nor from a follow-up meeting with Kirillin in London. I remember the first mainly because of the pleasure it gave me that our host was Duncan Wilson, who had been posted as UK Ambassador to Moscow, and the London meeting because of the formal luncheon given by the Government to the Soviet delegation. I was placed next to Academician Kotelnikov, a physicist, who was one of Kirillin's deputies.* He tried to tease me by asking why I was withholding the funds that would allow Bernard Lovell of Jodrell Bank to build the new radar dish that he wanted for his astrophysical researches. Clearly Soviet and British physicists knew more about each other's work than did my office. I assured Kotelnikov that it was not a matter upon which my opinion had been sought, and asked, just as lightly, what difference it made, one way or the other, to the USSR, given all the radar complexes they had built for the defence of Moscow. 'Oh,' said Kotelnikov, 'all that is military nonsense, second-class science, but they get all the money they want. We serious scientists are not so fortunate. Do you know,' he continued, 'our phased-array radar system outside Kharkov?' When I said I didn't, he started to pencil the layout on the back of his menu card, which quickly became covered. I

*Kotelnikov is today the senior Vice President of the Soviet Academy of Sciences.

passed him mine on which to continue the sketch, gradually easing his towards me. With a twinkle in his eye, he said, 'I see you would like to take this away.' He looked at what he had drawn, completed it, and then passed the cards to me, saying, 'You can have both.'

But if the scientific and technological exchange agreement between the United Kingdom and the USSR took up very little of my time, the setting up of the International Institute for Applied Systems Analysis (IIASA), in which the USSR was to play a major part, certainly did. The idea behind this venture surfaced during a period of détente, when President Johnson viewed it as a bridge-building exercise between East and West. McGeorge Bundy, who by then had left his post as Special Advisor to the President on National Security Affairs, successfully floated the idea in Moscow in 1967. He then saw a number of European leaders, including Chancellor Brandt of West Germany and Harold Wilson, all of whom promised support. That done, the United States and the USSR decided that the task of bringing the idea to fruition should be entrusted to one of the other countries that had said they were interested. The United Kingdom was chosen, and Harold Wilson passed the job to me.

It was a dreary undertaking, and dragged on for nearly two years. This was partly because the Russians insisted that the participating Western governments had to be matched by an equal number of Warsaw Pact states. Another reason was that the two superpowers had to agree to bear a bigger share of the cost than the others. A third reason was that there were many who were sceptical about the notion that 'systems analysis' could help solve any of the major problems of the developed world.

Bundy I knew well, and he was enormously helpful behind the scenes. The Russian negotiator was Gvishiani, whom I had not met before. He was a very energetic and firm character and, as another of Kirillin's deputies, and also a son-in-law of Kosygin, he carried weight. The Italian negotiator, Aurelio Peccei, was a retired industrialist and the mainstay of the Club of Rome, which was an informal group of men who firmly believed that there are absolute limits to economic growth which, with environmental pollution and unchecked population growth, spelt mankind's doom.* Gvishiani and Peccei quickly became

*The Club of Rome commissioned a group of computer specialists at MIT to produce

torchbearers for the American idea, believing that its implementation would really help solve the ills of the world. They also saw to it that my interest was not allowed to flag, and as a consequence I had to do a fair amount of travelling. On one occasion I wasted a day by flying to Rome in order to meet Gvishiani, only to receive a message, while waiting with Peccei, that he was not coming. I had to go to Moscow to confer for two days with a party of Russian experts led by Gvishiani, and one of Americans that Bundy had brought with him. What I remember best about that particular visit was an excellent dinner that Gvishiani had laid on at an inn some miles outside Moscow. He had his elegant wife with him, and as a Georgian he presided in what he told us was the role of 'tamala' – which meant that every ten minutes or so he would rise from his chair and, with a glass of vodka in his hand, point to a guest who, in turn, had to rise, say a few words as a toast, and then toss back the vodka in one go. I fear I was invited to make too many short speeches on that occasion, and was conscious of the fact that Bundy was being more circumspect than I. I kept wondering what the attractive Mme Gvishiani was making of it all.

The meeting that resolved the political and financial problems took place in Vienna between Bundy, Gvishiani and myself. We were alone, staying in different hotels, but conferring in the sitting room of Gvishiani's luxurious suite in the Bristol Hotel. On that occasion it was agreed that the Americans and the Russians would each pay a third of the total costs of IIASA, the remainder being shared equally by the other participating countries, whatever their number. To overcome the political difficulty of having East Germany as a participant, we also agreed that adherence would be through the agency of national scientific academies, which would be provided with the necessary funds by their governments. The Institute would thus not be an intergovernmental organization.

The Austrian Foreign Minister entertained us to dinner in a small party that included four of his officials. Some discreet hints had been dropped that the Austrian Government wanted the new Institute to be set up on their soil, and this was obviously the point of the dinner. The Minister had placed Bundy and me on either side of him, with

---

a 'model', and in due course they published a book called *Limits to Growth*, which was widely read in influential circles.

Gvishiani opposite, and in a quiet voice he told me that he had been Ambassador to Czechoslovakia in 1968 when the Russians moved their tanks into Prague, allegedly to forestall a counter-revolution that had been plotted in West Germany. To my surprise he said that he had been greatly relieved by the Russian move, for had it been delayed, World War III would most probably have broken out, and that would have meant the end of Austria. His words made understandable something that Smirnovsky, the Russian Ambassador in London, had said on one of the few occasions when, properly briefed, I had lunched alone with him. One day, he insisted, the world would thank the USSR for having acted against the Czechs when it did. I could now see that Smirnovsky was implying that the liberation fever that the Czechs had generated would have spread through Poland into East Germany, and that this would have brought in West Germany and, in due course, would have precipitated an all-out East–West conflict.

The agreement reached between Bundy, Gvishiani and myself entailed an enormous amount of paperwork – especially for Foreign Office officials. We now had to transform the idea of governmental participation into participation between national academies, one or two of which had to be invented for the purpose.

Something then happened which almost sent us back to the original concept of an intergovernmental institute. Willy Brandt, the German Chancellor, came to London early in March 1969 for exchanges on a number of matters, including the Common Market and his *Ostpolitik*. I had to sit in on the talks, and after an amiable exchange of views in the morning session, and just when the Prime Minister was about to adjourn the meeting for lunch, the Chancellor said that he wanted to raise one more matter. His government had no objection to the East Germans participating in the proposed IIASA. The item was not in our briefs, and the Prime Minister turned to me to comment. All I could say was that the statement was most welcome, and that it would certainly help speed the conclusion of our negotiations. What I could not say was that it would have been far better had we known the Chancellor's views before, but that we had already gone too far along the academic road to turn back. I had a feeling that Brandt did not know that we and the Americans had assumed – perhaps incorrectly – that he had vetoed the original proposal.

During the final phase of the negotiations, those countries that wanted to provide a home for the new institute began to lobby hard. Britain was a late starter, but we were hardly likely to be selected since we had just expelled about a hundred Russians from their various missions in the UK. France put in a late but powerful bid. In the end Austria won by promising to provide as a home for the Institute the magnificent royal palace at Laxenburg, not too far from Vienna. Gvishiani had always wanted Austria which, as he put it, was on the crossroads between East and West.

The final preparatory meeting took place in London under my chairmanship, and was attended by representatives of some twelve national academies. The agreement that formally established the International Institute for Applied Systems Analysis was then signed. I was thankful when it was all over, and when Gvishiani assumed the chairmanship of the Institute's Council, so allowing Bundy and me to bow out. I visited the Institute on two or three occasions, and was much impressed by the enthusiasm of the staff and by the splendour in which they worked. Early on in the Reagan regime, however, the United States withdrew its official support, with the UK following suit by stopping its much smaller annual payment. When that happened, a powerful group of American supporters, under the sponsorship of the American Academy of Arts and Sciences, raised funds from charitable sources in order to maintain the American connection. With the Royal Society now out of the picture, I tried, but unsuccessfully, to do the same through the British Fellowship of Engineering, which unfortunately failed to raise the money necessary to maintain a formal British link. Today, therefore, the USSR is the main supporter of the Institute. Only time will tell whether IIASA will succeed in fulfilling the main hope that brought it about – that of helping bring about East–West understanding. So far there is little to boast about.

If IIASA was not in the mainstream of my activities in the Cabinet Office, the idea of a European Technological Community, which Harold Wilson floated in 1967, certainly was. To the public, he never appeared to be a dedicated 'European', doubtlessly because he had to hold the ring between those members of his Cabinet who were openly anti-European – among them Edward Short and Dick Crossman – and those, like Roy Jenkins and George Brown, who were as staunchly 'pro'. Even had opinion among his ministers not been divided, I would doubt if he could have succeeded where Harold Macmillan and

Edward Heath had failed – to persuade de Gaulle that the UK was ready to become a loyal member of the European Community.

The trouble was that, when it came to action, it always seemed impossible to cut through the coils that bound us to the United States, particularly in the nuclear field. At the operational level, our weaponeers and Royal Navy officers understood and worked with their American opposite numbers – with the notable exception of their dealings with Admiral Rickover. As the father of the American nuclear navy, Rickover was a law unto himself, and despite (or perhaps because of) a host of eccentricities, he was an officer much admired in Congressional circles. When in the late fifties and early sixties the Royal Navy began to build nuclear propulsion plants for its submarines, it had frequently to turn to the US for help. In effect this meant turning to Rickover who, until he was retired from office by President Reagan in 1981, insisted that I had to be his main channel of official communication with the Royal Navy. Our naval staff were ready to accept this odd arrangement – even after I had moved from the Ministry of Defence to the Cabinet Office – lest the effort to establish a more conventional channel of communication led to its breakdown.

It was Rickover who started this personal relationship. He had read the article on nuclear warfare that I had published in *Foreign Affairs*[2] and, a few months after its appearance in January 1962, had arranged to meet me when he learnt that I was in Washington. My introduction took as unusual a shape as the relationship which followed. I was lunching with General Sir Michael West, at the time the head of the British Military Mission, when in came Rob Scott, with whom I had come to Washington, to say that an Admiral Rickover was in a car outside and wished to meet me, but that he refused to come in. Since Rob said it was important, I left the table and found Rickover sitting in a car with Gerard Smith, the State Department official who later negotiated the SALT treaties and the 1972 ABM Treaty. Rickover began by saying, 'That was a fine piece of yours in *Foreign Affairs*. Keep it up,' adding, to the amusement of Gerard Smith who had had Rob and Rickover to lunch, 'We military are not made to think. Keep in touch.' I returned to the Wests' dining room somewhat bemused.

Whenever I visited Washington, right up to 1986, the year of his death, I would spend an hour or two with Rickover. Scarcely in keeping with his usual way of life, he twice arranged a formal dinner on my behalf, on the first occasion inviting – commanding, would be a better word – Gerard Smith and a Supreme Court judge (I forget his name) together with their wives, and on the second, Senator Henry 'Scoop' Jackson.* The second occasion I remember well, first because I could not get the powerful Senator to share my enthusiasm for a comprehensive test ban, and second because a flurried marine, who had been imported as a waiter for the evening, came in to say that President Carter was on the line, and wanted to speak to the Senator. When the two had finished talking, Scoop said, 'Don't ring off, Rickover wants a word with you.' Rick grabbed the telephone, and opened the conversation by saying, 'Hi, Mr President, I've done you a good favour in your State. I said nice things about you.' I was taken aback by the nonchalant way both had dealt with their President.

When Rick visited Holy Loch to inspect the US submarines that were stationed there, he almost always did so over a weekend. He would telephone to say that he was coming, and would ask me to arrange a flight from Scotland to wherever I happened to be, the understanding being that he would stay the night. His return flight to America always had to be timed so that he could be back at his desk in Washington on the Monday morning. Even after my retirement it was to me that he sent the regular reports on radiation levels in Holy Loch which the US was committed to provide as an assurance that nothing untoward was happening there. These I would acknowledge simply by saying that I had sent them on to the 'right quarters'.

The UK's 'special relationship' with the US is not an institutional arrangement, but a reflection of the personal ties that exist between individuals, particularly in the US and UK nuclear and intelligence communities. Without these links, the 'relationship', whatever its political significance, would, I imagine, simply fade away. Unfortunately, the widespread belief that there is more to it than just that was a serious obstacle to Harold Wilson's idea of a European Technological Community. Another was the inevitable industrial and commercial rivalry that exists between the members of the EEC. While I never tried to keep up with the changing ramifications of the UK's political relations with France and West Germany, I was fascinated by the

*The first Mrs Rickover, a formidable lady, was hostess at the first dinner. After her death he married again, and it was the second Mrs Rickover whom I met at the dinner when Senator Jackson was his other guest.

conception of a Technological Community, as the Prime Minister spelt it out in a speech that he delivered at the Guildhall in November of 1967. I had always regretted the failure of anything practical to emerge from the work of the Armand Committee (p. 159). Here was another chance.

To the best of my knowledge the PM's text had not been seen by the Cabinet Office before it was delivered, and when a day or two later I asked him what happened next, he smilingly said that he had put the finishing touches to the speech in the car on his way to the Guildhall, and that it was now up to officials to add substance to his proposals. Then he ran through the dismal record of our failures. British manufacturing industry was not competitive in world markets. The industries of fragmented Europe undercut each other in their domestic markets as well as abroad. Europe was totally overshadowed by the American giant. There was little if any standardization of procurement within NATO. My own efforts to coordinate British defence R&D with that of the Pentagon had been a failure. While our aviation industry stumbled, that of America, with its vast and unified domestic market, flourished. The United States was challenging the world. That, according to the Prime Minister, was the situation, and it had to be changed. (At the time, few realized that Japan was also becoming a dominant industrial power, and one that would soon overshadow the USA.)

The speech generated a great deal of interest, not only in Europe, but also in America. Don Hornig was so keen to learn what our plan of action was – incorrectly believing that there was one – that he flew over with some of his Washington colleagues, including Gerry Tape, to confer with me. The big American multinationals were then moving into Europe, and it was being said that they – not the USA or the USSR – constituted a more powerful superpower than even the USSR. I made it plain to Hornig that Britain had no intention of restricting itself to the older conventional industries, as he had indicated we would have to do, so leaving to the Americans the cultivation of the emerging high-tech industrial fields.

Apart from the Jaguar and some helicopters, all our efforts to arrange that the British and French aviation industries cooperated in the production of military aircraft had failed. Julian Amery, when Minister of Aviation, had however succeeded in launching the civil

Concorde project as a joint Anglo–French venture. In 1968, a year after we had signed a 'protocol' to be a partner in a tripartite arrangement with the French and West Germans to develop a European 'airbus', the Government dropped out, leaving it to the Hawker company to take the enormous, but fortunately successful, risk of participating as a 'private' venture. Hawkers had hoped for government support, but they were in competition with the British Aircraft Corporation, which had plans to develop a purely British carrier, the BA-311, a plan which many officials in the Ministry of Technology favoured. The two European projects were therefore competing not only with each other but also with those of McDonnell-Douglas and Lockheed, the two giant American companies which could rely, even if indirectly, on enormous government aid.

As an official who would be called upon to advise the Prime Minister, I was lobbied fiercely both by those of our own people who favoured the BA-311 and by Henri Ziegler (p. 228), the chief executive of Sud-Aviation, the nationalized French company that was primarily responsible for the development of the Airbus. Ziegler had cooperated with George Edwards in the development of Concorde, but if the UK were to join in the Airbus, his British partner would be Arnold Hall, the head of the Hawker group. I was bombarded with figures about the specifications of the two designs, with estimates of cost and performance, and became convinced that the European Airbus was a better bet than the BA-311, particularly as it meant Anglo–French cooperation. I also doubted whether government money was going to be provided for either project. I myself then started lobbying. I had no doubt that the British Aircraft Corporation was not powerful enough to take on the American giants on its own. I spoke to Arnold Weinstock, the head of GEC – which then owned a substantial part of the British Aircraft Corporation – about the need to combine with the French, and arranged that he should see Wedgwood Benn, the Minister of Technology.

When they met, Benn was surrounded by a bevy of officials, of whom only one spoke up in favour of the idea of the British aviation industry 'getting into bed' with the French. Weinstock, who had insisted that I should be with him, even if I remained silent, was on his own, and we left with Benn promising that he would let Weinstock know whether the Government thought the proposal of a broadly based connection between the French and British aviation industries should be followed up. The meeting took place some six months before the election of June 1970. Weinstock later told me that during those months he never heard a further word – not surprising, perhaps, since Benn was far from enthusiastic about cooperation with Europe. He was also having to deal with the other problems of the aviation industry, particularly those arising from Rolls-Royce's determination to go ahead with its big RB-211 engine project, this time in competition with the two giant American engine companies.

I discussed the subject of Anglo–French cooperation with Christopher Soames on many occasions during the period he was our Ambassador in Paris. Christopher had lost his seat in the election that brought Harold Wilson to power. He had then joined the board of the Decca electronics company, and had got it into his head that I should leave my post in Whitehall – as well as resign my Birmingham chair – to join forces with him in the company. The idea had no attractions for me. But I shared Christopher's conviction that Britain's future lay with Europe.

One night Joan and I were invited to dine when he and Mary, his wife, were entertaining General Yigael Yadin, the Israeli archaeologist. Christopher and I got into a corner and started talking about the ambassadorship to France which was about to fall vacant, with Christopher in his usual confident way saying that if he were appointed, he would know how to turn de Gaulle's '*non*' to Britain's membership of the EEC into a '*oui*'. Why, he asked, didn't I put the idea into Wilson's head? I did, and in July 1967 arranged a small dinner party at the Zoo where the two of them, sitting on either side of Joan, got into a serious conversation about Europe. The Prime Minister clearly liked the idea, and duly passed the hint to George Brown, with the result that Christopher, an ex-Tory Minister, was appointed the Labour Government's Ambassador to France, a position that he held from 1968 until 1972, after which he became a member of the European Commission.

I do not know by what yardstick ambassadors are rated, but for my money Christopher did a marvellous job in very difficult circumstances. Macmillan, with the full support of his cabinet colleagues, had failed in his efforts to get the UK accepted as a member of the EEC, and here was Christopher trying to smooth the way for a Labour Prime

Minister who was having to do a balancing act between the European and anti-European members of his administration.

The French had more than one reason to be suspicious of the strength of Britain's commitment to the European idea. Nassau had convinced de Gaulle that Macmillan's Britain lacked the courage to become truly European. Harold Wilson had then tried to jettison the Anglo–French Concorde project, and had failed to follow up his declaration that he was going to 'upturn Nassau' and cooperate in the nuclear field with France. The UK had helped launch the ELDO organization (actually as a means of salvaging something from the Blue Streak fiasco), and then had in effect abandoned it. There were other cases of backsliding on our part. Needless to say we, in turn, drew attention to the occasions when the French had let us down, for example in the variable-geometry aircraft project. Christopher certainly started on his diplomatic ventures with the cards stacked against him.

But being Christopher, he shrugged off the difficulties, and with Mary set about making the Paris Embassy not only an enviable centre of social life, but also an effective focus of negotiation. I called there whenever I was in Paris, both to enjoy their hospitality and to discuss what I was learning from my friends in the French aviation industry. Christopher encouraged the informality of my contacts, despite the fact that the official links which the UK had with the French on aerospace matters were through the Ministry of Technology. He knew that much of the foundation of my easy friendships in France derived from my standing as a scientist, and from my relations with French research workers who were active in the same fields of enquiry as my own. Faint echoes of my pro-French activities during the war years also helped. What did not help was my poor French, based as it mainly was on a reading of every one of George Simenon's novels.* Nonetheless,

---

*I had once collected – with some difficulty – all the two hundred or so titles recorded in the '*catalogue raisonné*' of his books. Most of Simenon's characters addressed each other by the familiar term 'thou' – 'tutoying' as it is called. Sometime during the winter of 1944–5, I asked the hall porter of the Hotel Vendôme, where I was quartered, to send a telegram to Louise de Vilmorin, the beautiful and exotic French writer who appears so prominently in biographies of Duff Cooper. The porter raised his eyebrows at the '*tu*'s in the text I gave him, but I insisted on them being left in. I did not then realize that in the circles in which Lou-Lou moved, tutoying implied a degree of intimacy which, whatever its foundation, was not admitted publicly. She made this very clear to me when she returned to Paris.

Christopher did not regard this as a serious obstacle to my delivering in 1971 the Winston Churchill Memorial Lecture to the Association France–Grande-Bretagne.[3] It promised to be a daunting enough affair without the embarrassment of having Christopher whip my text from me when Joan and I arrived at the Embassy because, as he put it, the Foreign Office people who had translated my English text did not appreciate the nuances of the French language. Having been assured that I would have enough time to read a new translation before changing for the meeting, we sat down to talk about other matters.

As it turned out, I mounted the dais, in dinner jacket and black tie, with a text I had not seen before. After a flowery introduction by Christopher, I stumbled through my lecture for some forty minutes, to an awe-inspiring audience that not only included some prominent French political figures, but also Mary's mother 'Clemmie', Winston's widow, who had come over for the occasion. Alastair ('Ali') Forbes, who was also a guest at the Embassy at the time (and whose French is that of a Frenchman, bar the accent, which is Ali's in any language), said that of the many strange things I had ever done, my performance that evening was the bravest and funniest of all. But the Winston Churchill Lecture was Christopher's way of 'doing me proud'.

Harold Wilson's call for European cooperation did not get very far. The most immediate obstacles were Rolls-Royce's plan to develop its big RB-211 engine, and the clash between the BAC-311 and the European Airbus project. Rolls insisted that their big engine could power both a European Airbus and whatever airliner was going to capture the American market – Lockheed's or Douglas's or Boeing's. The French doubted this, while my American friends kept advising me that the Rolls engine stood no chance against Pratt and Whitney's corresponding 50,000 lb-thrust machine, which was in competition with one of General Electric. There was a limit to the market for engines of that size.

In addition to what I was learning officially about Rolls-Royce, I was being provided with information about the company by Whitney Straight, a close friend and a non-executive director of the Rolls-Royce board. He was very dubious about the course that was being pursued by the company's Managing Director. I also had talks with Lord Kindersley, the company Chairman, and with Mr Haughton, the Lockheed chief who used to visit London to press his case for help in

442

his battles with Douglas and Boeing. I kept warning Harold Wilson that the position of Rolls-Royce was damaging his European initiative and that the company had become a 'lame-duck'. But Rolls-Royce was too prestigious not to be supported by the State – even after the company went bankrupt, as Ted Heath was to discover when he became Prime Minister. I never did learn the true cost of the RB-211, but from the technological point of view it was and clearly remains a success.

I can recall only one major item of technological cooperation that gave any substance to Harold Wilson's dream – the tripartite agreement between the Netherlands, West Germany and ourselves to enrich uranium by the centrifuge process. Harold Wilson writes that Frank Cousins told him about the idea of the centrifuge shortly before his resignation from the Ministry of Technology, and that Cousins had learnt about it from 'Atomic Energy Authority scientists'.

As I remember it, the Prime Minister told me that Bill Penney had been to see him about a new centrifuge process to enrich uranium which was so simple that to me it sounded as if it could be carried out in any backyard. If that were the case, it was a development that clearly threatened the proposed Non-Proliferation Treaty. There was another consideration. Capenhurst, the plant that produced our enriched uranium, would need to be enlarged if it were to provide the increased supplies of fuel that were going to be demanded by our nuclear power programme. If Penney's story were confirmed, it might be cheaper to embark on the new centrifuge process than to increase the size of Capenhurst. The matter was extremely urgent, said the Prime Minister, and would I look into it? I was given permission to call in expert advice, on condition that I approached no-one who had not been cleared to deal with the most secret nuclear matters – and the fewer I brought in the better.

Bob Press helped me convene a small group of men who fitted the bill, including a few who were on the Central Advisory Council, and we went up to Capenhurst to inspect the prototype plant where the centrifuge was being tested. It turned out to be a chemical engineering development that was based upon a process that had been described in the scientific press by its German inventor, Zippe.

In the course of our enquiries, and while we were still arguing between ourselves about the technical and economic merits of the centrifuge process, Joseph Luns, at the time Foreign Minister of the Netherlands, flew over with his Prime Minister for an official visit. I was one of the members of the Cabinet Office staff whom the PM had with him for the talks, which included an item about technological cooperation. Luns, whom I had met a few times before with mutual friends in London, wanted to know how the idea of a European Technological Community was coming along. There was little the Prime Minister could tell him.

Luncheon had been laid on in Number 10, and as we left the Cabinet room to go to the dining room upstairs, Luns held me back saying 'All this talk about technological cooperation is getting us nowhere. Isn't there something that we could do?' Without hesitating, I told him that we knew that the Netherlands and West Germany were considering the formation of a joint company to enrich uranium by the centrifuge process. Why didn't we make it a tripartite affair? In those days the United States dominated the world market for the enriched uranium needed for power plants, and it was well known that West Germany did not like being dependent on the American monopoly. Joe expressed little surprise that we knew of his country's negotiations with the Federal Republic, and agreed that the idea should be pursued.

Harold Wilson was all in favour. Wedgwood Benn, the Minister who would be involved, was at first lukewarm. Our nuclear experts had given him the usual story. We were so far ahead that were we not to continue on our own, we would merely be helping our potential competitors.

But then came a serious snag. Despite Bill Penney's almost conspiratorial attitude when he saw the Prime Minister, there was nothing secret about the basic principles of the high-speed centrifuge process. We had discussed the technique some years before with the Americans under the umbrella of our nuclear exchange agreements, and in accordance with which, as I have already said, no information that the Americans might have provided could be passed on to a third party. Not long before, they had vetoed a deal that the engineering firm of Babcock and Wilcocks had made to supply the French Navy with a heat exchanger for a nuclear propulsion plant because, so it was claimed, the dimensions might provide a clue to the design of the rest of what was basically an American system.

In the way these things get known, the Americans learnt about our talks with the Dutch and the Germans. They wanted to be assured that no single feature of our prototype centrifuge plant, or of the design of the individual centrifuge cylinders, derived from anything we had learnt from them. Our Atomic Energy people assured me that I need have no fears on that score, and I so informed the Prime Minister, and then the Americans. But the US Atomic Energy Commission was not satisfied, and a team led by Gerry Tape flew over to discuss the matter, in the hope that they would also be allowed to inspect our small prototype plant. This our own Atomic Energy people at first refused.

At the end of the day the Americans proved to be right. There was a minor feature in our design that had been discussed at a low-level technical meeting between experts of the two sides, and whose disclosure, according to the Americans, violated our agreements. Regardless of the fact that it was so insignificant a detail that, so I was assured, it could have been deduced from first principles by any first-class engineer, I had to fly to Washington and, sitting at the end of a long table, offer my apologies to a full meeting of the American Atomic Energy Commission, with Glenn Seaborg in the chair, for having, out of ignorance, misled them. I congratulated them on knowing more than I did about the matter in dispute – which raised a smile. My apology was accepted, and no more was said.

The Dutch and the West Germans were greatly relieved at the outcome of the American intervention, and after I had visited Stoltenberg, the German Minister of Technology, and then Joe Luns, a final meeting was convened in The Hague, with Wedgwood Benn, now an enthusiastic supporter of the tripartite agreement, signing the necessary documents. So it was that URENCO, a tri-national company, came into being.

Joe Luns and I got to know each other fairly well during the course of the negotiations, in the middle of which he even sent me the draft PhD thesis of a young university friend of his, about which, as a personal favour, he wanted my opinion! He was as keen as I was that the European Technological Community should not end just with URENCO. But that is what it did. The vision of such a community does, however, remain alive, and in a sense has been resurrected in the French civil EUREKA project, which was put forward as a counter to the Americans trying to recruit European scientists in the furtherance of President Reagan's dream of a space-based defence against ballistic missiles. But such industrial and technological cooperation as has so far occurred between the countries of Western Europe has been mainly on a company-to-company basis. Its scale has not yet been large enough to halt the deindustrialization of the United Kingdom, a matter that has kept worrying me all the years since I ceased to be a full-time government servant.

PART IX

Epilogue

36

Retirement Years

Shortly before Harold Wilson's Moscow visit in 1966 (p. 429), I wrote to Rob Aitken saying that I wished to give up my university chair. Rob refused to accept my resignation. No-one, he said, regarded me as an absentee professor, and despite the unconventional direction that I gave it, my department continued to flourish. Moreover, as Vice Chancellor he did not want me to sever my connection with the University. It was all very flattering, but since I was insistent, he agreed to issue a public statement to the effect that I was resigning at a date that the University was arranging. It was nearly two years before my resignation took effect.

My departure from the Cabinet Office proved almost as protracted. No term had been set to my appointment, but when I reached my sixty-fifth year I told Harold Wilson that it was time that a successor was appointed. His reply was that he neither saw any reason why I should go, nor did he wish me to go. But if I was determined to leave, he would want me to go to the Lords. I decided to stay. I was worried because he would not give me any indication that a successor would be appointed, and at the time I was disinclined to join the small band of civil servants who are honoured in the way he proposed. Burke Trend, with whom I had already discussed the matter of a successor, had also been unwilling to commit himself that there would be one.

Two years later it was more than time that I retired. Ted Heath, now Prime Minister, also took the line that my appointment was not governed by civil service rules, and that despite my years, he would like me to stay on. If, however, I decided to retire, he hoped that I would still be available as a consultant, with a perch in the Cabinet Office. Then, very nicely, he added that he would be pleased if I would go to the Lords. This time I agreed. Alan Cottrell was appointed in my place, although at a civil service rank one rung below the top one to which I

had been recruited. Alan retired after three years, to become Master of
Jesus College in Cambridge, and Bob Press then assumed his duties at
a civil service rank one below Cottrell's, and without being designated
Chief Scientific Adviser. In the form that I knew it, the post of Chief
Scientific Adviser to the Government then lapsed.

Ted gave a dinner party to mark my retirement. I had no idea what
the occasion would be like until Joan and I arrived at Number 10, to
discover that Ted had invited some sixty guests – mainly ministerial,
military and civil-servant friends, with most of whom I had been
associated closely over the years. The biggest surprise was that among
them were Jerry Wiesner, Harold Brown, and Rickover from America.
No-one does these things more graciously than Ted. In an after-
dinner speech, he was so laudatory about the services that I had
rendered the State, that Joan felt that she was listening to a memorial
address. Ted then told the company that I had agreed not only to
continue as a consultant, but also to go to the Lords. He made it sound
as though I was doing him a favour rather than having an honour
conferred on me. In the circumstances, my reply was anything but
adequate. When we left the table I received many congratulations, and
Victor Rothschild excitedly wanted to know what I was going to call
myself. 'Why, Rothschild, of course,' I replied, to the amusement of
those standing around. Dickie Mountbatten said that it had to be Lord
Solly, as no-one knew me by any other name.

After dinner Rickover told me that he would now take the opportunity of telling the Prime Minister how to run the country, and sure
enough, there they were some minutes later, side by side on a sofa, with
Rick doing all the talking. Edwin Plowden once told me that in the late
fifties, when he was Chairman of the Atomic Energy Authority, Rick
was in England negotiating the sale to the UK of the nuclear propulsion plant that the Royal Navy wanted. Rick had barely met Plowden
before, but he insisted on Plowden accompanying him to the airport
when he went to board his plane for Washington. He had not yet had
time to tell Edwin how to run the Authority! Other than Congress, to
which Rick regarded himself as directly answerable, he refused to
allow any interference with his work, but he usually knew how others
should do theirs. He lectured Congressional committees endlessly
about the defects of the American educational system. That was
another field in which he regarded himself as an expert.

Portrait by Derek Hill.

OUT OF HARNESS

Facing page

1 A professional shrimper (S.Z in Norfolk).
2 Alec Todd (Lord Todd, President of the Royal Society) being indoctrinated into the art of shrimping. Antonia (Coney) Jarvis assists.
3 Sporting the hat of a member of the Commandeurie du Bontemps, with Nanou, Gaston Mayer's wife, looking on, France 1957.

4 William Walton and his wife Susana in Norfolk (S.Z. behind newspaper).
5 With Ira and Lee Gershwin when at Caltech, 1959.
6 With Anita Mandl at the author's seventieth birthday celebrations.
7 Peter Krohn.

This page

8 With Dickie Mountbatten and coconuts, Borneo 1965.
9 In Whitney Straight's motorlaunch in Majorca. Left to right, S.Z., Michael Renshaw, Douglas Fairbanks Jr., and Whitney.
10 With John Z. Young at the Shooting Box.
11 Terence Morrison Scott admires the author's seventy-fifth birthday cake.
12 With Ben Nicholson laying down the law at the Shooting Box.

Inaugurating the Burnham Thorpe village bowling green.

Ted's dinner party took place seventeen years ago, years that have been as full as any that went before, and in which I have never been able to keep out of my mind the main issues that concerned me when I was a full-time official, particularly the nuclear dilemma to which no answer has yet been found. My academic and zoological interests were also there to keep me busy. Until 1984, when I ceased to be President, I paid close attention to the affairs of the Zoological Society. It was easy, too, to slip back into the academic world. At the time of my retirement, there were still some strands of research in which I was directly involved, so that I did not publish my last strictly scientific paper until 1973, forty-seven years after the appearance of my first. I also set about the production of a second edition of my *New System of Anatomy*, and of my first book, *The Social Life of Monkeys and Apes*.

A suggestion that I should become the Master of a college in one of our ancient universities did not attract me. As a Norfolk resident I had, however, been a member of a 'promotions committee' that had sat under the chairmanship of Lord Mackintosh to urge the claims of Norwich as the seat of one of the new universities that were to be established in the post-Robbins era (p. 112). The committee met in Lord Mackintosh's house near Norwich, and only one meeting remains in my memory, not because of the discussion, but because when we left, the distinguished-looking Lord Mackintosh stood at his front door and solemnly presented each of us with a box of Mackintosh's toffees, the product that had made his a national name. It pleased me to see Lord Adrian, the Master of Trinity College, Cambridge, a Nobel Laureate and an ex-President of the Royal Society who, together with John Cockcroft and Roy Harrod, was also a member of the committee, accepting his box with a gracious smile as though he had never before received so generous a gift.

The Government having decided that Norwich should be the seat of a new university, the UGC then appointed a small Academic Planning Board on which I was asked to serve. My specific contribution to its work was a blueprint for a school of environmental sciences. Seven years after the University's foundation I was invited to become its 'Professor at Large', at a nominal salary and with no formal duties. It has been an association that I have enjoyed ever since. To help the new School of Environmental Sciences along, I encouraged the Ford Foundation to provide a sum of money with which to cover the cost of

451

six annual international seminars on environmental problems, the proceedings of which were later published in book form.

My academic interests and connections have also been kept alive by invitations to deliver lectures at other universities, the two most prestigious being the Romanes Lecture in Oxford, which I delivered in 1975 to the title 'Advice and Responsibility', and the Compton Lectures at MIT in 1972, when Jerry Wiesner was its President. Jerry was determined that the lectures, to which I had given the general title 'Sense, Science and Society', should be well attended, and had accordingly arranged for the first to be delivered in MIT's vast Kresge Auditorium. It was, however, a period of considerable unrest in all American universities, with demonstrations increasing as President Nixon, advised by Henry Kissinger, intensified the US bombing campaign in Vietnam. On the evening of my first lecture, the students had taken to the streets to demonstrate against the bombing of Hanoi and the mining of Haiphong. Only about a quarter of the hall was filled, and then mainly by members of staff and graduate students. Unrest intensified throughout the following day, and my second lecture began in truly dramatic fashion.

The taxi driver who was taking me to MIT's main administration building, where I was due to be picked up by the Provost, stopped some two hundred yards short and said, 'Hey, look at that. I can't go any further.' I paid him off, and turned to see a mass of students surging towards me, pursued by National Guardsmen. I smelt tear-gas, but carried on until I was stopped by a tall good-looking student who, realizing that I was a stranger, told me that I had no chance of going any further. He then led me, gasping and with a handkerchief over my nose and mouth, to a nearby students' hostel. Here I spent about an hour, in an atmosphere that became increasingly permeated with gas. I could not find out where Jerry was, and had assumed that my lecture was off until, without warning, a National Guard officer appeared from nowhere and led me out of a side door of the building, from where I was driven to a lecture theatre where Jerry and an audience were waiting. Jerry had no need to explain that circumstances beyond his control were responsible for the late start. Every now and then I caught a whiff of gas.

The next occasion that I sat in the Kresge Auditorium was in 1976, at the first of a series of lectures which MIT had organized to mark the bicentenary of the American Declaration of Independence. I was among those whom Jerry had canvassed for ideas about the way the event might be celebrated by MIT, and was pleasantly surprised when my suggestion was accepted. It was that a series of lectures should be organized, each to be delivered by someone who had, or who still exercised, a major influence on the international political stage, to the general theme of 'the most likely changes in international relations that could occur over the next decade or two' (a somewhat transformed version of what I first suggested). I also proposed that the speakers should be rewarded with a gold medal specially struck to mark the occasion, and, as medallist, I offered the name of Elisabeth Frink. This suggestion was also accepted, and I was authorized to confer with her about the design. I attended the first lecture, which was given by Roy Jenkins shortly before he assumed the presidency of the European Commission. All the lectures subsequently appeared in a book under the title, *World Change and World Security*.[1]

Another way in which my connection with the university world was kept warm was through what became known as the Technological Projects Scheme. This was launched in 1967 by the Wolfson Foundation, of which I had become a trustee. Universities were invited to compete for funds to further specific scientific or engineering projects which, if successfully pursued, might be exploited by industry. As its author, it fell to me to launch and implement the scheme, for the staff of the foundation was then restricted to a Secretary and a typist – the current quip about the Wolfson Foundation was that it was run by a retired general and a blonde. After I had got the scheme going, I managed to get Dr Leonard ('Larry') Rotherham to help me. We had known each other for years, and when I was CSA to Defence, I had failed to persuade him to join me as deputy. He had also been a member of the Central Advisory Council which I had set up. Larry later wrote a book about the Scheme.[2] It was the first of its kind to be launched in the UK specifically in order to help bridge the gap between academic researchers and the people responsible for innovation in industry.

An opportunity to learn in a more direct way about the industrial exploitation of science was presented to me by Harold Watkinson. When he retired from active politics in 1962, Harold had become the chief executive of the Schweppes company, which in 1969 joined forces with the equally renowned confectionery firm, Cadbury, headed by Adrian Cadbury. On my formal retirement as a civil servant, I was invited to join the new board, but Harold and Adrian understood when I said that I preferred to start as a consultant, so as to learn about the technical problems which faced the company. I was enormously flattered when, after a few enjoyable years as a member of the main board, the company attached my name to a large research centre that they had built on the campus of the University of Reading.

I was still one of the company's non-executive directors when in 1975 I was invited by Rhodes University in South Africa to deliver the Cecil Rhodes Memorial Lecture. I had not been back to the land of my birth for almost half a century, and Joan was to come with me. The Chairman of the company's South African branch undertook the task of arranging the trip, and our programme soon became crowded with meetings, speeches and dinners. The day after our arrival in Johannesburg, there was a 'black-tie' dinner where, much to our amusement, I was introduced in an after-dinner speech as Lord Watkinson. The following morning I was driven to Pretoria to meet Mr Vorster, the South African Prime Minister. I had no idea what I was supposed to discuss with him, and was bewildered when on my arrival, the head of the Prime Minister's private office handed me a note saying that the British Ambassador would like me to call on him after I left Mr Vorster. From his opening words I gained the impression that the Prime Minister thought that I had been briefed to discuss political matters – he and Ian Smith,* the last white Prime Minister of what was then Rhodesia, had just had their famous meeting on a train that had been halted on a bridge over the Zambesi River. But I had no brief, and was determined, if at all possible, not to touch on any sensitive issues. The conversation proceeded in a desultory way, and ended with our discussing the relative merits of rifles of different calibre when hunting lion. I knew about rifles, and I knew about lions, but nothing about the two together, which Mr Vorster apparently did. I enjoyed telling Sir James Bottomley, our Ambassador, that the substantive part of my talk with the South African Prime Minister was about lion hunting.

*The Rhodesian Prime Minister, who in his Unilateral Declaration of Independence had taken Rhodesia, as it then was, out of the British Commonwealth.

The trip by car through Durban down the east coast to Port Elizabeth and then to Rhodes University in Grahamstown was highly enjoyable. The theme I had chosen for my lecture was what a Cecil Rhodes of today would do were he to try to emulate the vision of the original Rhodes who had hoped that peace and understanding could be brought to the world through an international scholarship scheme. My lecture seemed to make little impact on my audience nor, after its obscure publication, did I ever hear it referred to.

After Grahamstown, we were driven to Plettenberg Bay on the south coast, where we were deposited in a luxurious hotel for the only few days of the whole trip that we were left on our own. The timing was perfect, for our stay coincided with the arrival in the bay of about a dozen of the extremely rare blue whales, the biggest of all living mammals – some say the largest vertebrate ever to have existed on earth. The animals were close in, and I spent hours studying them through binoculars. After a few days we drove on to Cape Town where we were looked after mainly by my widowed twin sisters and an old uncle. The twins were a year younger than me, and he was in his early nineties. There is only one twin left now, and my old uncle, alas, is no more.

Sir de Villiers Graaff, then the leader of the main, but small, opposition United Party, gave me lunch, and despite an absence of nearly fifty years, thought it was not too late for me to enter political life in South Africa! I visited my old school in its splendid new site outside Cape Town, and was amused when the headmaster pointed to a panel in the assembly hall where my name appeared alongside others, but with someone else's academic record attributed to me. The school's old boys association entertained me to dinner, but knowing no-one, I felt like a fish out of water. I gave a public lecture at Cape Town University before a large audience with, as I learnt afterwards, overflow meetings in two other rooms that were served by closed-circuit television. The title I had chosen was 'Direction and Misdirection in Science', and in illustrating one part of my theme, I referred to Eugene Marais, a popular Afrikaans writer, but a scientific impostor whose skilful pen had been steered by a lively imagination, sometimes fuelled by drugs. I should have been warned. The accounts of my lecture in the papers next day made it clear that I had committed something like sacrilege in the way I had referred to an Afrikaaner who had entered

South African folklore as a literary and scientific genius. The story of my gaffe was taken up by paper after paper during the rest of our stay in the country, as though the only purpose of my lecture had been to make an unfair attack on the memory of a great South African. Newspaper cuttings in the same vein followed me long after we had left South Africa, where, towards the end of our month's stay, we spent two delightful days in the Kruger National Park. Our guide, the Chief Education Officer, did not expect me to emulate Marais by discoursing on the theme of the animal soul.

My post-retirement academic activities have certainly given me pleasure. But the truth is that I have always remained mostly interested in the three major topics that had concerned me when I was the Government's full-time Chief Scientific Adviser – the encouragement of industrial R&D, the protection of the environment, and, most important, nuclear policy. After Ted Heath lost the General Election of 1974, I wrote to Harold Wilson to tell him that, at his predecessor's request, I had stayed on in the Cabinet Office as a one-day-a-week consultant. Did he want me to continue? The answer was yes. I wrote in the same vein to James Callaghan when he took over in 1977. I do not recollect receiving a reply. John Hunt, Burke's successor as Cabinet Secretary, advised me to carry on as before. In 1979 Margaret Thatcher replied to the letter I sent her. That is why I am still there. As Robert Armstrong, the recently retired Secretary to the Cabinet used to put it, when occasion demanded I could be wheeled out as an exhibit before a visiting dignitary as one might the oldest inhabitant of a village.

In my capacity as consultant, I saw Ted Heath every now and then, usually to discuss nuclear matters. He also called on me to undertake a few one-off enquiries that were not being dealt with either by Alan Cottrell or Victor Rothschild, head, for some three years, of the Think-Tank. The first enquiry that I did for Ted was to survey the research into cancer that was being carried out in the UK. The reason why he wanted this done was that Richard Nixon, not long after becoming President, had announced, with much beating of drums, that he was launching a research programme that he hoped would lead to the eradication of cancer during the term of his presidency – much in the same way as Ronald Reagan was later to declare that he wanted nuclear weapons made impotent and obsolete. Ted wished to know whether the UK could do more than it was already doing, to which, after enquiring widely, my answer was that I thought not. I had visited all the main centres of research in the country, and had not come across a single good idea that was not being followed up for lack of resources. What I did discover, however, was that thousands of people up and down the country died of cancer in conditions of great hardship, cared for only by relatives. If the Prime Minister could marshall any more resources than those that were already devoted to the disease, I hoped they could be diverted in that direction. My report was a personal one, but Ted decided that it should be published, together with a foreword that he penned.[3]

Another enquiry that I pursued for him was to see whether the UK's then pre-eminent position in toxicological science could be used as the basis of an international institution to service the whole European Community. The UK was the first country in the world to enact any general law to control the sale of food and drugs, a piece of legislation from which derive our present regulations that control the licensing of new drugs and food additives. The centenary of the Act was celebrated in 1975 at an international symposium organized by the Ministry of Agriculture Fisheries and Food, which I chaired.[4] I had not, however, got very far in my enquiries by the time of the 1974 Election, after which my initiative came to a halt. Harold Wilson's Government was not likely to go seeking closer links with our European partners.

Later I undertook another one-man enquiry, this time for Peter Walker when he was Minister of Agriculture in Margaret Thatcher's first administration. The subject was badgers, creatures which, while rarely seen, hold a special place in the affections of children – mainly because of that well-known book, *The Wind in the Willows*. The trouble was that in some parts of the country, particularly in the Southwest, outbreaks of tuberculosis in dairy cattle were often associated with the presence of tuberculous badgers on the land that the cattle grazed. The Government had therefore taken powers to gas the setts of badgers that were suspected of carrying the tubercle bacillus. This was done only two years after a law had been passed that forbade the cruel sport of badger-baiting. Violent protests followed. Gassing, it was said, was just as cruel as baiting, and anyhow there was no scientific proof that badgers did infect cattle. As the Minister who carried the statutory responsibility for seeing that TB was eradicated in dairy cattle, Peter had had to take action.

One day he telephoned to ask whether I would examine the evidence that linked the disease in cows with that in badgers. Believing that what he wanted was not a formal enquiry but an assessment of technical reports, I agreed. He then issued a press notice in which, having expressed his concern about the criticisms that were being levelled at his department, he announced that he had asked me to take 'an objective look' at the problem. The upshot was an enquiry that ended in the publication a year later of a lengthy report.[5] My conclusion was that the available evidence definitely indicated that the disease in badgers was connected with its occurrence in cattle, and that the gassing procedures which the department had instituted were consequently justified. I therefore recommended that they should be resumed under strict control, on the understanding that, after three years, a critical review should be made of the further evidence that would by then have come to light.

My report attracted widespread interest, and stimulated numerous articles and letters both in scientific journals and in the daily press. I was not the least bit surprised when it was rejected out of hand by badger-protection societies. A laudatory letter sent me by the recently retired Director of Research of the World Health Organization was adequate compensation. Three years later, after gassing had been resumed, the follow-up enquiry which I had recommended was carried out by a team of expert veterinarians. It provided further evidence to support the proposition that a direct association does exist between the disease in the two animals.

The problem in which I tried to get Harold Wilson interested during his third term as Prime Minister was that of devising fiscal and other measures to encourage manufacturing industry to increase its investment in R&D. The situation had been deteriorating for some time, with a downturn in R&D having preceded by a few years the fall in general industrial investment, and was far worse than it was at the time he launched the idea of a European Technological Community. An official working-party was set up to look into the matter, but apart from providing additional statistical material that revealed the situation more precisely than I had painted it, little if anything was done. The PM's attention was on many more urgent problems, including the referendum to decide the UK's continued membership of the Common Market. As we now know, he was also beginning to worry about hints of an MI5 plot to bring down his Government. But I went on pressing, and a few days before the formal public announcement (on 16 March) of his resignation and of his handover to Jim Callaghan, he invited me to lunch in order to discuss the problem with two of the younger members of his Government whose business it was. The PM arrived late, and when he joined us over a drink, John Hunt having acted as host until he arrived, he had some chit-chat with his two colleagues, from which I gained the correct impression that one thing that was not going to happen when he stepped down – which, it was widely known he was about to do – was that he would be succeeded by Roy Jenkins.

We had a lengthy discussion about the problem, and about the reasons why the tax and other concessions that had already been introduced had not checked the decline in industrial R&D, but no fresh ideas about what needed to be done were suggested. At the end of the luncheon, the PM asked me to prepare a paper on the subject. I sat down that afternoon and did this, putting in some of my own ideas. The PM acknowledged my paper in a note saying that it would be considered by his successor. As it turned out, I heard no more about the matter nor, during the three years that Jim Callaghan was Prime Minister, did I ever deal directly with him.

The member of Callaghan's Cabinet with whom I did deal was David Owen, who early in 1977 became Foreign Secretary after the sudden death of Tony Crosland. We had first met when he was the Navy Minister under Denis Healey. As Foreign Secretary, he became every bit as concerned as I was about the need for an urgent and successful conclusion to negotiations that were then in progress in Geneva to arrange a CTB (p. 340). Not since Harold Macmillan, whose interest, truth to say, was somewhat equivocal because of the issue of the UK's status as an independent nuclear power, had I dealt with a minister as interested intellectually as was David Owen in the problems of arms control. My belief that Jim Callaghan was uninterested in my views on nuclear matters, and unsympathetic to those of his Foreign Secretary, was, however, wrong. In 1982, three years after he had been succeeded as Prime Minister by Margaret Thatcher, I published a book under the title *Nuclear Illusion and Reality*.[6] It carried a blurb from his pen which began, 'The broad case made in this important book is unanswerable.'*

Unanswerable or not, it was not one that appealed to or was appreciated by Margaret Thatcher who, before she became Prime Minister, had not been concerned with nuclear matters, and in particular with nuclear strategy and nuclear politics. She had been unconvinced by what I had told her when she asked me to comment on a letter that Dickie Mountbatten had sent her shortly before he was assassinated (p. 303), and it was mainly because of her then conventional views on the subject that I decided to write *Nuclear Illusion and Reality*, and why I have continued ever since to spend as much time as I can in discussing and writing about the nuclear problem.

As a cross-bencher in the House of Lords, that is the subject which has been my main interest, although I have also participated in debates on a few other topics. My maiden speech was made in a debate that commended the UK's entry into the Common Market. I also participated in one that was stimulated by the publication, early in 1972, of the Think-Tank's report on the control of government-sponsored R&D, a report in which Victor Rothschild commended the 'customer–contractor principle' as being applicable to all government R&D, and not just to that sponsored by executive departments such as Defence. Not surprisingly, the recommendation that it should apply to the operations of the Research Councils was vigorously opposed in a report by the Council for Scientific Policy (the CSP), which was then under the chairmanship of Sir Frederick Dainton. Ted Heath asked me to glance at drafts of both reports before they were published. The CSPs I described as 'an exercise in sail-trimming' which, while acknowledging the need for, or the likelihood of, change, altered nothing. Victor's proposals I commended as being a step in the right direction, since I could see them leading to that close relationship of the Research Councils to executive departments for which I had been arguing so long. But Victor's paper, I also wrote, was framed in so provocative a way that if published as it stood, it would be bound to draw unnecessary fire. Some editing took place before it appeared.

The majority of those who spoke in a two-day debate in the Lords on

---

*Two other previous Prime Ministers, Alec Home and Harold Wilson, were equally generous.

the two papers were upholders of the Haldane doctrine of Council independence and, correspondingly, hostile to Victor's proposals. I participated with what I hoped would, in the circumstances, be regarded as a well-balanced speech. But I had not reckoned with Victor's sensitivity to criticism. He was much bruised by the way the debate had gone. I can still see him sitting in the 'box' – the little enclosure for civil servants to whom Government Ministers can refer for instant information – with his head down on his arms on the ledge. He had tried before the debate to explain his proposals in the scientific press but, inevitably, in trying to obviate possible criticism, he had equivocated at the expense of clarity. Whether it was my pointing this out that irked him, I never knew, but for some time after, our relations remained cool. Despite the way the debate had gone, Victor's recommendations were, however, adopted more or less as they were set out in his report, and the term 'customer–contractor principle', which had been used much earlier on by Wedgwood Benn, is still occasionally heard. I doubt, however, if anyone could claim that its operation has been either a success or responsible for the disarray of the scientific scene in Britain today.

I try never to miss a defence or arms-control debate, and I have participated in a few, having kept up to date with the strategic dimensions of the nuclear problem mainly with the help of information provided me by friends in the US scientific defence community.* My association with SIPRI – the Stockholm International Peace Research Institute – an organization that is supported by the Swedish Government, has also helped. So too has my participation in a series of informal and confidential international meetings in Geneva that have been organized by Martin Kaplan, the highly effective Director of the Pugwash movement, and through which I have been kept aware of the views of nuclear matters of countries other than the USA.

My connection with the Swedish institute SIPRI began when I was invited, together with a few other foreigners, to become a member of

---

*The Upper House is not a forum where one can delve into the all-important technical considerations that underlie nuclear doctrine. In so far as I have succeeded over recent years in contributing constructively to the nuclear debate, it has been through the medium of responsible American journals and newspapers that have invited me to write review-essays. Robert Silvers, the editor of the *New York Review of Books*, has been particularly generous in the space that he has allowed me.

the organization's scientific advisory board. When I was later asked to suggest a British military figure who might also join, I immediately thought of Dickie Mountbatten. He did not need much persuading. Neither of us could have guessed that a statement that he was later to deliver on SIPRI's behalf would become one for which he is widely remembered.

In 1979 he and I flew together to the only SIPRI meeting he ever attended. Dickie had arranged for us to stay in the Royal Palace as guests of his brother-in-law, King Gustaf. The King was a charming and highly cultivated man, an authority on the arts of the ancient Chinese as well as the Etruscan civilization, and an expert on fine porcelain. Herb York should have been told all this when he had asked Dickie a few years before what his brother-in-law had done to justify election to the Royal Society (p. 199). Other than ourselves, and two or three of his small entourage, there was no-one else at the King's dinner table. I have a pleasant memory of the ritual moment when, with an apron round him, the King himself made the crêpes suzettes, which he liberally drenched with a full half-bottle of Cointreau. That was the innocent and, so I was told, the only way in which alcohol ever passed his lips.

The meeting Dickie attended was chaired by Gunnar Myrdal, the famous economist and sociologist, and the husband of Alva, at the time her country's 'ambassador at large'. There was an embarrassing moment at the start when Dickie said that he wished to table a book that was relevant to what we had to discuss, and also the typescript of an article that he said was soon to be published. He said all this in a way that made it seem that he and I were joint authors.* When I saw that the book was my *Beyond the Ivory Tower*,[7] which I had dedicated to him, I suggested that we should first have a word to see if the article he proposed tabling was up to date. I was appalled when I saw that he was

---

*Many years later Dickie did the same thing when he took the chair at a Foyles Literary Luncheon that was organized to mark the publication of my first volume of memoirs. In a speech full of praise, he said that I would never have written the book had he not insisted, and that it was based on a record of our cooperation over the years – what record I could not imagine. The second volume, he told the company, would be more important than the first. It was all said light-heartedly and without much concern for the facts. When it came to signing copies of the book at the end of the luncheon, I was much amused as he added his signature to mine in a few. I wish I had picked up one that carries our joint signatures.

about to hand over the typescript of the UN report on the Economic and Political Consequences of Nuclear War, which all those present would have known was the work of an international panel. He had clearly not glanced at the copy of the text that I had given him before it came out in print. Dickie was not a great reader.

It was part of his charm that he often acted impulsively. Sometimes a small stimulus would elicit so massive a response that it caused endless trouble. That was what happened when, as Chief of Combined Operations, he had thrown himself so enthusiastically behind Geoffrey Pyke's vastly imaginative but totally unrealistic idea of building a huge aircraft carrier out of ice. That was how his notorious encounter with Cecil King, the press baron, came about, and about which so much is now being written.

At the time of the meeting, Hugh Cudlipp was Cecil King's main editor. He was also a friend of Dickie's, and he and I had long known each other. King I had met on no more than about three occasions, the last of which was a luncheon to which he had invited me. I had naturally assumed that I was to be one of a number of guests. Instead, I was on my own. King was utterly unlike any other newspaperman I have ever met. He was an unsmiling giant, and a forbidding host. Our 'conversation' consisted of a diatribe which he delivered on the subject of Harold Wilson as the architect of Britain's decline. I was not the only senior civil servant who at the time was subjected to the treatment.

I was unaware that Dickie and he had arranged to see each other until the morning of the day – 8 May 1968 – that the meeting took place. John Brabourne, Dickie's son-in-law, telephoned to say that I simply had to be present to see that nothing unwise happened. He did not explain what was worrying him, but in the light of what I now know, I realize that Dickie had told him about a conversation he had had the day before with Hugh Cudlipp. Dickie telephoned soon after to ask me to be there. What happened next, so far as I was concerned, is exactly as described by Cudlipp[8] and repeated by Ziegler.[9] Whether there had been any talk before I walked into the room in Kinnerton Street where Dickie and his two guests were sitting, I do not know, but the moment I had taken a chair, Dickie turned to King and said, 'Now you can start.' And start he did, to paint a picture of an England in economic disarray, utterly demoralized, and with an ineffective government and a Prime Minister no longer able to control events. Public order was about to

463

break down, there was a likelihood of bloodshed in the streets. There would soon be a need for machine guns at street corners. What was required was a new administration to restore order, with Dickie at its head.

Hugh Cudlipp never interrupted. He has written that he had arranged the meeting at King's behest – King later said that it was Dickie who had asked for the meeting. As King spoke, Dickie occasionally nodded his head. He then turned to me remarking that I had not said a word so far, and what did I think. I had listened aghast to what King had been saying about upturning the Government, about order breaking down, and about Dickie's part in a new administration. Without a second's hesitation, I stood up and, walking to the door, uttered the words recorded in Cudlipp's book, to wit, that King had been proposing treason, that as a servant of the Crown – as I said the words, I felt that 'servant of the Crown' must have sounded pompous – I would not listen to another word, and that neither should Dickie. For a second or two Dickie tried to restrain me at the door, but as I left the room, I kept repeating, 'Throw them out, throw them out.'

My pocket diary tells me that after leaving Dickie's flat I went to a cocktail party of Cecil Beaton's, before changing into 'tails' to attend a grand legal dinner in Lincoln's Inn. The meeting in Kinnerton Street had been a piece of theatre. But a few days later, an article signed by King appeared on the front page of the *Daily Mirror*, calling for a new leader to replace Harold Wilson. Within days Cecil King was deposed from his own lofty position and Hugh had taken his place.

Hugh Cudlipp's autobiographical memoir, *Walking on the Water*, in which he tells the story, was published in 1976. I therefore assume that he must have started to write it sometime in 1975. In November of that year he sent Dickie the few pages of typescript in which he gave an account of the meeting. Late that night, there was a ring on my doorbell. I was already in bed, and when I went down in a dressing-gown, there was Dickie with some sheets of paper in his hand. Before he was in the house, he said in a loud voice, 'You must read this straight away. Hugh Cudlipp has just sent it to me. You know him. Can we stop him publishing it?' 'For heaven's sake, come in,' I said. 'The whole street will hear you.' John Barrett, Dickie's private secretary, was standing by the car a few feet away. Once Dickie was in the house, I glanced at what he had given me, and immediately said that in general it looked all right to me. 'Being a newspaper man, Hugh will publish it whatever you say. It's too good a story for him to ignore.'

It was far too late to go over the pages carefully, and we arranged to get together the next day. Dickie then returned Cudlipp's text with suggestions for a few minor corrections, which Hugh acknowledged as giving a more precise account of what had happened and what had been said. As he put it in a letter to Dickie, 'It is immeasurably better with the *full* quotation of what Solly said, and my recollection of the words entirely coincides.'[10]

What I did not know then was that what was at stake was not just an argument between King and Cudlipp. The story of the meeting was to become inextricably entangled with rumours that there had been a real plot to overthrow the Wilson Government. When Hugh's book appeared, King declared that the account it gave of the meeting was a pack of lies, and that the initiative had been Dickie's, not his. I had left the meeting, King said, because I was embarrassed which, to put it mildly, I certainly was.

A few months later, in February 1976, I had to take the chair at the annual lunch of the Parliamentary and Scientific Committee, of which I was then President. As the main guest, Prince Philip was on my right. Harold Wilson was on my left and, believing Wilson and Cudlipp to be close friends, I asked whether he had seen the proofs of Hugh's book. I told him about the pages that had been sent to Dickie, and was amazed by his sharp reaction. What I now know is that apart from the *Daily Mirror*'s attacks on him, Wilson was already disturbed by rumours that a real 'putsch' was being planned.

One night in the summer of the following year, I ran into Wilson at a big party. He came up to me as I entered the room, and started to press me about the Kinnerton Street meeting. He knew, he told me, that I had agreed to see two journalists the following day to discuss the affair, and as a good civil servant, he assumed that I had made a note of what had transpired. No, I replied, it was not the sort of thing that needed a note. He carried on in the same vein until I asked what was going on; was someone out to 'frame' Mountbatten? When he replied no, I broke away.

Next day, two reporters, Barrie Penrose and Roger Courtiour, came round to see me. They had already spoken to Wilson and had been tipped off to make further enquiries. I was among those whom, I believe, Harold Wilson had suggested they should see. They began by referring to Hugh Cudlipp's account of the meeting. Were there, they asked, maps laid out in the room showing at which street corners machine guns should be posted? No – there were none. Did I know about the suspicions that were being focused on a section of the security services, and about the involvement of senior military people in a possible coup? No. Why had I used the word 'treason'? Because, I answered, King was talking treason. Had I ever heard seditious talk in the Ministry of Defence in the days when I was there? No. I kept telling them they were talking nonsense and that no senior military man to whom I had ever spoken had indicated by word or deed any disloyal intent. My secretary was in the room and made notes of all that passed.

A few months later, the two reporters published a highly colourful story about the 'coup' that never came off, and in which they brought in Dickie's and my name. The article generated a flurry of further comment in the newspapers, with talk of spies at the top of our security services. Chapman Pincher, who by now had made spy catching a hobby, had entered the lists, and made the affair even more exciting. Questions were asked in the Commons. The official reply was that the matter had been looked into thoroughly, and that there was no truth in any of the allegations. Once again I had to confirm that, so far as Dickie was concerned, Hugh Cudlipp's story was a true record of what had happened.

But good stories cannot be killed. Cecil King died in April 1987, at a time when the public appetite for spy stories had been greatly sharpened by daily accounts of a legal action that the UK Government had taken in the Australian courts to prevent the publication of the memoirs of Peter Wright, a retired MI5 official. The obituaries of King again referred to Dickie's part in a coup that had aborted. Today there are demands for further enquiries. If they are ever made, I have little doubt that the public will once again hear about that extraordinary meeting in Kinnerton Street.

As time passes, however, I am equally sure that less will be heard of it than about an important consequence of Dickie's association with SIPRI. After the meeting which he attended in Stockholm, I do not believe that he gave any further thought to the Institute until he was invited, early in 1979, to attend a ceremony in Strasbourg and, as a

466

member of SIPRI's scientific council, to accept a prize that the French Louise Weiss Foundation proposed to award the Institute. The occasion demanded a speech, and Dickie got in touch with me. He had spoken out on nuclear issues in public on only one previous occasion. Early in 1970, Denis Healey, still Defence Secretary, had stated that NATO's strategy depended on the early use of tactical nuclear weapons. This view was immediately challenged by George Wigg – who by then had retired from the Wilson Government – in an article in *The Times* that was headed 'The perils of defence on the cheap'. On the Saturday of the same week Dickie telephoned from Paris to ask me to try to arrange that a letter that supported Wigg should appear in the following Monday's *Times*. His short letter, which he dictated to me over the telephone, duly appeared, together with a supporting editorial. There was also a lengthy front-page piece by Charles Douglas-Home (later the Editor of the paper), headlined 'Mountbatten challenge on nuclear policy', which brought in my name as the person who some years before had provided the basis for Dickie's critique. A lively exchange of letters and articles followed in both the British and foreign press.

Dickie did not know why he had been asked to accept the award that was being given to SIPRI, and I suggested that he should find out from Frank Barnaby, then the Director of the Institute. It turned out that Barnaby had not been consulted. He was, however, pleased that SIPRI was going to be represented in so distinguished a way. Dickie then asked me to draft a speech, which he said he would later translate into 'Burmese' – a reference to the fact that in the Ministry of Defence the textual changes that he made to impart his style to the drafts of letters and minutes that his staff had prepared on his instructions were referred to as 'Burmese'. He wanted me, he wrote, 'to steam ahead in writing a really tough speech which will shake the conscience of the world'. Within a week I had sent him a few paragraphs on which I suggested he could build. He replied that he wanted me to 'complete the job'. The longer draft which I then sent he acknowledged by saying that he had read it 'several times with growing fascination' and that it was 'a work of art and stands completely by itself.'[11] He then set about 'personalizing' what I had written – which also meant telling the story of the horrors he had seen during his Service career, about his Presidency of the United World Colleges, about Prince Charles, and finally by referring to the sixteenth-century seer, Nostradamus who, among other things, is supposed to have predicted the Fire of London in 1666, and who foretold a great war that would occur in 1999. 'I have an uneasy feeling,' wrote Dickie, that 'you won't like my introduction of Nostradamus.' I didn't, nor could I see what Prince Charles or the World Colleges had to do with SIPRI and the nuclear arms race. In the end only Nostradamus disappeared. In a final session at his flat in Kinnerton Street, I helped him make a few final textual changes. But the core of the message he wanted to deliver remained unchanged. He found the idea that nuclear weapons 'could be used in field warfare without triggering all-out nuclear exchange leading to the final holocaust' more and more incredible. Nuclear weapons cannot be 'categorized in terms of their tactical or strategic purposes . . . As a military man I can see no use for any nuclear weapons which would not end in escalation . . . nuclear devastation is not science fiction – it is a matter of fact.'[12]

Dickie was deeply disappointed by the lack of any reaction to his speech. On his return to London, he wrote to tell me that his audience had been very small, and that despite the efforts of our Ambassador in Paris to get British correspondents to attend, there were only a half dozen or so 'locals' at the press conference, and that they were mostly interested in putting questions about SIPRI, which were dealt with by the SIPRI team. 'It was simply a damp squib,' he wrote.

I replied saying that I was 'not surprised that the press conference was a flop'.[13] The trouble, I said, is that 99 per cent of people now seem to accept, without worrying, that they live in an irrational nuclear world. To illustrate my point, I told him that the Paris *Herald Tribune* had just devoted a considerable amount of space to a piece that was headlined: 'Study says fewer would die in Soviet Union: – US and Russia Seen Surviving Nuclear War'; the piece went on to say that given a nuclear war, *only* up to 165 million of the 220 million people in the USA would die, a fate which would befall *only* 100 million of the 261 million in the USSR. The study had been commissioned by the Senate Foreign Relations Committee. What it did not say, I went on to tell Dickie, was 'that there would be nobody around even to dispose of the dead; that pestilence and plague would follow; that even if a tenth of the number of people they talk about were killed instantly, the disaster would be beyond anything previously experienced.'

Dickie's speech was later circulated to the world's press, where again it attracted only slight interest. Part was also published in the American quarterly *International Security*. The main reaction came only a year later, when Lord Noel-Baker initiated a debate in the House of Lords 'to call attention' to the speech, which he used to trigger a wide review of the international failure to stop the arms race.[14] It was a good debate in which most who participated endorsed, and no-one disavowed, the main points that Dickie had made.

Following on the debate, selected excerpts of the speech appeared in a CND advertisement. That was what really sparked the reaction that Dickie had hoped for. In the course of an exchange of letters in *The Times* commenting on the way Dickie's name had been used, it was made clear that he had not set out to espouse the cause of CND, but to explain that the idea of actually using nuclear weapons was madness, and that what was wanted was a balanced reduction of the nuclear and conventional forces of the two sides. Numbers of other top military men then came out publicly to support the proposition that the most likely consequence of the use of any nuclear weapons in a NATO conflict would be escalation to all-out nuclear war. On both sides of the 'iron curtain' one started to hear it said that while nuclear weapons deter, they are not weapons of war. Dickie's speech had brought about the reaction for which it was designed. Not surprisingly, there are those who then began to ask why our military leaders have to wait until after they retire before they state the obvious.

Rereading the story that I have told in these pages, I get the feeling that I have packed a great deal into my life. It has never seemed that way. Obviously, had I not become as deeply involved as I did in the affairs of the Zoo, there would have been more time for other things. That would have been even truer had I not been caught up in the wheels of Whitehall. I might have spent my working life at the laboratory bench, trying to unravel the cellular mechanisms that underlie the specificity of hormonal action – a fundamental question that has always intrigued me, and to which no answer of any intellectual merit has yet been suggested. I might have gone on with my critical studies of the hypothalamic–pituitary connection. Dozens of other questions demanding answer would have been bound to crop up as I pursued one of my various research interests.

But even though the way in which my life unfolded may have denied me the continuous excitement of work in the laboratory, the last thing I can do is regret the course that it did take. I have never lost my interest in all things creative. My memory is still fairly sharp. There is a lot more that I still want to write. I have been fortunate in my relations both with my research students, and with the staff and colleagues with whom I have worked. I have enjoyed a happy marriage and family life, and the warmth and riches of great friendship. What other life could have been better?

APPENDIX

MINISTERS AND DEFENCE CHIEFS 1957 ONWARDS

Prime Ministers
Harold Macmillan, January 1957 to October 1963
Sir Alec Douglas Home, October 1963 to October 1964
Harold Wilson, October 1964 to June 1970
Edward Heath, June 1970 to March 1974
Harold Wilson, March 1974 to April 1976
James Callaghan, April 1976 to May 1979
Margaret Thatcher, May 1979 –

Chiefs of the Defence Staff
Admiral of the Fleet Lord Mountbatten, 1959–65
Field Marshal Sir Richard Hull, 1965–7
Marshal of the RAF Sir Charles Elworthy, 1967–71

Permanent Secretaries to the Ministry of Defence
Sir Richard Powell, 1956–9
Sir Edward Playfair, 1960–1
Sir Robert Scott, 1961–3
Sir Henry Hardman, 1963–6
Sir James Dunnett, 1966–74

Secretaries of State for Defence
Duncan Sandys, January 1957 to October 1959
Harold Watkinson, October 1959 to July 1962
Peter Thorneycroft, July 1962 to October 1964
Denis Healey, October 1964 to June 1970

GLOSSARY

ABM	Anti-Ballistic Missile
ABRC	Advisory Board for the Research Councils
ACARD	Advisory Council for Applied Research and Development
ACDA	Arms Control and Disarmament Agency
ACSP	Advisory Council on Scientific Policy
AEA	Atomic Energy Authority
AFVG	Anglo–French Variable Geometry (aircraft)
AGARD	Advisory Group for Aeronautical Research and Development
ANF	Atlantic Nuclear Force
AORG	Army Operational Research Group
ARC	Agricultural Research Council
BBSU	British Bombing Survey Unit
CDS	Chief of the Defence Staff
Caltech	California Institute of Technology
CIGS	Chief of the Imperial General Staff
CIP	Committee on Industrial Productivity
COCOM	Coordinating Committee for Export to Communist Areas
COSI	Chiefs of Staff (Informal) meeting
CSA	Chief Scientific Adviser
CSP	Council for Scientific Policy
CTB	Comprehensive Test Ban
DDR&E	Defense Development Research and Engineering
DRPC	Defence Research Policy Committee
DSIR	Department of Scientific and Industrial Research
ELDO	European Launcher Development Organization
ESRO	European Space Research Organization
EUREKA	A European Communities Programme of Research in Advanced Technology
ICBM	Intercontinental Ballistic Missile
IIASA	International Institute of Applied Systems Analysis

473

JCS	Joint Chiefs of Staff
JIGSAW	Joint Inter-Service Group for the Study of All-Out Warfare
LCC	London County Council
MinTech	Ministry of Technology
MIT	Massachusetts Institute of Technology
MLF	Multilateral Force
MOD	Ministry of Defence
MRBM	Medium Range Ballistic Missile
MRC	Medical Research Council
MWDP	Mutual Weapons Development Program
NASA	National Aeronautics and Space Administration
NPT	Non Proliferation Treaty
NRTC	Natural Resources (Technical) Committee
OPEC	Organization of Petroleum Exporting Countries
OSRD	Office of Scientific Research and Development
PEP	Political and Economic Planning
PSAC	President's Science Advisory Committee
R&D	Research and Development
SAC	Strategic Air Command
SACEUR	Supreme Allied Commander, Europe
SALT	Strategic Arms Limitation Treaty/Talks
SDI	Strategic Defense Initiative
SHAPE	Supreme Headquarters Allied Powers, Europe
SHAPEX	Supreme Headquarters Allied Powers, Europe Annual Exercise
SIPRI	Stockholm International Peace Research Institute
UGC	University Grants Committee
USAF	United States Air Force

NOTES

ABBREVIATIONS USED IN NOTES

Macmillan 1   Macmillan, H., 1971, *Riding the Storm, 1956–1959*, London: Macmillan.

Macmillan 2   Macmillan, H., 1972, *Pointing the Way, 1959–1961*, London: Macmillan.

Macmillan 3   Macmillan, H., 1973, *At the End of the Day, 1961–1963*, London: Macmillan.

Mountbatten   Ziegler, Philip, 1985, *Mountbatten*, London: Collins.

FAW   Zuckerman, S., 1978, *From Apes to Warlords*, London: Hamish Hamilton and 1988, London: Collins.

CHAPTER 1
pages 3–9

1 An account of the life of the Bishop of Birmingham, *Ahead of his Age*, by his son, Sir John Barnes, was published in 1979 (London: Collins).

CHAPTER 2
pages 10–18

1 Zuckerman, S., 1947, Revision of the anatomical curriculum at Birmingham University, *Lancet* (29 March), p. 395.
2 Zuckerman, S. (with H.P. Gilding), 1954, *Proceedings of the First World Conference on Medical Education* pp. 243–52.
3 Zuckerman, S., 1961 and 1981, *A New System of Anatomy*, Oxford University Press.
4 Zuckerman, S., 1951, Research in the Department of Anatomy, *Queens Medical Magazine*, **44**, 15.

CHAPTER 3
pages 19–28

1 Zuckerman, S., 1965, The natural history of an enquiry, *Annals of the Royal College of Surgeons*, **37**, 133–49.
2 E.E. Cummings to S.Z., 28 December 1953.
3 Corner, G.W., 1981, *The Seven Ages of a Medical Scientist*, Philadelphia: University of Pennsylvania.
4 Zuckerman, S., 1970, *Beyond the Ivory Tower*, London: Weidenfeld & Nicolson, pp. 46–60.
5 FAW, p. 135.
6 Zuckerman, S., 1954, Art and science in anatomical diagnosis, *Manchester University Medical School Gazette*, **33**, 137.

CHAPTER 4
pages 29–46

1 Published in 1968 as 'Scientists in the arena', *CIBA Foundation and Science of Science Foundation Symposium on Decision Making in National Science Policy*, London: J. & A. Churchill, pp. 5–25.
2 J.D. Bernal to S.Z., 26 April 1968.
3 Gardiner, Margaret, 1982, *Barbara Hepworth. A Memoir*, Edinburgh: Salamander Press. *See also* FAW p. 49 ff.
4 Zuckerman, S., 1958, *'Les relations hypothalamo-pituitaires'*, *Journal de Médicine de Bordeaux et du Sud-Ouest*, **135**, 121–47.
5 Zuckerman, S., 1973, The great Bordeaux magnetic machine mystery, *Sunday Times* (7 January).
6 Zuckerman, Joan (with Geoffrey Eley), 1979, *Birmingham Heritage*, London: Croom Helm.

CHAPTER 5
pages 49–54

1 John Durant has given a fairly detailed account of the foundation of the Society for the Study of Animal Behaviour in *Animal Behaviour*, 1986, **4**, 1601–16.
2 I provided an account of the work of this committee in Brooke Crutchley and the scientific world, *Tributes to Brooke Crutchley*, Cambridge: University Printing House, 1975, pp. 1–5.
3 Zuckerman, S., 1932, *The Social Life of Monkeys and Apes*, London: Kegan Paul.
4 Zuckerman, S., 1933, *The Functional Affinities of Man, Monkeys and Apes*, London: Kegan Paul.

CHAPTER 11
pages 97–101

1 Zuckerman, S., 'Need for a Science Secretariat', 16 September 1945. FAW App. 7.
2 *Scientific Man-Power*, 1946, London: HMSO (Cmnd 6824).
3 *Scientific and Engineering Manpower in Great Britain*, HMSO 1965.
4 *First Annual Report of the Advisory Council on Scientific Policy (1947–8)*, London: HMSO (Cmnd 7465).

CHAPTER 12
pages 102–9

1 *Scientific Man-Power*, 1946, London: HMSO (Cmnd 6824).
2 Zuckerman, S., 1968, Scientists in the arena, *Ciba Foundation and Science of Science Foundation Symposium on Decision Making in National Science Policy*, London: J. & A. Churchill, pp. 5–25.

CHAPTER 13
pages 110–3

1 *Scientific and Technological Manpower in Great Britain 1962*, London: HMSO (Cmnd. 2146), 1963.
2 Gannicott, K.G. and Mark Blaug, Autumn 1969, *Higher Education Review*, p. 56.

CHAPTER 14
pages 114–30

1 Committee on Industrial Productivity, *First Report* (Cmd 7665) April 1949, *Second Report* (Cmnd 7991) July 1950, London: HMSO.
2 FAW, App. 1.
3 *Report of the Commission on Mining and the Environment*, London: Land Use Consultants, 1972.
4 *Forestry, Agriculture and Marginal Land*, London: HMSO 1957.
5 *The Sheep Industry in Britain, 1958*, London: HMSO 1958.
6 *Scale of Enterprise in Farming*, London: HMSO 1961.
7 Agriculture in the British Economy, *Proceedings of ICI Conference*, Brighton (1956), 1957.
8 Zuckerman, S., 1960, Natural resources and the national estate, Chapter 2 of *Land Ownership and Resources*, Dept of Estate Management, University of Cambridge.
9 Zuckerman, S., 1958, The national need for increased self-sufficiency, *Report of the 12th Oxford Farming Conference*.

10 Bevan, Aneurin, 1952, *In Place of Fear*, London: Heinemann.
11 Wilson, Harold, 1952, *In Place of Dollars*, London: Tribune Publications.

CHAPTER 15
pages 131–44

1 Report from the Committee on Toxic Substances in Consumer Goods, *Fourth Annual Report of the Advisory Council on Scientific Policy (1950–1)*, July 1951, London: HMSO (Cmnd 8299).
2 *Toxic Chemicals in Agriculture*, London: HMSO 1951.
3 *Toxic Chemicals in Agriculture. Residues in Food.* London: HMSO 1953.
4 *Toxic Chemicals in Agriculture. Risks to Wildlife.* London: HMSO 1955.
5 Political and Economic Planning, 1955, *World Population and Resources*, London: PEP.
6 S.Z. to R.G. Snider, 25 November 1955.
7 *Ninth Annual Report of the Advisory Council on Scientific Policy (1955–6)*, 1956, London: HMSO (Cmnd 11).
8 Zuckerman, S., 1955, 'Asia's Other Need', *The Observer* (11 December).
9 Zuckerman, S., 1957, Foreword and postscript in *The Next Hundred Years*, eds Harrison Brown, *et al.*, London: Weidenfeld & Nicolson.

CHAPTER 16
pages 145–53

1 British Bombing Survey Unit, 1946, *The Strategic Air War against Germany 1939–1945*.
2 Zuckerman, S., 1952, Vulnerability of human targets to fragmenting and blast weapons, *Textbook of Air Armament*, London: Ministry of Supply.
3 Zuckerman, S., 1953, Biological effects of explosions, Chapter 11 of *Medical Research*, Eds Green & Covell, in *History of the Second World War* series, London: HMSO.
4 O.H. Wansbrough-Jones to S.Z., 8 July 1952.
5 Ashton, E.H. and J.T. Eayrs, 1970, *Ciba Foundation Symposium on Taste and Smell in Vertebrates*, Eds Wolstenholme & Knight, London: J. & A. Churchill, pp. 251–63.
6 Zuckerman, S., 1982, 'Why dogs can never be the mine hunter's best friend', *The Times* (3 September).

CHAPTER 17
pages 154–64

1 FAW, p. 216.
2 FAW, p. 283.
3 *Scientific and Technical Co-operation in NATO*, Paris: NATO [1957].
4 *Increasing the Effectiveness of Western Science*, Brussels: Fondation Universitaire, 1960.
5 Zuckerman, S., 1948, The recovery of the French railways, *The Adventure Ahead*, London: Contact Publications.
6 *NATO and Science*, Brussels: NATO, Scientific Affairs Division, 1973.
7 Office of the Minister for Science, 1961, *Report of the Committee on the Management and Control of Research and Development*, London: HMSO.

CHAPTER 18
pages 165–76

1 Gowing, Margaret, and Laura Arnold, 1974, *Independence and Deterrence: Britain and Atomic Energy, 1945–52*, Vol. I *Policy Making*, London: Macmillan.
2 US Scientific Laboratory of Los Alamos, 1950, *The Effects of Atomic Weapons*.
3 Smyth, H.D., 1945, *Atomic Energy*, Washington, D.C: US Government Printing Office; London: HMSO.
4 Glasstone, S. (ed), 1957, *The Effects of Nuclear Weapons*, Washington, D.C: Atomic Energy Commission, Washington, D.C: US Government Printing Office.

CHAPTER 19
pages 179–93

1 Zuckerman, S., 1945, 'New Horizons for Atoms and War'.
2 British Bombing Survey Unit, 1946, *The Strategic Air War against Germany 1939–1945*.
3 Kenneth Harris, 1982, *Attlee*, London: Weidenfeld & Nicolson, p. 277.
4 Perrin, Michael, 1982, *The Listener* (7 October).
5 Blackett, P.M.S., 1948, *Military and Political Consequences of Atomic Energy*, London: Turnstile Press.
6 Oliphant, M., 1947, A Military Policy for Great Britain (19 March 1947).
7 M. Oliphant to S.Z., 23 April 1947.
8 FAW, p. 358.

9 Zuckerman, S., 1958, in *Operational Research in Practice*, London: Pergamon Press, pp. 6–16.

10 *Defence: Outline of Future Policy*, London: HMSO (Cmnd 124), 1957.

11 Debate on Defence White Paper in *Hansard* (Commons), 16 April 1957.

12 Zuckerman, S., 1958, Liberty in an age of Science, *Nature, London*, **185**, 135–8.

13 Zuckerman, S., 1959, Mechanisms involved in conception, *Science*, **130**, 1260. Later republished as the introduction to *Mechanisms Concerned with Conception*, ed Carl G. Hartman, London: Pergamon Press, 1963.

14 Williams, Philip M., 1979, *Hugh Gaitskell*, London: Cape, p. 449.

CHAPTER 20
pages 194–208

1 Watkinson, Harold, 1986, *Turning Points*, Salisbury: Michael Russell.

CHAPTER 21
pages 209–29

1 Watkinson, Harold, 1986, *Turning Points*, Salisbury: Michael Russell.

2 Hastings, S., 1966, *The Murder of TSR2*, London: Macdonald.

3 Crossman, R.H., 1976, *The Diaries of a Cabinet Minister*, Vol. 2, London: Hamish Hamilton and Jonathan Cape.

CHAPTER 22
pages 233–54

1 *Defence: Outline of Future Policy*, London: HMSO (Cmnd 124) 1957.

2 *Hansard* (Commons) 29 February 1960.

3 *Hansard* (Commons) 13 April 1960, Cols 1265–6.

4 Macmillan 2. See also Harold Watkinson, 1986, *Turning Points*, Salisbury: Michael Russell.

5 *Hansard* (Commons) 27 April 1960, Col. 232.

6 *Hansard* (Lords) 3 May 1960, Cols 278–9.

7 *Hansard* (Commons) 27 April 1960, Cols 222, 279–82.

8 Macmillan 2.

9 Kistiakowsky, George B., 1976, *A Scientist at the White House*, Cambridge, Mass: Harvard University Press, 1976, p. 206.

10 Macmillan 2.
11 McDougall, Walter A., 1985, *The Heavens and the Earth*, New York: Basic Books.
12 Ball, George, 1982, *The Past Has Another Pattern*, New York: Norton.
13 Neustadt, Richard E., 1970, *Alliance Politics*, New York: Columbia University Press, p. 48.
14 Brandon, Henry, 1963, *Sunday Times* (8 December).
15 Rubel, John, personal communication.
16 *Hansard* (Commons), 22 June 1960, Col. 395.
17 Brandon, Henry, *op. cit.*
18 Neustadt, Richard E. *op. cit.*
19 *Ibid.*

CHAPTER 23
pages 255–69

1 Ball, George, 1982, *The Past Has Another Pattern*, New York: Norton.
2 Macmillan 3.
3 Schlesinger, Arthur, 1965, *A Thousand Days. John F. Kennedy at The White House*, London: Andre Deutsch, p. 738.
4 Ball, George, *op. cit.*
5 *Ibid.*
6 Macmillan 3.
7 Ball, George, *op. cit.*

CHAPTER 24
pages 270–91

1 Quoted in B.H. Liddell Hart, 1960, *Deterrent or Defence*, London: Stevens.
2 *Hansard* (Commons), 1 March 1955, Col. 1895.
3 Kistiakowsky, George B., 1976, *A Scientist at the White House*, Cambridge, Mass: Harvard University Press.
4 Defense Annual Report to Congress for the Federal Year 1981, quoted in R.H. Ellis, 1980, *Building a Plan for Peace*, Washington, D.C: Joint Strategic Planning Staff.
5 Kistiakowsky, George B., *op. cit.*
6 FAW p. 75.
7 FAW p. 142.
8 UN Department of Political and Security Council Affairs, 1968, *Effects of the Possible Use of Nuclear Weapons*, New York: United Nations.

9 Macmillan 2.
10 *Mountbatten.*
11 Zuckerman, S., 1962, Judgment and control in modern warfare, *Foreign Affairs*, **40** (2).

CHAPTER 25
pages 292–304

1 *Mountbatten.*
2 *Ibid.*
3 McNamara, Robert, 1986, *Blundering into Disaster*, New York: Pantheon Books; London: Bloomsbury Publishing (1987).
4 *Mountbatten.*
5 O'Keefe, Bernard, J., 1983, *Nuclear Hostages*, Boston: Houghton Mifflin.
6 Zuckerman, S., 1979, 'Working with a man of destiny', *Observer* (2 September).

CHAPTER 26
pages 307–23

1 Seaborg, Glenn T., 1981, *Kennedy, Khrushchev and the Test Ban*, Berkeley: University of California Press.
2 *Ibid.*
3 Macmillan 2. He was quoting Dante on 'the great refusal' made by Pope Celestin V when he abdicated from the papacy and so opened the way to Boniface who, according to Dante, brought moral disaster on Church and Christendom. What Eisenhower made of having Dante quoted to him in Italian, Macmillan does not say.
4 Seaborg, Glenn T., *op. cit.*
5 Macmillan 2.
6 Kistiakowsky, George B., 1976, *A Scientist at the White House*, Cambridge, Mass: Harvard University Press, p. 133.
7 Seaborg, Glenn T., *op. cit.*
8 Macmillan 3.
9 Seaborg, Glenn T., *op. cit.*
10 *Ibid.*

CHAPTER 27
pages 324–42

1 Macmillan 3.
2 Seaborg, Glenn T., 1981, *Kennedy, Khrushchev and the Test Ban*, Berkeley: University of California Press.

3 *Ibid.*
4 Macmillan 3.
5 Seaborg, Glenn T., *op. cit.*
6 *Ibid.*
7 Zuckerman, S., 1966, Technological aspects of proliferation, *The Control of Proliferation*, Adelphi Papers No. 29.
8 The Atomic Energy Authority, 1965, *The Detection and Recognition of Underground Explosions*, London: HMSO.
9 Thirlaway, H.I.S., 1973, Forensic seismology, *Q.J. Roy. Astron. Soc.*, **14** (3), 297–310, and in *The Vela Program*, ed. Ann. Kerr, 1985, Defence Advanced Research Projects Agency.
10 Owen, D., Speech at a Lunch for Senior Ambassadors in Geneva on the third day of the Non-Proliferation Treaty Review Conference on 29 August 1985.
11 Macmillan 2.
12 Seaborg, Glenn T., *op. cit.*

CHAPTER 28
pages 343–50

1 UN Department of Political and Security Council Affairs, *Chemical and Bacteriological (Biological) Weapons and the effects of their possible use*, New York: United Nations, 1969.
2 UN Department of Political and Security Council Affairs, *Economic and Social Consequences of the Arms Race and of Military Expenditures*, New York: United Nations, 1972.

CHAPTER 29
pages 353–65

1 Henderson, Nicholas, 1982, *The Birth of NATO*, London: Weidenfeld.
2 *Central Organization for Defence*, London: HMSO (Cmnd 476) 1958.
3 Macmillan 1.
4 *Mountbatten.*
5 *Ibid.*
6 Macmillan 3.
7 *Ibid.*
8 *Central Organization for Defence*, London: HMSO (Cmnd 2097) 1963.
9 Zuckerman, S., 1979, 'Working with a man of destiny', *Observer* (2 September).

10 Hough, Richard, 1980, *Mountbatten. Hero of Our Time*, London: Weidenfeld & Nicolson.

CHAPTER 30
pages 366–72

1 Castle, Barbara, 1984, *Castle Diaries 1964–70*, London: Weidenfeld & Nicolson.

CHAPTER 31
pages 373–85

1 *Hansard* (Commons) 26 February 1964, Cols 480–1.
2 Wilson, Harold, 1971, *The Labour Government 1964–1970*, London: Weidenfeld & Nicolson.
3 *Statement on the Defence Estimates 1965*, London: HMSO (Cmnd 2592), 1965.
4 Williams, Geoffrey, and Bruce Reed, 1971, *Denis Healey and the Policies of Power*, London: Sidgwick & Jackson.
5 Wilson, Harold, *op. cit.*
6 Williams and Reed, *op. cit.*
7 *Ibid.*
8 *Statement on Defence Estimates 1966, Part I, Defence Review*, London: HMSO (Cmnd 2901), 1966.
9 *Mountbatten*.
10 Williams and Reed, *op. cit.*
11 Gordon-Walker, Patrick, 1970, *The Cabinet*, London: Cape.
12 Crossman, R.H., 1976, *The Diaries of a Cabinet Minister*, Vol. 2, London: Hamish Hamilton and Jonathan Cape.
13 Wilson, Harold, *op. cit.*
14 Williams and Reed, *op. cit.*

CHAPTER 32
pages 386–99

1 *Our Bomb – The Secret Story*. London Weekend Television, 6 April 1986.
2 Wilson, Harold, 1971, *The Labour Government 1964–1970*, London: Weidenfeld & Nicolson.
3 *Hansard* (Commons) 14 December 1967, Col. 620.
4 Owen, D., 1981, *Face the Future*, London: Cape.

CHAPTER 33
pages 403–17

1 Williams, Marcia, 1972, *Inside Number 10*, London: Weidenfeld & Nicolson.
2 Wilson, Harold, 1971, *The Labour Government 1964–1970*, London: Weidenfeld & Nicolson.
3 *Ibid.*
4 *The Torrey Canyon, Report of the Committee of Scientists.*, London: HMSO, 1967.
5 Ministry of Agriculture, 1954, *Report of the Departmental Committee on Coastal Flooding*, London: HMSO.
6 Wilson, Harold, *op. cit.*
7 Crossman, R.H., 1975, *The Diaries of a Cabinet Minister*, Vol. 1, London: Hamish Hamilton and Jonathan Cape.
8 Wilson, Harold, *op. cit.*
9 *Ibid.*
10 *Ibid.*
11 *Ibid.*
12 Zuckerman, S., 1973, Science, technology and management, *Who Speaks for Earth?*, New York: Norton.
13 Zuckerman, S., 1974, in *Population and the Quality of Life in Britain*, London: Royal Society of Arts.
14 Zuckerman, S., 1971, *Technology and Society* (Background report to 23rd Congress of ICC, Vienna), Paris: International Chamber of Commerce.
15 Minutes of Evidence to Select Committee on Science and Technology (Sub-Committee C), London: HMSO, 1970.

CHAPTER 34
pages 418–28

1 *Report of The Committee of Enquiry into the Organization of Civil Science*, London: HMSO, October 1964 (Cmnd 2171).
2 Crossman, R.H., 1976, *The Diaries of a Cabinet Minister*, Vol. 2, London: Hamish Hamilton and Jonathan Cape.
3 The Comptroller and Auditor General, 1986, *MOD: Control and Management of the Development of Major Equipment*, London: HMSO.
4 Ministry of Technology, 1970, *Industrial Research and Development in Government Laboratories. A new organization for the Seventies*, London: HMSO.
5 Central Advisory Council for Science and Technology, 1968, *Technological Innovation in Britain*, London: HMSO.
6 Prior, Jim, 1986, *A Balance of Power*, London: Hamish Hamilton.

7 Zuckerman, S., 1986, Chapter VIII in *Star Wars in a Nuclear World*, London: William Kimber.

CHAPTER 35
pages 429–46

1 Wilson, Harold, 1971, *The Labour Government 1964–1970*, London: Weidenfeld & Nicolson.
2 Zuckerman, S., 1962, Judgment and control in modern warfare, *Foreign Affairs*, **40** (2).
3 Zuckerman, S., The Role of the Scientist in Modern Government, delivered in Paris, 6 May 1971.

CHAPTER 36
pages 449–69

1 Dahl, Norman C., and Jerome B. Wiesner (eds), 1978, *World Change and World Security*, Cambridge, Mass: MIT Press.
2 Rotherham, L., 1984, *Research and Innovation*, Oxford: Clarendon Press.
3 Zuckerman, S., 1972, *Cancer Research*, London: The Cabinet Office and HMSO.
4 Ministry of Agriculture, Fisheries and Food, 1976, *Food Quality and Safety: A Century of Progress,* London: HMSO.
5 Zuckerman, S., 1980, *Badgers, Cattle and Tuberculosis*, London: HMSO.
6 Zuckerman, S., 1982, *Nuclear Illusion and Reality*, London: Collins; New York: Viking Press.
7 Zuckerman, S., 1970, *Beyond the Ivory Tower*, London: Weidenfeld & Nicolson.
8 Cudlipp, H., 1976, *Walking on the Water*, London: Bodley Head.
9 *Mountbatten.*
10 Hugh Cudlipp to Lord Mountbatten, 11 November 1975.
11 Lord Mountbatten to S.Z., 13 March 1979.
12 Mountbatten, Louis, 1979/80, A Military Commander surveys the Nuclear Arms Race, *International Security* **4** (3).
13 S.Z. to Lord Mountbatten, 10 May 1979.
14 *Hansard* (Lords) 23 April 1980, Cols 818, 864.

INDEX